I0210919

I DON'T UNDERSTAND IT.
ONE MINUTE I'M THE GUY EVERYBODY LOVES,
THE NEXT I'M THE GUY EVERYBODY LOVES TO HATE.
- ROSCOE ARBUCKLE -

THIS ONE IS FOR SKIP — ANOTHER "FUNNY FAT GUY"
WHO OFTEN MADE SOME REALLY BAD DECISIONS
BUT NEVER STOPPED BEING ONE OF THE BEST
FRIENDS YOU COULD EVER WANT.

SAY GOODBYE TO HOLLYWOOD

SCANDAL, SIN, SPIRITS & THE RISE AND FALL OF ROSCOE "FATTY" ARBUCKLE

TROY TAYLOR

AN AMERICAN HAUNTINGS INK BOOK
ALTON, ILLINOIS

✔AY GOODBYE TO HOLLYWOOD

SCANDAL, SIN, SPIRITS & THE RISE AND FALL OF ROSCOE "FATTY" ARBUCKLE

© Copyright 2025 by Troy Taylor

All Rights Reserved.
ISBN: 978-1-958589-29-8
First Edition

Published by American Hauntings Ink
301 Piasa Street - Alton IL - 62002
www.americanhauntingsink.com

Publisher's Note:
No part of this publication may be reproduced, distributed, or transmitted In any form or by any means, including photocopying, recording, or other electronic or mechanical methods, without the prior written consent of the publisher, except in case of brief quotations embodied in critical reviews or other noncommercial uses permitted by copyright law.

Cover Design by April Slaughter
Interior Design by Troy Taylor
Author Photo by Stephanie Susie

Printed in the United States of America

THE STORY OF ROSCOE "FATTY" ARBUCKLE IS A STORY THAT'S ALWAYS BEEN CHRONICLED IN THE TRUE HOLLYWOOD TRADITION — IN OTHER WORDS, STICKING TO THE FACTS AS LONG AS THE FACTS DON'T GET IN THE WAY OF A GOOD STORY.

BUT I'VE DONE MY BEST TO GET THIS ONE RIGHT AND TO MAKE SURE THAT, THIS TIME AROUND, THE TRUE STORY IS ACTUALLY TRUE. I THINK, AFTER ALL THESE YEARS, ROSCOE HAS EARNED IT.

LABOR DAY WEEKEND 1921

THE DRIVER DOWNSHIFTED AS THE PIERCE-ARROW ROUNDED another sharp curve. There were the steep cliffs of the coastline on the right and the Pacific Ocean on the left. Seagulls wheeled above him in the bright sunshine as he worked the shifter and tromped down on the gas pedal for the straightaway. The engine of the custom touring car responded with a roar, and its tires gripped the paved surface as it chewed up the miles between Los Angeles and San Francisco – the driver's destination for the weekend.

The state of California had started paving the winding road that would someday be Route 101 back in 1912. As it was pieced together, planners used several already well-established routes, like El Camino Real. This historic Spanish trail connected the 21 major California missions. But nine years later, many stretches of the road remained unpaved, and the narrow road was often treacherous for the average automobile of the day.

But Roscoe Arbuckle didn't drive an average automobile. The Pierce-Arrow was just one part of his fleet of cars, which included a silver Rolls-Royce, a Renault roadster, a Cadillac town car, a Hudson limousine, and a Locomobile Sportif. But the Pierce-Arrow was his favorite, especially for road trips. The auto had set him back a cool $34,000, and despite the false rumor that the car included a backseat toilet, it did have more than its share of luxuries, including a cabinet often used for hiding bootleg liquor. Painted an iridescent blue with a gray cloth convertible top and all-white tires fitted with silver rims and vanished wood spokes, the huge and flamboyant Pierce-Arrow drew attention wherever it went.

And Roscoe was behind the wheel of it on that Saturday before Labor Day, September 3, 1921. At 34 years old, he was the number two actor in the world, only slightly behind Charlie Chaplin. He'd directed

Roosevelt Highway
Santa Monica Bay

at least 78 films and had appeared in more than 150 of them – starring in all but the first few – and known best by his adopted nickname of "Fatty," he was one of the most famous men in the movies. He was also the first screen actor to sign a contract that was worth $1 million a year. This had made the former vaudeville performer rich beyond his wildest dreams.

As part of that contract, Roscoe had made nine feature-length films for Paramount Pictures by Labor Day weekend. All of them had been produced over the last 21 months. He'd wrapped production on one of them just three weeks earlier and was already planning the next one. He was tired, and he needed a break, even though his bosses at Paramount had demanded that he stay in L.A. for the holiday weekend.

It was the fourth annual "Paramount Week," starting on Labor Day weekend and running for the next seven days. During the celebration, Paramount Pictures pulled out all the stops to publicize their films, and many more theaters than usual booked the studio's movies exclusively. On Labor Day, the studio's stars were expected to parade through Los Angeles, with the highlight being Fatty Arbuckle in his famous Pierce-Arrow. Later that same day, he was supposed to appear at a screening of his film *Gasoline Gus* at the lavish Million Dollar Theater downtown. But despite orders from Paramount studio head Adolph Zukor, Roscoe wouldn't be making those appearances. He was on vacation, and the long weekend was the perfect time to jaunt up the coast to San Francisco.

Adolph Zukor would not be pleased.

Roscoe wasn't making the trip with those closest to him that weekend. His wife, actress Minta Durfee, was elsewhere. She and Roscoe had been married for 13 years by 1921, but they'd been separated for the past four and a half. Another who was not along for the ride was his best friend, comic actor Buster Keaton, who'd been his companion on other San Francisco trips in the past. Keaton had married actress Natalie Talmage three months earlier and had decided to sail a yacht to Catalina Island for the weekend.

They'd invited Roscoe to come along, but he declined. He wasn't up for sailing, and he didn't want to spend the weekend with newlyweds. He wanted to let loose and have a party, and for that, San Francisco was the perfect place.

It was still the biggest city on the West Coast – fancying itself the "Paris of the West" for decades – and had world-class hotels and restaurants. But with that designation came a sense of entitlement and disdain for the people down south in Los Angeles, which was mostly filled with transplants from small towns in the Midwest. They also resented the "new money celebrities" of the moving pictures who treated their city as a personal playground, which was precisely what Roscoe Arbuckle planned to do that weekend.

When a party was on the agenda, Roscoe was always accompanied by an entourage. He was the main attraction, and they were his supporting cast. He made the plans, he got all the attention, and he paid for the tabs. Buster Keaton and the usual members of his posse didn't accompany Roscoe up the coast that weekend, but he certainly wasn't planning to celebrate alone. The two men riding with him – Lowell Sherman and Fred Fishback – were not close friends, but they were usually additions to the pack during late nights in L.A. They knew that Fatty always seemed to find the best parties.

Lowell Sherman, 34 years old, was a handsome young actor who mostly played dashing playboys, dastardly villains, or a combination of the two. He had only recently started to distinguish himself, most prominently in a film called *Way Down East*, which had been a smash hit in 1920.

Fred Fishback, who was 27, was born in Bucharest, Romania, and started as a film actor and then became Roscoe's assistant director. In September 1921, he was under contract to Universal Pictures, writing and directing comedies.

No one knows what was discussed during the trip. Service stations and roadside cafes were rare but welcome sights in those days, and Fatty's Pierce-Arrow got attention whenever it stopped. They might have talked about movies – Douglas Fairbanks and a new actor named Rudolph Valentino were hot at the box office – or they might have chatted about sports, especially since Babe Ruth was having the best year of his career so far.

They might have had a drink or two during the long trip up the coast. The basement of Roscoe's L.A. mansion was stocked with the finest liquor, and 20 bottles were stashed away in the car for the ride. They'd buy more in San Francisco,

Lowell Sherman

And Roscoe's other pal, Fred Fishback (Left)

even though Prohibition was the law of the land. It had been in effect for almost two years by then, which meant buying, transporting, or selling intoxicating beverages could earn you a stiff fine or six months behind bars. But for the wealthy, like Roscoe and other Hollywood celebrities, booze now had a bit of outlaw glamour to it. There were

secret knocks and passwords to get into speakeasies. There were private parties and underworld connections.

A weekend of wine, women, and song was worth the trip from L.A. The three men didn't care much about the music, and they preferred hard liquor to wine, but there were plenty of women in San Francisco. All three of the men were married, but the wives had all been left at home.

The destination of the trio that weekend was the St. Francis Hotel, one of the most prestigious lodging establishments west of the Mississippi. The 450-room St. Francis was modeled after the grand hotels of Europe, and after two years of construction at a cost of $2.6 million, it was an immediate sensation when it opened in 1904. Construction of a third wing was started almost immediately to meet the demand for more rooms. The fire that occurred in the wake of the

The St. Francis Hotel in San Francisco

great 1906 earthquake decimated the interior of the hotel, but it suffered no structural damage. It reopened just 20 months later. In 1913, a fourth wing raised the room count to 629.

The St. Francis was state-of-the-art for the time. It featured pneumatic tubes that allowed guests to exchange messages with the front desk. Each room had its own telephone, which was a luxury in 1921. Engines in the basement fed vacuum outlets in each room, replacing the hotel's climate with fresh air every eight minutes. The hotel had its own orchestra, which played on the mezzanine. It had its own school for young guests and its own Turkish bath with heated saltwater pumped in from the bay.

The St. Francis also had the finest restaurant in the city, and from 1904 to 1926, the head chef was Victor Hirtzler, who had been the personal chef of Nicholas II, tsar of Russia, and oversaw the kitchen at the Waldorf-Astoria in New York before coming to the St. Francis. His menu was noted for its variety – traditional French dishes, American favorites, and local foods like bay oysters, artichokes, and avocados. For breakfast, guests could choose between 203 egg dishes! By publishing cookbooks, naming dishes after himself, and greeting celebrity guests, Hirtzler became the most famous chef in America.

And there were plenty of celebrity guests to greet. Thanks to its grandeur and luxury, it attracted the rich, the famous, and the powerful. The list of those who had stayed there before 1921 includes Presidents Theodore Roosevelt, William Taft, and Woodrow Wilson, and such Hollywood celebrities as Charlie Chaplin, Mary Pickford, Douglas Fairbanks, John Barrymore, and Cecil B. DeMille.

The hotel's brochure in the early 1920s listed only three famous guests, however. They were names likely chosen to represent the caliber of the guests who had stayed there – World War I General John Pershing, famed evangelist Billy Sunday, and Roscoe "Fatty" Arbuckle.

Room 1219 at the St. Francis, which Roscoe shared with Fred Fishback.

After the Labor Day weekend of 1921, however, one of those names would be discreetly removed from the next set of brochures that went to the printer.

ROSCOE, LOWELL, AND FRED ARRIVED AT THE ST. FRANCIS late in the afternoon of September 3. Fatty's live-in secretary had reserved three adjoining suites on the top floor of the hotel's south wing – rooms 1219, 1220, and 1221. Each room had a door that opened into the hallway, and a door connected each room in a line.

Room 1219 was a rectangular room that faced south and had a bathroom and a closet. Room 1220 was a larger, square room with one window that faced south and a second window that faced east. It had a fireplace but no bathroom or closet. Room 1221, another rectangular room, had two windows that faced east and another facing north. It had a bathroom, but no closet. Room 1220 was typically used as a second bedroom for one of the other suites, which is why it didn't have its own bathroom, but on this weekend, the bed had been removed. It was going to be used as a lounge for the party, with furniture that included two couches. A single bed had been added to 1219 for Fred, while Roscoe slept in the room's double bed. Lowell slept in the double bed in room 1221.

On the evening of their arrival, a deliveryman dropped off four bottles of gin and scotch from nearby Gobey's Grill. If any of the hotel staff noticed, nothing was said. They were highly skilled at looking the other way when it came to their guests. Besides that, one of the unadvertised additions to the hotel was the fully stocked speakeasy in the basement.

On Sunday, after spending an afternoon sightseeing in Roscoe's Pierce-Arrow and visiting local friends, the three pals dined and danced at the Tait-Zinkland Café, located a block from their hotel. It was, in addition to the restaurant at the St Francis, one of the finest eateries in the city. The café also offered a cabaret show, and alcohol was served to discreet customers.

Chorus girl "Alice Blake," whose real name was Alice Westphal, daughter of a prominent local businessman

The trio from Los Angeles stayed late and, during the festivities, Lowell Sherman invited one of the café's chorus girls to come to the St. Francis the next day for drinks. Her name was Alice Westphal, but she used the name "Alice Blake" to keep her café career quiet. The 26-year-old Alice was the daughter of a prominent flour mill owner from Oakland. In 1912, when she was just 17, she made news thanks to an unsuitable elopement that her father promptly had annulled. She now had aspirations for a singing and dancing career, and by accepting Lowell's invitation, she probably thought the hotel party would be a chance to rub shoulders with Hollywood producers. She had a dancing rehearsal the following afternoon but promised to stop by the hotel beforehand.

On that same Sunday evening, three other visitors from L.A. checked into the nearby Palace Hotel – small-time film publicist Alfred Semnacher, his friend Maude Delmont, and a film actress named Virginia Rappe.

The German-born Semnacher was 43 years old and had been estranged from his wife

The nearby Palace Hotel, where Al Semnacher was staying with Maude Delmont and Virginia Rappe.

for nearly a year. He had filed for divorce because of her affair with another man, and a hearing was scheduled for September 15. He'd known Maude Delmont for years and had run into her a few days earlier as he was leaving the Pig'n Whistle restaurant in Hollywood. She was either 38 or 39, her real age unclear. She'd admired his car and suggested a trip. Alfred also invited his friend Virginia to ride along and stay a week in San Francisco. The young actress, who had turned 30 that summer, was thrilled. She'd spent too much time alone recently, and a vacation in her former home of San Francisco sounded wonderful. Semnacher had introduced her and Maude just before the three of them left to drive up the coast.

Another guest at the Palace Hotel was Ira Fortlouis, a 34-year-old salesman who'd formerly peddled hardware and sewing machines but now focused on women's clothing. And he knew Fred Fishback.

On Monday morning. Fortlouis was leaving the Palace for an 11:00 A.M. meeting with Fred when he saw Semnacher, Maude, and Virginia in the lobby. Always on the lookout for women to model the dresses he sold, he asked a bellboy about the dark-haired beauty in

Al Semnacher

Newspaper image of actress Virginia Rappe

an eye-catching green outfit and was told she was "Virginia Rappe, the movie actress."

Fortlouis walked over to the St. Francis and went up to the twelfth floor. He knocked on the door of room 1220, and it was Fred who opened the door. He was fully dressed, but Lowell and Roscoe were still in pajamas and robes. The four men chatted, and Ira asked them if they knew the actress that he'd spotted in the lobby at the Palace – Virginia Rappe. They all did, having run into her on either a studio set or at a Hollywood party. Fred placed a call to the Palace and had the concierge pass a note to Virginia, inviting her to the party at the St. Francis. She agreed to come and told her friends, "I'll go up there and if the party is a bloomer, I'll be back in 20 minutes."

Maude Delmont dressed for court, undoubtedly looking more severe than she looked on the day of the party.

Virginia arrived at the suite around noon. A former model and fashion designer, she was wearing the same outfit she'd been wearing in the Palace lobby – one that she'd made herself – a jade skirt and jade sleeveless blouse over a white silk shirt and a string of ivory beads. Her hair was up and was tucked under a white Panama hat with a jade ribbon.

Virginia called Maude on the telephone about 20 minutes later. She invited her to come up to the suite. It wasn't much of a party yet, but there was plenty of alcohol, and more people were coming. Maude walked over from the Palace, and soon after she arrived, another guest showed up – Alice Blake, the chorus girl that Lowell had invited the night before. About 20 minutes later, her friend Zey Prevost also arrived. The pretty aspiring actress was also a chorus girl whose real name was Sadie Reiss. She thought "Zey Prevost" gave her a bit of Hollywood glamor. Unlike her friend, Alice, she came from a modest family of Portuguese immigrants. When not trying to get jobs dancing and acting, she worked in the pantry of a cafeteria.

"Let's have some music, a piano or something," Virginia suggested.

Roscoe asked the group, "Who can play the piano?"

None of them could. So, Roscoe ordered a Victrola, which was soon delivered, along with some records. The crank was turned, and the brass horn on the phonograph began playing popular tunes like "St. Louis Blues" and "Ain't We Got Fun."

Alice Blake's friend and fellow chorus girl, Zey Prevost, whose real name was Sadie Reiss

Now it was a party! They drank and danced, and everyone started to relax and have a good time.

Fred left the shindig at about 1:30 and took Roscoe's Pierce-Arrow to a nearby beach to look at some seals that he was considering filming for an upcoming movie. That left four women and three men in room 1220. Roscoe asked Lowell to tell one of those men, Fred's acquaintance Ira Fortlouis, that it was time for him to buzz off. The salesman had overstayed his welcome, and he soon left.

Soon after he departed, a friend of Roscoe's named Julia Mae Taube arrived at the party. Mae was the wife of a cattle buyer and the daughter-in-law of popular evangelist Billy Sunday, a vocal supporter of Prohibition. The day before, Mae had stopped by the suite, and Roscoe had invited her to take a ride in his Pierce-Arrow that afternoon. He later described her as "peeved" when she arrived to find a party in full swing.

"Who are all these people?" she asked him.

Roscoe's friend, Mae Taube, who was married to the son of prominent evangelist, Billy Sunday.

Roscoe Arbuckle – although not in the pajamas and bathrobe he was wearing during the party.

Roscoe shrugged. "Search me. I don't know them."

But he did introduce Mae to Virginia. Not wanting to join in the drinking, Mae said that she'd return later for the promised auto ride.

Meanwhile, Al Semnacher appeared with the intention of picking up Maude and Virginia, but both women were having too much fun to leave. Virginia was drinking orange blossoms – Fatty's favorite cocktail, made with gin, sweet vermouth, and orange juice – and Maude, who'd changed into a pair of Lowell's pajamas, had downed more double scotches than anyone had counted. Instead, Al drove Alice Blake the one block to her dance rehearsal. When they got to Tait's, though, she found out rehearsal had been canceled and returned to the party.

Alice's need to attend that rehearsal was likely the reason the party had kicked off as early as it did. It was probably just intended as a pre-party gathering. Roscoe had planned to spend the afternoon taking Mae for a drive, and most of the invited guests were supposed to arrive at the suite later in the afternoon. But as the afternoon wore on and the drinking continued, the casual gathering turned into the main event.

By now, those present in the suite were Roscoe, Lowell Sherman, chorus girls Alice Blake and Zey Prevost, Virginia Rappe and her traveling companion, Maude Delmont. Food was ordered from downstairs, along with more orange juice and ice. The deliveryman from Gobey's Grill returned with more booze – mostly Canadian whiskey but also some local moonshine.

Roscoe was still wearing the pajamas and purple bathrobe that he'd put on when he got out of bed that morning. This would later be used to paint him as some sort of playboy who was looking to get out of the pajamas and into bed with one of the women – and perhaps this was at least somewhat accurate, although the long-sleeve shirt and pants, covered by the robe, revealed no more skin than a suit and tie.

Still, with Maude wearing a pair of Lowell's pajamas – supposedly because she was hot – and Lowell still in his night clothes himself – it had become a sort of fraternity-style pajama party.

In private conversations, Fatty was an introvert and prone to shyness, but he came alive when performing in front of a group, especially after a few drinks. He knew how to captivate an audience, large or small, and he had everyone in stitches with his humorous showbiz stories. With a drink in one hand and a cigarette in the other, he was fox-trotting to jazz records on the Victrola while he entertained the partygoers.

Roscoe jokingly announced that he would jump out of the suite window if anyone wanted to join him. He laughed, "If I jump out of the twelfth-story window, they'd talk about me today, and tomorrow they would go to see the ball game. So, what is in life after all?"

Virginia Rappe

At some point, Roscoe and Virginia sat together on the sofa, chatting quietly. Most likely, they talked about show business. Fatty was at the top of his game, but Virginia's acting career was considerably slower. They had moved in the same Hollywood circles. They knew some of the same people, especially director Henry Lehrman. He and Virginia had dated for more than two years. They'd broken things off after an argument earlier in the spring, but there were still many emotions between them. Roscoe had been directed by Lehrman many times. Virginia may have thought getting to know Fatty could help her career, as had her relationship with Henry. Back then, just like now, success in show business was often about the people you know.

They may have also talked about San Francisco. Both had lived there in the past, and Virginia, like Roscoe, had been to Tait's and other local night spots. They possibly talked about Los Angeles, too.

They'd likely danced in the same nightclubs, dined at the same restaurants, and attended some of the same parties.

They had other things in common, too. They'd traveled to the same cities and had both lived in New York City. They'd lost their mothers at nearly the same age. She never knew her father, and he had been absent for most of his childhood and had since passed away. They'd both started their careers when they were young – she was a model and he was a stage actor, then a singer.

As they sat together in room 1220, with the music playing, it's likely they flirted a little. Roscoe probably started some of his sentences with "Gee" – his favorite expression, and one that made him endearingly childish, like his film characters. But he may have also made some risqué jokes, as he often did, and this was also like his most popular movie roles because the on-screen Fatty may have seemed childlike, but his character's tastes were always adult in nature.

At some point, Virginia tried to enter the bathroom in room 1221. The door was locked. She could hear Maude inside and asked if she could come in. The answer was no – Lowell was in the bathroom with her. Virginia walked back through 1220, where Roscoe, Alice, and Zey were sitting. She entered room 1219 to use the bathroom there.

A short time later, just before 3:00 P.M., when Mae Taube was supposed to return for that car ride, Roscoe entered room 1219, the room he'd been sharing with Fred Fishback.

He closed and locked the door behind him.

ONE

ASK ANYONE... THEY'LL TELL YOU IT'S TRUE.

When Roscoe Conkling Arbuckle was born on March 24, 1887, he topped the scales at a massive 16 pounds. At more than twice the size of a normal infant, he nearly killed his mother and left her in such frail health that she wasted away until she died 12 years later.

Actually, aside from the name of the newborn and his birth date, not a word of that is true. But these were the legends of Fatty Arbuckle, later dreamed up to explain not only his size but his larger-than-life persona.

In truth, Roscoe was a normal-sized baby when he was born in a farmhouse near Smith Center, Kansas, to parents William and Mary. He was the last of five children – a sixth child had died at birth – and his oldest sister, Lola Belle, who was 17 at his birth, married and moved out when Roscoe was an infant. His other siblings were Nora, 16; Arthur, 11, who was already helping their father in the fields; and William Harrison, known as Harry, who was eight.

Roscoe's parents had both grown up in farm families in Indiana before they'd gotten married in 1867. Along with their first four children, the couple had left Indiana in 1880 and gone in search of new opportunities

Early days in Smith Center, Kansas, where Roscoe spent the first year and a half of his life.

in the West. They staked out a homestead just outside of a new township called Smith Center in north-central Kansas, about 15 miles from the Nebraska border. Smith Center was the only hint of civilization for a 900,000 square mile county that had exploded from 66 people in 1870 to nearly 14,000 just a decade later. In 1883, the town had 19 stores and three hotels, but no saloon. Kansas was the first state to prohibit liquor sales in 1881. Almost every building in town was brand new because nearly everyone had just arrived there.

Life was tough on the Great Plains. Wheat was the major crop, cultivated at a time when horses pulled plows and reapers, and most work was done by hand. Children who were old enough to swing a sickle or tie a bushel worked from dawn to sunset. Lumber was scarce, so families lived in earthen dugouts at the mercy of the weather. The Arbuckle home was later described as "a sod house of the most primitive kind."

Though he would romanticize his Kansas birthplace later in life, Roscoe lived there for only his first year and a half and remembered the place only from stories from his family. There was later to romanticize – the family was poor, cold, hungry, and his father was frequently drunk and abusive. In the fall of 1888, the Arbuckles sold the farm and the farming equipment and headed west again.

Traveling by horse-drawn wagon, they ended their journey in Santa Ana, California, 30 miles southeast of Los Angeles. Founded in 1887 during a California real estate boom, Santa Ana became the county seat of Orange County around the time the Arbuckles settled there in 1889. Its population had grown to nearly 4,000, and businesses were thriving because the town was an important stop on the Santa Fe Railroad "Surf Line," which connected L.A. with San Diego. Tracks for

Santa Ana, California, in 1889, when the Arbuckles arrived there.

horse-drawn streetcars ran along the unpaved streets, and buildings as tall as four stories seemed to sprout overnight.

The Arbuckles bought a double house, and they crowded into the front half of the bottom floor, renting out the rest of that floor and all the second floor to tenants. It was a good way to ensure a steady income, but it wasn't enough for William.

Almost as soon as they settled, Roscoe's father wandered off again, heading to Northern California in search of more lucrative business opportunities. Later, Arthur and Harry went to work for him.

It's unknown what effect William's abandonment had on Mary, who was a devout Baptist, but Roscoe later said that he never felt loved as a child. His father remained out of the picture for most of his childhood.

Roscoe, age 7

Financially, William's absence undoubtedly had an impact on the son he left behind – Roscoe had to start earning money for his family running errands for shopkeepers at the age of five. Schoolmates later remembered him also pulling around a little red wagon, delivering clothing to neighborhood families that his mother had washed.

Most of his time he spent alone. Like his brothers, his sister Nora left home in the early years after the family moved to Santa Ana, and his oldest sister, Lola, died as a young adult. He was, essentially, the youngest child of a single mother. The time that most children used to build relationships with others, for Roscoe, was used to make nickels and dimes that were contributed to making sure he and his mother were able to eat.

Even so, some would recall him gathering with friends to play with marbles in the street. In a photo of him taken at age eight, he looks much like he would when he was an adult – round head, plump cheeks, and chestnut hair parted from the left. He was teased by other children, who gave him a nickname dreaded by overweight kids everywhere – "Fatty." He hated it. The teasing he endured caused him to withdraw further into his own little world.

Santa Ana had one school, which Roscoe seldom attended after the second grade. Instead of going to class, he slipped into vaudeville theaters, watching the rehearsals, laughing at the antics of the performers, hearing the applause, and daydreaming about escaping

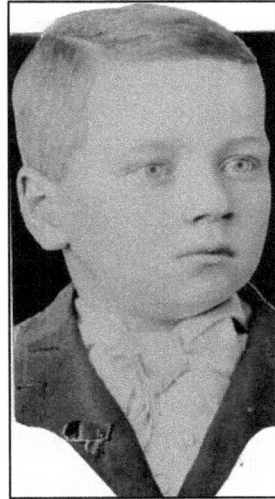

into this make-believe world of costumes, music, pratfalls, and, most of all, making audiences laugh. Adults in Santa Ana looked down on the vagabond actors who performed in places like Santa Ana, but the lonely and curious Roscoe would have done anything to join them.

ROSCOE'S FIRST BREAK CAME ALONG THANKS TO A MAN named Frank Bacon. Before turning to acting when he was in his twenties, Bacon had been a sheepherder, newspaper publisher, and a failed political candidate. In the final four years before his death in 1922, he was probably America's most popular stage actor, and his obituary was splashed across the front pages of every paper in New York. In between, he was a character actor with his own stock company based in San Jose. He struggled for years for his later fame, barnstorming from town to town with a cheap repertoire company and living on the cheap. It's estimated that he played 1,000 parts over his theatrical career.

In 1895, during the lean and hungry years, the Frank Bacon Stock Company arrived in Santa Ana to stage a comedy and musical revue called *Turned Up* at the Grand Opera House. A local boy was cast for a small role, but he failed to show up for the final rehearsal just hours before the show was supposed to open. On that day, a chubby eight-year-old boy was waiting on the side of the stage, just waiting for Frank Bacon to find him.

Roscoe in his first vaudeville role as an "African American boy" for Frank Bacon

The part was for an African American boy. Well, not really. In those days, black roles were almost always played by white actors in exaggerated makeup. Roscoe's acting debut was to be performed in "black face." Because he was wearing short pants and was barefoot, Bacon told him to run home and bring back some black socks to cover his calves and feet. Roscoe knew that he couldn't show up at home when he was supposed to be in school, so he started to cry. Quickly, Bacon found a solution. He used greasepaint to blacken Roscoe's lower legs and feet, along with his face. That evening, he stepped onto stage under the glowing lights of the theater's new electric carbon arc lights to face the first audience that ever paid to see him.

He received 50 cents a week for three weeks of shows and told his tired and overworked mother that he'd earned it by sweeping floors. Meanwhile, the women in the acting troupe fawned over the chubby little boy. Roscoe was stagestruck. At just eight years old, he'd caught the show business bug.

Mary eventually found out what he'd been doing. Somehow, though, he managed to overcome her religious objections and convinced her that acting was a better-paying job than selling newspapers on the streets, working in a factory, or working any of the other jobs that children performed in those days. He was, after all, her only child in a house with no adult male, and money was always tight. Over the next four years, he took most of Santa Ana's child acting roles, performing as an accomplice to a hypnotist, playing a little girl, and every other part imaginable.

Offstage, Roscoe remained shy around other children because of his weight, but he was better than most kids at athletics despite it. He loved to swim, and was good at it, and he was also amazingly limber and acrobatic, which would later serve him well.

On Sunday, he sang with his mother in the church choir. Though as an adult he shunned religion, the public performances and choir singing proved beneficial during his early career. Nevertheless, it seemed at the time that he would grow up to be just another anonymous man who, as a child, happened to have acted on the stage and filled out the background of theater shows that were long forgotten.

A poor little fat boy from a whistle stop like Santa Ana simply didn't become famous.

AS THE OWNER OF A BOARDING HOUSE, MARY DEVOTED most of her time to her struggling business and little of what time she had left to her child. And Roscoe was dependent on her. She was the one person who hadn't left him – and then he lost her, too. He was 12 years old when his mother died at age 50 in 1899. It's no surprise that he continued a search for a mother's love as an adult. His first wife was very nurturing, and he developed a close bond with his first mother-in-law.

After Mary's death, he stayed in Santa Ana for several weeks with his sister, Nora, her much older husband, Walter St. John, and their five-year-old son, Alfred, who would later become a reliable supporting actor in his uncle's films.

Watsonville, California train station

Soon, though, Roscoe was sent north to live with the father who had abandoned him. William owned a small hotel in Watsonville, a small town of about 3,500 on California's central coast. He had no idea what to expect as he took that lonely train ride, and though he would make other gut-wrenching trips from Southern to Northern California, this was his first.

As he'd been told to do, when the train stopped at the Watsonville station, he stayed in his seat until he was ushered off. He sat down on a bench in the station with his cardboard suitcase and waited forlornly for his father, who never came to get him. Hours later, a railroad employee took pity on him and took him to William's hotel, which was a few blocks away. When he got there, Roscoe learned that his father had sold the establishment and moved away. He was now all alone in a strange town with $2.50 in his pocket. The desk clerk kindly arranged for him to eat with the hotel staff and gave him a small room off the dining hall. He was told that he could earn his room and board by doing odd jobs around the building.

The hotel staff enrolled Roscoe at the local school, although he rarely went. Encouraged by the hotel restaurant's singer, who believed the young boy had a beautiful voice, Roscoe sang for tips from guests when he wasn't taking care of his chores. He also practiced juggling and pratfalls, which came in handy when he entered an amateur talent contest at the local theater. When he took the stage, he sang two songs and then, uncertain about what to do when the audience demanded an encore, he improvised. He danced, rolled, flipped, and jumped around the stage, much to the amusement of the crowd.

This was the first time he'd experienced the feeling of making an audience laugh on his own, and it may have also been when he realized that his size, which had been the cause of so much distress, could be used to his advantage.

Admiring his acrobatic skills and his self-effacing good humor, the crowd rooted for the chubby, baby-faced boy. Unwilling to leave the stage while people were still laughing and applauding, Roscoe continued until the giant hook, a vaudeville staple, reached for him from offstage. Roscoe dodged it and somersaulted into the orchestra pit, earning him even more love from the audience. He won the first prize of $5, and he was soon an amateur night regular.

Stories vary about how William Arbuckle returned to his son's life. Shortly after Mary's death, he had married another woman, also named Mary, but who went by Mollie, who was a widow with six children of

Santa Clara, California, in the early 1900s

her own. They would have two additional children together, in 1900 and 1903. The census in 1900 listed 11 family members at the Arbuckle's rented house in Santa Clara, including 13-year-old Roscoe, who found himself with a father figure for the first time since he was an infant.

Santa Clara was located about 45 miles south of San Francisco and was devoted to citrus farming. Once again, Roscoe was teased about his weight, a torment that was compounded by his father's insistence that he wear overalls every day. One Santa Clara resident later recalled, "Whenever a baseball went over the fence or out of the lot, the other lads put up a cry of 'Go get it, Fatty,' and with kicks and punches, sent the big boy on his way after the ball. He always was punched and kicked by the other boys."

It was a much different life than the one he'd enjoyed at the hotel in Watsonville, basking in applause and laughter from theater goers.

Again, Roscoe seldom went to school. He fished and swam in a nearby pond instead. He worked on the farm with his father and brother Harry. He cleaned a saloon and served coffee and donuts at the restaurant of another hotel that his father bought. These years would later become part of the characters that he played – lazy country bumpkins in overalls and lowly laborers who worked in hotels and restaurants.

Roscoe still managed to pursue show business, in any case. He shilled for medicine shows and traveling magic acts, and he danced jigs and belly-flopped onto saloon floors for beer and cigarettes. In his early teens, he sang again in amateur shows, this time at the Victory Theater in nearby San Jose. On stage, he easily overcame his shyness and replaced his loneliness with the adoration of the crowd, and through cheers and applause, he found the love that he didn't feel at home.

His stepmother, Mollie, later remembered his time growing up. "He was aggravatingly lazy as a boy. Neither his father's cuffing nor my pleading would cure it." She also spoke openly about what a terrifying, violent, and loveless home it was for Roscoe. "His father used to beat him, and he often deserved it."

In a horrifying recollection of the brutality, Mollie claimed she once saved the boy's life when "his father was choking him and beating his head against a tree."

When Roscoe was lucky, his alcoholic father would only insult him for his excess weight and not pull out his belt or raise his fists. Still, the sting of his words – especially William's claim that someone else must have fathered the worthless boy – lingered into his adulthood.

Roscoe Arbuckle desperately dreamed of an escape.

William Arbuckle, Roscoe's abusive and alcoholic father, who made his life miserable as a boy.

IN 1903, HIS CHANCE FINALLY ARRIVED.

He received an offer from father and son theater owners Sid and David Grauman. The two men had migrated to Canada's Yukon Territory in 1898 during the Klondike Gold Rush, and while they staked a mining claim, they found greater fortune staging vaudeville shows and boxing matches for the miners. One of their favorite boxing referees, by the way, was former lawman Wyatt Earp.

Two years later, they made their way to San Francisco, bought a downtown store, moved in 800 chairs, and started a vaudeville house called the Unique Theatre. In February 1903, they opened another Unique Theatre, this one in San Jose. They'd heard Roscoe sing at the Victory, and they soon enticed him to perform at the new Unique, singing what were called "illustrated songs" for $17.50 a week.

Illustrated songs were precursors to music videos. A singer performed onstage, accompanied by either a pianist or a record, while a series of slides that combined photography and paintings were projected on a screen, illustrating the lyrics. Illustrated songs were popular, mainly because they had the advantage over early motion pictures, having both color and sound, and ran between vaudeville acts and movies, which allowed time for the changing of backdrops or film reels. Audiences often sang along, and the shows fueled sheet music sales, just the same way that music videos would boost record sales eight decades later.

This may have also been Roscoe's first extended exposure to early films. Between their first public projections in 1895 and the rise of nickelodeons in 1905, movies were seen primarily during vaudeville shows. Typically, they were travelogues, prize fights, or gag reels that lasted for less than a minute. Their novelty waned quickly, so the "flickers" were usually wedged into the middle of lineups that consisted of dancing girls, jugglers, comedians, and illustrated song singers like Roscoe – just another diversion in the theatrical lineup.

Sid Grauman, the theater impresario who gave Roscoe his first big break

But as Roscoe witnessed the impact of such life-changing inventions during his early years – not just movies but also electric lights, telephones, phonographs, and automobiles – he developed a curiosity about technology that stayed with him for the rest of his life.

The next purchase by the Graumans was San Francisco's Portola Café, which offered singing waiters. They asked Roscoe to take a position as the headwaiter and a soloist, and so, in 1904, the 17-year-old escaped his father's grasp and moved to the big city – a rapidly expanding metropolis of over 350,000 inhabitants from all over the world. Singing to the city's moneyed crowds, he was generously tipped for his tunes. He worked late into the night and slept away the daylight hours.

In the same year that he moved to San Francisco, Roscoe's baritone voice impressed another ambitious theater impresario, Alexander Pantages. A Greek immigrant who ran away to the sea when he was only nine, Pantages had been a sailor, boxer, gold prospector, and had helped dig the Panama Canal. While searching for gold in the Yukon, he got into the theater business and then did the same in Seattle. Pantages would, in just a few years, build an empire of vaudeville and movie theaters, but when he met Roscoe, he only had two of them, both in Seattle. He also had a vaudeville troupe that traveled the West Coast, which Roscoe joined at the invitation of Pantages.

Roscoe – still only in his teens – became the star singer on the Pantages circuit, performing with the troupe in big and small theaters all over the west, spending much of his time in railroad cars. Unlike most other Americans at the time, who rarely ventured far from their hometown, in his first 18 years, Roscoe had seen a considerable slice of the country. He'd lived on farms and in the largest city west of St. Louis. He'd traveled 1,000 miles from his hometown of Santa Ana. He answered fan letters, greeted admirers, and signed autographs, all while making an impressive $50 a week, which is the equivalent of about $1,800 today.

Alexander Pantages

While playing in Portland, Oregon, in 1905, Roscoe agreed to join two burlesque comedians – Leon Errol and Pete Gerald – during a tour of the upper West. It was a gig that, even though it was half the pay, allowed him to sing untethered to a slide show and, even better, to try his hand at comedy.

He later said that it was Leon Errol "who persuaded me that I had a voice, ability, and that I would make a good actor. He also taught me several valuable things like how to fall all over the place without making myself a candidate for the hospital."

With Errol as his teacher, Roscoe became a student of stunts, soft-shoe dancing, comedic timing, creating characters and costumes, and applying makeup. Other than dodging the hook at an amateur show, Roscoe didn't really have a chance to be funny. He was shy and backward, only coming out of his shell when he sang. But at age 18, he started to develop the skills he needed to become a comedian.

In Butte, Montana, a rough-and-tumble copper town known for its massive vice district of brothels, saloons, and gambling halls, the trio performed with a blonde singer of large proportions and ribald character who was popular with overwhelmingly male audiences. She tended to drink a lot before the shows and often missed her entrances. One evening, she was nowhere to be found, so a new woman took her place, dressed in the regular singer's white gown. This new performer was sporting a blonde wig and sang "The Last Rose of Summer" in a sweet, falsetto voice.

The substitute singer was none other than Roscoe Arbuckle. The audience loved it – and loved what happened next even more. The theater roared with laughter as the enraged female singer finally showed up and started chasing Roscoe around the stage.

As the tour continued, the trio began to understand why the upper West circuit was known as the "death trail" in vaudeville circles. Not only were the venues spread far apart, but it wasn't as lucrative as other circuits. When Leon Errol accepted another job, Roscoe attempted to fill his role with Gerald, but things went badly. He wasn't yet a skilled

Leon Errol

comedian, so Gerald was forced to find a new partner. This sent Roscoe back to the dying medium of illustrated songs, which earned him little more than enough for a train ticket back to San Francisco.

He was back in the city on April 18, 1906, when the Great San Francisco Earthquake awakened him. Fires, caused by broken gas mains, burned for another four days and nights.

Discouraged by his failure on the road, Roscoe returned to work for Alexander Pantages, who booked him as a singer in the prospecting town of Vancouver, British Columbia. When this engagement ended, he joined a stock company performing classic plays for appreciative audiences in Alaska. The heavy costumes kept the performers warm in the chilly theaters, just as the beards and bearskin coats did for those who attended the shows. By the end of the year, Roscoe was in Seattle, singing and doing comedy roles in each show. He created several characters and put them into regular rotation. They included Jasper the Janitor, Little Willie Wilkinson, and Private Roundhouse, each helping him to keep refining his comedic talents.

In February 1908, Roscoe, now 20 years old, returned to San Francisco. Over the previous four years, he had traveled extensively, starting as a teenager and returning as a young adult. However, he ultimately ended up where he began, no wealthier nor better established, and still alone. There had been little time for relationships on the road. His life as a vagabond entertainer, appearing in the red-light districts of mining and farming towns, had grown exhausting. He

Outside the Byde-A-Wyle Theatre, where Roscoe went to wait for his next big break in vaudeville

now wanted to stick somewhere long enough to establish his singing career.

After an audition, he was signed as a singer with the Elwood Tabloid Musical Comedy Company, which moved south in June to the new Byde-A-Wyle Theatre across the street from the Virginia Hotel in Santa Ana.

Roscoe was now back in Southern California as a featured performer in a first-rate venue. It seemed his next big break was on the horizon.

AS IT TURNED OUT, THE NEXT LIFE-CHANGING EVENT IN Roscoe's life had nothing to do with show business. One day, while returning to Long Beach from a sightseeing trip to Los Angeles, he noticed a young woman sitting across from him on the train. He offered a smile to the small, blue-eyed, auburn-haired girl, but she quickly turned away. Roscoe wasn't ready to give up yet. When her suitcase began to slip in the luggage rack above her, he reached up and pushed it back into place.

The young woman looked up. "Please don't touch my suitcase," she said to him. "I don't like blonds or fat men. I can manage for myself."

"Gee, I'm sorry," Roscoe muttered, and he moved to another seat. The words had stung, especially coming from such a lovely girl.

But later, the woman recalled that she'd regretted what she said to him that day. "I don't know what got into me. Actually, I was attracted to him, but I couldn't let myself be picked up, could I?" She described Roscoe as heavy but handsome, and he "looked like he'd been scrubbed to death." She remembered his "clear, smooth complexion, blond hair, and his meticulous clothing – white trousers, white shoes, blue coat, and straw hat."

The young woman was Minta Durfee. She came from a working-class family that lived near downtown Los Angeles. Before the movies came, L.A. was a city of manufacturing and oil production. Her father, Charles "Buck" Durfee, was a railroad brakeman, and her mother,

Flora, was a seamstress. The couple had six children together, the fourth of whom, Araminta, was born on October 1, 1889.

Going by the shortened name of Minta, she was 17 and dreamed of her own life in show business. Until recently, she'd appeared only in school productions but then, a family friend had helped her to get a slot in the chorus of a play at the Burbank Theater in L.A. She'd now secured a new chorus job with the Elwood Company in a new show at the Byde-A-Wyle – the same show in which Roscoe was about to appear.

On that June day, on her way to stay at the Virginia Hotel with the rest of the company, Minta and her bulging suitcase boarded the train headed south to Long Beach.

Minta Durfee, the young women who would soon be Roscoe's wife

Much to her surprise at her first rehearsal, Minta saw the hefty, good-looking man once again. But then, when Roscoe laughed at her irritation with being called a "dame" by her boss, she decided that her first bad impression of him was accurate. That opinion soon changed. During their first performance, as Roscoe's baritone voice and soft-shoe dancing succeeded in delighting the crowd, Minta's feelings about him began to thaw.

The show ran twice daily, and after each second show, some of the company members drank and danced, but Roscoe and Minta strolled the boardwalk along the beach. Impressed with his singing voice, she encouraged him to try for higher billings and large venues. But Roscoe had his own suggestion – why didn't they sing a duet in a Byde-A-Wyle show? Minta agreed and, holding hands at center stage, the young man with his melodic voice and the tiny redhead next to him crooned "Let Me Call You Sweetheart" to each other.

Roscoe had won her over. Decades later, Minta wrote:

His ability to do everything naturally, humorously, artistically, and with ease made me realize he was a genius. His way with audiences, his poise, lack of vanity and jealousy amazed me. I was overwhelmed by his personality and talent. He was all artist on stage, but off the stage he was the big boy who played leapfrog on the beach, swam

Roscoe and Minta were married after only knowing each other for less than two months in 1908

like a champion, shot billiards to perfection, and while he did so, drank huge pitchers of cold buttermilk.

The show closed at the end of July, and Minta planned to spend time with her family before returning to the chorus lines. After the final performance, Roscoe and Minta walked to the end of the pier, standing hand in hand, with the waves shimmering in the moonlight. They professed their love to one another – the first romantic relationship for either of them.

Roscoe had always believed that if two people were in love, they should get married. He got down on one knee and proposed. "Will you marry me?" he asked.

Minta was nervous and noncommittal, so he scooped her up and dangled her over the water, laughing and telling her that he'd drop her if she said no. It was the gesture of a young boy, playful silliness to hide his insecurity. Minta said yes, and he subsequently asked her father for her hand in marriage. He was also won over by the charming young man and quickly agreed.

On August 5, 1908 – six weeks after they met – the couple married on the stage at the Byde-A-Wyle. The wedding was turned into a for-profit, "special, once-in-a-lifetime" event by the theater company. Accompanied by a 12-piece orchestra, Roscoe sang "An Old Sweetheart of Mine," while a photograph of the newlywed couple was projected onto a screen. The audience followed the song with a five-minute round of applause.

It likely seemed fantastical to a 21-year-old Roscoe to be marrying an 18-year-old girl that he'd only known for a month-and-a-half, and onstage before a paying audience, but by then, the often-awkward young man was most comfortable bathed in the hot lights with all eyes on him. Perhaps turning his wedding into another performance was making such an extraordinary event feel more ordinary, not less.

The honeymoon that they'd planned had to be cancelled so they could be part of a one-month run with a show in the farm town of San Bernardino, about 60 miles east of Los Angeles. While Roscoe was singing the dreaded illustrated songs, Minta was bedridden with pleurisy, an inflammation of the lining of the lungs that causes sharp chest pains.

It must have been an eye-opening few weeks for the young couple as they lived together in cramped quarters. Minta was still getting to know the man she had married so soon after meeting him. In private, he was sometimes shy and brooding, but at other times, he was romantic or playful. He could be filled with insecurity and doubt, yet he was always very confident whenever he was singing. Onstage or off, he was happiest when he was performing.

The pair had little in common besides their mutual love for show business, yet they settled into a comfortable routine and an easygoing mixture of love and friendship that would endure for years to come.

TWO

ON JULY 7, 1891, VIRGINIA CAROLINE RAPP WAS BORN IN Chicago. Even though almost every source, including her tombstone, shaved four years off her age and stated she was born in New York in 1895, it was on that day in the Windy City that Virginia arrived in this world.

Destroyed two decades earlier in the great fire of 1871, Chicago had risen from the ashes bigger and better than before. New buildings of wood and masonry, alongside skyscrapers of steel, reached for the heavens next to Lake Michigan. Between the devastating fire and 1900, the city hosted a World's Fair, and its population exploded from 300,000 to nearly 2 million, becoming the second largest in the country, behind only New York City. It became America's industrial heart, the "Hog Butcher to the World," and the "City of Big Shoulders." Waves of immigrants arrived from Eastern Europe, and after the Civil War, a steady stream of rural Americans migrated north in search of factory, construction, and meat-packing jobs. Away from the towering structures on State Street, the department stores of the Loop, the mansions of Prairie Street and Lake Shore Drive, and the monuments of the World's Fair, Chicago was a city of ethnic neighborhoods with rows of brown and gray houses squeezed tightly together and crowded tenement buildings filled with both families and despair.

Virginia grew up in one of those tenement houses. The only child of Mabel Rapp, Virginia was born out of wedlock when Mabel was either 17 or 18. She never knew her father and initially believed that her mother was her sister and that an older woman who used the name Caroline Rapp was her mother. She later thought that Caroline was her grandmother. She wasn't – she was probably no relation at all.

Tracking down information about Mabel is difficult, to say the least. A search of the newspapers reveals a few anecdotes. For

*Two early modeling photos of Virginia, which appeared in an article about
Chicago artists' models in the Chicago Tribune*

instance, two days before Christmas 1892, Mabel, who was described
as "a pretty girl of nineteen," was accidentally locked in Chicago's
Veterans' Building by a janitor. She was in the news again in 1898 when
she was arrested for passing bad checks in association with "the most
dangerous gang of forgers the police have dealt with for years."
Mabel was a part-time chorus girl and occasional model. For some
time between 1900 and 1905, she and her daughter lived in New York
City. Mabel died just before her 30th birthday.

Orphaned at age 11, Virginia lived with her "grandmother,"
Caroline Rapp, and she was also looked after by Kate Hardebeck, who
later called herself Virginia's "adopted aunt," claiming Mabel had
asked her, on her deathbed, to look after her daughter. Friends later
described Virginia in childhood as a "rollicking schoolgirl, addicted to
roller skates, short skirts, bobbed hair, and athletic sports of all kinds."
In addition to sports, she took dancing lessons, perhaps hoping to
follow her mother onstage.

In 1907, Virginia turned 16 and began her modeling career,
changing her name from Rapp to the more exotic Rappe –
pronounced "Rap-Pay." The teenager was entering into an almost
brand-new industry. London designer Lady Duff Gordon is credited
with training the first couture models in 1894 and staging the first
runway show in 1904. From that time until World War II, Paris and, to a
lesser degree, London, dominated high fashion. When Virginia began

in the field, American women were just starting to earn an income modeling dresses and hats at live shows, primarily in department stores, and in newspapers and magazines. Like the early motion picture actors, models were widely perceived as being disreputable and were virtually all anonymous.

However, from the start of her career, the ambitious Virginia wanted publicity. In 1908, an article in the *Chicago Tribune* asked in a bold headline, ARE THE ARTISTS' MODELS OF CHICAGO MORE BEAUTIFUL THAN THE MOST FAMOUS MODELS OF PARIS? And it featured two photographs of Virginia. The article that accompanied, written by a man, of course, painted the 17-year-old as both innocent and manipulative:

> It is predicted by the artists of the city that Virginia Rappe will be one of the world's famous models after the years have mellowed her and taken from her posing the slight touch of childish gaucherie which still remains. She is unreservedly beautiful and, young as she is, shows a remarkable understanding of and sympathy for the subjects she represents.
> She is a simple little girl of 15 years...

Virginia was already shaving years off her age, even at only 17. By the time she was 24, four years had been subtracted, and at 28, it was seven.

> ...who looks out on the world with the clear, dewy eyes of a child just awakened from sleep. She lives at home, where she is the pet of the family, and she poses because she is extremely pretty and she "wants to." What Miss Rappe has wanted to do, she generally has done. She is not spoiled; she has merely a happy faculty for making others see things in the same light in which they appear to her.

In 1912, Virginia worked at the Mandel Brothers Department store in downtown Chicago, sometimes as a model but usually as a clerk

Virginia spent 1912 working at the massive Mandel Brothers

department store in downtown Chicago, sometimes as a model but mainly as a salesclerk.

This was the same year that Virginia entered a pact with sisters Gladys and Ethel Sykes, each promising never to get married. For Gladys, it was to get married *again*. She had recently divorced Arthur Greiner, a race car driver, remembered for a horrific crash in the first Indianapolis 500 in 1911. First to break the vow, she agreed to remarry him a year later.

By October 1912, the three young women had moved to New York City, where their beauty was "attracting considerable attention in the theaters and restaurants of the Longacres Square district" in midtown Manhattan. By then, Virginia was a full-time model and was one of the first American women who give her occupation as "model." When she appeared at fashion shows in the largest department store in Omaha, Nebraska, in September 1913, a newspaper interview noted, "Miss Rappe spends most of her time in New York when she is not touring the country to appear at style shows in big stores."

In 1913, an article was published in newspapers across the country that focused on Virginia's advice to young women. The suggestion of Virginia Rappe, "who as a commercial model travels over the United States and Europe at a salary of $4,000," was that women avoid becoming stenographers – there were too many of those – or waiting in line for poor-paying jobs and instead, think outside the box. Specifically, she encouraged working for wealthy families and doing tasks such as shopping, which are the sorts of jobs employers may not have known they could hire someone to do. "Be original – every girl can be that," Virginia concluded.

Today, the idea of aspiring to do domestic work as a novel solution to unemployment seems quaint at best, but at a time when only 18 percent of American women were working for wages – and when their most common jobs were seamstress, teacher, nanny, or maid – the idea of women creating their own positions and approaching employers rich enough to need such positions was considered news. Virginia followed her own advice by networking with people much wealthier than herself. It's also worth noting that at a time when the average salary for employed men and women was $1,296, Virginia claimed to make $4,000 – more than $90,000 today.

She traveled abroad in ways that were mostly reserved for the moneyed class at the time. A front-page story in 1914 focused on Virginia and a female friend returning to New York City from Europe on an ocean liner. The headline of the story reads: "Girls in Pink Bloomers Mystify Ship's Passengers." The two young women, smiling in the photo, but with their bloomers covered, managed to stir up some publicity, much like being famous for just being famous in the modern day, for their underwear.

Taking her advice to be original, Virginia began designing her own line of clothing in early 1914. This led to a move to San Francisco, primarily to market her fashions at the World's Fair, which kicked off in February 1915. There, she became friends with a dancer named Sidi Spreckels, who had married a millionaire, and she ushered Virginia into high society.

Virginia continued to use the press for publicity. If she were designing fashion today, she would undoubtedly be a social media influencer, but back then, she supplied a steady stream of stories about her designs to the papers. In May 1915 alone, there were four syndicated newspaper articles about her latest clothing creations, each with photographs.

At only 24 years old, Virginia established herself as an entrepreneur, demonstrated a creative method of using the press to her advantage, adeptly demonstrated her independence, and provided career advice to other women.

All of this would sharply contrast with the way she began to be portrayed in courtrooms, newspapers, and tabloids in 1921 – a harsh view of her that has only grown in the decades that followed.

EVEN THOUGH VIRGINIA KEPT HER PROMISE AND NEVER married, she did repeatedly become engaged. She

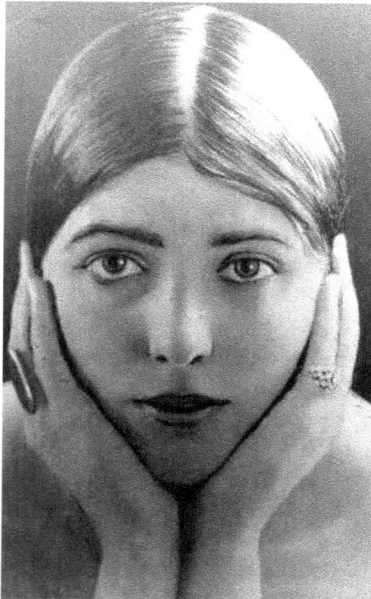

committed to marry at least three men, and possibly two others. In 1910, she met Harry Barker, a real estate developer from Gary, Indiana, in Chicago. After her death, Barker denied having been engaged to her. However, she did wear a diamond ring he gave her, and a witness testified that she broke off the engagement.

Her first confirmed engagement was to 40-year-old sculptor John Sample, who reportedly broke things off with her. In July 1915, she was engaged to Argentine diplomat Alberto d'Akalaine, but it was Virginia who ended it. She told friends he was "nice but old enough to be my grandfather." He was followed by dress designer Robert Moscovitz, who died in a trolley accident in San Francisco.

Her engagement to d'Akalaine seems to indicate that social climbing affected some of her romantic choices. At that time, her best friend was Sidi Spreckels, who was notorious for marrying an older, very wealthy man. As we'll soon see, one more powerful man claimed he was also engaged to Virginia, and if his story was true, it ended only because of her death.

The tragic death of Robert Moscovitz may have been one of the reasons that Virginia decided to move to Los Angeles in the spring of 1916. More likely, though, she was probably motivated by the same reason that thousands of other beautiful young women came to L.A. each year – Hollywood. The so-called "movie struck girls," most still teenagers, poured into Los Angeles from all over America. They came seeking the kind of fame and fortune that girls like Mary Pickford and Lillian Gish had already found. Each of those girls was likely the prettiest girl in her hometown and, of course, imagined that the studios would jump at the chance to make her a star. All but a few, though, were destined for an endless string of cattle calls and often faced poverty and hunger. In a way, they were following Virginia's advice to "be original." However, their journeys inspired fear and alarm in the small towns those girls left behind because, as everyone seemed to know, Hollywood was a seething den of sin, sex, drugs, and prostitution.

Virginia moved into the Hollywood Hotel, a palatial resort in the heart of Tinseltown that was a home and office for actors, producers, directors, and writers – or, more accurately, to the famous, the soon-to-be famous, the never-going-to-be famous, and the used-to-be famous. She later moved in with her "adopted aunt," Kate Hardebeck, and her husband, Joseph, who then lived at the southeastern edge of Hollywood.

There were likely days when Virginia felt that fame and fortune would remain as elusive for her as it was for thousands of other movie-

Hollywood Hotel, where Virginia lived after she arrived in Los Angeles, hoping to break into the movies – like thousands of other

struck girls, most of whom were younger than her and many of the other actors who had come from the stage. However, since films were silent at the time and had no spoken dialogue, being a great actor was less important than it would be when sound came to moving pictures. Beauty and personal connections could be the deciding factors in casting.

Virginia's modeling career slowed considerably after she moved to Hollywood, but she continued to travel and model when she could. In the spring of 1917, she landed a gig modeling gowns in an Atlanta department store. It was also that same year that she scored her big movie break when she won the lead role in the film *Paradise Garden*. The film is now lost, but a review in *Variety* noted that Virginia was a "vamp" who "possesses a dreamy pair of eyes, with the black hair of this type. It will take a number of like roles before she reaches a number of other established vamps."

If you're wondering about the "vamp," which was so popular at the time, it was a new and trendy word that was derived from "vampire" and described a woman who used her sex appeal to entrap and exploit men.

Ironically, in the film, the male lead, Harold Lockwood, is initially infatuated with Virginia's character. But when he learns of her promiscuous nature, he becomes violent and "tears her dress in the rear, leaving her practically nude down to the waist."

The following year, the director of *Paradise Garden* cast Virginia again, this time in the anti-German World War I film *Over the Rhine*. But when the armistice between Germany and the Allies was signed on November 11, 1918, the movie was shelved. Two years later, it would be recut and released as *An Adventuress*, but it received little attention. Two years after that, in 1922, it was recut again and released as *The Isle of Love* to take advantage of the recent fame of two actors who had been unknown when the film was shot – Virginia and Rudolph Valentino.

This version of the film is the only one that exists today. It's an incoherent mess that mixes bathing beauties, biplanes, a cross-dresser, and a lengthy fist fight in the back of a speeding convertible, with a convoluted plot about schemers taking over an island resort that inexplicably hides German soldiers. The cuts are startling, and the title frames seem to contain dialogue from another, equally bad film. But it does live up to its name with surprisingly risqué content, including topless women in a stage show getting in and out of a swimming pool.

Virginia in "Pyjamarama" in 1915

Virginia is nearly as revealing when she steps out of the same pool dressed only in a sheer, sleeveless gown. Her role as Valentino's love interest is stretched out with repeated shots of them riding together in an automobile. Introduced with "Just about the nearest of all the fair femininity on the isle is Vanette," Virginia is first seen lounging on a couch with one leg up, smiling slyly, casually smoking, with her flapper's hairstyle – the perfect example of an independent woman.

PERHAPS THE GREATEST AFFECT ON VIRGINIA'S CAREER AT this time was her relationship with director Henry Lehrman.

Born in the Austro-Hungarian Empire in 1881, Lehrman had immigrated to America from Vienna in late 1906. Three years later, he

Henry Lehrman

began working at Biograph Studios in New York City. According to legend, the thickly accented immigrant told pioneering director D.W. Griffith he was an agent with Pathe studios in France, which was then the largest film production company in the world. When his ruse was discovered, Lehrman was christened with the nickname "Pathe." He was soon appearing as a bit player in Griffith's films before collaborating on Biograph comedies with actor/writer/director Mack Sennett. When Sennett left Biograph in 1912 to start Keystone Studios in Los Angeles, Lehrman went with him.

At the time, comedy films were one-reelers, lasting about 10 to 12 minutes, and were quickly churned out. Lehrman directed 28 of them in 1913 alone, overseeing new and future stars like Ford Sterling, Mabel Normand, Charlie Chaplin, and Roscoe Arbuckle. He also earned another nickname – "Suicide" – because he often pushed his actors to do dangerous stunts. He formed his own production company, called L-KO, which stood for "Lehrman-KnockOut" – and made a string of better-than-average comedy shorts, then moved over to the Fox Film Corporation to head up its comedy division. Doing very well for himself, he spent money lavishly on expensive automobiles and became a regular fixture in Hollywood nightclubs.

Virginia became involved with Lehrman in late 1918, and two years later, they were sharing an address. She was now living the high life in Hollywood, complete with her own driver and a personal trainer. Dating the head of a production company had another perk, too – Lehrman cast her in at least four films, all comedy shorts. The first, a 1919 Fox production, *His Musical Sneeze*, starred Lloyd "Ham" Hamilton, then a comedic star on the rise.

After more than two years with Fox, Lehrman went out on his own again in early 1919, formed Henry Lehrman Productions, and constructed his own $200,000 studio. In a newspaper article from September 1919, the company announced the signing of Virginia and called her "one of the wealthiest and most beautiful young women of western America" and the "richest girl of stage and screen." The announcement also strangely claimed she was both an "heiress" and "the owner of more than 800 acres of the richest oil lands of Texas," with her "wealth computed in the millions." The story was complete fiction, likely concocted by Virginia or Lehrman to garner publicity. It was also made up of stories that aligned with Virginia's many dreams for her future.

The new production company's first film was *A Twilight Baby* in 1920, and again, it starred Lloyd Hamilton and featured Virginia in a supporting role.

But the company wouldn't last for long. It started to drown in bills before it could really get established, causing Lloyd Hamilton to abandon the sinking ship. Virginia appeared in two more Lehrman productions without him – *The Punch of the Irish* and *A Game Lady* – but by the time the second film was released, Lehrman had lost his studio and his house. Debts would haunt him for years.

The company closed for good in early 1921, which was also when Lehrman's relationship with Virginia faltered. He signed a deal to direct four films in Fort Lee, New Jersey, and moved alone back to New York City.

Virginia moved back in with the Hardebecks, but she was unhappy. She probably hoped to rekindle the romance with Lehrman eventually, so she seldom socialized. Kate Hardebeck later said, "Her chief delight was tramping in the hills around Hollywood with her dog."

On July 7, 1921, Virginia turned 30, although she refused to celebrate that as her actual age. Even so, it likely depressed her, as did the death of her friend Billie Ritchie on July 6. Billie had acted in at least 60 films – all made with Henry Lehrman – and he and Virginia had been close.

She had other reasons for being glum. Her design and modeling careers had stalled, and even though she'd had a promising film debut in 1917, she had still failed to establish herself as a movie star four years later. There may have been legitimate reasons for this, including the fact that, based on reviews, she was not a particularly gifted screen performer. It's also likely that her reputation in the industry was harmed by her relationship with Lehrman and the resulting belief that she was not earning her roles through acting talent alone. Also, after at least three engagements and one lengthy relationship, she remained unmarried. The financial success that she sought, which friends like Sidi Spreckels and celebrated screen vamp Louis Glaum enjoyed, had eluded her.

But maybe, as she hiked over the Hollywood hills, alone with her dog and her thoughts, the innovative and independent young woman who urged others to "be original" was planning the next phase of her life.

As August 1921 came to a close, a low-level movie publicist named Al Semnacher, who was ending a failed marriage, asked Virginia if she wanted to ride along with him to San Francisco. She'd known Al for about five years, but only well for the previous six weeks or so. Virginia said yes. Like her friend, she was in need of a vacation. A woman named Maude Delmont, whom Virginia had never met, would also be coming along.

They left early on Saturday, September 3, traveling in Al's automobile on future Highway 99 up through Bakersfield, passing orange groves, lettuce farms, and herds of sheep and cattle. They had sandwiches and coffee, packed by Kate Hardebeck, and Maude had brought along a pint of whiskey that she sipped on. Her fellow travelers didn't partake.

On the way, they stopped in the town of Selma and spent the night at a ranch owned by one of Maude's friends. Virginia mailed a postcard to Kate, saying that she was having a "very pleasant time." They left at 1:30 P.M. the next day, arriving in San Francisco and checking into the Palace Hotel at 9:30 on the evening before Labor Day.

At 11:30 the next morning, while eating breakfast with her traveling companions, Virginia received a message from Fred Fishback, a movie director that she knew. He was at the nearby St. Francis Hotel with actor Lowell Sherman and famous comedian Roscoe "Fatty" Arbuckle. The three men had a suite of connected rooms on the top floor, and a party was going to be happening that day.

Would Virginia like to stop by?

THREE

THE MOVIE INDUSTRY DIDN'T START IN AMERICA – IT WAS JUST in America where it was perfected. After animated motion pictures began to be screened in Paris, Thomas Edison assigned his company's photographer to create a machine for viewing moving photos. That machine, the Kinetoscope, was unveiled in 1893 and established the principles of modern projectors – even though it wasn't a projector. It was more like a peep-show device, a novelty, and the uniqueness quickly wore off.

The race for a true projector ended in 1895, nearly in a three-way tie between the Lumiere Brothers in France, a former employee of Edison named Eugene Lauste, and yet another Edison man, Thomas Armat, who ended up selling his invention to his former boss, who renamed it the Vitascope so that he could continue doing what he did best -- taking other people's inventions and claiming them as his own.

On April 23, 1896, the American motion picture industry was launched when a Vitascope machine projected movies onto a screen at a musical hall in New York City. The series of one-minute flickers played between vaudeville acts and included a shot of waves breaking on a beach, which caused the audience to recoil in fear, afraid of getting drenched.

Edison, the American Mutoscope Company – which later became Biograph – and American Vitagraph were the initial "Big Three" studios, producing most early American movies. Each sold its own projector and churned out a stream of artless films to vaudeville houses. Audiences quickly got tired of them, dismissing moving pictures as a fad that would never last.

But then came along the first "story films," which managed to bring movies into the modern era. Audiences flocked to theaters to

Small nickelodeon theaters became all the rage as Americans began to embrace the movie industry. Change came rapidly to the business.

watch actual narratives on film and nickelodeons began springing up across the country. For just five cents, you got a seat and a continuously repeating program of silent shorts accompanied by piano or organ music. The little theaters catered to the working class who couldn't afford tickets to a play.

The movie business then, however, was much different than it would be even a few years later. One policy was to present no onscreen credits, which was a way to keep the salaries of the nameless talent very low. Movies were marketed on the strength of each company's name and reputation instead. The first movie star, Florence Laurence, became world famous but was known only as "the Biograph Girl." Directing, writing, and acting in motion pictures were considered routine chores, and they paid accordingly.

In 1908, the Big Three studios formed a trust to try and ruin the studios that refused to purchase their licensed cameras and projectors. Edison sued one company after another, charging them with infringing on his copyrights, and East Coast studios went looking for greener pastures – and sunnier skies.

At a time when the sun was important to even indoor filming – via glass ceilings – the short, drab days of winter made it difficult for productions to stay on schedule. The potential for bad weather made exterior shooting impractical, first on the East Coast and then in Chicago, where some movie makers fled to stay one step ahead of Edison.

Some studios began to winter in Cuba or in Florida, but soon, they went in search of another sunny and temperate area, which they found on the other side of the country in a little town just outside of Los Angeles called Hollywood.

The Selig Polyscope Company, started by former magician William Selig, was one of the companies that first fled New York for Chicago. It shot mostly comedies and travel shorts but then in the winter of 1907, director Francis Boggs and a small crew journeyed west. Though the interior scenes were filmed in Chicago, they shot the exteriors on the beach and on a roof in downtown Los Angeles.

Former magician William Selig, who started the Selig-Polyscope Company – one of the first film companies to venture west to Los Angeles in the early 1900s

Boggs resettled in L.A. in March 1909 and set up an outdoor studio for Selig in the drying yard behind a downtown laundry. The third movie he shot there was a western called *Ben's Kid*, which featured comic relief by a young actor named Roscoe Arbuckle.

By that time, Roscoe and Minta were living with Minta's family and local vaudeville bookings had dried up. Roscoe, newly married and barely 22, was anxious to prove to his wife and her parents that he was able to provide, even if that meant the star singer was reduced to working in the lowly moving picture business. At Selig, he earned $5 a day, which was a pittance compared to his future Hollywood salary but acceptable then since he was doing very little work.

By the time he made his second film, *Mrs. Jones' Birthday*, he was the star. He played a husband who kept comically breaking the presents he bought for his wife's big day. A review of the film noted: "The Jones of the picture is a fat fellow, a new face in picture pantomime, and the earnestness of his work adds greatly to its value. There are times when he plays to the camera, but there are other actors more experienced than he in this line of work who do the same thing."

The inexperienced actor was already receiving good marks, but he was ashamed of what he was doing. Stage performers – even those who cut their teeth in vaudeville – considered the movies to be

Roscoe and Minta at home

beneath them. Because of that, he didn't tell Minta where he was earning that $5 each day – the equivalent of $125 today. So, one morning Minta and her mother took the next streetcar after his and found Roscoe in a red satin shirt and a cowboy hat with a guitar, performing in front of a hand-cranked movie camera.

"My god! They're making a motion picture!" Minta exclaimed, as if she had caught her husband with another woman.

When Roscoe saw them, he was furious. "Go home! Go home!" he yelled at the pair. Later, his mother-in-law asked him why he'd hidden what he was doing. Embarrassed, he explained, "Because I didn't want Minty to know or come down there. I'm afraid they will ask her to work. They need people, but I'm not going to permit her to work there. It isn't show business. I'm ashamed of this kind of work, but we need the money."

Later, of course, Roscoe would change his mind, and Minta would carve out a place in the movie business herself, but it was different for everyone in those early days. He later admitted, "There was nobody breaking in then. Everybody was doing as I did – sneaking in."

BEFORE ROSCOE HAD BEEN FORCED INTO MOVIE MAKING to earn a living, he's been part of a theatrical troupe that staged pays based on fables and literary works at the Auditorium Theater in L.A. Most of the shows only lasted a week, allowing him to hone his acting skills in a variety of roles. Most of his reviews were positive, though the *Los Angeles Times* once quipped, "He sings much better than he acts."

In the same theater company with Roscoe was Walter Reed, a veteran vaudevillian who exaggerated his Irish background in his comedy. This was a second chance for Roscoe to learn to deliver laughs, after failing when paired up with Pete Gerland three years earlier. With more practice, he'd started to grow more confident with his comedic skills.

In May 1909 – soon after his making his first films with Selig – Roscoe and Walter were booked into the Orpheum Theater in Bisbee, Arizona, a booming mining town that was only a few miles from the

Mexican border. At that time, the residents of Bisbee numbered over 20,000, mostly men, and when not working in the mines, they wanted entertainment. This turned drinking, gambling, and whoring into the town's most popular pursuits. The notorious Brewery Gulch was jammed with some 50 saloons, brothels, and opium dens that literally never closed.

During his time in Bisbee, Roscoe became a regular in "Brewery Gulch," the vice district of the rough-and-tumble mining town. While booked at the Orpheum Theater, he performed comedy, sang, emceed wrestling matches, and umpired baseball games.

This seemed to be no place for lady, so Minta stayed home in Los Angeles until her mother admonished her, telling her that she needed to be with her husband. So, Minta boarded a train headed east and moved into a Bisbee boarding house with Roscoe. She quickly became an important part of the Reed & Arbuckle company, acting and singing, often in duets with her husband. The company changed its musical comedies every few days and became very popular – so popular that they were asked to stay at the Orpheum for most of 1909.

In Bisbee, they ingratiated themselves with local politicians and with mining executives who lived high above the town in the exclusive "Quality Hill" houses. Roscoe sang solo at an Elks Club Funeral, he and Reed sang and boxed three comical rounds – it was declared a draw – at an Eagles Club event, and the entire company sang at a country club dinner.

At other times, they bonded with the miners who lived in the valley in crowded barracks. Reed was the timekeeper and Roscoe the play-by-play announcer at an Orpheum wrestling match attended by 700 locals, during which the Swedish champ defeated California's best, the Big Indian.

Roscoe became a regular in the Brewery Gulch saloons – much to Minta's dismay – but both she and Roscoe regularly visited the new Warren Ballpark, where the Bisbee Muckers baseball team played. Roscoe umpired one game. After another game, the press noted, "Roscoe Arbuckle and the rest of the Orpheum bunch were again on hand making things lively in rooter's row, especially the ladies.

Roscoe and Minta performed an exhausting schedule of shows at the Princess Theater in Los Angeles

Arbuckle gave a free eccentric dance act when his hopes ran high in the seventh. None of the thespians ever miss a game and are among the loyalist of the loyal legion."

Other than a short stint performing for American miners in northern Mexico, the company remained in Bisbee for eight months. After their final, standing-room-only performance on December 27, the *Bisbee Daily Review* wrote: "At the close of the performance, members of the entire company lined up across the stage and said 'Auld Lang Syne' as a fitting climax to their long, successful engagement here. The company left yesterday for Clifton, and Bisbee will now be a 'sure enough' lonesome town during the intervals between road shows." And with that, the Reed & Arbuckle Arizona Territory tour came to an end.

In the spring of 1910, Reed went back to Bisbee, but Roscoe and Minta were in Los Angeles, living with her parents again. Roscoe organized his own vaudeville company. He wrote the shows, produced them, and starred in them, with Minta in supporting roles. They played at the Princess Theater downtown, cranking out three shows each day, seven days a week, changing the content weekly. The grueling schedule ran from April to mid-July, earning many positive reviews.

By the time the run ended, worn down by the manic pace of producing and performing in 21 vaudeville shows every week, Roscoe decided to focus solely on his acting, which led to his fourth Selig move in Fall 1910. It was called *The Sanitarium* and one review stated, "It may have been slammed together in one night." On that not-so-happy note, he joined the Burbank Theatre stock company, acting in drama and musical comedies.

On top of a very busy professional life, Roscoe was not just sharing a home with Minta and her parents, but also with his wife's 17-year-old sister, Marie; her 13-year-old brother, Paul; and a male lodger. But Roscoe didn't mind the arrangement. He was especially close with

Minta's mother and brother. Flora was kinder and more nurturing than his own mother had ever been, and Paul was the younger sibling that he'd never had.

He played baseball and tag with Paul and the neighborhood kids, or they pitched corn cobs at tin cans and other targets. Minta later remembered: "Roscoe's swinging off the streetcar was always a 'come on' for the kids in the neighborhood. They would yell, run, and jump on him. We always had studying for the new week's role and song to do, but watching him tumble in the grass, throwing a baseball or playing marbles made you know he had very little fun in childhood."

While living with Minta's family, Roscoe got a taste of the family life – and childhood – that he'd never had

In contrast to an early life filled with abuse and neglect, during which he had to go to work, the adult Roscoe found the childhood that he'd always wanted – one with a loving mother and father, and siblings, and friends who wanted nothing more than to play with him.

That overgrown boy, the one that frolicked with the kids who lived down the street, would have a tremendous influence on the character he would play on the big screen.

AROUND THE SAME TIME THAT ROSCOE WAS RUNNING himself ragged with his vaudeville company, the industry that would truly make him famous was starting to come together into what is now its familiar form. In 1910, the Selig Polyscope Company established the first permanent movie studio in Los Angeles.

With 320,000 residents, the city was then in the middle of a population explosion. California was still a semi-recent addition to the United States and eastern newspapers were promising sunshine, warm weather, and easy living on the west coast.

During the late 1800s and early 1900s, thousands of new immigrants had arrived in Southern California, where the new arrivals found plenty that sunshine, but not much else. The city was built in the desert, so there was no natural water supply. It had to be piped in – under very questionable methods – and even today, there still isn't enough to go around.

Hollywood, circa 1910

Of all the reasons for the rapid growth of L.A., Hollywood was undoubtedly one of the biggest ones. It wouldn't be long before the mere mention of the name would guarantee readers for any newspaper story in the nation. In just a few short years, thanks to stars like Mary Pickford, Douglas Fairbanks, Charlie Chaplin and many others, Hollywood would manage to set itself apart from the rest of the world, because everything there seemed larger than life.

In addition to great weather, the Hollywood region provided movie studios with a landscape appropriate for virtually any story – deserts, forests, mountains, lakes, and ocean, from endless vistas of undeveloped scrub land to a rapidly growing city. Los Angeles was also a non-union town, jammed with laborers who were happy to do any job, including building stages and sets, sewing costumes, and making movies. Workers could be hired for half of what it cost in New York and land was even cheaper. Soon, every American movie studio of note established a base in Los Angeles and Hollywood, while former East Coast giants like Edison went bust.

After Selig, the second film company to make the move to Los Angeles was Nestor, which left New Jersey in October 1911. It was the first studio to open in Hollywood itself – a city within a city since it had been annexed by L.A. in 1910. The name stuck around, though.

When Nestor opened its studio there, it was a farm community with dirt roads and fields filled with lemon and orange trees. No one would have suspected then that this sleepy community was soon going to become known all over the world as the place where movies were made – and where dreams came true.

Well, perhaps not always, because on the very day Nestor's studio opened, the Hollywood film industry suffered its first tragedy.

Over at Selig Polyscope, a caretaker burst into a meeting between William Selig and his director, Francis Boggs. With a revolver in his hand, the caretaker fired five times, hitting Boggs twice and Selig once. Boggs died on his way to the hospital, but Selig survived.

The murderer was quickly captured but he offered no explanation about what he fired the shots at the two men. He was convicted and sentenced to 26 years in prison – his motivations forever a mystery.

Perhaps it should have been seen as an omen that a tragic death of mysterious circumstances occurred on the very day that Hollywood as we know it got its start.

There would certainly be many more to come.

Francis Boggs, the movie industry's first murder victim

BUT ROSCOE STILL WASN'T COMMITTED TO MAKING THE movies that would eventually turn him into a household name. Instead, he and Minta joined the traveling troupe of Ferris Hartman, a veteran vaudeville performer and producer who was well-known on the West Coast for first-rate shows. He opened a new show every Sunday, in fact, other without a rehearsal.

Roscoe won star billing with the company, typically singing two solo songs, performing in two dance numbers, and acting in two sketches. In many cases, ads for upcoming revues noted "Special Appearance by Roscoe Arbuckle" and brag that he was a favorite performer in whatever town in which they appeared.

In September 1911, Roscoe and Minta were on a train to Sacramento when Minta started experiencing cramps. She soon discovered she was pregnant, but the couple's happiness turned out to be short-lived when she suffered a miscarriage a short time later. They were devastated by this turn of events. Roscoe blamed himself, as he always did when anything bad happened to those around him. Afterward, Minta stayed in Sacramento for a week alone to convalesce while the tour company moved on to Denver. They were young, she told herself, and they were certain to have other chances to become parents.

When the company reached Chicago, Roscoe found himself the furthest east that he'd even been in his life. The troupe had a critically and commercially successful run in the Windy City and when they were finished, the Arbuckles returned to L.A. before heading back to the Bay Area for Hartman's next production.

In the summer of 1912, a review of one of their shows in Oakland made special mention of "a nice little chap named Roscoe Arbuckle" and added, "He is a positive scream, one of the funniest fat farceurs that has caused chortlings for many a month." Once again, Roscoe's star was rising – though now it was his comedy that was earning praise and his singing. After years of practicing, he was just as comfortable with pratfalls and wisecracks as he was with belting out a tune.

Though only 25, Roscoe had worked in theater for a decade – singing, dancing, joking, and acting – and he likely had started to feel like fame and fortune were always going to elude him. Whether on the road or living in his wife's parents' house, his employment was always at risk of ending without notice. He seemed destined to spend his entire career in the theater, mostly getting by but sometimes not, and always addicted to the same bright lights, makeup, and applause that had first hooked him when he was only a boy.

IN LATE SUMMER 1912, ROSCOE RECEIVED A NEW OFFER FROM Ferris Hartman – and it was an astounding one. Not only would it allow Roscoe to travel to exotic places that few Americans had ever seen, but he would also be the headliner. He couldn't deny the fact that he was stunned – and so was Hartman.

Ferris had been shocked when a Manila-based American tycoon extended an offer for him to bring his entire company to the Orient for an extended tour. Perpetually in debt, Hartman had to scramble to put together the necessary cast, costumes, props, and scripts. The troupe of 43 singers, actors, dancers, musicians, and stagehands set sail on August 12 on a Pacific Mail steamship headed west. It was an ocean voyage of over 7,000 miles. None of the cast members had ever been that far away from home.

One room on the steamship was occupied by the Arbuckles. Minta later recalled their excitement in the early days of the trip: "Roscoe and I made it a habit to stand together at the rail late at night, staring at the running sea. We were extremely close in those moments, closer perhaps than at any other times in our lives. We were happy, truly happy."

Ferris Hartman

Their first stop was Honolulu. Hawaii was then a U.S. territory with a governor and an abdicated queen. At the company's first performance, Queen Lili'uokalani – who was a singer, songwriter, and musician herself – was coaxed out of the royal box to the stage, where she gracefully performed a native dance.

During their three-week stay on Oahu, Hartman said that he and his troupe were "serenaded by bands and royally entertained." Roscoe, always an avid swimmer, spent as much time as he could in the water, sometimes with Olympic gold medalist Duke Kahanamoku.

From Hawaii, the company sailed next to Japan, performing in Yokohama and then Tokyo. The Japanese often stared at Roscoe – a

Minta and Roscoe

man of large girth was presumed to have equally great wealth – but he accepted the attention good-naturedly. The company performed an old favorite of Hartman's, Gilbert and Sullivan's *The Mikado*. The all-white cast was made up to look Japanese with Roscoe as the title character of the emperor. It was a huge hit.

In Shanghai – then considered the "Paris of the East" with a large mix of cultures and American and British districts – members of the company often found themselves surrounded by begging children in the street. There was a stark contrast between the impoverished majority in the city and the native and foreign aristocrats who attended their performances. Reviews complimented Roscoe in blackface as "a quaint old negro servant" and in a love scene with his wife.

However, there was more romance onstage between the Arbuckles than there was in real life at this time. Memories of the "extremely close" moments on the voyage had faded and months living in strange cities far from home had taken their toll. Frequently after a show, Roscoe drank with others in the company, then returned drunk to Minta and complained about how little money he was making as the star of the show. They argued as he groaned about how much better things would be if they'd stayed in California.

If the trip to the Orient had been among the best times in their marriage, his drunken complaints in the Far East were some of the worst.

The tour continued to two westernized cities – Hong Kong and Manila. The company remained in the Philippines for six weeks, over the Christmas holidays, and Roscoe contracted a throat infection, likely caused by his late-night drinking. Three weeks of shows had to be canceled, causing his popularity with the rest of the cast to plummet. This, in turn, made his insecurity and gloominess worse. All he wanted was to be liked by his castmates and his drinking was largely motivated by his desire to fit in with them.

The final performances for the company were back in China, at Tientsin and Peking. Then, finally, on January 31, 1913, Hartman's company boarded a ship and sailed east.

When the ship docked in San Francisco 25 days later, the Arbuckles had been away from home for six months. They spent a little time sightseeing in Northern California, repairing a marriage that had been frayed by Roscoe's drinking and his behavior in China and the Philippines. Able to relax for the first time in weeks, they boarded a train south toward Los Angeles.

Having traveled further than most Americans then or now, they had many stories to tell but the ride south was a bittersweet one. Their luggage was loaded with exotic gifts for Minta's family, but they'd had to borrow the money for the train tickets. The Far East tour had been a once-in-a-lifetime adventure and Roscoe had been the star of the show – a role that had gone to his head at times – but they were poorer because of it. And to make matters worse, they were also unemployed.

FOUR

ITS OFFICIAL NAME WAS KEYSTONE STUDIOS BUT IT WAS better known around Hollywood as the "Fun Factory." And it's chief operating officer, Mack Sennett? The "King of Comedy," of course, but admittedly, it was a moniker he'd earned.

It was at the Fun Factory that the tropes of cinematic slapstick were both invented and perfected – car chases, foot chases, frantic pacing, gravity-defying feats, bumbling policemen, and custard pies to the kisser. The Factory offered a working-class aesthetic that appealed to nickelodeon audiences, including millions of recent immigrants who didn't have to speak English to laugh at the universal language of buffoonish cops and pratfalls.

It was at Keystone Studios where technical innovations were made in editing, stunts, and set design, and during a mere five years developed the careers of some of the greatest acting talents of the silent era, including Charlie Chaplin, Mabel Normand, Harry Langdon, Ford Sterling, Chester Conklin, Charley Chase, Harold Lloyd, Gloria Swanson – and Roscoe Arbuckle.

Mack Sennett had been born Michael Sinnott in 1880 to Rish immigrants. He was raised in rural Quebec, where his father was the town blacksmith, and when he was 17, his family moved to Connecticut, then Massachusetts. He worked as both a boilermaker and in a pulp mill for several years before he got tired of manual labor. Inspired by a vaudeville show he snuck into, he started taking singing lessons and moved to New York City in 1902.

It was during an audition for a theater impresario at the Metropolitan Opera House that he had a revelation that would become a prominent theme for his films. He later recalled that the man told him that he wasn't suited for high-class theater but was better-suited performing in burlesque shows on the Bowery. To Sennett,

Mack Sennett

this introduction to show business laid bare the divide between the leisure class who attended shows on Broadway and the working class, who were entertained on the Bowery. This created a lingering resentment within him toward the producers of "highbrow" entertainment that would become a theme for every film he ever made.

Sennett struggled to eke out a living in the Bowery burlesque houses for a few years but then, in 1908, he turned his attention to moving pictures. He found a job with Biograph and joined the company around the same time as a writer and actor named David Griffith, who – as D.W. Griffith – became Biograph's head director a few months later. Many of the films Griffith made starred Mack Sennett. The director thought the burly, dark-eyed man had a memorable appearance and used him in many bit parts like "gypsy" and "peddler." The two men shared a passion for walking and while strolling the streets of Manhattan, Sennett absorbed all he could from Griffith about the new art of moving pictures. Of Griffith, he would later say, "He was my day school, my adult education program, my university."

But Griffith had nothing to teach him about comedy. The great director wasn't known for his sense of humor – that was all Mack Sennett. He was the one who began directing and writing comedies for Biograph in late 1910. He began devouring everything he could find about comedy, reading short stories and plays, and soaking up everything he could find that was funny. Through trial and error, he figured out the timing that was necessary for generating laughs on film without sound.

In July 1912, having directed more than 100 shorts for Biograph but frustrated with the low pay and lack of control over his work, Sennett left the studio and accepted an offer to run a new comedy film company for Charles Baumann and Adam Kessel. The two producers had been poaching Biograph talent for two years by then and when Sennett partnered with them, he brought along not only Virginia Rappe's future boyfriend, Henry Lehrman, actor Ford Sterling, and Sennett's own girlfriend, Mabel Normand. Baumann and Kessel supplied $2,500 in seed money and, as equal partners with Sennett,

Keystone Studios in Edendale

they launched Keystone Pictures Studio, which made a handful of movies in New York and New Jersey before they packed up and headed west.

Keystone opened up shop at a former horse ranch east of Hollywood, in a part of L.A. that's now Silver Lake but then was called Edendale. They purchased and built a mixture of buildings on the farm, and it became known as the Fun Factory, a plant devoted to churning out comedies as efficiently as Ford was assembling cars.

Sennett later wrote: "Overnight, our place was busting its seams with idiotics. Anything went, and every fool thing you might think of under the influence of hashish, or a hangover went big. We were awash with pretty women, clowns, storytellers who couldn't write. We made a million dollars so fast my fingers ached from trying to count."

Sennett and the rest of the gang created a persona for Keystone that the studio rewrote the rules of comedy by subverting the conventions on-screen as well as off. A constant stream of press releases presented Keystone as a madhouse and its employees as both victims and instigators of chaos – a script editor working on a pile of logs; Sennett and actor Fred Mace chased through a park by a bear; Ford Sterling nearly blown up in an exploding taxicab. The industry press greeted the stream of "shocking but true stories" with some skepticism but printed them anyway. Keystone even shot "behind-the-scenes" films that made it seem as though its casting calls and productions were filled with slapstick antics.

Whether the atmosphere at Keystone was all fun and games or not is open for debate, but there was at least one true eccentric at the studio – Mack Sennett himself. He reveled in his persona as a small-town rube who came to the glitzy big city of Los Angeles. He wore a Panama hat with the crown cut out, believing that sunshine on his prematurely gray and perpetually chaotic hair would prevent baldness. Stains from the tobacco he chewed stained his poorly fitting shirts. His breakfast each day consisted of radishes and onions, washed down with whiskey shots – a meal he believed preserved his health. He rode around the lot on horseback each morning. He had a massive marble bathtub installed in his office on the top floor of the tallest building on the lot and, while bathing, he made phone calls, took business meetings, gave orders, and drafted letters. After each lengthy bath, he was given a rubdown by a former Turkish wrestler.

Thanks to the fact that all the films were silent at the time, there was no dialogue to worry about our microphones to shoot around. This allowed most of Keystone's films to be improvised after sketching out a threadbare plot. All Southern California became the studio's backlot. Filmmakers shot performers amid public events big and small, from fairs to fires. The lakes, streets, and houses near the studio appeared in movie after movie.

Sennett's greatest innovation was speed – the quick editing pace of chase scenes and fights and the breakneck repetition that turned chuckles into belly laughs. Coming years before the animated shorts that so many of us grew up with, the violence in the films was completely over the top with collapsing houses, falling brick walls, boards cracking over heads, guns firing, bombs exploding, and yet the victim always got up again with no greater damage than a blackened face and maybe some tattered clothing. Critics called the films vulgar and yet that vulgarity – just like with vaudeville and burlesque – appealed to the audiences flocking to the theaters to see them. Keystone

Sennett and his crew quickly became famous for their wild, slapstick comedies, especially those featuring the Keystone Kops

comedies had a logic all their own – there were essentially live-action cartoons for adults.

And I don't care how cultured you think you are – they're funny, even more than a century later. But, of course, their weaknesses when we watch them now are as apparent as their strengths. The plots are thin enough to see through and are endlessly recycled. The acting veers into wild pantomime. Racial and ethnic stereotypes are everywhere. The screen time between rounds of mayhem is obviously filler. And yet, you can't help but wait for the infectious moment when the stuck-up heiress falls in the lake or the Keystone Kops give chase in car and wagons, on bicycles or on foot but can't quite catch the crook.

We can't help but laugh, just like we do when, again and again, the funny fat man falls down.

IN EARLY APRIL 1913, ROSCOE ARBUCKLE STEPPED OFF A trolley car wearing his best white suit and walked onto the Keystone Studios lot. He met Mack Sennett, he met Mabel Normand, and he was hired for a salary of $3 a day – quite a bit less than what he'd made for his film debut four years earlier. By that time, though, the popularity of film was rising and Roscoe likely felt that movies were going to provide him with better financial security in the long run than vaudeville would.

Roscoe was introduced to Keystone thanks to his nephew, Al St. John. Thanks to his acrobatic vaudeville career, the 19-year-old got his foot in the door at Keystone doing bit parts and was able to introduce his only slightly older uncle to Mack Sennett. Al, Henry Lehrman, and Sennett himself all acted in Roscoe's first Keystone film, *Murphy's I.O.U.*, which came out just two weeks later, on April 17.

Sennett called Keystone "a university of nonsense where, if an actor or actress had any personality at all, that personality developed in full blossom without inhibition." But initially, he seemed oblivious to Roscoe's skills. He was usually relegated to background roles – until another Keystone innovator spoke up on his behalf.

Mabel Normand

Mabel Normand was the undisputed Queen of early comedy. Born to a poverty-stricken family in New York City in 1893, she was an accomplished athlete as a teenager and labored in a garment factory sweatshop before getting a break in modeling and as a bit player at Biograph. It was there she met Mack Sennett. Seeking bigger roles, though, she moved to Vitagraph, where she usually played a mischievous comic character named Betty, but Sennett encouraged her to return to Biograph. By August 1911, she was back in the fold, acting first in D.W. Griffith's dramas and then almost exclusively in Sennett's comedies. Mabel was a dark-haired, soft-eyed doll with a coy smile, and the camera loved her.

And so did the man behind it. Tumultuous romantic relationships between directors and actresses are now a Hollywood cliché, but Mack and Mabel were the first. He was a gray-haired bear of a man in badly fitted clothes, and she was short, slender, fashionable, and 14 years younger – but they shared a contagious sense of humor, dedication to their craft, and a breezy attitude toward many of life's concerns.

When Sennett left Biograph to start Keystone, Mabel was a minor star, and she moved to the west coast with the promise of $125 a week. Her fearless physicality was on full display in early Keystone comedies like *Mabel's Lovers* (1912), the first of dozens of films with her name in the title.

It's hard to explain to a modern audience just how much of a trailblazer Mabel Normand was. Before her – and even for some time after – female comics were rare. Women rarely appeared in comedies and when they did, they were typically overweight and unattractive. Comedy was considered a man's work – even if that man wore a dress.

But "Madcap Mabel," as she was known, was petite and pretty. She battled the male villains and often rescued her male rescuers. She did all her own death-defying stunts. She played middle-class

"Madcap Mabel" – a trailblazing woman of early Hollywood

characters and had the perfect persona for a studio whose principal audience was the working class. The kind of man who worked all day in a factory thought she was an attainable beauty, and the kind of woman who, as Mabel did, worked all day as a seamstress revered her. In 1914, the readers of *Photoplay* magazine voted her their favorite film personality. She was also one of the first female movie directors.

Mabel was pretty much the same offscreen as she was in front of the camera. She craved excitement. She bought a sports car and a 60-foot yacht used for deep-sea fishing and party trips to Catalina Island. She learned to fly an airplane. She on dance contests, ocean swimming contests, and horse races. She purchased a summer house in the California wilderness, where she and her friends fished and hunted. Her adventurous exploits were frequently reported in the press, but there was never any mention of a boyfriend. Instead, a notice in August 1914 clarified that, despite reports, she had not recently married "the director general" of Keystone.

To her fans, she seemed to be a woman as free and independent as the characters she played, one of the first stars to live the Hollywood lifestyle, and with no greater concern than which car she wanted to drive and how fast she wanted to go.

And it was Mabel who leaned on Mack Sennett to cast Roscoe in bigger roles, convincing him that the fat man was funny. In *Peeping Pete* – one of the six films in which he appeared in June 1913 – he plays

Roscoe and Mabel made for an amazing comedy team – the funny fat man and the petite female comic

a housewife whose husband (Sennett) spies on his neighbor's more attractive wife. Mabel coached Roscoe to ignore the noisy, cranking camera and play to an invisible audience. He was excellent and, as the summer wore on, he became her co-star, replacing Ford Sterling, and his salary was bumped up to $5 a day.

It had been a calculated plan to pair Roscoe with Mabel – the oversized funny man with the petite female comic. In 1913, Keystone's chief competition was film's first comedy duo, John Bunny and Flora Finch, who had starred in more than 160 comedies for Vitagraph in just three years. They were just as odd of a couple as Roscoe and Mabel – Bunny was short and fat with a bulbous nose and jolly demeanor while Finch was skinny and stork-like with a long neck and beaklike nose. Together they played husband and wife, and their physical contrast was a big part of their comedy. So, when Sennett teamed up Roscoe with Mabel, he hoped to duplicate the success of Vitagraph's money-making couple.

In July, the pair filmed *A Noise from the Deep*, playing lovers who fake Mabel's drowning so they can elope. During the shoot, they improvised a gag that would be repeated thousands of times in the years to come when Mabel hurled a custard pie from a catering table

into Roscoe's face. The splat of pies would become a standard component of slapstick comedy, and no one was better at throwing them than Roscoe. The ambidextrous actor sometimes accurately hurled two pies in opposite directions at the same time.

Roscoe's athletic abilities were finally put to good use in the movies. He

In "A Noise from the Deep," Mabel threw the first custard pie in a comedy film.

was fearless with stunts – running, swimming, and climbing – and became an expert at taking falls and absorbing and throwing fake punches. Comedic acting had not come naturally to him – he'd struggled with it on stage at first – but now he practiced playing to invisible crowds, just as Mabel taught him. Because big screens could exaggerate expressions, he discovered that less could be more. He learned how to virtually "wink" at the audience through the camera lens, treating the viewer as his confidant, and not hamming it up like other actors who virtually "shouted" at their audience.

Roscoe appeared in at least 36 movies in 1913, the year he went from background actor to headliner and when his screen persona began to take shape. All those films gave the public a chance to get to know him. His name wasn't important – people recognized his round face and portly body on the street, the beach, and in the saloon.

They loved Fatty before they even knew who Roscoe Arbuckle was. He was one of the first film stars to experience this – one of the first to be recognized on sight and to be beloved wherever he went.

THE FIRST TRUE "FATTY" FILM WAS RELEASED IN SEPTEMBER 1913. It was called *Fatty's Day Off* and it paired him with Mabel again and Sennett tossed in a Kops chase. In the title credits, he was Roscoe "Fatty" Arbuckle. The nickname he'd hated so much as a kid had followed him to adulthood, but he accepted it now as the price of doing business. He never used it himself. Friends called him Roscoe, except for Mabel, who teasingly called him "Big Otto," after a public zoo elephant that William Selig had recently opened in conjunction with his movie studio.

Fatty's Day Off also featured a 23-year-old actress who was making her big-screen debut – Minta Durfee. Roscoe's wife later remembered this as a big moment in their marriage. They were working together with Roscoe's nephew, Al St. John, making new friends in the new movie industry, and living in a city they now thought of as home. They developed an especially close friendship with Mabel

Normand. Thanks to his growing fame, Roscoe's salary rose to $200 a week by the end of 1913.

Another film, *Fatty Joins the Force*, had Roscoe reluctantly saving the police commissioner's daughter and being given a job as a cop. He's harassed by kids, one of whom hits him in the face with a pie. After jumping in a lake to wash off, the kids steal his clothes, and his fellow police officers assume he drowned. Afterward, he runs about in his underwear, and a hysterical woman tells policemen, "There's a wild man at large!" Fatty is arrested and the film ends with him in a jail cell, disgraced, sobbing, and praying for a release.

While it's a minor film on his list, *Fatty Joins the Force* illustrates the emerging "Fatty" persona – cowardly when rescuing the daughter, childlike, surprisingly agile when an inadvertent fall from a punch turns into a backflip but clumsy and prone to stumbles and falls, generally happy-go-lucky but capable of anger when things don't go his way. It's easy to understand his appeal to children -- most of his characters have the personality of a bratty 10-year-old boy – but his adult motivations for sex, money, and success make him a boy-like figure that adults could laugh at, too.

But Roscoe was eager to take on another role – director. Seeing how others, like Mabel, had progressed from acting to calling the shots, he was excited about doing the same. Many of the Fatty films were directed by Henry Lehrman, who Roscoe credited with teaching him all about the mechanics of pictures. When Lehrman and Ford Sterling left Keystone in February 1914, Roscoe, who had already taken over Sterling's role as the studio's go-to lead, filled the void Lehrman left behind in the director's chair.

Roscoe, who was always curious about technology, dismantled and reassembled a film camera one night before his directing debut to better understand how this essential moviemaking tool worked.

And Roscoe's star rose a little bit higher.

BUT BY THE TIME HE CALLED "ACTION!" THERE WAS ANOTHER star on the rise at Keystone.

The story goes that Roscoe and some of the other Keystone actors and crew members were playing cards in the studio dressing room one day when the actor started working on the costume for his new character. They laughed as he modeled a bit of crepe under his nose until he found the mustache that he liked. He then slipped on a pair of Roscoe's pants, swimming in the excess fabric. The snug coat he slipped on belonged to Mabel, one of the few performers at the studio who was slimmed than the English newcomer. The bowler hat that he perched on his head belonged to Roscoe but had originally been owned by Minta's father. The clownishly large shoes had been used in chases by the Keystone Kops. Then, with the addition of a bamboo cane, the actor began to shuffle about, drawing more laughs from his coworkers as he pantomimed an impoverished bumbler in ill-fitting clothes who was trying to maintain his dignity.

Charlie Chaplin had just given birth to the "Little Tramp."

The character that he created in January 1914 had truly originated in Charlie's youth. Back then, living in Victorian London, his mentally unstable mother was placed in an institution, which sent him to a workhouse and a

Charlie Chaplin

rural orphanage before living briefly with his alcoholic father, who died when Charlie was 12. After that, he toured England with a professional dance troupe and then spent most of his teenage years playing child characters on British stages. Approaching 20 years old in 1908, he joined the company of former acrobat Fred Karno, who was to stage comedy what Mack Sennett would be to movie slapstick. Karno's rehearsal space was even called "the Fun Factory," and there his troupe practiced gags until every gesture was perfectly timed. After he discovered that melancholy and mayhem were a great comedic mix, Charlie fleshed out his characters, developing precise timing and a need for perfection.

In 1912, the Fred Karno Company was winding down a tour of North America when Sennett and Mabel – both still at Biograph – attended a show. The following spring, Sennett told his Keystone partners in New York to find the little English fellow in Karno's show, who was named something like "Chapman."

They found him. Charlie was signed to Keystone for $150 a week – three times his best salary with Karno, a big investment in an actor who'd never appeared in film – and he reported to work with Keystone in December 1913.

By then, he was 24 years old, slender, and boyish. He was humble, shy, and tossed into the assembly line of another "Fun Factory," this one dedicated to breaking all the rules he'd learned in the first.

Comedy was fast, emotions were broadly expressed, and rewriting and rehearsals were luxuries that the breakneck schedule simply didn't allow. One day, he told Minta, "I'm too shy, and I feel uncomfortable around here. I feel lost. I'm in a foreign country, and I don't know anyone."

He starred as a shifty swindler in his film debut, *Making a Living*, which pitted him against Henry Lehrman, who was soon to leave the studio. They clashed offscreen, too, when the slow-working newcomer resisted the frantic Keystone pace.

But soon, the Little Tramp made his first appearance, wearing Roscoe's pants and hat. The character caught on with the studio's target audience – a poor man that the poor could laugh at. In *A Film Johnnie*, the Tramp is a movie fan who sneaks into a studio and encounters actors who play themselves, including Roscoe. The bashful Tramp compliments Roscoe, even nervously patting his protruding belly, and Fatty hands him a coin before walking away. The Tramp subsequently bumbles onto a film set and infuriates the director. It's impossible to miss that the film is an in-joke about Charlie's troubles fitting in at Keystone.

Unlike others at the studio, Roscoe didn't resent Charlie or perceive him as a threat. Roscoe wasn't a jealous person; he was much more likely to worry about his own faults. In addition, he was open to Charlie's slower comedic pace and he himself often lobbied for a greater variety of humor styles in Keystone films. Charlie also had a great working relationship with Minta, who frequently acted with him, and this made Roscoe like him even more.

Including two cameos, Roscoe was in six films with Charlie in 1914. But at the end of the year, Charlie's contract with Keystone expired. The Essanay Film Manufacturing Company was a small studio looking to get big, and it offered him a weekly salary of $1,250 and a $10,000 signing bonus. This was more than Mack Sennett paid himself and there was no way that he could match it. So, with a final wave goodbye, the Little Tramp shuffled away from Keystone.

Roscoe and Charlie did six films together in 1914. Their partnership ended when Charlie's contract expired and he moved to Essanay Studios

ANOTHER REASON THAT ROSCOE FELT NO ILL WILL ABOUT the rising stardom of Charlie Chaplin was that his fame, fortune, and celebrity were also rising quickly throughout 1914. When he started directing in March, Sennett gave him his own comedy unit, which included Minta and his nephew, Al. He ended up directing 31 of the 50 films that he appeared in that year, typically working from 8:00 A.M. to 6:00 P.M. six days a week. Although uncredited, he also wrote many storylines, sketching out plots and stunts. He set comedies in the Wild West, cities, farms, amusement parks, a seaside resort, on an Indian reservation, and elsewhere. Unlike other directors on the Keystone lot, he repeatedly delivered his completed films on schedule.

Nine of those 1914 films featured "Fatty" in the title, so that just as moviegoers were buying tickets to see Charlie Chaplin pictures, they were showing up to see Fatty movies, too. Most featured Al as some sort of creep, Minta as the love interest, and Roscoe as the goofball character who stumbles into trouble.

Fatty seemed to be everywhere – in the movies, the newspapers, and the movie magazines, which were also gaining in popularity. One magazine profile about Roscoe appeared in June 1914 with a provocative title that was also a little less hurtful thanks to that question mark -- "Nobody Loves a Fat Man?" In the story, Roscoe joshed back and forth with the interviewer about his weight, his attractiveness to female fans, and the skill of the Keystone baseball team, of which

Roscoe and Minta at the movies

he was a member. About his acting, he joked, "But outside of falling on my ear, being surrounded by snakes, chased by bears, and made to do fifty-foot fives off the long wharf at Santa Monica, my work has been rather uneventful."

But all jokes aside, it was obvious that Roscoe loved his work, and it showed. Even when his onscreen characters were at their worst, he still managed to delight audiences because his joy was contagious.

For instance, there was *Fatty's Magic Pants*, which opens with Roscoe and Minta outside a boarding house, learning about a dance. Charley Chase arrives on the scene and finds the couple dancing on the sidewalk. Charley, who is carrying a tuxedo, informs Fatty that he can't attend the dance without formal wear, so Minta decides to go with Charley instead. Trying to steal the suit, Fatty knocks down Charley, and then Minta knocks down Fatty, and the two woozy men start to fight.

Charley Chase

Later, after his mother beats him instead of lending him 50-cents, Fatty steals Charley's tux off a clothesline. He is decked out in the too tight suit as he attends the benefit dance with Minta. Charley sneaks in and unravels the stolen pants, leaving the embarrassed Fatty in his underwear. Charley then shoots Fatty several times, although the bullets strike with all the effect of a slap. Fatty leaps out a window to the street where a cop, noting his state of undress, places a barrel around him and beats him with a club. The final image is

Charley and Minta laughing at a crying Fatty as the cop herds him off to jail.

Unlike Chaplin's Little Tramp, there's not a lot of sympathy to be had for the title character of *Fatty's Magic Pants*. He is insincere, mean, and lazy. When he greets him, Charley Chase offers his hand, and after they shake, Fatty's smile turns into a scoff. A minute later, Fatty distracts Charley and hits him with a board wrapped in newspaper, only then to laugh heartily at his rival lying on the ground. Though he steals the formal wear, he doesn't appear to be poor. His only legitimate attempt to get his own tux is to beg his mother for the money. The punishment for his minor theft – public humiliation, hit by bullets, police brutality, and jail – doesn't really fit the crime but we don't have much sympathy for Fatty's downfall.

The spoiled man-child isn't that bad, so we smile at his innocence when he naively gives the hatcheck man not just his hat and cane, but also his shoes, and we laugh out loud when, among high society, he dances about with unbridled happiness.

But he's not that good either – he's a grown-up delinquent – so, like his girlfriend and his girlfriend's new beau, we laugh at the end as Fatty cries.

IN 1914, ROSCOE AND MINTA RENTED A LARGE HOUSE NEAR the beach in Santa Monica. After years of traveling, they were happy to finally be settled in one place. They lived there with their dog – a pit bull named Luke – who was a gift to Minta from Keystone director Wilfred Lucas (the dog's namesake) after Minta performed a dangerous stunt for a film. They hired a Japanese servant, Oki, who lived in the guest house. Roscoe often stayed up late, writing plots, planning stunts, figuring out camera angles, smoking, and drinking.

The couple – who'd been broke the year before – now spent their lavish paychecks on luxuries that befitted the movie stars they were. Minta bought designer clothes and perfumes,

Roscoe and his beloved dog, Luke

and Roscoe bought expensive jewelry for her and an automobile for himself – a secondhand Stevens-Duryea Model C-Six touring car. It was something he'd wanted for years but never dreamed he'd ever be able to afford. His love of cars was shared not only by Mabel Normand but also by a new friend, race car driver Barney Oldfield, co-owner of the Oldfield-Kipper Tavern in downtown Los Angeles, which was a trendy spot for sports and movie celebrities, including Roscoe.

Mabel was a frequent visitor to the Arbuckle home. Her relationship with Mack continued to be hot and cold, so it was likely a relief to be with friends and to get time away from the grueling shooting schedules at Keystone. She spent most Sundays with Minta and Big Otto, often with Minta's family, eating dinners cooked by Minta's doting mother.

Mabel on the beach at Santa Monica

Roscoe and Mabel also swam in the ocean together almost every Sunday and while Minta was content to merely watch her husband and friend in the water, she and her husband often enjoyed the local nightlife together. She later recalled: "If either of us went anywhere in the evening, the other always went along. I was brought up in the belief that a wife's place was to suit herself to her husband's wishes, and to go where he wanted to go... Perhaps we made a mistake by being so much together. It is the safest thing for married couples to take an occasional vacation from each other. I know that now, but you couldn't make me believe it then."

It's not hard to imagine Roscoe and Minta as 1914 came to an end, walking along the beach as they had six years earlier when they fell in love. They talked about the future, even if their marriage was sometimes strained as his drinking would darken his mood and cause arguments. But at least they had a marriage, unlike their friends, Mack and Mabel, and unlike their first years together – spent mostly in strange towns and cities – they now had the comfort of financial security and a beautiful home with friends and family nearby. They had wonderful careers, doing what they loved, and even with a few bumps in the road, life was good.

There seemed to be no way that it could ever come to an end.

FIVE

IT HAD BEEN IN 1912 THAT MOVIES HAD STARTED TO CHANGE. They were no longer merely short, novelty films relegated only to storefront nickelodeons. The first full-length American films had been screened that year. They lasted for an hour or more and commanded two or three times the nickel admission price of shorts and were certainly of greater prestige.

And then came *The Birth of a Nation* in 1915. It ran for more than three hours and brought in bigger audiences than any other film of the silent era. Even though it was a racist propaganda piece for the Confederacy and the Ku Klux Klan, it rewrote the language of films and was a monumental business gamble that struck it rich like no motion picture before or since. Frequently banned, legally challenged, and either loved or hated, everyone knew about it, and everyone was talking about it.

As running times grew and movies migrated to those larger venues with larger ticket prices, the old vaudeville houses vanished. They were converted into movie palaces and in the best of them, full orchestras played, and choruses sang. Shades of gray were replaced with tinted color – amber for daylight scenes and blue for night scenes, lavender for scenes of passion, and green for danger, red for fury. The audience was no longer just the working class. By 1915, everyone wanted to go to the movies.

Movie stars weren't just famous faces anymore --- familiar onscreen but otherwise anonymous. Audiences knew their names and their stories and hungered for details about their personal lives. The Biograph Girl, Florence Lawrence, had been the first to have her name marketed, but she soon had company. By 1914, Mary Pickford's name was displayed boldly across theater marquees above the titles of her films. She became the first real movie star. Hollywood went into the

PHOTOPLAY

MAGAZINE *for August*

"Writing" Co...

Fatty Arbuckle

DANCE WITH
ONE WOMAN
AT A TIME

Mabel Normand

The Fastest Growin
Magazine in America
Read It and See Why

15 Cents

fame business and
the studios started looking for ways to promote not just their movies,
but their performers, too.

Studio publicity worked hand in hand with that new presence in
the industry – the movie fan magazines. The first such publications,
Motion Picture Story and *Photoplay*, had been launched in 1911, but
were mostly filled with movie-based short stories until *Photoplay*
reinvented itself in early 1915 with a new focus on the offscreen lives
of actors. It became the first true celebrity magazine, and it brought
more women than ever into movie theaters. Before the end of 1915, 13
additional magazines about Hollywood celebrities were available on
newsstands.

An article in the August 1915 issue of *Photoplay* called
"Heavyweight Athletics" delved into the eating habits of Roscoe
Arbuckle. It claimed that his idea dinner started with a martini and
included "crabmeat cocktail, dozen raw oysters, thin soup, stuffed
celery Parisienne, cold artichokes with mayonnaise, fried salmon steak
or sand dabs, Hungarian goulash with homemade noodles, roast
turkey with dressing and cranberry sauce, fresh asparagus, green
peas, stewed corn, fresh pastry, Roquefort cheese with toasted
crackers, large cup of coffee."

Of course, there was not a shred of truth to this -- Roscoe had an
average appetite – but it made for exciting reading for his fans. The

celebrity press, along with Keystone's own publicity, presented an image of Roscoe that was more in line with the toles he played onscreen than real life – a man of unchecked and oversized appetites. They exaggerated his weight, athletic ability, and gambling habits, and implied that he had a seemingly unquenchable thirst for alcohol. In that same *Photoplay* article was a suggestion from Roscoe: "Do not drink more than six steins of beer during the course of a meal."

More publicity followed Roscoe to San Francisco in April 1915. Kitty Kelly, a columnist for *Flickerings from Film Land*, caught up with him in the lobby of the St. Francis Hotel – six years and six months before that fateful Labor Day – where he was sitting in a plush chair drinking a highball.

While much of the world was embroiled in World War I at the time, San Francisco was staging a World's Fair, allegedly to celebrate the recent completion of the Panama Canal but really to advertise the city's recovery from the 1906 earthquake. It was the same fair that attracted an ambitious model and fashion designer named Virginia Rappe to San Francico.

Roscoe was there with a Keystone cast and crew to shoot two films, both directed by Roscoe and starring him and Mabel Normand. When the interview took place, Roscoe, Mabel, another Keystone actress, and Keystone moneyman Adam Kessel were in the lobby waiting for some rainy skies to clear off.

Kessel told Kitty Kelly that while dramatic films were all the rage, Keystone had a special formula for its comedy shorts – attract the children and their parents will follow.

Roscoe agreed. "I cater to the kids," he said, before explaining how a famous opera singer waited 20 minutes to meet him because her eight children "are so crazy about these Keystone pictures. I really felt much complimented."

But that wasn't the focus of the article when it came to Roscoe. It was him "blinking unconcernedly at his highball." It's likely this cocktail consumption was encouraged by

Kessel but if his image demanded the indulgence, the movie star was happy to oblige.

The publicity machine was so busy building a flamboyant, hard-drinking, life-of-the-party, larger-than-life image for Roscoe that when the time came for him to be taken seriously, no one had any idea what to believe.

So, naturally, they believed the worst.

AFTER CHARLIE CHAPLIN LEFT KEYSTONE, ROSCOE AND MABEL became the studio's top box office draw. Sennett returned to the "husband and wife" formula for them and highlighted the pair in titles like *Mabel and Fatty's Wash Day*, *Fatty and Mabel's Simple Life*, and *Mabel and Fatty's Married Life*. They weren't exactly must-see films, but the two of them together meant childish playfulness and slapstick shenanigans and, as always, audiences loved them.

Both Keystone stars were making $500 a week, but Roscoe was feeling some discontent. Sennett had offered Chaplin $750 a week to renew his contract, only to have him defect to Essanay for even more. He'd paid Broadway star Marie Dressler, a film rookie, $2,500 weekly to headline *Tillie's Punctured Romance*, cinema's first full-length comedy. The 1914 production had been directed by Sennett and featured, with one exception, the entire Keystone company at the time, including Chaplin, Mabel, Minta, and Al St. John. The exception was Roscoe. According to the story, the full-figured Dressler insisted that the rotund star not appear on screen because she was afraid that he'd upstage her. True or not, Roscoe was feeling underpaid and unappreciated.

Roscoe's paycheck was spent as quickly as he got it. Minta later remembered: "Roscoe bought me a Rolls-Royce, the first one in Hollywood with a genuine silver radiator. And jewels, like you've never seen it. He was the most generous man on earth. I never knew a man as generous as he was, not only to me but to everybody. He couldn't say no to anyone. Roscoe used to give me all the money he didn't spend himself. I've sat with thousands of dollars in my purse. Roscoe always said, 'I'll make it, darlin', and you spend it.'"

And he wasn't the only one in the family making a movie star salary. In addition to the money Minta was making, their dog was making many times more than the average working man. Luke's cinematic debut came in January 1915 and two months later, he was headlining in *Fatty's Faithful Fido*, stealing scenes and pulling off stunts, including ladder climbing, for which the pit bull had an almost eerie proficiency. Luke appeared in 10 Fatty movies over five years, and whether the pair were sharing a sandwich or drinking from the same garden hose, the affection between Fatty and Luke was obvious in every scene. It was a love story, both on the screen and off it.

While most critics scorned such silliness, those who worked in the movie industry rarely shared this dismissive attitude about slapstick comedy. When even the most serious dramas required actors to use broad pantomime and show exaggerated emotion to overcome the lack of sound, an oversized comedian getting hit in the face with a custard pie earned the respect of fellow actors and directors. Roscoe was invited to join the prestigious Photoplayer's Club, the first social organization of the movie industry. He and Minta were among the 2,000 who attended the club's 1915 Valentine Day ball, and he became a semi-regular at its Wednesday night dinners.

Roscoe acted in 20 short films in the first seven months of 1915, directing 15 of them. Most paired him with Mabel and many featured what had become his family stock company – Minta, Al, and Luke.

However, none of them appeared in *Miss Fatty's Seaside Lovers*, where Roscoe played a woman being pursued by three men, one of whom was a 22-year-old unknown actor named Harold Lloyd, who would soon have a big career of his own.

They didn't co-star in Fatty's *Tintype Tangle* either, which ups the violence to such heights that it plays like a parody of other Keystone comedies. A jealous husband has two six-shooters that seem to never need reloading, and every bullet seems to connect with Fatty, but they have no lasting consequences. Only a point-blank shot to Fatty's chest knocks him down, but he gets up unbloodied to run the shooter's hand

A publicity shot for "Fatty's Tintype Tangle," showing off the wires from Roscoe's dangerous stunt work in the film

through a meat grinder. Afterward, in perhaps his greatest stunt, Fatty shimmies up a telephone pole and dances about on the suspended wires.

And yes, like a silent film Tom Cruise, he actually performed this stunt, which would've killed him if he had fallen.

With the grueling film schedule and the fact that Roscoe and Minta were together at work as well as at home, the couple's marriage started to get strained. Minta recalled: "We were both busy, and busy people are often nervous and irritable, not because of any dislike, but simply because they get on each other's nerves, and neither one, because of the continual strain of work, has the time to acquire sufficient calmness to meet the other's needs."

She later added: "He wasn't a man who could say, 'I'm sorry.' And that hurt me in some of the disagreements we had before and after the trials. We'd have an argument, and the next day he'd make up for it by buying me a diamond ring or necklace or just some little present. But all he had to do was say, 'I'm sorry.' But he never did."

Mack and Mabel

BY THE SUMMER OF 1915, THE ROCKY RELATIONSHIP BETWEEN Mack Sennett and Mabel Normand had stretched out for more than four years. It remained unacknowledged in the press and even friends were loathe to ask about it, not knowing the status of it. In June 1915, they finally – although privately – became engaged.

But in mid-September, it all ended with a crash.

One night, an actress telephone Mabel and told her to go to Sennett's place immediately. She knocked on his door and he opened it in his underwear. She recognized a woman in a negligee trying to hide behind a sofa – 23-year-old Mae Busch, who had arrived in L.A. early that year and by summer was headlining Keystone movies. Busch hurled a vase at Mabel, which slammed into her forehead. Sennett tried to the blood that immediately began to flow but Mabel pushed him away and staggered out the door.

Roscoe and Minta were in chaise lounges on the porch of their house in Santa Monica when a taxi drove up and stopped. The door opened and the driver, carrying Mabel in his arms, walked up to the porch. There was blood all over her face, in her hair, and streaming down her neck and onto her clothes. Roscoe slipped the driver a little something extra, hoping he'd keep

Mae Busch

the secret. They checked Mabel discreetly into a hospital.

More than a week later, a story finally appeared in the newspaper:

It was learned yesterday that Miss Normand was injured during the staging of a wedding scene at the Keystone studio. It was a typical wedding, which means there was considerable "rough stuff." Roscoe Arbuckle, the heavyweight comedian, was the bridegroom and Miss Normand the bride... There was a general bombardment of old shoes and rice after the ceremony, and some enthusiastic celebrator hurled a boot at the bridal couple. Arbuckle dodged the boot, and it struck Miss Normand on the head.

Mabel playing a bride adds a bitter irony to the story cooked up by the studio publicity machine. For years, it had been generating a stream of publicity about Mabel's dangerous exploits. In recent weeks, she had supposedly been killed by a rattlesnake, stopped a studio burglar with a piece of athletic equipment, bested 20 other athletes in a five-mile ocean swim race, and fended off an octopus that had become attached to her leg. But this time, Mabel went off script,

TRIANGLE KEYSTONE

ROSCOE ARBUCKLE
with Mabel Normand in
FATTY AND MABEL ADRIFT
MACK SENNETT PRODUCTION

purposely giving a less credible explanation, when she told *Photoplay* the following April: "Roscoe sat on my head by mistake. I was unconscious for 12 days and laid up for three months. Don't talk to me about being killed – I've been through it."

Mabel acted in only one other film in 1915 – *Fatty and Mabel Adrift*. It was written and directed by Roscoe and became the pair's best collaboration and a huge financial success. It has all the usual elements – Fatty and Mabel as newlyweds, Al St. John as the villain, and Luke the dog as the hero. But the film has an ambitious plot with the couple cast on the ocean in their barely floating house. The convincing aquatic effects are pulled off with a larger-than-usual budget, filming in a studio water tank and the Pacific Ocean. Roscoe's growing skill as a director is apparent in the creative touches in the film when his shadow kisses a sleeping Mabel, when he and Mabel appear framed by hearts, and when the heart frame of the jealous Al crumbles.

It's a bit of delightful whimsy that hasn't been seen at the movies for at least a century.

BY 1915, ROSCOE HAD TRAVELED MORE WIDELY THAN MOST Americans of the era – Alaska, Hawaii, the Philippines, and the Far East – and yet, he had never been east of Chicago. Despite spending 18 years in vaudeville, he'd never seen New York City, the heart of American theater, a place he'd come to love.

So, Roscoe was excited when a train carrying a dozen members of the Keystone company arrived at Grand Central Station in New York on December 30, 1915. In the group that traveled with him was Minta, Mabel, Al, and another man, Ferris Hartman, who'd been with Roscoe and Minta when they'd toured the Orient years earlier. Roscoe had given him the job of assistant director – a kindness because Hartman had fallen on hard times. He subsequently directed a few movies, most starring Al St. John, but attempts to resurrect his theatrical career failed. In 1931, at age 70, he starved to death in a San Francisco hotel room.

The group, in town to make movies in New Jersey, was met at the station by executives from the Triangle Film Corporation, formed in July to finance, distribute, and exhibit movies produced by three Hollywood heavyweights – D.W. Griffith, Thomas Ince, and Mack Sennett. A

The Keystone crew in New Jersey in late 1915

crowd of fans swarmed the players from Keystone as they strolled along the concourse.

The Keystone group was taken to the Hotel Claridge, which was located in the bustling center of the city on Boardway in Times Square. Limousines were available at their beck and call. On their second night in Manhattan, New Year's Eve, they attended the musical *Peter Rabbit in Dreamland* as guests of the *New York Globe*. The 2,000 people in attendance applauded them when they took their seats in a special box.

For Roscoe and Minta, the stay at the Claridge was short. On one of their first night's there, a drunk and belligerent Roscoe tried to make the kitchen staff cook a meal for him at 3:00 A.M. When they wouldn't, he shouted, "Then I'll find a hotel that does!" And he did – the Cumberland, a few blocks away, which provided them with a larger suite and around-the-clock attention. Minta was not happy with her husband's behavior. She later said: "Roscoe knew he was good for publicity, and the Cumberland manager knew it. Roscoe also knew that money could buy anything – except good manners."

The filming was done just across the Hudson in Fort Lee, New Jersey. Edison and the other New York studios began filming in Fort Lee in 1907, and independent studios appeared there over time, building facilities, and buying equipment to shoot, edit, and process film. It had been nicknamed "Hollywood East" and Triangle had leased studio space there.

The main reason for the cross-country trip was to get try and get some publicity from the New York press. During the first production

"Hollywood East" in Fort Lee, New Jersey

in New Jersey, a writer from *Picture-Play* magazine spent a day on the set and interviewed the stars for a lengthy article called "Behind the Scenes with Fatty and Mabel," which provided a close-up look at Roscoe and Mabel at work. The reporter was taken on a wild ride with Mabel from New York out to Fort Lee and as the day's shoot got under way, the reporter marveled at how the "surreal" the experience was.

After the sound of pistol shots rang out, Roscoe assured the writer not to worry, saying it was just his nephew Al shooting apples off a co-worker's head, testing out the stunt so that Roscoe could try it in his next film. Apparently, the reporter didn't understand that Roscoe was joking.

But he did understand just how hard the Keystone players worked, watching them take falls and absorb punches without complaint. One of the lasting images of the article was Roscoe falling off a banister – once landing on his face – during take after take, cracking heads with an actor while searching for a button and doing this repeatedly despite the pain.

"How many times can you do the same scene?" the reported asked.

"Until I can't do any better," Roscoe replied, as one assistant straightened his bow tie and another combed his hair. "Often, I use 10 or 15 thousand feet of film for a two-reel production. Generally, I take a month or more to produce a picture that runs less than thirty minutes on screen."

The film that Roscoe, Mabel, and company were making that day was *He Did and He Didn't*, an unusual departure for the team. How unusual was it? Well, it's alternate title was *Love and Lobsters*, and in a sequence near the end, jealous Fatty shoves the man he suspects of cheating with his wife out of a window and strangles the wife (Mabel) before he's shot to death. But in case you think they'd started making horror films, this happens in a nightmare, brought on by consuming some bad shellfish.

Roscoe went on to write, direct, and star in seven films made in Fort Lee, but only one more featured Mabel. She left Keystone, but Mack Sennett – who himself wanted to get free of his New York partners – offered his ex her own independent production company, complete with facilities, back in L.A. Wanting to start making dramatic films, she took the

Roscoe's nephew, Al St. John

deal. Rehearsals began in June for her feature, *Mickey*. That summer, Mabel held a "burial at sea" on her yacht. Inside the casket was her slapstick career. As a funeral dirge played, "Madcap Mabel" wished a final goodbye to her old friend and the casket was dumped into the sea.

Roscoe's wife, Minta, returned to Los Angeles, too. Mabel had offered her a part in *Mickey*, and she also wanted to mourn with her family. Her father had died while she was in New York.

Roscoe stayed behind in Fort Lee, though, to make three more films. These pictures featured 20-year-old Alice Lake, a tiny brunette who was a former dancer. She looked like a younger and more spirited version of Minta, the woman she was replacing onscreen – and may have been replacing offscreen, too.

BY THE TIME THAT ROSCOE STARTED MAKING PLANS TO return to Los Angeles, he couldn't help but notice that the country – perhaps the entire world – was in the grips of what the newspapers were calling "Chaplinitis."

While at Essanay in 1915, Charlie Chaplin made 14 films, including his classic *The Tramp*, and his vagabond character grabbed hold of the public like nothing before or since. Syndicated comic strips kept readers up to date on the Little Tramp's daily adventures, while all kinds of Little Tramp merchandise flooded stores. Wearing the costume and mimicking the mannerisms of the beloved character became so popular that theaters sponsored "Charlie Chaplin Nights" with every seat filled with some version of the Tramp.

In his career, Charlie had turned out to be as vagabond as his character. He left Essanay, as he had Keystone, after one year. In February 1916, he signed with the Mutual Film Corporation for a record $10,000 weekly and received a $150,000 signing bonus. In return, he only had to make one comedy short per month for month.

As "Chaplinitis" continued to spread, and as Charlie signed a deal worth $670,000 a year, Roscoe Arbuckle – who had been, a few years earlier Charlie's more famous co-star – was still at Keystone with an annual salary of just $26,000.

But Charlie knew what he was doing – or rather his older half-brother, Syd, knew his way around a contract. Charlie was one of the four biggest stars in Hollywood and Syd wanted to make sure the studio he worked for appreciated that fact.

The other three stars – Mary Pickford, Douglas Fairbanks, and Roscoe Arbuckle – negotiated their own contracts and thanks to this, they were far behind what Charlie was making.

Talent agents, like Syd, had played supporting roles in the theatre business since the 1890s, but they didn't become a major part of the film industry until the late 1920s.

Roscoe, however, like Charlie Chaplin, ended up getting ahead of the pack. He may have never encountered an agent in Los Angeles, but in New York, he met Max Hart, the leading vaudeville talent rep.

Lou Anger

Hart specialized in boosting the careers of his clients – including W.C. Fields and Will Rogers – to Broadway. Roscoe's singing voice was silenced in the movies, but he still loved the stage, so the two men had a lot in common. Hart managed to secure Roscoe a new contract with Metro Pictures that was worth $200,000 annually and it brought along both Minta and Al St. John.

But before Roscoe could accept the deal, fate intervened in the form of Lou Anger, a short and portly vaudeville comedian who had toured with his songstress wife for about a decade. Lou was searching for a career change, and he saw Roscoe as a connection to the film industry that he could exploit.

Promising a better deal than Hart's, Lou talked Roscoe into attending a secret meeting in Atlantic City with a man named Joseph Schenck.

Schenck was born in Russia in 1878 and was 14 when he came to America with his family. They settled in New York and he and his brother, Nicholas, began operating a beer concession in an amusement park, offering free vaudeville shows to keep thirsty customers buying drinks. In 1910, they purchased controlling interest in the Palisades Amusement Park in New Jersey, a small, rundown dump that the brothers managed to make popular by adding better attractions.

Joseph Schenck

The man who financed the operation for them was Marcus Loew, who was then the owner of a chain of vaudeville theaters and nickelodeons. So, when the amusement park started making a profit, they invested their money in the fledgling movie business, buying and operating nickelodeons in a partnership with Loew and financing low-budget movies, some of which were distributed by Paramount Pictures.

Founded in 1914, Paramount was the first national distributor of feature films. Previously, features were leased to regions or screened in rented theaters, but Paramount cultivated its own coast-to-coast theater network. Among the production companies whose movies were distributed by Paramount, the biggest was Famous Players Film Company, run by Adolph Zukor and Jesse Lasky. In May 1916, the pair

Paramount Pictures was founded in 1914 by Adolph Zukor (Left) and Jesse Lasky (Right)

acquired half of Paramount's stock. Lasky became Paramount's vice president and creative force, while Zukor assumed the role of president and began consolidating the company's production, distribution, and exhibition branches into one increasingly powerful entity.

When Jesse Lasky was running Famous Players, he often raided Broadway looking for movie talent. He did the same thing with Paramount, and the studio became known for its prestige feature films, many of which were directed by Cecil B. DeMille. He now began a quest to sign as many of Hollywood's big stars as he could. The first to sign was Mary Pickford. He then tried to entice Chaplin, but his price was too high, so in the summer of 1916, he turned to the second-biggest comedy star – Fatty Arbuckle.

By this time, Joe Schenck was looking for a route for himself to the Hollywood big time, and he proposed that a company be formed to produce Roscoe's movies, which would then be distributed by Paramount. Roscoe would get script and casting control and a salary of $5,000 a week, plus 10-percent of the profits. Schenck would head the company and pocket 20 percent of Arbuckle's take, plus his own share of the company's profits. Lou Anger would serve as Roscoe's agent, and he'd get 10-percent of the star's remaining $4,000 weekly take. This would mean that Roscoe's annual salary – minus Schenck's and Anger's shares – would be $187,200, which was more than seven times what he was making at Keystone, and, with shares of the profits, it was potentially much more lucrative than what he'd make from the Metro deal Max Hart had negotiated for him.

It was an enticing deal for Roscoe. He'd not only have his own production company, but he'd have distribution through Paramount, too. He accepted the offer and Schenck paid Hart $20,000 to let the actor out of his deal. The signing bonus was a Rolls-Royce Silver Ghost touring car.

After at least 122 films over three years, Roscoe's career at Keystone was over. Mack Sennett never forgave him.

He wasn't the only one unhappy with his Paramount deal. Minta was dismayed when she learned of it, even though he failed to tell her about it until he returned to Santa Monica in August. He'd kept her in the dark about the biggest decision of both of their careers.

Years later, she said: "I was greatly upset at how quickly Roscoe had succumbed to the ruthlessness of a Joe Schenck. Joe was all about money, and Roscoe was suddenly all about money to the extent that in cutting ties with Max Hart, her was ruining Al's chance and my chance of earning a living."

Roscoe told her that he would get her something, meaning some kind of movie deal, but Minta recalled: "But I knew there wouldn't be something. I knew it was the beginning of the end for us."

ROSCOE'S RETURN TO SANTA MONICA CAME WITH MORE problems than just Minta's unhappiness about his Paramount deal. In the weeks after he came back, a skin infection near his left knee became infected and inflamed. It probably began as an insect bite that he scratched too many times, but by Labor Day weekend it was much more than just an itch. His knee was now severely swollen, and he could barely walk on it because of the extreme pain. Minta called

Roscoe and Minta were smiling in this publicity photo, but all was not well at home after Roscoe landed the Paramount deal.

neighbor Hobart Bosworth, a friend, actor, and director, to get his advice. He took one look at Roscoe's knee and encouraged him to go to the hospital. Roscoe refused. He didn't want the bad publicity, fearing it might put his new contract in jeopardy. So, Hobart began making telephone calls and finally spoke to a hospital intern who agreed to make a discreet house call.

The intern diagnosed a staph infection that was putting his leg at risk and if it spread through his bloodstream, it could kill him. He injected Roscoe with morphine and incised the wound, leaving it open to drain the pus. He gave Roscoe a prescription for morphine to help with the pain.

And soon, one of the movie industry's first big stars became one of its first drug addicts.

At a time when aspirin didn't yet exist, morphine was sold over the counter as a pain reliever, just like heroin and even cocaine. Reputable pharmaceutical companies sold kits that contained vials of drugs, syringes, and needles, which allowed customers to self-administer for pain. Doctors and pharmacists recommended such drugs for even minor ailments. It was estimated in 1911 that one in every 400 Americans was addicted to an opiate. In 1915, a federal law restricted the sale of opiates and cocaine without a prescription. Doctors, however, still readily prescribed them.

The intern continued to inject Roscoe with morphine each time he returned to inspect the open wound and lengthen the incision, but because the painkiller was to be administered every few hours, Roscoe injected the drug when the intern wasn't there.

Morphine works quickly, racing through the bloodstream from the injection site to the brain. About 30 seconds after injecting it, Roscoe felt a pleasant rush, a tingly sensation that passed within a few minutes. Morphine mimics the effects of endorphins, though in much greater qualities, connecting with receptor sites in the brain and central nervous system and blocking the transmission of pain signals. Roscoe became drowsy, his muscles numb, and his body heavy. His pain vanished, replaced with a warm sensation and the feeling that he was close to sleep, where he'd hang for the next few hours. He'd been lost in a haze during that time, unaware of the people around him until it faded away, the pain returned, and he started craving the needle and his next fix.

Roscoe rarely moved while he was in the throes of his addiction. He lost his appetite – a common side effect of the drug – and as his tolerance grew, doses had to increase to be effective. As the days blurred, the man known as Fatty started losing weight. He no longer wanted to eat. He only cared about the syringe.

His leg was horrific. The open wound was not healing. When the intern decided that amputation was the only thing that might save Roscoe's life, Minta contacted Bosworth, who called a friend, Dr. Maurice Kahn. The doctor diagnosed Roscoe's morphine addiction and checked him into the Kaspare Cohn Hospital near Hollywood. His leg was saved.

But his drug addiction turned out to be more problematic. The science of addiction didn't yet exist. There was simply no research. Morphine had been used for alcohol addiction. Cocaine had been used for morphine addiction. And then there was the "non-addictive" cure for everything – heroin. In Roscoe's case, the most prudent course was the most intimidating – cold turkey.

To kick his cravings, he had to do it locked in a padded cell in a hospital – although, officially, he wasn't there. Officially, he was at home in Santa Monica, swimming in the ocean, playing with Luke, romancing his wife, and drinking, of course. Keystone publicity and the movie industry press, which printed whatever the studios told them to, Roscoe was a borderline alcoholic, but drugs were viewed as degenerate, a vice only for the lowest class.

The first withdrawal symptoms began within hours of the door to his padded room closing behind him – watery eyes, diarrhea, runny nose, sweating. The opiates brought on a rush of euphoria, but now he suffered the opposite. He was restless, irritable, sad, anxious, and, of course, still craving the drug. As the hours crawled by, the initial symptoms got worse, accompanied by involuntary twitching, hot and cold flashes, stomach cramps, and muscle and bone aches. He screamed and moaned for hours at a time. He was unable to sleep, eat, or stop the revolt of his body and mind. His blood pressure soared, his temperature rose, and he was violently sick.

On the second day, his symptoms worsened to the point that they were unbearable. His vomiting, diarrhea, and urination became involuntary, and when there was nothing left, his shaking body continued to try and wring every drop from him. Roscoe collapsed into a fetal position, shaking, and racked by pain that electrified his entire body. He wept but had no tears.

The symptoms peaked three days after his last injection and then, mercifully, subsided after 10 days in Hell.

From the day when he'd received his first morphine injection to the day that he returned home from the hospital, "Fatty" had lost more than 80 pounds. His clothing hung off him, and so did his skin. His eyes were sunken into his skulk, the outline of which was now eerily visible. Unable to walk or even stand on his left leg, he wheeled into the house in a wheelchair.

No one who knew him – whether friend or fan – would likely have recognized him at that point. Roscoe Arbuckle was a ghost of his former, famous self. Uncertain he would ever easily walk again and with the body that had brought him celebrity and wealth in ruins, he suddenly realized how quickly and cruelly his fame and fortune could be taken away.

This is the worst thing that could ever happen to me, Roscoe thought to himself, unable to predict what the future could bring.

SIX

IN FEBRUARY 1917, PARAMOUNT CAME UP WITH A PLAN TO promote its newest star. They'd put him on a train in a private car and send from him the Pacific to the Atlantic on a 23-stop tour, meeting with local exhibitors at banquets, promoting his future with Paramount Pictures.

But there were a few problems.

When the departure date for the tour arrived on February 17, Roscoe's left leg was still in rough shape. He was still in pain and was limping around with a cane. And having lost those 80 pounds, the actor beloved as Fatty remained notably undersized.

But the show must go on. A sendoff party was held on Friday evening at the Hotel Alexandria in downtown Los Angeles and it was attended by Hollywood's elite. Paramount bosses Jesse Lasky and Adolph Zukor were there. The L.A. district attorney served as toastmaster. A giant red banner was painted with bright yellow letters: HE'S WORTH HIS WEIGHT IN LAUGHS, it read. When the guest of honor entered the ballroom – illuminated by a spotlight, accompanied by an orchestra, and greeted with a standing ovation – he was supported by Minta on one side and Lou Anger on the other.

Ironically, they were also the two competing influences on his life. Minta was his motherly nurturer, who always supported him, and because she was more careful about money matters, she'd often served as Roscoe's business manager – until Lou Anger came along. Lou was six years older than his client, a fellow comedian, and they shared a love for vaudeville and baseball. He'd positioned himself to be Roscoe's fun-loving pal and big-brother figure. The trip to come would determine which one of their influences won out.

On the morning after the party, Roscoe boarded the private train car with Lou, Minta, Minta's sister and her husband, friend Joe Bordeaux, a masseur, and a doctor.

The train first went north to San Francisco and then traveled east, stopping in towns both small and large, including Milford, Utah, and Chicago. At each stop, a banquet was held at night and Zukor, Lasky, or Schenck would be there to make a speech about how happy they were to be there, talk about some upcoming Paramount films, and introduce Roscoe. Minta later recalled that Roscoe would always just thank people for attending, "but they laughed as if he'd just told them a lot of jokes."

He greeted crowds outside the train station in Chicago, was "chairman of the reception" at a free screening of Paramount's *Snow White* in Pittsburgh, and was the guest of honor at a Motion Picture Operators Union Ball in Washington, D.C. In Philadelphia, he placed a wreath on the Liberty Bell after a parade was held for him at the train station, followed by a banquet that evening.

As the trip continued, the daily public luncheons and dinners continued. During each one, Fatty was expected to load his plate, and he began packing his trademark pounds back on.

Boston was the last stop on the tour and on the evening of March 6, dinner was served at the luxurious Copley Plaza Hotel. Zukor, Lasky, Marcus Loew, and the Massachusetts attorney general were among the dignitaries in attendance when Roscoe was enthusiastically received by more than 125 of Paramount's New England exhibitors.

That was the official party. It was not the party that would become infamous. That came later, in the early morning hours of March 7, when several prominent members of the Arbuckle reception attended an event in nearby Woburn, Massachusetts, at a brothel called Mishawum Manor.

Hush money would keep the secret of what happened that night quiet for the next four years, but by that time, the story of the "Mishawum Chicken and Champagne Orgy" became too good to keep.

THE STORY OF THIS NOTORIOUS NIGHT EVENTUALLY LEAKED in July 1921 and initially, Roscoe was painted with the same brush as everyone else involved, dragging him into the scandal that shocked Hollywood and the rest of the country. Thankfully, though, on July 13, a story in the *Los Angeles Times* cleared his name. It appeared under a headline that blared, "FATTY" NOT AT PARTY IN ROADHOUSE – "roadhouse" was a stand-in for "whorehouse" – and the sub-headline assured everyone, "Arbuckle Did Not Go to Frolic That Caused Scandal."

Of course, the "chicken and champagne orgy" scandal would be eclipsed two months later by a much greater one, but that summer, Roscoe was in the clear.

The same couldn't be said for those who actually were there on the night in question.

After the dinner to mark the end of Roscoe's publicity tour at Boston's best hotel, 15 of the attendees – including Jesse Lasky and Adolph Zukor – traveled 11 miles north to Mishawum Manor, a stately home that had been converted into an upscale bordello. Since Roscoe was traveling with Minta, he used her presence to decline the invitation to come along. Joseph Schenck also avoided the affair.

The party had been arranged by Hiram Abrams, who Zukor had installed as Paramount's figurehead president. He'd later regret that after Abrams began treating the position as something other than honorary. But for now, he used his clout to set up the night with Lillian Kingston, a madam who went by the name Brownie Kennedy. It included fried chicken, 52 bottles of champagne, which was all allegedly consumed, and 16 women, who were euphemistically referred to as "actresses," when the story later broke. It began at midnight on March 7, and some of the men didn't leave until daylight. Abrams paid the bill of $1,050.

Two months later, Lillian Kingston was arrested, tried, and convicted for "liquor nuisance" and keeping a "house of ill fame," after the brothel's female piano player and one of the prostitutes testified against her. She was fined $100 and sentenced to six months in prison. She appealed, which was when the names of Paramount executives who'd attended the party appeared in the Boston papers, plus a story was mailed to the wife of one of the men. But this turned out to be merely the first rumble of what was going to become a deafening explosion.

The husbands of two female party "attendees" and the father of another – who was a minor – hired lawyers to bring civil complaints against the film executives and to press county District Attorney Nathan Tufts to file criminal charges. Abrams hired Boston lawyer

Daniel Coakley, who met with Tufts to steer the executives clear of the storm. This was accomplished with $100,000 in Paramount hush money and some company stock. Coakley made payments of between $7,000 and $16,500 to potential plaintiffs in exchange for signed agreements stating they would not pursue legal measures against Paramount executives.

On appeal, Kingston entered a guilty plea to the liquor charge and paid the $100 fine. The brothel charge was dismissed when the paid-off complainants refused to come forward again and by then, Mishawum Manor was closed.

No charges were filed, criminally or civilly, against the Paramount men and the night of drunken debauchery remained a local story that was quickly forgotten.

And it stayed forgotten for the next four and a half years.

District Attorney Nathan Tufts, who prosecuted brothel madam Lilliam Kingston – and was later removed from office when the news of the studio executives involved in the "Chicken and Champagne Orgy" were revealed

Then, on July 11, 1921, the story exploded when a hearing was held in Boston to remove Tufts from office. Though none of the hush money was traced to him, that likely just proved that he was adept at covering his trail.

During the hearing, Tufts was found in dereliction of his duty in not fully investigating potential crimes at the "orgy" and for conspiring with Coakley and Kingston's attorney to extort the Paramount executives under the threat of indictments. Eventually, several months later, Tufts was removed from office by the Massachusetts Supreme Court and Coakley was disbarred.

More importantly, though, as far as Hollywood was concerned, the scandal became big news. The hush money had kept Zukor, Lasky, Abrams, and the rest out of court in 1917, but now they had been placed at the heart of a widely reported and humiliating event.

The news of the scandal would have a terrible effect on the fate of Roscoe Arbuckle – even though he wasn't even there.

Roscoe and Minta put up a loving front during the film tour but the troubles between them had worsened, mostly thanks to Roscoe's drinking and other bad behavior

ON MARCH 7, THE ARBUCKLE ENTOURAGE – UNAWARE OF what had occurred at Mishawum Manor – took a train to New York City, where Roscoe and Minta moved back into a suite at the Cumberland Hotel.

Roscoe was finally feeling better. He'd put on some weight, and he was moving around much better on his left leg. He started planning comedy shorts for his new production company – none of which included his wife. Minta would always blame Lou Anger for forcing her out of her husband's film plans, effectively ending her acting career and damaging her marriage beyond repair.

Anger may have hastened the end of their marriage, but the romantic relationship had been troubled for a few years. Roscoe liked drinking with his pals and wild nights on the town; Minta liked reading books and quiet nights at home. They argued frequently and in private, fueled by liquor, his insecurities often boiled over into a rage. And by Minta's own accounts, her husband, still in pain from his injury, hadn't been able to perform sexually during the cross-country tour. She recounted one rampage after he failed to have sex with her in which he threw dresser drawers and ripped a telephone off a wall.

"I'm a star! I'm not supposed to be married! I can't be hampered by a wife!" he yelled at her, before kicking a table and cutting his leg. He then locked himself in the bathroom, remorseful and ashamed.

Alice Lake, one of Roscoe's co-stars and an actress he'd likely been unfaithful with

"I never heard a man cry so hard in my life," Minta said. "It was terrible."

Roscoe had likely been unfaithful, almost undoubtedly with Alice Lake and possibly with others, too. He had married young, with little experience with women, when he was poor and was a virtually unknown singer in a stage show. Eight and a half years later, he was one of the most famous men in the world. He was wealthy and was soon to be even wealthier. He was also a film director capable of launching the careers of an almost endless number of beautiful young actresses. He'd told Minta that he was a star – he wasn't supposed to be married. He wanted to experience everything it meant to be a movie star.

On March 24, Roscoe turned 30 and as a gift, Minta bought him memberships in the Friars Club and the Lambs Club, exclusive all-male New York theatrical societies. Soon after, he moved into the Friars' new Manhattan clubhouse – dubbed the "Monastery" – claiming that the massages and baths available there were ideal for his recovery.

Minta moved into a Manhattan apartment with her sister and brother-in-law. The Arbuckle marriage was over in every way but on paper.

But that paper was still very important. In 1917, a divorce was sure to do damage to Roscoe's image, especially at that crucial point in his career. So, the couple separated instead. Minta signed an agreement that paid her $500 weekly while the couple privately lived apart.

Minta wouldn't work for more than a year. When Mabel Normand's film, *Mickey,* was finally released in August 1918, it was well-reviewed and popular, and she had a plum supporting role. The following year, she starred in a series of two-reel comedies for a small New York film company, but hardly anyone noticed.

She slipped out of the public eye after that, only to emerge again in September 1921, defending the husband from whom she'd been separated from for more than four years.

IN THE SAME MONTH THAT ROSCOE EFFECTIVELY LOST HIS wife, he gained a best friend.

Joseph Keaton was born on October 4, 1895, as his parents were passing through the small town of Piqua, Kansas, while working for a traveling medicine show. The story of his early years grew more in the telling than Roscoe's did – a cyclone blew away the town where he was born. When he was not yet two, he lost a finger in a clothes wringer. His head was split open by a brick he tossed. He was sucked

A young Buster Keaton performed with his parents, Joe and Myra

out of his bedroom window by another tornado and dropped out of the sky a block away. And the nickname that his career would make famous was given to him by Harry Houdini after he fell down a flight of stairs when he was a little boy and suffered no injuries. "That was a buster," the great magician announced.

But little of that was true. Houdini was a family friend, but if we can believe the original version of the story told by Keaton's father, another entertainer gave the boy his nickname after just such a tumble. And while a too-curious Buster did shred his right index finger in a clothes wringer, the tale of misfortune was embellished to further the legend of the seemingly indestructible child.

Keaton began his stage career even younger than Roscoe did. His parents, Joe and Myra, moved with their son to New York City in 1899, and they began establishing an acrobatic table act that Joe performed in vaudeville theaters. Myra played a coronet while dodging Joe's kicks and table twirls.

In October 1900, they were playing in Delaware and Joe placed his five-year-old son onstage as part of the show. Soon, Buster was getting laughs and the act began to focus on Joe's hilarious efforts to control his rambunctious son. When Buster repeatedly interrupted his father's monologue, Joe tossed him around the stage and into the orchestra pit. What seemed to be slapstick child abuse initially caused the audience to recoil and squirm, but that discomfort turned to laughter and applause when Buster reappeared unhurt – only to be playfully punished again.

Joe realized the biggest laughs came when a pratfall went unacknowledged, so he coached his son not to smile or make a face, no matter how funny or painful the gag. This was the beginning of the stone-faced persona that Buster would make famous in his films.

The pint-sized comedian quickly became well-known on the vaudeville circuit. He would always claim he enjoyed the professional roughhousing and learned early how to break his falls, rarely suffering more than the kind of abrasions he could have gotten playing with friends. But New York's child labor laws restricted young performers and the Keatons played a cat-and-mouse game with enforcement agents for years before getting caught in 1907 and being banned from New York theaters for two years.

Finally, on October 4, 1909, a piece in *Variety* announced his sixteenth birthday and his legal return to the stage. He was actually 14, but regardless, he had grown too big to be easily tossed about so the act had to evolve. Now father and son traded blows as physical equals and Buster sang parodies of hit songs and poked fun at other acts on the bill.

Buster Keaton

But real life wasn't always filled with laughter.

Over the next several years, resentments and grievances between father and son grew, made worse by Joe's growing fondness for alcohol. Sometimes the onstage violence was as real as it appeared to be. The three Keatons continued working together until January 1917, but by then 21-year-old Buster was exhausted by the three-times-a-day shows and was sick of his father.

He signed with Max Hart, who secured a role for him on Broadway, but Buster's relationship with Hart was as brief as Roscoe's – and was ended by the same man. In mid-March, Buster was walking through Times Square when he ran into Lou Anger, with whom he'd been on the same vaudeville bills. Anger was now getting into the movies as the manager of Fatty Arbuckle, who was starting production on his new company's first movie. He invited Buster to stop by the set in the morning and see what he thought about making films.

Joseph Schenck's Colony Studio occupied a warehouse on East Forty-Eighth Street. On the day that Buster Keaton dropped by, the Norma Talmadge Film Corporation was on the first floor, making a new drama picture starring Norma herself, who was also Schenck's wife. On the top floor, under a glass roof, was Roscoe's Comique Film Corporation. He hadn't chosen the name, which meant "comic" in French. Roscoe loved to annoy Schenck by pronouncing it "com-eeky."

The crew was hard at work that morning building a general store. When Buster arrived, the crew was setting up the next shot while Roscoe – the film's director and star – was going over gags for a

scene with Al St. John and other
actors who were playing store customers. Roscoe was in a costume
that had become almost as recognizable as Charlie Chaplin's – plaid
shirt, suspenders, pants pulled up too high, and a bowler hat, several
sizes too small, perched atop his head.

Roscoe recognized Buster right away. He was familiar with his
family act, and he invited him to join in the onscreen mayhem. But
Buster hesitated. Though he'd grown up sharing vaudeville bills with
moving pictures and had sat in the dark and watched his share of
films, his father always considered movie acting to be beneath a
theatrical performer. But perhaps, finally ready to break free of his
father's control once and for all, he joined the scene when Roscoe
asked him again.

Dressed in overalls and a straw hat, Buster plays a customer who
buys a bucket of molasses from Fatty but gets his foot stuck in a
puddle of sticky goo. Fatty then knocks him free and tosses him out of
the store.

Buster had been thrilled with his first experience performing for
a camera lens and like Roscoe, he was also fascinated by mechanical
inventions. Roscoe took the camera apart for him so he would
understand how it worked and what it could do. He showed him how
the film was developed, cut, and then spliced together. Buster was
hooked, finding everything about the new business to be exciting –
including the company secretary, Norma Talmadge's sister, Natalie,
who he met that first day and married five years later.

The next morning, Buster told Max Hart that he was going to withdraw from the show he'd lined up with him so that he could pursue movie acting with Roscoe Arbuckle. Twice thwarted by Lou Anger, Hart tore up the contract – presumably for another fee – and Buster was free to become a film star.

When Buster showed up later at the Colony Studio set, Roscoe looked at him nonchalantly and told him, "You're late" – and one of the most entertaining pairings in early comedy history began.

Their first film together, *The Butcher's Boy*, was a two-reeler that was told in two parts – the first in a general store and the second in a girl's boarding school with both Roscoe and Al St. John in drag. Keaton's three-and-a-half-minute segment is the highlight, building up to a baking flour fight between Roscoe, Al, and Buster. When compared to the films that followed, this one was really just a retread of a Keystone comedy, but it did well. This was Roscoe's first movie in over nine months and since his audience had been used to getting a new Fatty flick every two weeks, they were hungry for something new. Paramount's publicity machine created a buzz, and moviegoers turned out in droves.

By this point, Al St. John had created a niche for himself as the villain in his uncle's films, a role he played in all five of the initial Comique shorts and most of those that followed. Usually, he played an unhinged rube who was trying to steal Fatty's girl.

When the camera started rolling on *The Butcher's Boy*, Al was 23 years old, married, and had appeared in almost 100 movies. He was never a leading man and even Roscoe laughingly noted that he had a "supremely terrible face." Still, it was mostly makeup that gave him

Buster Keaton, Roscoe, and Al St. John

(Right) Al playing one of the unhinged characters that showed up in his uncle's comedy shorts

his distinctive creepiness. His teeth were blackened to look lost. His lips were darkened, and his cheekbones were contoured so that his face looked narrow. He typically wore the clothing of a country yokel, and he used his gangly form to great advantage, weaving around on rubbery legs as he mugged for the camera with bug eyes and ghoulish grins. He was a talented actor but one who the audience immediately accepted as a sinister foil. Al had always been an acrobatic athlete, too, which meant he could perform his own amazing stunts. His skills made every one of Fatty's films better and, in hindsight, it's hard to imagine them without Al in them.

Over the next six months, four more shorts followed and while working with Buster, Roscoe's artistry dramatically improved. In an extended scene during *The Rough House*, Fatty lazily fights a fire in his burning bed using one cup of water at a time, then he wrangles a limp garden hose as though it's an out-of-control fire house. It's the kind of surreal comedy in which Buster would later specialize when making his own movies.

In *His Wedding Night*, Roscoe and Buster inadvertently put the first same-sex marriage ceremony on film when Fatty nearly weds, by mistake, Buster, who had earlier put on a wedding dress. The movie contains a scene in which Fatty kisses a woman while she is unconscious – becoming just one of the numerous onscreen moments in which a horny Fatty behaves badly toward women. The memories of this kind of cinematic behavior only helped the public form a quick opinion about the star in September 1921.

There's more of the same in *Oh Doctor!* With Roscoe playing a character who is unbelievably called "Dr. Fatty Holepoke," who brazenly tries to cheat on his wife. Buster plays the doctor's abused son, but with each blow from his father, the son seems mortally injured and cries uproariously, making fun at his old job performing with his father. Roscoe also laughs at his own past, slipping into a Keystone Kops uniform and even a Chaplin-style mustache.

The fifth and final Arbuckle/Keaton film was shot on location and called *Coney Island*. The opening shots are of Coney Island's Luna Park and were filmed the same way Keystone did it – secretly, while the park was in operation. It would've been too expensive to do with permission.

At the beach, following Luke the dog's lead, Fatty not only digs in the sand but buries himself to escape from his shrewish wife, played by Agnes Neilson. In the park, Buster attempts to rescue his lost date, played by Alice Mann, after she's stolen away by Al St. John. After Fatty helps to get Al arrested, Buster's date ends up with Fatty instead and, after a wild water ride, the two enter a bathhouse.

When Fatty tries to rent a bathing suit, the man behind the counter says, "Can't fit you. Hire a tent." Fatty steals a woman's bathing suit and then breaks cinema's fourth

Buster swung the hammer, and Roscoe took it on the chin in "Coney Island"

wall when he sees the camera about to show him naked and tells it to shoot him from the chest up.

At the beach, Buster and Mann reunite, while Fatty and Al fight in the ocean. The police are called and thrown into the same jail cell; the fight starts again but they knock out the cops instead of each other. After they escape, Fatty locks up his wife in his place. Outside, he and Al swear off women – the cause of all their troubles – and vow to make sure their friendship comes first. The vow lasts only until two pretty women pass by.

Written by Roscoe, Coney Island has a cynical view of romantic relationships. Fatty cheats on his wife, a woman leaves her date for the first man who can better take care of her and then does it again, while Al pursues every female – and a cross-dressing Fatty – without regard to their availability. Only Keaton's character remains out of the romance mess. When he sees Alice Mann in her swimsuit, he faints, but Fatty leers at her and grins. Buster wins the girl back, but the final image of the film is of Fatty and Al once again on the prowl.

At one point in the movie, Fatty drops a coin in a fortune-telling machine that promises an answer to the question: "When will I marry and have a happy home?"

Fatty – married in real life and in the film – receives a card from the machine that reads: "There ain't no such animal."

ROSCOE WAS ON HIS OWN IN NEW YORK DURING THE spring and summer of 1917. He was famous, wealthy, and living a bachelor lifestyle that ensured he got to experience everything that came with his life as a movie star. He also had a new best friend in Buster Keaton. Unlike his onscreen persona, Buster was quick to smile and laugh and he and Roscoe shared an irreverent sense of humor that included a love of practical jokes. They also shared a fascination with trains and fast cars. Though the pair worked long hours at the studio or on location, they spent their evenings on the town, impeccably dressed and motoring around the city in Roscoe's Rolls-Royce.

They became regulars at a place called Reisenweber's, a massive dining and entertainment complex in Manhattan. It occupied half a block and was four stories tall with a rooftop garden lounge and a dozen dining rooms. It boasted 1,000 employees and could hold as many as 5,000 guests. Its tropical-themed Hawaiian Room featured hula

Reisenweber's in Manhattan, Roscoe's and Buster's favorite hangout while in New York. It was closed by Prohibition raids in 1922.

dancers, while its lavish Paradise was a ballroom that showcased a cabaret revue and imposed the city's first cover charge – 25-cents. When Reisenweber's opened in January 1917, it booked the Original Dixieland Band, which promptly turned the club into the hottest place in the city and helped popularize a new form of music straight from New Orleans called "jazz." Reisenweber's became tremendously popular but would only last five years. As a prime target for Prohibition raids a few years later, it was closed in 1922.

On weekends, Roscoe and Buster attended Gatsby-like parties at the waterfront estate of Joe Schenck and Norma Talmadge in Bayside, Queens. They sailed on Long Island Sound, ate the steaks Schenck barbecued, drank champagne, played croquet, and rubbed shoulders with business tycoons and celebrities, almost always including Irving Berlin, a childhood friend of Joe Schenck.

Roscoe made numerous appearances at public events, sometimes for charity and sometimes for profit. In May, at the Motion Picture Charity Ball – a Red Cross benefit attended by more than 5,000 and included "almost every prominent film actor and actress in New York – he led the grand march and generated laughs with a little comical dancing.

The weekend after the ball, he traveled with 75 others on a private train to attend the opening night of a minor league baseball game in Portland, Maine. The team – called The Duffs – were owned by Hiram Abrams, then president of Paramount.

On April 6, 1917, the United States had entered World War I and in June, the draft was instituted for all men between the ages of 21 and 31. That month, Comique purchased nearly $50,000 in war bonds to support America's efforts, although Roscoe declared that he likely wouldn't be much help on the front lines. He did, however, joke that he be useful when it came to stopping bullets "or providing a human fortification behind which my entire company could hide."

On June 5, both he and Keaton registered for the draft. When asked if they might be exempt from service, Buster – who was missing most of his trigger finger, left the line blank. Roscoe wrote "yes," but offered no specific reason about why he shouldn't serve.

In August, Roscoe sold his Rolls-Royce to Hiram Abrams and purchased his first Pierce-Arrow. Three months later, he bought his manager, Lou Anger, a surprise gift of a new Cadillac. As Minta later recalled, "Roscoe was a poor boy, abandoned as a kid by his father, who was an alcoholic. So, I guess he had to make up for his impoverished childhood. He spent money wildly. He was the first star to have an entourage."

That entourage was a group of men – of course – most of whom worked in the movie industry but were less famous and less wealthy than Roscoe. Among them were Buster, Lou Anger, and Joe Bordeaux, but other members changed from night to night and from nightclub to nightclub. Roscoe loved the company and liked nothing better than getting together with the boys, singing, laughing, and partying like they were in college. In effect, Roscoe had created the family that he never had --- and they were *his* family. He was in charge, and he picked up the tab. He led and they followed. At age 30, he was finally enjoying the kind of lifestyle that he'd missed out on when he was a younger man.

Some of the money that Roscoe wildly spent went toward new suits, hats, and shoes. He loved fine clothes and was quoted as saying, "There's nothing in the world more repulsive as a fat man who isn't well-dressed."

But he had the money to blow on clothes, generous gifts for co-workers and friends, and nightly food and drinks from Reisenweber's and other hot spots. His weekly income – minus Schenk and Anger's shares and Minta's $500 and not counting his share of box office profits

– was $3,500. That was more than twice the average *annual* household income in America at the time.

Roscoe Arbuckle had finally arrived. He now had the money to match his fame and had established himself as a genuine Hollywood celebrity.

Balboa Studios in Long Beach

TWO YEARS EARLIER, ROSCOE HAD SPENT A WINTER FILMING in New York, and it was not an experience that he wanted to repeat – it was time to go home.

In October 1917, he and his company relocated to Southern California and to the rapidly growing community of Long Beach, where he'd performed and had gotten married nine years earlier. Two brothers, Herbert and Elwood Horkheimer, had purchased Edison's small studio in Long Beach in 1912 and started expanding.

By the time Roscoe and company arrived, Balboa Studio occupied 20 buildings on eight acres in downtown Long Beach, just six blocks from the ocean. The studio had gained attention for its modern facilities and technical innovations, including the largest glass-enclosed stage on the West Coast. With an many as 10 production companies shotting at the same time, Balboa had become the city's largest employer and a tourist attraction. It was a major achievement to lure Roscoe there and away from Hollywood.

Roscoe rented a house on the ocean about a mile from the studio, sharing it with a former vaudeville performer named Herbert Warren who was now an editor at Comique, Warren's wife, and Luke the dog. Buster rented an apartment with his parents. Seeing his son's rapid rise in the movies, Joe Keaton changed his mind about films, and he appeared in the first three Comique films made at Balboa.

Having gotten used to the New York City nightlife, Roscoe sought out the same thing in and around Los Angeles. He and his entourage made the rounds, dropping in at Al Levy's Tavern in Hollywood, the Cabrillo Ship Café off the Venice pier, the Café Nat Goodwin on the Santa Monica pier, and every other glitzy and glamorous spot in the area. A typical night, like a Tuesday, usually began with dinner at the Hotel Alexandria downtown, moved to ringside seats for prizefights at Jack Doyle's arena in Vernon, and ended with drinking and dancing

Some of Roscoe's favorite nightspots in Los Angeles included the Ship Café (Above Left), Café Nat Goodwin on the Santa Monica Pier (Above Right), and Al Levy's Tavern

at the nearby Vernon Country Club, where the waiters drew straws to serve Roscoe because of his generous tips.

The entourage slowly grew as the night progressed. Casual acquaintances and even strangers learned they could be pals with Fatty by the end of the night if they joined the group somewhere along the way. And, as always, the movie star always picked up the bill.

Celebrity writer Louella Parsons wrote of Roscoe and his entourage: "Some men might resent such a thing as putting them in the easy-mark class, but it is one of the nice things about Roscoe Arbuckle that he is like a big boy in wanting to share with his friends the good things which have come his way."

AT THAT TIME, WORK WAS ALMOST AS FUN AS ROSCOE'S After-hours events. The first Comique film at Balboa, *A Country Hero*, featured a scene in which a train crashed into two cars, ballooning the budget. They also constructed a rural town on the lost, dubbed "Jazzville," and while the name captured the hot new music genre, the town itself was a reproduction of Roscoe's birthplace of Smith Centre, Kansas.

His next film was *Out West*, Roscoe's first western and a spoof of that style of film. One of the standout scenes takes place on top of a speeding train. Since both Roscoe and Buster were fans of macabre humor, much of the comedy in *Out West* is dark. Keaton's saloon owner character casually shoots a card cheat in the back multiple times, kicks the dead man through a trap door in the barroom floor, drops a corset onto the corpse, removes his hat for a one-second blessing, and slams the door shut.

This was something new for a comedy short – bullets that actually do damage. Part of the way that *Out West* spoofed the westerns of the time was by exaggerating their violence.

As Roscoe continued to innovate what was essentially celluloid pantomime, Comique comedies became increasingly surreal. *The Bell Boy* includes a random scene involving a mysterious man with a long beard who is looking for a barber. Fatty the bellboy uses scissors, a razor, and hats to turn the customer into a dead ringer for first General Grant, then Abraham Lincoln, then Germany's Kaiser Wilhelm.

Moonshine features a shot in which 45 men come out of a Model T and another of a wrecked cabin reassembling itself. In *The Cook*, chef Fatty instantly prepares food and drinks that he then flips across the kitchen for Buster the waiter to effortlessly catch without spilling a drop – even as both are dancing "Egyptian-style" in a spoof of Theda Bara's title role in *Cleopatra*.

His most surreal film, though, was *Good Night Nurse*. It opens with a drunken Fatty in a torrential rainstorm watching people literally blow past him. Fatty rips the skirt of the woman (Keaton) he's trying to help, and she promptly high kicks him in the face. While helping a fellow drunk get home, he sticks postage stamps all over the man's face and drapes him over a mailbox. Other clever moments include Roscoe in drag and Buster bashfully flirting in a hallway and a hospital orderly catching two items – a saw and a human leg – tossed out of an operating room.

Motion Picture Magazine complained, "It borders over much of the vulgar. The parading of a man in a supposedly blood-spattered physician's apron is not at all our idea of a comedy situation." But it's this kind of humor that makes *Good Night Nurse* hold up so well today.

Roscoe in "Good Night Nurse"

Many of the biggest laughs in these short films came via the title cards – the way that dialogue was inserted in silent films – that came onscreen between scenes. They were generally written after filming and with a slower production schedule than at Keystone, Comique's titles were much funnier. Sometimes they functioned as a comical commentary track. In Moonshine, the fourth wall is broken when, after the moonshiner's daughter leaps into Fatty's arms, Fatty tells her father, "Look, this is only a two-reeler. We don't have time to build up love scenes." The father replies, "In that case, go ahead, it's your movie."

The shorts that Roscoe made with Buster Keaton were the best of his career and this was in part because of his generosity as an actor, director, and friend. While lesser comedic stars would have felt threatened by Buster's talent, Roscoe welcomed his pal's ability to generate laughs, and he gave him the time and space he needed to improvise. The team-up of the portly and expressive Roscoe with the slight and reserved Buster was inspired and in films like *The Cook*, they feel like equals. Roscoe also encouraged Keaton's contributions to writing, directing, and editing, and he became his friend's unofficial assistant director.

Buster later wrote about Arbuckle:

The longer I worked with Roscoe the more I liked him. I respected without reservations his work as both an actor and a comedy director. He took falls no other man at his eight ever attempted and had a wonderful mind for action gags, which he could devise on the spot.

Roscoe loved the world and the whole world loved him in those days. His popularity as a performer was increasing so rapidly that he soon ranked second only to Charlie Chaplin. Arbuckle was a rarity, a truly jolly fat man. He had no meanness, malice, or jealousy in him. Everything seemed to amuse and delight him. I could not have found a better-natured man to teach me the movie business, or a more knowledgeable one.

Roscoe used his fame – and sense of humor – to sell thousands of dollars' worth of war bonds at every appearance during the war

IN MID-1918, THE WAR WAS STILL RAGING IN EUROPE AND America was sending as many as 10,000 soldiers each day to fight. Publicly, Roscoe stated that his extra weight kept him out of uniform so, instead, he used his celebrity and wealth to support the war effort. Her performed at military and Red Cross benefits, "adopted" an army company, and invited American and Canadian soldiers, back home from the front, to visit him on set at Balboa Studios. He and the cast from Comique frequently performed free vaudeville shows at army camps across Southern California.

Roscoe had purchased war bonds at the start of the conflict and continued to do so, while also encouraging the public to support the military in the same way. In May, he was the surprise participant in a Long Beach war bond parade, waving an American flag as he was mobbed by children. In films financed by the American and Canadian governments, he touted the benefits of each country's bonds. As a longtime smoker, he made it his cause to ensure that soldiers had plenty of cigarettes to smoke on the front lines. His contributions to the New York Sun "Tobacco Fund" helped them ship cigarettes overseas, and every time he bought a carton of cigarettes into one of the drop-off boxes on the Balboa Studios grounds, which were there "to gather smokes for the boys in France."

Buster Keaton didn't just support the soldiers – he became one. He was drafted into the army in July 1918 and on night before he left for Camp Kearney, near San Diego, Comique threw him a farewell dinner at the Jewel City Café in Seal Beach, a café that was popular

Buster entered the military during the war and was stationed in France.

with movie stars working or staying in Long Beach. You couldn't buy booze in Long Beach at the time, but Seal Beach was wet.

When Buster's outfit shipped out to New York three weeks later – after training camp was completed – Roscoe, Al, and Lou Anger traveled to Camp Kearney to see him off.

While in New York, waiting for a ship, Buster was visited by Natalie Talmage, and they spent a day dining and dancing at some of Long Island's finest spots. This marked the beginning of their romance.

Keaton was stationed in Amiens, France, and saw no combat. It was cold and frequently rainy, and he slept on the ground or on equally dirty floors, developing an ear infection that permanently damaged his hearing. The war ended on November 11, 1918, but Buster's military service did not. He was transferred to a town near Bordeaux, and there he organized entertainment for anxious young men waiting for ships to take them home. He remained in France, performing for his fellow soldiers, even as his audience was continuously shipping back to America.

ROSCOE, OF COURSE, CONTINUED TO WORK IN HIS FRIEND'S absence, recruiting a Comique gag writer, Mario Bianchi, to step in front of the camera as Monty Banks, who'd go on to a prolific comedy career of his own. After completing a film called *Camping Out*, his second movie without Buster, Roscoe spent two weeks in San Francisco, looking for more nightlife than Los Angeles could offer him.

The press made note of the trip, but there was no mention of Minta's absence or the presence of another female companion – though it's unlikely Roscoe slept alone on his two-week holiday. He was subsequently romantically linked with Alice Lake and friends claimed that the relationship was on and off for several years. It stayed out of the fan magazines because Roscoe was still married.

The press was careful about his privacy, but his audience was sometimes more demanding. When out in public, he was frequently

mobbed by fans. Around the time when the war came to an end, *Photoplay* noted:

> The people adore Fatty, I soon discovered – young and old. They felt somehow, he was a rock to cling to, a prop against shadows that are falling too heavily in these days of stress. He represents the way of escape – he and his merry-making crew – the defiance that we humans must hurl at woe. In a way he typifies the happy, serious spirit of the American – the ability to see the funny side of everything, however seemingly tragic.

✒EVEN

BOTH DURING AND AFTER THE WAR, ROSCOE ARBUCKLE WAS A generous man. He supported the troops, he donated to good causes, and he even gathered a group of Comique players who, accompanied by armed guards, performed shows for incarcerated prisoners at several California prisons.

Roscoe was charitable even when others weren't looking. In fact, he went further than most of his fellow movie stars. Louella Parsons recounted how kind he was to individuals behind the scenes. She mentioned an instance involving a "certain little girl whom Fatty had given his friendship and advice" about which she wrote: "To those who think the Arbuckle life is one round of continual pleasure, it might be well to hear how he went out of his way to befriend this girl when things looked black for her. I shall always like him for that, though he modestly refused to admit he had done more than any other man would do when I spoke to him of this young woman."

By mid-1919, Roscoe was in a position to be particularly generous. Just a few months earlier, he'd signed a deal worth $3 million.

For Roscoe, the seed for something new had been planted the previous year when *The Cook* became the last film ever made at Balboa Studios. The Horkheimer brothers had declared bankruptcy just before it was completed. The studio buildings weren't demolished until 1925 but long before that it was clear that Long Beach was never going to topple Hollywood as the movie-making capital of the world.

And that wasn't all. When Charlie Chaplin, Douglas Fairbanks, Mary Pickford, and William S. Hart were together promoting war bonds, there was discussion about why, considering their power and popularity, they couldn't oversee distribution of their own films? That way, they could maintain creative control and ownership from the

United Artists was created by some of the biggest stars in Hollywood

start to finish. D.W. Griffith joined them and as negotiations progressed, the press began calling them the "Big Five."

Hart eventually dropped out, but on February 5, 1919, Chaplin, Fairbanks, Pickford, and Griffith launched United Artists. With neither contract players nor acres of soundstages, the very idea of United Artists was an insult to the increasingly powerful studio system. The so-called "studio" was a film exchange that incorporated four independent production companies that was run by artists to distribute their own work. It was a huge threat to how things were "supposed to be done."

Only three United Artists films were released in 1919. None of them were Chaplin's. He still had obligations to his First National Pictures contract so he wouldn't make his United Artists debut for another four years. Nevertheless, the news of the studio's formation rocked the major studios, including Roscoe's employer, Paramount, which was by then at the top of the Hollywood heap.

It didn't help that United Artists was assisted with its start-up by former Paramount president Hiram Abrams, who became the new company's managing director, or that Fairbanks and Pickford had only recently decided not to renew their Paramount contracts.

This meant that Roscoe was the brightest star left at the studio and -- more bad news for Paramount -- his contract was about to expire. Rumors swirled that the "Big Five" was soon to become the "Big Six" − or remain five after Hart dropped out − with Roscoe joining his friends Chaplin, Fairbanks, and Pickford. It would be a major victory for Abrams, with whom Roscoe had remained friendly, to steal the biggest moneymaker that Paramount had left.

After the formation of United Artists, Roscoe was the biggest star left at Paramount

Heated negotiations began but on February 21, Roscoe met with Adolph Zukor in Kansas City, where he signed a three-year Paramount contract that landed him $1 million a year. The big contract – the first $1 million Hollywood deal – accomplished its immediate intention, which was stirring up nationwide publicity for Paramount and its star. This launched another Fatty Arbuckle publicity tour, traveling by train to New York City, Washington, D.C., and New Orleans.

During a brief stay in Manhattan, Roscoe met opera legend Enrico Caruso – they were each a fan of the other – and spent time with Louella Parsons, the celebrity gossip pioneer. She was in a screening room with Roscoe, Zukor, Schenck, and several others as actresses were considered for Fatty's love interest in future Comique comedies. Parsons also accompanied them to Sherry's, a French restaurant popular with the society crowd. Over oysters, chicken, and cocktails, Roscoe confessed that if he wasn't in show business, he'd want to be a surgeon. He had a friend at Los Angeles County Hospital who allowed him to witness appendix removals. Charlie Chaplin had accompanied him on these trips a few times, which meant the world's two greatest comedy actors spent more time than seems normal watching a doctor slice open human bodies.

But while Roscoe wasn't celebrating with wine, women, and song or watching appendectomy operations or betting on prizefights or buying another round for friends and hangers-on, He was making movies without his best friend, Buster Keaton, who was still stuck in the army.

ROSCOE'S BIG CONTRACT CALLED FOR A NEW HOUSE. HIS excuse was that he needed a new place that was closer to his new workplace since Comique had moved from Long Beach, but in truth, he had a lot of money burning a hole in his pocket and he wanted to spend it.

In the first decades of the twentieth century, the most exclusive area in Los Angeles was the West Adams district near downtown. The

Victorian mansions located there were home to the wealthiest businessmen in Southern California. The homes were massive and expensive, built for large families and for parties thrown for hundreds of guests. They were as "old money" as you could find in L.A. and the newly rich movie stars of the era took notice.

Roscoe's home in the West Adams District of Los Angeles, which was originally owned by screen "Vamp" Theda Bara (Below)

The first movie star in the neighborhood was the original "vamp," Theda Bara, who rented a large Tudor Revival home from U.S. Navy officer Randolph Huntington Miner in 1917 when he and his family were in France and Theda's fame and fortunes were starting to rise. Theda had been born Theodosia Goodman in Cincinnati, but Fox publicized her as an Egyptian-born occultist with an affinity for snakes and a taste for raw meat. The Jewish's star's new name was supposed to be an anagram for "Arab Death." She played along, filling the mansion's elegant room

with mummy cases, crystal balls, and all kinds of exotic décor. The house was portrayed in the press as a place you'd be wise to steer clear of. But her unusual fame was short-lived. When her contract with Fox ended in 1919, Theda retired and moved out of the West Adams District.

Meanwhile, Roscoe's production company had moved from Long Beach to a studio in Edendale, next door to Keystone. He was looking for a home closer to work and Joe Schenck encouraged him to move into the mansion abandoned by Theda Bara. He moved in – also renting from the Miners – and quickly removed the ghoulish décor she'd left behind and re-decorated in a style that could be described as that of a wealthy movie star – or a bachelor college boy with too much money to spend.

In addition to thousands spent on furniture, he also stocked his basement shelves with a collection of booze that grew to epic proportions – gin, scotch, rye, rum, and wine. This was his "doomsday shelter," meant to protect him against the coming shortages that would be caused by Prohibition. It's unlikely that his regular parties, which typically lasted until dawn, put much of a dent in his supply, but it wasn't because he didn't try.

And it wasn't just liquor and fast cars that Roscoe was spending his money on. His other great love was baseball.

The rapid rise in the popularity of movies during the first two decades of the twentieth century coincided with America's passion for baseball. Grand stadiums – like Fenway and Wrigley Field – opened and players like Honus Wagner, Ty Cobb, "Shoeless Joe" Jackson, and Babe Ruth made headlines and attracted a constant stream of new fans for the game.

Roscoe was one of those fans. He had played the game when he was a kid and on Keystone's team and had regularly attended games since his arrival in California.

Until the late 1950s, baseball teams traveled by train, which made the West Coast a very long trip from eastern cities. That's why in 1919, there were 16 major league teams but none farther west than St. Louis. The West Coast had the Pacific Coast League. Unaffiliated with major league clubs, the PCL was sort of a shadow league for the first half of the century, although it created legends like Ted Williams and Joe DiMaggio. Until 1958, when the Dodgers moved to Los Angeles and the Giants to San Francisco, the PCL was the big league for baseball fans in California.

This made it big news in 1919 when Roscoe bought a controlling interest in the Vernon Tigers and made himself the president. The team had started in 1909, but the Tigers had never made any money. Their location was not exactly family friendly. Vernon was better known for its nightclubs and a boxing arena and the Tigers' ballpark was located adjacent to Doyle's Bar. It was billed as "the longest bar in the world," with 37 bartenders working 37 cash registers with space to serve more than 1,000 drinkers at a time. It wasn't the kind of place that L.A. parents were likely to take the kids – well, until Fatty Arbuckle bought the team.

Once the sale to Roscoe was final, Lou Anger, whose wife was the sister-in-law of the Tigers' pitcher, became the general manager – despite having no baseball experience whatsoever.

Roscoe admitted, "I'm just going into it for the sport of the thing and nothing else." His job with the team, he said, was to "sign the checks."

But as the first celebrity owner of a sports team, he ended up with a windfall of publicity. Game reports referred to the Tigers as "Fatty's team." He appeared in team photos and on the covers of the game programs. He even had his own baseball card, on which he was dressed in a Tigers' uniform, biting into a baseball like an apple.

He was the biggest attraction at every game and even when the team lost – which was often – he was no less a hero. Parents brought their children to fill up the ballpark seats and mothers pointed out Roscoe to their sons as the kind of man they should aspire to be. At one game, Roscoe, Al St. John, and Buster Keaton – finally home from his military stint – performed a sketch in Tigers uniforms, pitching and hitting with paster-of-Prais bats and balls that exploded when they met, much to the delight of the crowd. By the end of the summer, the press had nicknamed the Tigers the "Custard Pies" in a nod to Fatty's slapstick roots.

On August 8, Roscoe and his entourage – including Buster and Lou Anger – traveled to San Francisco by train for several games that pitted the Tigers against the San Francisco Seals and the Oakland Oaks. The

Roscoe may not have made a lot of money as a baseball team owner, but it was a gold mine for publicity.

actors performed baseball sketches in front of record crowds of as many as 30,000 people.

Roscoe stayed at the Hotel St. Francis, which started using him in their advertising soon after. The nights in San Francisco were spent at parties in Roscoe's honor and drinking and dancing at the Tait-Zinkland Café. One night started at Tait's by the by and ended, at some point in the morning, at Tait's downtown. As always, Roscoe picked up the bill for everyone, which ran as high as $2,000.

On October 5, the Tigers won their first-ever Pacific Coast League title, squeaking past their main rival, the Los Angeles Angels. But in the same year that the Chicago White Sox suffered a gambling scandal, the Tigers' championship celebration was dampened by a scandal of its own. It was reported that five players were bribed to throw games in Vernon's favor. They were all expelled from the league.

Roscoe wasn't implicated in the mess, but the publicity for "Fatty's Team" had gone from good to bad. Owning the team had taken a lot more time and money than he'd planned and when he should have been celebrated as the president of the league champions, his name was being dragged through the mud thanks to its connection with cheating.

He sold the Vernon Tigers after being the owner for just a single season.

CORPORAL BUSTER KEATON HADN'T LEFT FRANCE UNTIL February 1919, more than three months after the armistice was signed that ended the war. Suffering from a hearing impairment, he convalesced in military hospitals in New York and Baltimore. He was finally discharged at the end of April, when he returned to Los Angeles – and to the movies.

The acting roster had changed at Comique while Buster was away. Molly Malone was now with the company, while Alice Lake was out. Jackie Coogan – father of the Jackie Coogan that thrilled audiences alongside Charlie Chaplin in *The Kid* – was also a new member of the troupe, but Al St. John was gone. He left Paramount and went to Fox, where he achieved fame on his own as an actor and director.

Roscoe and Buster made three shorts together in 1919 and all three were hits. In *Back Stage*, Roscoe performed a stunt in which the front of a house falls toward Fatty, but it misses him as an open window passes over him. Buster later repeated this gag in his first short without Roscoe, *One Week*, and, of course, most famously in his feature *Sherlock, Jr.*

The second film, *The Hayseed*, presents Fatty as his most likable and is a subdued, more character-driven comedy.

The Garage includes gags involving the use of too much motor oil and a giant turntable for washing and drying cars. The best part is a bit in which Buster hides from a cop by walking, stride for stride, in front of and behind the much-wider Fatty. Released in 1920, *The Garage* was the fourteenth and final comedy short with Roscoe and Buster together.

It's worth noting that this short was filmed at Henry Lehrman's studio. It was made while a young actress named Virginia Rappe was also at the studio, appearing in a film called *A Twilight Baby*.

Offscreen, when not watching a Tigers game, partying, or betting on a boxing match, Roscoe and Buster were reveling in practical jokes.

When Adolph Zukor attended a dinner party at Roscoe's West Adams mansion with Sid Grauman, Alice Lake, and others, he was the only one there not in on the joke that the clumsy butler who spilled the turkey dinner everywhere was Buster Keaton, even after an "outraged" Roscoe shattered a breakaway bottle on the terrible butler's head.

When Marcus Loew came to town, Buster played Roscoe's chauffeur, taking the theater owner on a horrifying ride through Los Angeles.

Pretending to be gas company workers, Roscoe and Buster pretended they were just about to destroy the pampered front lawn of actress Pauline Frederick's Beverly Hills mansion. They also convinced Vic Levy, a Belgian dressmaker, that the king and queen of Belgium wanted to have dinner at his home. At the dinner that followed, Levy was the only one there who was unaware the royal couple were actors.

Years later, Buster Keaton wrote: "Few of us in that whole Hollywood gang had had time to acquire an education. I suppose we were doing the things in our twenties that we would have done earlier if we'd gone to high school and college."

While the pair would remain close friends, with plenty of good times still ahead of them, their business relationship soon changed. After six years in the film industry, Roscoe had still not appeared in a movie that was longer than two reels. Comedy was the genre of shorts, and those shorts played prior to features on the same bills. By the fall of 1919, Roscoe was eager to start appearing in features, but those longer films were beyond the scope of his current production company.

So, Joe Schenck shifted Roscoe's contract from Comique to Paramount, the studio that was already paying handsomely to distribute Roscoe's movies. Buster would become the new solo star of Comique's shorts while Roscoe would star in Paramount feature films written and directed by that studio's top talents.

It seemed like a simple business deal and a golden opportunity for Roscoe Arbuckle, but it would turn out to be the moment when his world began to completely shift on its axis.

ROSCOE WOULD ALWAYS REMEMBER WHERE HE WAS DURING the early morning hours of Thanksgiving 1919. He was at the Hotel Alexandria – along with pretty much everyone else in show business – dancing, drinking, and dining at the Director's Ball, then Hollywood's most glamorous annual event. On most evenings he was enjoying things like boxing, gambling, and jazz dancing, but when Hollywood's formal galas occurred, he was almost always there.

A few weeks later, he spent the Christmas holidays with his wife. He and Minta remained on good terms, writing affectionate letters back and forth and making frequent long-distance telephone calls.

But looking back, he'd remember that party at the Alexandria because it was the last big event at which he'd been able to enjoy a legal drink for a very long time.

At the stroke of midnight on January 17, 1920, Prohibition went into effect in America, making it illegal to manufacture, sell, or transport "intoxicating liquors." But the law couldn't stop America's thirst and Prohibition became the greatest thing that ever happened to organized crime. Vowing to "give the people what they wanted," more than 200,000 speakeasies opened across the country where anyone could get a drink. As one man put it at the time, "If you say you can't find a drink, then you just ain't trying."

Not long before Prohibition took effect, Roscoe bought the West Adams mansion from the Miners for $250,000, joking that he had to do it to protect his cellar filled with booze.

According to the census records, Roscoe lived in the house at that time with a 37-year-old male cook and a 27-year-old female maid, both of whom were Japanese immigrants. His secretary, housekeeper, butler, chauffeur, and gardener lived elsewhere. The other movie star in the house – Luke the dog – wasn't counted in the census. Roscoe now had three dogs. Minta later said, "He and the big St. Bernard have wonderful times. Roscoe gets into his bathing suit, and puts a tub in the garage, and he and the dog are perfectly happy there for half a day."

He continued decorating the house in a manner he felt fit the image of a movie star. He imported a carved front door from Spain and purchased mahogany paneling, gold-leafed bathtubs, crystal chandeliers, Oriental rugs, marble counters, antique dishes, a red lacquer dining room table with gold clawed feet from China, and a Hawaiian royal chair. Always fascinated with the latest gadgets, he had his closets and dressers wired with lights that came on when a door of drawer was opened.

But as ostentatious as his house was, it was always overshadowed by his cars, especially the one that was essentially built for him in 1919. The massive frame and motor of a Pierce-Arrow was delivered to Don Lee Coach & Body Works in Los Angeles, to whom Roscoe paid more than $28,000 to have the vehicle customized. They reshaped the hood and cowl of the already luxurious car and then added features like a backseat liquor cabinet, silver pot-shaped headlights, and a radiator cap monogrammed with an A. The work was completed in April 1920

Roscoe, Luke, and his special customized Pierce-Arrow in 1919

and for the next week, more than 10,000 gawkers crowded into the company's showroom to marvel at the $34,000 machine.

Roscoe continued to host a string of house parties, slowly depleting the stockpile of booze in his basement to the sound of jazz records. He threw lawn parties, stag parties, dinner parties, and early morning parties. He staged a party around a dog wedding, at which Luke served as the "best man."

His favorite haunts in Venice and Vernon had gone dry, so he often journeyed to Tijuana. He was among the Hollywood celebrities who spent Halloween 1920 at Tijuana's Sunset Inn. A news story said that a "spirited" night was assured in the Mexican village. More than nine months into Prohibition, the quotation marks around the word "spirited" – even at Halloween – were a knowing wink.

THERE WERE THREE THINGS THAT MARKED THE END OF 1920 FOR Roscoe Arbuckle – the release of his first feature film, the death of his father, and a trip to France.

The film was called *The Round Up* and the poster featured Fatty in cowboy clothing and his name in letters as large as the title, although "Fatty" was squeezed between much bigger spellings of his first and last name. Although the film includes his signature bit of rolling a cigarette with one hand and a few other minor gags – like Buster Keaton, uncredited, as a Native American – the film is otherwise short on comedy. It's a western romance with too many subplots.

It wasn't well-received by fans of slapstick comedy, but it accomplished its goal of establishing Roscoe as a feature film actor. The story is tedious, but Roscoe brought a surprising amount of drama

to the part of Sheriff "Slim" Hoover, and it turned out to be the role that gave him his signature line.

At the end, unable to get the girl, he forlornly rested his head on a fence post, followed by the last dialogue card that read: "Nobody loves a fat man."

In November 1920, William Arbuckle died from cancer at the age of 71. Roscoe paid his father's final medical bills, but it's unknown whether he ever saw the man again after leaving their unhappy home in Santa Clara when he was 17. Whether he did or not, he didn't attend the funeral.

He couldn't because he was in New York City, planning to board an ocean liner on its way to France with his friend, a former actor named Fred Ward. Unfortunately, though, Roscoe partied so hard – Prohibition be damned -- that he literally missed the boat and he and Ward had to take another ship five days later.

This was Roscoe's first trip across the Atlantic and when he reached Europe, he found out just how famous he had become. Movies were a major American export, especially after the war, which had decimated the European movie industry.

Paris went wild for Roscoe from the time he landed until he sailed for home. He was wined, dined, and celebrated during the entire trip. Hundreds of fans lined the streets just to get a glimpse of him. They followed his chauffeured car wherever he went. There were banquets, dinners, lunches, and dances. Most of the official thanks offered to Roscoe was for the comfort his comedies had provided the French during the four bloody years of the war. He reciprocated when, at the

Arc de Triomphe, he placed a bouquet on the spot where the Tomb of the Unknown Soldier would be located a few weeks later.

The final nine days of his trip were spent in London. He stayed at the luxurious Hotel Savoy and hosted a dinner attended by 150 British notables. Once again, fans followed him everywhere and Roscoe was happy to smile, pose for cameras, and sign autographs. He knew the greatest product he had to sell himself and that every day, everywhere he went, he had the chance to sell it.

He returned to New York on December 22 and again spent Christmas in Manhattan with Minta.

THE ROUND UP WAS THE FIRST OF FIVE FEATURE FILMS THAT Roscoe made in 1920, though since they required more post-production and publicity than his comedy shorts, they didn't make it to the screen as fast as those films did.

Only one other was released that year. In it, Roscoe plays an unsuccessful attorney who runs for political office. In an unfortunate subplot, a woman tried to entrap Fatty and start a scandal that will ruin his reputation.

Originally released in December 1920, it was still playing in theaters 10 months later when a real-life scandal came along and ruined the life of the film's leading man.

The title of the film turned out to be an ironic one – *The Life of the Party.*

EIGHT

THE END OF THE GREAT WAR SHOCKED AMERICA. NOT ONLY WAS the country forced to deal with scores of deaths caused by the Spanish Flu pandemic, but peace sent the economy into a nosedive. Manufacturing had ramped up during the war, and the military employed millions, but afterward, factories closed, and the returning soldiers flooded an overwhelmed job market. After a mild recession, a depression hit at the start of 1920 that lingered for the next year-and-a-half. The value of the stick market was cut in half, and unemployment soared to nearly 12 percent.

The bad times wouldn't last. The economy would bounce back, only to freefall again nine years later, much worse than before. But that was far off in the future.

America survived and one of its saviors was Hollywood. The movies could always be counted on to provide a distraction from real life. Maybe a working man couldn't afford a ticket to the theater, but he almost always had a nickel or a dime to go to the movies – and Hollywood was always happy to let them spend it.

In 1921, there were 854 films produced by Hollywood studios, more than any other year, before or since. By 1922, nearly 40 percent of Americans went to the movies every week. They saw Charlie Chaplin's first feature, *The Kid.* The packed theaters for *The Four Horseman of the Apocalypse*, a smash hit that launched the tango craze and Rudolph Valentino's career. They watched Douglas Fairbanks, Mary Pickford, Lillian Gish, and D.W. Griffith's last major commercial success, *Orphans of the Storm.* And they paid to see five feature films from Roscoe "Fatty" Arbuckle, a number that would have been greater if not for that Labor Day weekend in San Francisco.

The movies were where Americans went to laugh, cry, and dream together, to forget about their tenement apartments and their bleak prospects for a good job. And when they left the theater, many of them bought the latest issue of one of the movie magazines that filled the newsstand racks. The dreams the movies had given them continued as they turned page after page, comforted by the knowledge that their favorite starts were living lives of luxury in the perpetual sunshine of Southern California. They were relieved to see there had been no end to the star's lavish paydays, parties, mansions, and servants. They still had their charity balls, fashionable clothes, international trips, and blissful days of pretending to be someone else.

Movie stars were America's royalty, and Americans paid attention to everything they did – as Roscoe Arbuckle was soon going to find out.

ROSCOE MADE FOUR FEATURE FILMS IN THE FIRST EIGHT MONTHS of 1921. It's often been said that the last three were shot without a break – supporting his need for the Labor Day vacation – but this isn't correct. *Brewster's Millions, The Dollar-A-Year Man*, and *The Traveling Salesman* were shot in 1920 with overlapping schedules and were released in 1921. The four features produced in 1921 – *Crazy to Marry, Gasoline Gus, Skirt Shy*, and *Freight Prepaid* – had three week breaks between one production ending and another starting, and three weeks had passed between when *Freight Prepaid* wrapped and Roscoe went to San Franciso.

But even so, acting in nine five-reel feature films over 21 months was still a rough schedule. Chaplin made one six-reel feature and one two-reel short during this same period. But Roscoe was neither writer nor director on any of the nine features, so his Paramount schedule was not as grueling as his workloads had been at Comique when he was the director, star, and usually the writer or co-writer.

Paramount no doubt wanted as much output from Roscoe at it could get. He was their star attraction and by having him focus on acting alone, the studio became so flush with Fatty movies that *The Traveling Salesman* was not released until almost a year after production wrapped.

Though they made plenty of money when they were released, Roscoe's features aren't nearly as entertaining as the shorts he made for Comique. Unlike Chaplin, he never found the right balance of comedy and drama that made it possible to flesh out longer stories. Plus, also unlike Charlie, he was now dependent on the writing and directing of others.

Roscoe was at the start of the development of feature length comedies, and his efforts would've undoubtedly improved as the genre matured into the middle 1920s. He may have even made films that became just as memorable as the classics of Chaplin and Keaton – but, of course, he never got the chance.

LIKE PARAMOUNT STUDIOS, AUDIENCES WANTED AS MANY FATTY films as they could get – and they anxiously waited for news about Fatty himself. In April 1921 alone, there were stories about his appearance at a Knights of Columbus charity benefit; about his posing for photos with Buster Keaton, Alice Lake, and Viola Dana; and about him writing a 10-word telegram to an actress jailed for speeding. That last one became part of a huge publicity coup.

Reports about Roscoe's ongoing speeding stops were a running joke in local newspapers. His sportscars weren't just for show – he drove them fast, especially on what were then the quiet streets of Santa Monica. In most cases, the cops – dazzled by his customized cars and celebrity – let him go without even a warning.

Bebe Daniels, actress with a lead foot

But it was his friend Bebe Daniels who made his lead foot famous. Though only 20, Bebe was a film veteran. Previously the onscreen and very young offscreen love interest of comic Harold Lloyd, she was a quickly rising star at Paramount in 1921 when she was arrested in Orange County, California, for driving 56 miles-per-hour at a time when that was considered outrageously fast.

At her jury trial on March 28, more than 1,500 people showed up to get a glimpse of the star, who arrived in a limousine and wore a fur coat and veiled hat. She'd already made the mistake of taunting Judge John Cox by singing "Judge Cox Blues" at a benefit a week earlier and he got his revenge by sentencing her to 10 days in jail. She lost the case but won via a windfall of publicity.

On April 15, Bebe arrived at the jail with a huge pile of luggage. The next day, a furniture store delivered a bedroom suit to her cell, along with a Victrola and 150 records. Local musicians serenaded her, and guests arrived – 792 guests over the 10 days, including numerous celebrities who garnered their own publicity.

Roscoe sent her a telegram, written for public amusement: "Dear Bebe, Houdini is in town. Can we help? Love, Roscoe."

After her release, Bebe began her next film, *The Speed Girl*, a comedic account of her "ordeal." She managed to use the trial and her incarceration to great advantage and while her crime was a minor one, it did show how hungry the public was to see their favorite stars as real people – even when they were on trial.

ROSCOE, MEANWHILE, WAS CONTINUING HIS LAVISH SPENDING. High-end shopping was an addiction that was as comforting to him as food and booze. In addition to that customized Pierce-Arrow, he filled the six-car garage at his mansion with the best automobiles on the market – a Rolls-Royce, a Locomobile, a Cadillac, a Hudson, and

a Renault – all painted in colors that were guaranteed to get attention.

He bought more imported suits and shoes than he could fit in his closets and more artwork than he could hang on his walls. He lavished designer clothing, French perfumes, and expensive jewelry on women. He hosted elaborate parties. He bought on extended credit from stores that were eager to say they'd sold to Fatty Arbuckle, a plan that would prove to be a bad one, and he made risky investments, which later devastated his finances. He could never spend the money as quickly as it arrived – and it seemed like it would continue to arrive forever.

His sister, Nora, said: "Since he had made his fortune, he had always been generous to his own people. He has done many kind things for me and my family and for my brother in Fresno."

Roscoe's wife, Minta, had an opinion about his spending that wasn't nearly as glowing as that of his sister:

I know of many cases – men who have persuaded him to give them money, girls with whom he was friendly who have actually made him a joke because it was so easy to get money away from him. Ever since he was a boy – and he practically grew up with our family – he has been careless with money. He never considered expense. Money simply meant the means of getting what he wanted, of enjoying himself, or helping other people. Incidentally, helping other people is the way a great deal of his money has gone. He has been most generous to me ever since our separation. He has supported relatives. He has always been ready to help anyone who needed it. He has half a dozen pensioners about whom nobody but his own people know.

In public, he willingly played the clown, as was expected of him. At an American Society of Cinematographers ball, he stole the show by pretending to lead the orchestra for part of the evening and closing the night by pretending to fall asleep while dancing with a lovely Ziegfeld Follies girl, resting his head gently against her cheek, and continuing to move his feet occasionally to the music.

*Buster Keaton's wife,
Natalie Talmage*

On July 3, he was one of the biggest stars at a charity rodeo on the grounds of Pauline Frederick's Beverly Hills mansion. Buster Keaton and his new bride, Natalie Talmadge, were there, along with Tom Mix and Will Rogers, who were on horseback. Roscoe, who was on foot, pretended to get caught in the middle of thew action in the ring. It took him some time to make his way past the horses but had the grandstand convulsing with laughter by the time he arrived in his seat.

Roscoe was, as always, the life of the party.

LESS THAN TWO WEEKS AFTER THE BEVERLY HILLS RODEO, THE news broke about the "chicken and champagne" party that had been held at Mishawum Manor four years earlier at the end of Roscoe's publicity tour.

The hush money that had been paid had kept Adolph Zukor, Jesse Lasky, and Hiram Abrams out of court at the time, in July 1921, they were now in the middle of the scandal. Although the press was careful not to place Roscoe at Mishawum Manor, the affair was frequently described as "a party in his honor."

This would have a serious effect on his fate a few months later when he became involved in a sex scandal of his own, convincing Paramount to sever ties with him. By September, Abrams was the managing director of United Artists, but Zukor and Lasky were the top executives at Paramount. The earlier negative publicity resulting from their involvement in the "orgy" in a "roadhouse" compounded their stress when Paramount's biggest star became mixed up in what newspapers were calling an "orgy" turned deadly in San Francisco. They left it to Joe Schenck to support Roscoe publicly while those at Paramount made no comment but suspended his contract and recast his upcoming films. They wanted ticket buyers to stop associating Fatty with their studio. When the Mishawum story broke, the press frequently mentioned "Paramount executives" but two months later, the press rarely referred to Roscoe and Paramount together. Zukor and Lasky wanted that disconnection to continue.

What's more, the Mishawum Manor "orgy" story portrayed crass, wealthy visitors from Hollywood and Manhattan preying on poor, vulnerable women and then hiring and paying off slick lawyers so they could buy themselves out of trouble. The way the story was reported made it seem like movie industry big shots didn't think criminal laws or basic morality applied to them.

When Roscoe ended up in trouble in September, this kind of portrayal made him look bad, but was it true? He wasn't present at Mishawum Manor, and he didn't seem like the kind of celebrity who'd purposely mistreat ordinary people. There were plenty of stories about Roscoe on the train playing dice and drinking with African American waiters, suggesting he went out of his way to treat common workers as equals. In addition, he gave a lot of time and money to charities. He helped friends and even some strangers in need – and friends and hangers-on who weren't in need. He was also such a bigger tipper that waiters drew straws to see who'd get to serve him.

But bad behavior toward the "little people" only had to happen a few times to start people talking. One such occasion occurred in July, when Roscoe was in Chicago shooting scenes for *Freight Unpaid* and staying at the Congress Hotel on South Michigan Avenue.

This newspaper story appeared immediately after – and it would come back to haunt him a couple of months later:

"FATTY" ARBUCKLE $50 OUT AFTER HAVING REAL FIGHT
Movie Funny Man Has Trouble with Bellboy and Forfeits Court Deposit

Chicago, July 20 (Special) – Though the first reel was a riot, "Fatty" Arbuckle's latest feature, "Ouch, My Eyes," limped to a pepless finish in police court today. Arbuckle was to have stood trial on a disorderly charge lodged against him by Joe Greenberg, a bellboy at the Congress Hotel, who complained that "Fatty" hit him in the eye. "Fatty," it was alleged, had engaged the bellboy to do some work, but they could not agree on the wage. Words, as is the movie custom, were followed by blows. The bellboy got the worst of it, he said. The judge heard Greenberg's story and forfeited the $50 bond put up by "Fatty" when the celebrity failed to appear.

In mid-September, when every newspaper was screaming about Roscoe's other troubles, the *Los Angeles Examiner* published a very different version of the Congress Hotel story, which reads like a Keystone comedy come to life.

The setting was changed to the hotel's restaurant, Greenberg was recast as a waiter, and the plot revolved around Roscoe entertaining his lunch guests by flattening a sandwich on Greenberg's head and whizzing another past his nose before smashing a plate of creamed chicken into the waiter's face like he would with a custard pie. Outraged, Greenberg summoned two policemen, but instead of a madcap chase, they escorted Roscoe to the police station for booking. The ending remained the same – the movie star skipped his day in court and lost his $50.

In her gossip column back on August 8, Louella Parsons mentioned "the row he

had with a waiter back in Chicago," which made the L.A. version of the story, published a month later, easier to believe. But the story is ridiculous, especially since it allegedly occurred in a public setting and the Chicago papers didn't report it at the time. Regardless, it was a violent act attributed to Roscoe in another hotel in another city, even though no mention was ever made of Roscoe's side of the story. It had people asking, though, was it just a heated episode that Roscoe quickly regretted, or did it reveal the wealthy star's contempt for the background players in his privileged life?

Assuming it happened the way it was reported in the Chicago article – and we don't know since, again, we don't know Roscoe's side of the story – I believe this was an anomaly when it came to how the actor normally behaved. Evidence shows that Roscoe paid an unusually high amount of respect toward the working class from which he came. They were his biggest fans, and he was one of them – he'd even performed menial jobs in a hotel when he was a kid.

At worst, whatever happened at the Congress Hotel seems like his drawer-throwing, table-kicking outburst in front of Minta at the Cumberland Hotel four years earlier – a flash of Roscoe's temper. Mosty of the time, he was as easygoing as one might expect of someone enjoying his comfortable lifestyle, but he never completely gotten past his childhood insecurities – his feelings of abandonment and neglect, his unattractiveness, and his need for a loving family – and they could still fuel am anger that would sometimes erupt.

ON WEDNESDAY, AUGUST 31, THREE DAYS BEFORE HE LEFT TO make the drive up the coast to San Francisco, Roscoe attended the West Coast premiere of *The Three Musketeers*, starring his friend, Douglas Fairbanks. The screening was held in a theater downtown, and the audience of movie stars, moviemakers, and movie executives repeatedly broke into applause, thrilled by the action and romance onscreen.

Soon after, the *Los Angeles Times* announced the West Coast premiere of another film:

"GASOLINE GUS" ARBUCKLE SHOW AT GRAUMAN'S

Roscoe Arbuckle in "Gasoline Gus" ... combined with several special attractions, ushers in Paramount Week in Los Angeles, beginning Monday.

Although he was originally supposed to be at that film opening, the star of *Gasoline Gus* had made other plans for Labor Day Weekend 1921.

NINE

WHEN THE MORPHINE WORE OFF JUST AFTER MIDNIGHT ON Tuesday morning – the day after Labor Day – Virginia Rappe woke in the darkness, screaming in agony again. A light came on, and she saw that woman, Al Semnacher's friend, Maude Delmont.

Virginia lay on a single bed in room 1227 of the Hotel San Francis but she didn't know it. She had no idea where she was or why that woman was with her. All she knew was pain, relentless, merciless pain – like she'd been stabbed in the stomach. Curled up in a fetal position, twisting and turned in the sweaty sheets, she cried, wailed, and begged for relief.

Virginia Rappe

Maude, groggy after being awakened, asked the hotel physician, Dr. Arthur Beardslee, to return to room 1227. He was the second doctor to examine Virginia and, as he had five hours earlier, he injected her with morphine and again, she fell silent. She quickly fell back into a stupor. The doctor checked her pulse and examined her body, still finding her abdomen to be sensitive to his touch. When he left the room, he switched off the light, and it became quiet and dark once more.

Then, at 5:00 A.M. the morphine wore off, and Virginia began to scream. Again, that woman was nearby and again, the doctor returned, and another shot of morphine was administered. Maude told Dr. Beardslee that Virginia had last urinated 15 hours earlier, so he catheterized his patient, producing a small amount of urine that was tinged with dark blood. The color meant it was older and not from an open wound. He believed the catheter would treat Virginia's ailment and that she would recover after some rest. And with that, he left again.

Frustrated with the hotel doctor, Maude telephoned a physician she knew, Dr. Melville Rumwell, and he agreed to take over Virginia's care. Rumwell, in addition to his private practice, was also an assistant professor of surgery at Stanford University's medical school and was the head of Stanford's outpatient clinic.

Dr. Arthur Beardslee, hotel physician at the St. Francis

He arrived at the hotel just after 9:00 A.M. and examined Virginia carefully. He found no visible signs of injury, despite the sordid story that he was told by Maude Delmont, and Virginia, during moments of clarity, said she didn't remember anything that happened. She had lost consciousness while in room 1219 with Roscoe Arbuckle and when she woke up, she was in agony. She continued to feel pain from her abdomen to her chest. Rumwell diagnosed her with alcohol poisoning and left without prescribing anything to treat her other than hot compresses to her abdomen.

In his opinion, she wasn't suffering from anything serious.

THAT SAME MORNING, SEPTEMBER 6, ROSCOE SPOKE WITH AL Semnacher about Virginia. Both men surmised that she was sick from drinking too much the previous night. She as was sick and hungover – they'd both been there and knew what it was like.

Around noon, Roscoe paid the $611.13 tab for the three connected rooms and room 1227, where Virginia was then laying, then he, Fishback, and Sherman checked out of the St. Francis.

Roscoe drove his friends to Pier & on the San Francisco Bay, and they boarded the steamship *Harvard*. The boat, which had been used or troop transport during the war, had just completed its first month of service, making two roundtrips weekly between Los Angeles and San Francisco. Roscoe's Pierce-Arrow was also on board for the 14-hour journey, which began at 4:00 P.M.

During the trip, Fishback ran into a friend, who introduced him and Roscoe to a young woman and her mother. Doris Deane, who was

21, was just starting her acting career and that evening, at Arbuckle's invitation, she and her mother joined the three men for dinner in the stateroom. Doris was charmed by the famous actor, and he found himself attracted to the young brunette.

Before the ship docked in Los Angeles the next morning, they made arrangements to go out together on Saturday evening – but that was a date that Roscoe wouldn't make.

Doris Deane

THROUGHOUT THE NIGHT AND INTO THE NEXT DAY, VIRGINIA was attended by three nurses at various times – Jean Jameson, Vera Cumberland, and Martha Hamilton. They each encountered a young woman who sometimes screamed in pain and at other times, calmly offered her medical history. The nurses understandably blamed alcohol for her condition. For one thing, she admitted to drinking a lot on Monday afternoon and for another, home-brewed and bootleg liquor had already caused many problems during Prohibition. They believed that might be the cause of her stomach pains. They treated her with catheterization, enemas, and hot compresses.

Nothing seemed to help for long.

On Thursday, September 8, Dr. Rumwell returned to check on his patient. He found that her condition hadn't improved, which made him suspect she might have a kidney infection or perhaps a venereal disease.

Around noon, he had her admitted to the sanitarium of Dr. Francis Wakefield, who specialized in obstetrics and gynecology. Maude Delmont and one of the nurses, Jean Jameson, rode with Virginia in the black ambulance.

The fact that Virginia was sent there instead of being admitted to a hospital was later questioned, but the Wakefield sanitarium was the closest medical facility – just six blocks from the St. Francis – and Dr. Rumwell had privileges there. It was also common at the time, even for those with serious problems, to be treated outside of hospitals. Wakefield, which specialized in women's medicine and high-risk births, had two operating rooms as well as the staff and equipment to treat emergency patients.

The more important question is – why was Virgina left to suffer in a hotel room for three days in serious pain and blood in her urine? She was offered no other treatment than hot towels and morphine to deaden her pain, even though she was examined by three doctors – including an assistant when Dr. Beardslee wasn't available – and three nurses, all of whom shrugged off her condition as too much to drink.

If she had been properly treated during this time, it's likely we'd never know anything about what Roscoe Arbuckle was doing over Labor Day Weekend 1921, and the lives of Fatty and Virginia Rappe would have turned out very differently.

ROSCOE RETURNED HOME ON THE MORNING OF WEDNESDAY, September 7. He drove the Pierce-Arrow into the six-car garage and went into the house. His butler later retrieved his luggage from the car. When Roscoe entered the house, he was greeted by his three dogs, including Luke, who was almost as famous as his owner was. He checked in with his manager, Lou Anger, who informed him that *Gasoline Gus* was a huge hit. Another feature, *Crazy to Marry*, was about to go into wider release. Two other films, *Skirt Shy* and *Freight Prepaid*, had wrapped and were being cut and edited for theaters.

JESSE L. LASKY *presents*
Roscoe 'Fatty' Arbuckle
(By Arrangement with Joseph M. Schenck)
in
'GASOLINE GUS'

On Thursday, Roscoe went to the Paramount lot and met with the director of his previous four films, James Cruze, and they watched the final editing of *Freight Prepaid*, then sketched out some ideas for *The Melancholy Spirit*, a comedy about a drunken ghost that Roscoe and Cruze planned to make next.

Roscoe suggested the young woman that he'd made a date with, Doris Deane, for a role in *The Melancholy Spirit*, and Cruze agreed they should meet with her the following week. Roscoe called her with the good news, but this meeting, like their scheduled date, would be canceled.

And Roscoe wouldn't be appearing in *The Melancholy Spirit* either. The film was retitled *One Glorious Day* the following January when it went into production with legendary humorist Will Rogers in the role intended for Fatty Arbuckle.

Dr. Melville Rumwell

(Below) *Dr. George W. Reid*

ON THE AFTERNOON OF SEPTEMBER 8, DR. RUMWELL EXAMINED Virginia again at the Wakefield sanitarium. He now believed that her condition was the result of alcoholism and a resulting kidney lesion and infection. He arranged for a saline drip to replenish her electrolytes and for morphine to be injected every four hours.

When the doctor returned to see Virginia at 9:00 P.M., he found that her condition had rapidly deteriorated. Her pain was now severe, her pulse was elevated, and her abdomen was swollen.

Alarmed, he called in Dr. Emmet Rixford, a professor of surgery at Stanford University, vice president of the American Surgical Association, and one of the foremost physicians on the West Coast. After his examination, Rixford came up with a new diagnosis – peritonitis, an inflammation of the peritoneum, the abdominal lining and cavity. The likely cause was an infection created by a ruptured fallopian tube or bladder.

A third doctor, George W. Reid, concurred but all three men believed that in her present, weakened condition, Virginia would not survive surgery to correct the problem. They began administering antibiotics in hopes they could fight off the infection.

While coherent, Virginia asked Maude Delmont to telephone her San Francisco friend, Sidi Spreckels. Like at Virginia's request, Maude asked Spreckels to telegram Henry Lehrman in New York and inform him of his former partner's condition. Maude also telegrammed Kate Hardebeck with the bad news.

Sidi Spreckels was at Virginia's side on Friday morning. She was shocked by her condition – Virginia's skin was pale and clammy, her eyes sunken, and her lips cracked. She was so weak and in and out of consciousness that Sidi was uncertain her old friend even recognized her.

But Virginia allegedly said to her, "Oh, to think I led such a quiet life, and to think I would get into such a party."

When Sidi returned later with a return telegram from Henry Lehrman, Virginia had slipped into a coma. Sidi telephoned Pastor James Gordon of the nearby First Congregational Church, and he came to the sanitarium immediately. He dropped to his knees in the room and prayed for the very sick young woman's recovery – but apparently, no one heard his pleas.

On September 9, 1921, at 1:30 P.M., Virginia Rappe died in her room at the Wakefield Sanitarium.

*Virginia's friend,
Sidi Spreckels*

LATER THAT SAME AFTERNOON, DR. WILLIAM OPHULS, THE German-born and educated dean of medicine at Stanford University and one of the country's leading experts on pathology and bacteriology, received a telephone call from his Stanford colleague, Dr. Melville Rumwell. He told Dr. Ophuls that a woman had just died from an apparent case of peritonitis.

Within the hour, in the presence of Dr. Rumwell and nurse Grace Halston, Dr. Ophuls was examining Virginia's corpse on a table in a white-walled operating room at the Wakefield sanitarium. There was no morgue at the sanitarium, so they used what they had.

He checked Virginia's face, scalp, neck, front and back of her torso, her arms and hands, legs and feet, and her genitalia. He found no evidence of sexual assault but noted two bruises on her upper right arm and two more bruises on her thighs. He poked at her bloated abdomen.

A block was placed under her back to raise her chest. With scalpel in hand, an incision was made from her pubic bone to her sternum, carefully slicing through the abdominal wall so that the organs beneath were untouched. There was little bleeding, but body fluid leaked from her open abdomen. With no autopsy table to collect it, the fluid dripped to the floor and ran

Dr. William Ophuls

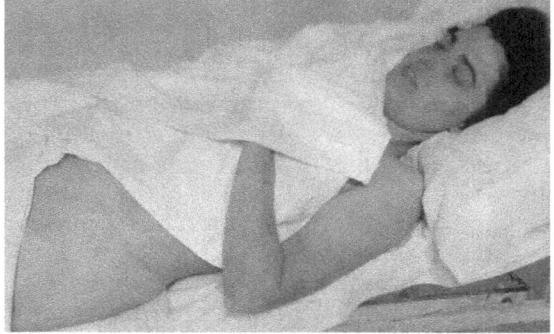

Morgue photos of Virginia Rappe

into a drain. Two additional incisions, as deep as the rib cage, were made from the sternum to each shoulder, curving under her breasts. Together, the three cuts formed a large Y on Virginia's torso. Three large flaps had been rendered – one on either side and one above – and the skin, muscle, and soft tissue were pulled back. The ribs were cut away with a saw and shears.

The inner patchwork of Virginia's body was revealed under the bright lights of the operating room. Dr. Ophuls examined her organs, searching for abnormalities. Blood had congested in her lower abdomen, though he did not yet see what had caused the bleeding. He removed the intestines, which looked normal and were virtually empty. The pericardial sac was cut open, revealing her heart inside. Arteries were sliced and searched for clots. Each of her lungs were cut open and prodded for signs of pneumonia or other issues. The lower lobes of one were congested, likely the effects of a common virus. Though stained brown and black – Virginia was a smoker – her lungs were functional.

Whenever asked, the nurses handed him a scalpel, knife, scissors, or forceps. The peritoneum was inflamed, and its thin membrane was stretched outwards. The doctor examined her liver and kidneys. The stomach, pancreas, duodenum, and spleen were also studied. Dr. Rumwell observed and assisted as Dr. Ophuls inventoried and inspected the organs he removed from the body. The two doctors examined Virginia's ovaries, fallopian tubes, uterus, rectum, and bladder, removing each of them.

Under the glaring light overhead, Dr. Ophuls, Dr. Rumwell, and Nurse Halston looked closely at the pinkish-red bladder, the ball of smooth muscle that collected urine from Virginia's kidneys.

It was unusually small and appeared to be the organ that failed, causing her body break down. The proof of that was right before their eyes – in a bright red area on the bladder's outer wall was a hole, about one-eighth of an inch in diameter.

A scalpel was placed in Dr. Ophuls' hand, and he made an incision next to the tear. The two doctors saw there weas a small clot of blood inside the organ. There was also a tear in the bladder's inner wall, about three-quarters of an inch long, which corresponded to the outside hole.

Dr. W. Francis Wakefield was called into the room to examine the bladder. There was no doubt. This was the wound that led to the agonizing death of Virginia Rappe.

AT 8:15 THAT EVENING, A SECOND AUTOPSY WAS PERFORMED, this one by Dr. Shelby Strange, autopsy surgeon for the San Francisco coroner's office.

He also examined Virginia's body and noted 11 bruises on her right upper arm, torso, and legs, as well as a small puncture mark on the left arm. The bruises and puncture marks were likely from the morphine injections given to her at the hotel and the sanitarium. Photographs were taken. The bladder and what Dr. Strange later called "the female organs" had been removed, but Dr. Ophuls brought them to the coroner's office in specimen jars. Examining them with a microscope, Dr. Strange noticed chronic inflammation in the tissue of the ruptured bladder. He sent the stomach to the city chemist for further analysis.

Unless the chemist discovered signs of poison in the body, his conclusion was the same as the one reached by Dr. Ophuls, although he reversed the cause and contributing factors. The cause of death, he stated, was acute peritonitis resulting from the rupture of the bladder. Due to how rare it was that a bladder could spontaneously rupture, Dr. Strange came to a logical conclusion.

As he later testified, he believed the rip in Virginia's bladder was caused by "some external force."

TEN

NEWSPAPER JOURNALISM IN 1921 – ESPECIALLY WHEN IT CAME to crimes that were worthy of eight-column headlines – was all-out war.

When the Fatty Arbuckle story broke, there were five daily newspapers in Los Angeles and just as many in San Francisco. Except for those owned by the same company, they were rabid competitors, divided by political parties and by the way they covered the most sordid criminal stories. There were morning papers, evening papers, ands to make sure everyone received the results of the day's final horse races, late editions. And when the news warranted it, extra editions were published – and there might be many of them throughout the day, depending on new developments in the case that was hot at the time. The main purpose of them was to get the "scoop" and beat the competition to the newsstand. Today, we think of the last of the print newspapers as a slow medium, often caught unawares when a big event occurs, but newspapers in 1921 were closer to the 24-hours-a-day news cycle that we have today – along with the fast responses, strong opinions, divided politics, and relentless competition that we have, too.

With radio still in its infancy, the papers were the *only* place to get news in September 1921. Newspaper editors, columnists, and publishers were celebrities – like television commentators today – and none were bigger than publishing tycoon Willam Randolph Hearst, who had a nationwide media empire of 24 papers. His L.A. and San Francisco *Examiners* began sharing information on the fast-developing Arbuckle case and they reveled in the salacious and the scandalous.

The news industry had recently started to become more sensational, and this development was accelerated by the Arbuckle case – much to the detriment of Roscoe. For the most part, this change was the result of competing wire services. The United Press Associations – later UPI – was formed in 1907 to take on the Associated Press. Hearts formed the more sensationalistic International News Service in 1909 and created the morning-edition Universal Service in 1917. So, by 1921, papers around the world could use content from multiple wire services, as well as the content from other papers, to spin stories as big as they liked. Each wire service fought for greater sales largely by pulling stories that could run with startling headlines.

Another big reason for the shift to sensationalism was because of the huge success of New York City's *Daily News*. Launched in 1919, America's first modern tabloid adopted the subheading "New York's Picture Newspaper," and its emphasis on photos, little text, and provocative headlines appeared to the working-class folks who had always been Fatty's biggest fans. Lured in by big headlines and the cry of the newsboys, they scooped up a copy to peruse on the subway, going to and from their jobs. After just one year of operation, the *Daily News* had over 100,000 readers, and a year after that, as the Arbuckle scandal loomed, the number had grown to 400,000 and other papers were copying their style.

To meet the growing demand for headline-worthy material, crime reporters managed to weasel their way into police stations, jails, hospital rooms, morgues, and law offices. They had paid informants everywhere and using expense accounts provided by their editors they worked hard to outbid their competitors to get details. Often, they arrived at crime scenes before the cops did and they followed leads that took them to the doors of witnesses, suspects, and victims, often before detectives could make an official inquiry.

Sometimes, reporters even detained suspects and obtained confessions. Many of them carried shiny badges and pistol permits and often represented themselves as detectives, but when the story came out in the papers it invariably read, they'd "made the arrest as citizens." They shared tips with the police, defense attorneys, and prosecutors, and paid all of them to throw their competitors off the trail. In cities were competition as fiercest, the police tailed the best newsmen – just as reporters trailed the best detectives – and each might wear a disguise recognizable only tot hose with whom they had a working relationship.

Less scrupulous reporters might make up a story or report one of dubious veracity – also just like today. For instance, a few days after the Arbuckle/Rappe story broke, the *Los Angeles Evening Record*, citing anonymous sources, claimed that members of a "Hollywood dope ring" made up of minor actors and studio employees planned

Oakland Tribune

"FATTY" ARBUCKLE CHARGED WITH ACTRESS'

FILM STAR

Tragedy Wipes Smile from Arbuckle's Face

DEATH CAR CRASHES INTO AUTO; MAN HELD

The Times

NEW SENSATION IN ARBUCKLE CASE!

LATEST NEWS FILM CLOWN'S TRIAL STARTS WITH A CLASH

ANTA CONSTITUT

Pretty Victim in Arbuckle Gin-Frolic
Remembered as Model in Atlanta Store

to kill Roscoe because of the negative light shining on the "dope peddling" because of the scandal. Needless to say, there was no truth to that one.

But when a newspaper devoted its resources to a story, those resources included not only the $25-a-week crime reporters but also the freelancers who were paid by the column inch and received bonuses for any front-page stories.

Every reporter of every kind wanted a piece of this story and on September 10, the feeding frenzy began.

A REPORTER FROM THE *LOS ANGELES TIMES* NAMED WARDEN Woolard beat the police to Roscoe's mansion on Friday evening, September 9, and he informed the movie star that Virginia had died a few hours earlier. Roscoe told the reporter that Virgina had become ill at his hotel party, but he knew of no injuries that could have caused her death. "After Miss Rappe had a couple of drinks, she became hysterical and I called the hotel physician and the manager," he told the reporter. He denied that he'd hurt her and added, "This is assuming serious proportions."

"Yes, it is," Woolard agreed.

Soon after, the reporter left, the telephone rang – another reporter, this one from the *San Francisco Chronicle*. Roscoe lied, saying "there were no closed or locked doors" to room 1219. He also implied that Virginia "threw her fit in the presence of everyone" in room 1220 before being moved into 1219.

Roscoe decided that two reporters were two reporters too many and he called Joe Schenck, who suggested a midnight meeting at Sid Grauman's office with the unofficial suspect and then three potential witnesses – Lowell Sherman, Fred Fishback, and Virginia's friend, Al Semnacher.

On his way there, Semnacher stopped at the home of Kate and Joseph Hardebeck. "His face was grave. Something terrible had happened. And I knew before he spoke that my Virginia died," Kate later reported.

When the men arrived at Grauman's office, they were met by Lou Anger. They discussed Virginia's death. Semnacher later testified, "We all thought it was very unfortunate, and we could not understand it."

As a friend of Virginia's who was only slightly acquainted with Roscoe, Al was the outsider in the group. It's been suggested that the men coordinated a strategy, agreeing on what would be said and what wouldn't be said to the press and the authorities. It seems likely this was the reason for the meeting, but was there a promise of money or career advancement made to Semnacher for his cooperation, as some have claimed? There's no evidence of that but depending on what you choose to believe about what happened, it could have happened.

From Grauman's office, Roscoe telephoned a police detective in San Francisco and offered his outline of events, including the claim that he was never alone with Virginia. He also asserted that anyone saying he was responsible for her death were motivated by "ill feelings" toward him. The detective told him to report to the San Francisco Hall of Justice so Roscoe then tracked down his attorney, Milton Cohen, who was out of town. Cohen called his partner, Frank Dominguez, who agreed to represent Roscoe in San Francisco.

After the meeting, Roscoe told his friend Viola

Attorney Frank Dominguez

Joe Bordeaux was an Arbuckle pal and bit studio player. He is the Keystone Kop in the front row to the right

Dana that he had to return to San Francisco but couldn't say why, adding, "For God's sake, don't die on me."

JUST AFTER 3:00 A.M. ON SEPTEMBER 10, ROSCOE'S PIERCE-ARROW was headed north again, its owner behind the wheel. With him were Lou Anger, Frank Dominguez, and Joe Bordeaux, who worked on both sides of the camera in Fatty's films and was a steadfastly loyal friend who Roscoe knew he could depend on. He usually referred to Roscoe as "Chief." The Pierce-Arrow was followed by Fred Fishback, Lowell Sherman, and Al Semnacher in Fred's car. The two groups stopped at a diner in Bakersfield for breakfast.

By then, the news had started to break. The press had pounced on the story and headlines were appearing in morning editions.

DETAIN ARBUCKLE!
FAT COMEDIAN IN TROUBLE AS GIRL DIES FROM ORGY
San Jose Morning News

ACTRESS DIES AFTER HOTEL FILM PARTY!
Los Angeles Examiner

GIRL DEAD AFTER WILD PARTY IN HOTEL!
San Francisco Examiner

GET ROSCOE IS DEATHBED PLEA!
San Francisco Bulletin

ROSCOE ARBUCKLE FACES INQUIRY ON WOMAN'S DEATH!
New York Times

MYSTERY DEATH TAKES ACTRESS!
Los Angeles Times

Only one newspaper seemed optimistic:

"FATTY" ARBUCKLE TO HELP CLEAR ACTRESS' DEATH!
Pittsburgh Press

But sensationalism would come out on top before the weekend was over.

According to one paper, the police had received two different accounts of Virginia's death. The first was "an affidavit given by Miss Alice Blake, actress" – one of the chorus girls at the party. The second was "a statement said to have been telephoned to them from Los Angeles from Roscoe Arbuckle, motion picture comedian, who denied portions of Miss Blake's affidavit."

According to Miss Blake: "About half an hour later, Mrs. Delmont tried to get into the room, but the door was locked. She banged on the door and Arbuckle came out. As he opened the door, we heard Miss Rappe moaning and crying, 'I am dying, I am dying.' Arbuckle came out and said to us, 'Go in and get her dressed and take her back to the Palace. She makes too much noise.'"

But the newspaper reported, Arbuckle's statement said, "We sat around and had some drinks and pretty soon Miss Rappe became hysterical and complained she could not breathe and began to tear her clothes off... At no time was I alone with Miss Rappe. There were half a dozen people in the room all the time."

Roscoe's Pierce-Arrow was easy to track for reporters that morning. When the group stopped in Fresno, Roscoe was quoted by newsmen as saying he had never met Virginia before Monday. "She had a few drinks, then it became necessary to call a physician and to have her removed," he said, leaving out everything that happened in between.

That same article listed Virginia's age as 23 and quoted San Franciscos's night captain of detectives, Michael Griffin: "No charges will be placed against Arbuckle, but he will be detained until after the inquest."

The Arbuckle convoy reached Oakland at 7:00 P.M. and, waiting there for the ferry to San Francisco, a weary Roscoe made a more diplomatic statement to the press, likely at the suggestion of his attorney: "I am coming here to do all I can with the investigation of the case." At the ferry dock, he bought a new newspaper from a newsboy while Dominguez made a telephone call.

"They're saying some rotten things about you, Fatty, but I'm for you," the newsboy told him.

"Thanks, son, I'm glad to know it," Roscoe replied sadly. He walked back toward his car, scanning the front page for the newspaper's account of the St. Francis party.

A few minutes later, he was cornered again by the

Roscoe with San Francisco attorney, Charles Brennan

press. "I don't know why they're saying these things," he scoffed. "I wasn't alone with Miss Rappe at all. There was someone else in the room during the entire affair. These tales of me dragging her into another room are false. She had two or three drinks and became hysterical. We did everything we could to revive her."

Roscoe clammed up when Dominguez returned to the car. A descendant of one of California's original Spanish families, Frank Dominguez resembled an older version of Roscoe, every bit as large but with white hair rimming his bald head. Regarded as one of the top attorneys in Los Angeles, he had the money and the celebrity friends that proved it. His telephone call had been to Charles Brennan, an experienced San Francisco lawyer who knew the local officials and the press. When Roscoe and the others arrived at the Palace Hotel in San Francisco, Brennan was waiting for them – and so were the police and the press.

While the reporters fired off questions that mostly went unanswered, detectives ushered Roscoe, Dominguez, and Brennan to the Hall of Justice. When they arrived there, they had to push their way through newsmen and photographers to get to the door. In the case the worst occurred, and Roscoe was charged with manslaughter, Brennan had

San Francisco Hall of Justice

a briefcase with him that contained $5,000, more than enough for any bail. But both attorneys were sure this spectacular show of wealth wouldn't be necessary.

Roscoe signed a statement regarding the events in room 1219. In it, he contradicted what he'd originally said by saying, "I have known Miss Rappe for the last five years." He'd later say that he was misquoted when he claimed

Assistant District Attorney Milton U'Ren

he'd only just met her at the party. Other than that, his previous recollection of events stayed the same – after "a few drinks" Virginia became hysterical and complained of difficulty breathing and began ripping off her clothes. Two "girls" disrobed her and placed her in a tub. When that failed to help, he called the hotel manager, adding, "I was at no time alone with Miss Rappe."

He and his attorneys were ushered into room 17, where assistant district attorneys Milton U'Ren and Isadore Golden informed them they had sworn affidavits from witnesses Alice Blake, Zey Prevost, and Maude Delmont, all claiming Arbuckle had assaulted Virginia and was responsible for her death.

Dominguez immediately instructed his client to admit only to Prohibition violations and to not say anything to the prosecutors or the detectives. It's unlikely that Roscoe could have talked his way out of being arrested – not with a rabid San Francisco press just outside the door – but as the interrogation progressed, the district attorneys became angry with Roscoe's silence. Sworn witnesses had said one thing – Roscoe said nothing.

He was as silent as his films.

Dominguez put a fine point on it. "Roscoe Arbuckle will not even admit his name is Roscoe Arbuckle," he declared.

After three pointless hours, Roscoe was allowed to leave the room. He consulted with Dominguez while the district attorneys conferred and then, shortly after midnight, Roscoe was arrested for the murder of Virginia Rappe.

He had, the prosecutors stated, violated section 189 of the California Penal Code, which defines first-degree murder to include a killing "which is committed in the perpetration of, or attempt to perpetrate rape." There would be no bail – bail wasn't allowed for a murder charge in California.

Roscoe was stunned. Murder?

From that moment on, there would be his life before the arrest and his life after. Nothing would ever be the same again.

ROSCOE WAS STANDING IN THE HALLWAY, TRYING TO MAKE sense of what was happening as reporters crowded around him, demanding a statement but he couldn't say anything. He was in shock. Photographers fired off boxlike cameras while holding up trays of

magnesium flash powder that ignited with bright bursts of light and smoke. As the corridor filled with haze, Roscoe blinked in confusion. When photographers shouted at him to smile, he managed to reply, "Not on an occasion of this sort."

He was unsmiling in his mugshots, which labeled him with the prisoner number of 32052. His bow tie was badly uneven.

Roscoe said nothing after his arrest, but Captain of Detectives Duncan Matheson did: "This woman, without a doubt, died as a result of an attack by Arbuckle. That makes it first-degree murder without a doubt. We don't feel that a man like Fatty Arbuckle can pull stuff like this in San Francisco and get away with it."

It seemed as though Roscoe had already been tried and convicted instead of merely arrested and in other statements, both Assistant D.A. U'Ren and Chief of Police O'Brien made it clear that Roscoe had refused to answer questions about the charges against him.

The top floor of the Hall of Justice was the jail and its "felon's row" was a long corridor lined with cells. Cell 12 became Roscoe's temporary home. It was six-foot by six-foot with three walls of solid streel and a fourth wall of steel bars. There were three wooden bunks stacked vertically, a wooden bench, and a washstand. As he stood just inside the door, he realized he didn't have his wallet. He'd given it to his lawyers. He asked for some of his money and his jailer replied, "You don't need money in here."

"Are you going to give me a partner in here?" Roscoe asked.

"Do you want one?" the jailer questioned.

"No, I guess I'll sleep better alone."

The door swung shut and was locked. Roscoe figured out a way to hang his overcoat and jacket, and he sank down onto the bottom bunk with a sigh. Eventually, when all was dark and quiet, he stretched out on the bunk and pulled the rough, woolen blanket up over him. But he didn't sleep. He couldn't. He sat up several times to smoke cigarettes and tried to sleep again.

But there was no rest for Fatty that night.

ON SUNDAY MORNING, ACROSS THE NATION, THE FIRST condemnations of Roscoe Arbuckle began to be read in morning newspapers and heard from church pulpits. Fatty Arbuckle had long been representative of onscreen Hollywood – the unruly, not-so-innocent, but funny fat man – but now he'd come to symbolize Hollywood offscreen, which was the Hollywood that so many feared. It was Sodom and Gomorrah combined, unrestrained by Christian morality.

"The shame of it all," preached Rev. John Snape of Oakland's First Baptist Church, "is that good people like you in this congregation make possible the continuance of such a man before the public."

The first cancellation of an Arbuckle film had occurred in San Francisco on Saturday as its star was on his back to the city when *Crazy to Marry* was pulled from two theaters. By Sunday afternoon, San Francisco theater owners joined together to ban Fatty movies across the city.

But it wasn't just San Francisco. That same day, *Gasoline Gus* was pulled from the Million Dollar Theater in downtown Los Angeles – a theater owned by none other than Sid Grauman, whose office Roscoe had met with witnesses and advisers at midnight the day before. Sid

ARBUCKLE'S C... ...FS N.Y. POLICE

PASSAGE OF PLEASURE F... CAFE MEN ...OF SUBPENA

Los Angeles Examiner

FINGERS BLAMED FOR RAPPE BRUISES; HUNDREDS HUNTING SLAYERS OF TWO 2 Men I...

Woman Accuser to Face Arbuckle Today

ACTOR SAFE IN MURDER TRA... CLAI...

SCRIPT

BRITISH Wounded mb Riot; Street

ON U. FIELD

FATTY GLUM AS DOCTORS TAKE STAND

FIVE IN JURY BOX TO HEAR FATTY CASE

Grauman and his father had known Roscoe for years. They'd even cultivated his singing career when he was a teenager. The swiftness with which Grauman pulled *Gasoline Gus*, a popular film with only one day left on its scheduled run, sent shockwaves through Hollywood.

Grauman made no comment about why he did it but likely feared that midnight meeting might tarnish him and his theater and hoped to diminish criticism – but it was a betrayal from which a friendship that dated back many years would never recover.

Grauman's action served as proof to the studios that their worst fears were coming true. The public outrage had only just begun, and it was already cutting into box office grosses. The fear was the greatest at Paramount Pictures. Its biggest star had been accused of murder. Paramount had released two of his films in the last month, had two more in the can, and had four in development. There was panic felt throughout the studio.

But, on vacation in London, the most prominent member of the motion picture community came forward to support his friend on that first Sunday. Charlie Chaplin told reporters, "There's nothing like that in his makeup. On the coast, Fatty is popular with everybody, and I hope he will be proven innocent."

THROUGHOUT THE DAY, INVESTIGATORS TOOK DEPOSITIONS from witnesses and searched for any available evidence.

In one of the strangest developments in the investigation, cops in Los Angeles, acting on instructions from San Francisco, went to the home of Al Semnacher and took possession of a woman's silk shirt that was missing three of its five buttons and a pair of woman's torn silk undergarments. They had been worn by Virginia Rappe at the party. Semnacher said he'd found them on the floor of room 1219 and took them to dust his automobile.

Virginia's other clothing – the jade skirt and blouse she had made herself and the white hat with the jade band – were in a closet in a Hotel St. Francis guest room occupied by Virginia's other travel companion, Maude Delmont.

WHEN ROSCOE AWAKENED IN JAIL SUNDAY MORNING, HE had no toiletries, but a fellow inmate loaned him some soap, a towel, and a comb.

Prisoners in the San Francisco City Jail who could afford it were allowed to order food from outside, so Roscoe had eggs, toast, and coffee delivered from a nearby restaurant. He was shaved by the prison barber.

He was the most famous resident ever locked up at the jail and this notoriety turned into a sort of meet and greet with the other inmates. Chatting with other accused felons, he answered their questions and accepted their sympathy.

"He's just a regular guy," one of them noted.

Later that evening, Roscoe met with his attorneys, which then included his usual lawyer, Milton Cohen. A request was made for better accommodations for the film star, but the request was denied.

When he told a jailer, "It's too lonesome alone," he was allowed to choose a cellmate and Fred Martin moved in with him. The press described Martin as "a laborer accused of contributing to the delinquency of a minor."

The man who made the whole world laugh told others in his cellblock that this day had been the worst one in his life.

But his life was just about to get a lot worse.

ELEVEN

ON MONDAY MORNING, SEPTEMBER 12, 1921, REPORTERS ARRIVED at Cell 12 of the San Francisco Jail to find Roscoe having breakfast with his new pal, Fred Martin. The movie star was well-dressed, especially compared to his cellmate in his work clothes, and was sharing boiled eggs, toast, and coffee delivered from a local restaurant. Other prisoners lurked nearby, jealously watching the celebrity and his cellmate eat something better than jail chow, but guards ordered them away. The newsmen crowded into the corridor hoping for a great quote from Roscoe.

But Roscoe shook his head at them. "Nothing I could say now would do any good," he told them. "My attorneys have asked me to remain silent at present. What I have to say will be said in my own defense later. Everything that I have said in the past while I was on my way up here seemed to have been distorted and made to appear against me. I am not as black as I have been painted, and when I go into court the public will have a different opinion of me. You can easily see that a man in my position should remain silent as this time, because words are liable to be twisted into a meaning other than you intended."

Although this was the only thing Roscoe said to reporters that morning, this headline appeared on the front page of the *San Francisco Call & Post* that day:

ARBUCKLE DANCES WHILE GIRL IS DYING, JOYOUS FROLIC AMID DEATH TRAGEDY!

The jail barber had shaved him the day before, but after breakfast, Roscoe sent for a more skilled razor-and-scissors artist from outside the jail. When that man arrived, her shaved and trimmed the hair of both Roscoe and his cellmate and the movie star also arranged for a massage.

He was in jail, sure, but Roscoe wasn't all that interested in doing hard time.

DURING THE WEEKEND WHEN THE ARBUCKLE CASE BROKE, THE District Attorney of San Francisco, Matthew Brady, was out of town. But on Monday morning, he took over the case from his assistants.

Born in San Francisco in 1875, Brady, who was 46 when the case broke, had been a lawyer in private practice before securing appointments to the Civil

San Francisco District Attorney Matthew Brady

Service Commission and then the police court bench. He narrowly defeated a scandal-ridden incumbent to become the city's DA in January 1920. He positioned himself as a reformer, eager to rebuild his office's reputation. It was speculated that he had his eye on the city's mayoral office or perhaps even the governor's office.

Brady began by assessing the quality of the case. Though there were sworn affidavits from Alice Blake, Zey Prevost, Maude Delmont, and nurse Vera Cumberland, the first two were showgirls who had willingly come to a booze party held by men they had only just met, and the last only had secondhand knowledge of anything that occurred in Arbuckle's suite. Brady decided that Maude Delmont, the apparently selfless woman who had befriended Virginia Rappe in her final days, was his strongest witness.

That would not turn out to be a great strategy, no matter how it seemed on paper.

But for now, Brady saw that Maude alleged that Arbuckle had lured a cautious Virginia to the part with the promise of "something big" for her film career, only to have Virginia reject his "proposition."

Newspapers had widely printed her allegations that Roscoe Arbuckle "dragged" Virginia in 1219, but her less volatile affidavit read as follows:

Miss Rappe went into the bathroom off Room 1219, leaving the rest of the party in Room 1220, and when she came out Arbuckle took hold of her and said, "I have been trying to get you for five years."

After he took hold of her and made this remark he then closed and locked the door of Room 1219, leading into Room 1220, leaving the rest of the party in Room 1220.

I felt anxious about Miss Rappe. When she did not return to our party I became very anxious about her. I called to her several times, no answer, then kicked against the door with the heel of my shoe at least a dozen times during the next hour. When I told her what I had done afterwards, she said she must have been unconscious immediately after he locked the door, otherwise she must have heard me.

D.A. Brady initially believed Maude Delmont would be his strongest witness, but that opinion would later change

After an hour's wait, I became alarmed, took down the receiver to the telephone and called for help from the office. Mr. Boyle, the assistant manager, came up. When Arbuckle heard our conservation he opened the door, standing in his pajamas, west with perspiration, and had Miss Rappe's Panama hat on his head.

The bed where she lay was saturated wet and she was semi-conscious and tearing her clothes. She tore the cuffs of her white silk shirtwaist and threw them on the floor, screaming: "He did it, I know he did it. I have been hurt, I am dying." This was said in the presence of Arbuckle.

She further told of Virginia's pains in her neck, left leg, and especially, abdomen, and of "monkey bites" on Virginia's neck and big marks on her right arm and left leg.

Early on Tuesday morning, Virginia, in severe pain, allegedly told her: "Maude, Roscoe should be at my bedside every minute and see how I am suffering from what he did to me."

And while D.A. Brady didn't know it, Maude's affidavit was filled with lies and exaggerations. Just for example, she didn't see Roscoe and Virginia go into 1219, had no idea what went on in the room, and they were not in the room for anything remotely close to an hour.

While on the courthouse elevator on the morning of September 12, reporters overheard her begging, "Oh please don't make me face Arbuckle. I don't even ever want to lay eyes on him again."

But then, a short time later, she told a newsman, "If I have to do it, I will. I will try to nerve myself to the ordeal, but it will be terrible."

The defendant was not in the courtroom when, shortly after 11:00 A.M., Maude stood beside the district attorney and swore under oath to the accuracy of her transcribed statement. After this short formality, she suddenly collapsed, nearly fainting – or at least that's how it appeared. Hysterical, she was led from the courtroom.

When a downtrodden-looking Roscoe appeared in court with his attorneys at 11:30 A.M., he was greeted by an explosion of camera flashes and chatter from the mostly male spectators who packed into the gallery, standing up, trying to get a better view. Accused men waiting for their turn in front of the judge, pressed against the steel fencing of the prisoner's dock.

When he was called to the bench, Roscoe approached, hands clasped and face downturned. Grimly, he listened to a clerk read Maude Delmont's complaint.

When it was over, Brady told the press, "I desire to state that I will spare no effort to punish the perpetrator of this atrocious crime, although I know I will be opposed by the cleverest lawyers and the greatest influence which money can purchase."

ON THE OTHER SIDE OF THE COUNTRY IN NEW YORK CITY, HENRY Lehrman had received the news about his old friend and former co-worker, Roscoe Arbuckle, and his former girlfriend, Virginia Rappe. From his Manhattan apartment, he fired off a statement to the press:

From information I received from San Francisco, I believe Arbuckle is guilty. For his sake, I wish that he will receive full measure of justice so there will be no other crime necessary. You know what the death of Virginia means to me. I will not attempt to express it. She died game, like a real woman, her last words being to punish Arbuckle, that he outraged her and she begged the nurse not to tell this, as she did not want me to know.

Would I kill Arbuckle? Yes. I feel just as any other man with red blood in his veins. I will not deny that I have said I would kill him if we were to meet. I hope the law will punish him and that he will receive full justice for the crime.

Arbuckle is the result of ignorance and too much money. He was originally a bar boy, although he had been in the chorus and done other things. I directed him for a year and a half, and I had to warn him to keep out of the women's dressing rooms. There are some people who are a disgrace to the film business. They get enormous salaries and have not sufficient balance to keep right. They are the kind who resort to cocaine and opium and who participate in orgies that are of the lowest character. They should be driven out of the picture business. I am no saint, but I have never attended one of their parties. Virginia's friends were decent people, and I know she would not have associated with anyone she knew to be vile.

It was a big surprise to everyone – and would have been to Virginia, too – when Lehrman claimed that he and Virginia were engaged to be married at the time of her death.

His malicious attack on Roscoe Arbuckle – filled with rumors and outright lies – became a sensation. Lehrman achieved the greatest fame of his career with this statement, using the tragic death of a woman who once loved him for all the publicity he could milk from it.

AT THE SAME TIME THIS WAS HAPPENING, ROSCOE'S FILMS WERE quickly being banned all over the country – by theater organizations, by theater chains, by censorship boards, and by police commissions. In other instances, individual theater owners followed Sid Grauman's lead and removed the films on their own.

In Jersey City, the commissioner of public safety contacted every theater town in town, inquiring about Fatty's movies. Every theater had pulled them. The commissioner told the press, "I know of no legal method to prevent the showing of Arbuckle features, but I think it would be common decency on the part of motion picture theater owners not to show the pictures until Arbuckle is cleared of the charges."

At least the commissioner stated the possibility that Roscoe could be "cleared of the charges" – most people weren't seeing that as a possibility. When some theater owners, who valued the idea of "innocent until proven guilty," didn't remove the films, protests were organized, marquee billboards were defaced, and lobby posters were torn down.

On the other hand, there was suddenly a demand for the films in which Virginia Rappe appeared. In death, she was finally given the star billing that she never received in life.

THE CORONER'S INQUEST INTO VIRGINIA'S DEATH, ORIGINALLY scheduled for later in the month, had to be moved forward to stay ahead of the grand jury that was scheduled to convene on the evening of Monday, September 12. So, at 2:00 P.M. that afternoon, the inquest began in an office of the country morgue, conveniently also located in the Hall of Justice.

A coroner's inquest has one goal – to determine the manner of death. In San Francisco in 1921, a jury of citizens sat in judgement and could ask questions of witnesses, though most of the questioning was done by the attorneys and the coroner.

The proceedings began with a heated argument between Assistant D.A. Milton U'Ren and defense attorney Frank Dominguez.

The prosecution argued that they were still gathering information and wanted to delay Maude Delmont's testimony so she could first be heard by the grand jury, away from the ears of defense attorneys and reporters. Convinced she was going to be coached by the prosecution, the defense demanded to question their chief accuser. Dominguez argued, "We want the full facts placed before the people and we want it done today at this inquest!"

The prosecution's only argument was that Roscoe's silence was not contributing to such transparency.

Overseeing the proceedings, San Francisco coroner Dr. Thomas B.W. Leland took offense to the implication that a coroner's inquest was unworthy of important evidence, but after deliberation, he agreed that Delmont's testimony could be delayed but ordered her to be on the stand the next morning.

The first witness at the inquest was Hotel St. Francis assistant manager Harry Boyle, who testified to being

San Francisco Coroner Dr. Thomas B.W. Leland

called to room 1219, carrying Virginia to 1227 with Arbuckle, and calling Dr. Olav Kaarboe – the second witness.

Dr. Melville Rumwell and Dr. William Ophuls recalled performing the first postmortem exam, and they bolstered the defense by saying they saw no evidence of violence other than the lacerated bladder. To the assertion that they conducted an illegal autopsy, Dr. Rumwell claimed he called the coroner's office and learned that Dr. Leland was out of town and could not be reached. Asked about the cause of Virginia's torn bladder, Rumwell ruled out a puncture created by a catheter and a spontaneous rupture caused by the bladder expanding too far.

After Dr. Emmet Rixford and Dr. George Reid spoke about their consultations with Rumwell in the sanitarium prior to Virginia's death, the proceedings adjourned for the day.

The press reported that Roscoe was "an almost unnoticed figure at the inquest."

ROSCOE MAY HAVE BEEN "UNNOTICED" AT THE INQUEST, BUT HIS presence loomed large in Hollywood.

When pressed for comment, most in the film industry steered clear of opinions about Roscoe's guilt or innocence. They cowardly went with "this is unfortunate" banalities. If you're thinking not much has changed in Hollywood, you'd be right.

Alice Lake emphasized her friend's compassion, though: "He was always doing kind things, and he certainly was always one of the first to help at benefits for poor people and other unfortunate ones."

Buster Keaton was one of the few to stand up for his friend: "I don't believe he is guilty. I never saw him pull any such parties. I think it's wrong to ruin a man before he is even heard."

From his office in New York, Joe Schenck was equally supportive, and he even went on the offensive against prosecutor Brady: "Arbuckle is a big, good-natured, lovable sort of chap, and I think that he is not guilty of the charges that certain California public officials seeking notoriety are trying to hang on him."

But the Los Angeles Athletic Club, home away from home to the city's celebrities and elite, held an emergency meeting and voted Roscoe out. The club president stated: "I have little to say regarding the action except it was the unanimous belief of the directors that such a step should be taken. We do not want that kind of men in the club fore we do not care to associate with that class."

That kind of bravery – based on rumors and conjecture -- was not exactly inspiring.

WHEN THE GRAND JURY HEARING BEGAN AT 7:30 P.M. ON Monday evening, a throng of reporters and spectators crowded into the hallway and pressed as close to the closed doors as guards would allow. Throughout the rest the evening hours and into the next morning, witnesses, flanked by police officers, were brought in and out to loud voices, camera-powder flashes, and assorted commotion.

Reporters, observers, defense attorneys, defendants who aren't testifying, and judges aren't allowed in a grand jury room. All the questions are asked of the witnesses by the prosecutor or by the jurors. The sole mission of the grand jury is to determine if there is enough evidence against the defendant for a trial. The prosecution has all the power in the room, which is why the joke is often made that they can convince a grand jury to "indict a ham sandwich."

The first witness at the hearing was Maude Delmont, who was questioned for more than an hour and then later, was brought back for an additional 15 minutes. When she emerged from behind the closed doors, she was leaving heavily on a police matron and was said to be ill "due to the shock induced by the death of her friend."

You know, the "friend" she'd just met that weekend.

Al Semnacher, Zey Prevost, and Doctors Rumwell, Ophuls, and Rixford testified next, as did the surgeon from the coroner's office who performed Virgina's second autopsy, Dr. Shelby Strange.

Two floors above in Cell 12, Roscoe was sitting nervously on the edge of his bed when guards approached him just before 1:00 A.M. He was wanted in the grand jury room, they said. He quickly got dressed and went downstairs with the guards.

A reporter described him as he trudged to the courtroom: "He looked nervous, his comedy face was far gloomier than that of a tragedian, and beads of perspiration sparkled on his brow."

Inside, the jury foreman asked Roscoe to give an account of the events in question, but he quickly replied: "My attorneys have advised me to say nothing at this time." He was in the grand jury chamber for three minutes before he was led back to his cell by the guards.

After the prosecutors left the room, the grand jury deliberated for nearly an hour. At around 2:00 A.M., the foreman announced that jury had decided against voting on the matter and instead wanted to give "District Attorney Brady more time in which to secure certain information which we desire."

Brady addressed the press after that, claiming that the case had not been weakened by the grand jury's indecision. But he did then make an announcement that would make huge headlines on Tuesday.

Zey Prevost, who changed her story about the party in front of the grand jury

"We have sent Miss Zey Prevost home under police surveillance," he said. "The girl changed her story completely before the grand jury. Whether or not we shall arrest her and charge her with perjury depends on further developments. I am convinced that undue influence and pressure has been brought to bear on her and other witnesses, one of whom, Alice Blake, has mysteriously disappeared from her home in Berkley. We have been unable to find her."

It was the first crack in the prosecution's case. It wouldn't be the last.

BUT IT ALMOST DIDN'T MATTER. AS THE NEWSPAPERS OF THE DAY soon proved – it was much easier to create evidence than it was to find it. Although I think calling what the newspapers and rumor mongers were concocting about Roscoe could hardly be called "evidence."

The amount of ink being spilled by the papers that first week seemed to be enough to float a battleship. And while most of the newspaper coverage was in San Francisco and Los Angeles, there were stories being printed everywhere, from Seattle to Miami, in big cities and small towns, and even across the Atlantic and Pacific Oceans – anyplace where Roscoe and his films had traveled.

The wave of coverage reached its peak on Tuesday, September 13, when the *San Francisco Examiner* printed a mind-boggling 17 stories about the case and the *San Francisco Chronicle* and *Los Angeles Times* weighed in with a staggering 16 each. The stories that day covered both the coroner's inquest and the grand jury hearing in progress, new evidence and witnesses introduced, as well as charges of perjury, missing witnesses, and "undue influence and pressure."

But it wasn't enough to simply cover the legal proceedings – everyone was printing Brady's statement – a good reporter had to dig up with the competition didn't have.

For instance, an interview appeared that day with Roscoe's housekeeper, who said her boss was just a "big, good-natured boy."

Another story reported that the inmate in the cell next to Roscoe's was a convicted murderer, who'd soon be returning to Maryland, where he'd escaped from prison. The headline for that one blared, ARBUCKLE WILL LOSE NEIGHBOR IN JAIL.

Another headline read, GRAVE OF ARBUCKLE'S MOTHER IS NEGLECTED and claimed that the wooden slab that marked Mary's final resting place in a Santa Ana cemetery was so faded it was unreadable, and the plot was "overrun with grass and weeds." This took a shot at – gasp – Roscoe's love for this mother, even though he repeatedly paid for the plot's upkeep.

Minta Durfee made her first public statement on Tuesday, offering support for Roscoe. His sister, Nora, as also supportive and her comments were widely published – "He has the kindest, tenderest heart in the world." His brother, Harry, told reporters he had "no comment," which led to a misleading headline of BROTHER IS NEUTRAL.

So, Roscoe's housekeeper, mother, wife, sister, and brother – who could be next?

BULLDOG MOURNS FOR ARBUCKLE
Faithful Pet Waiting at Door for Return of Comedian

Fatty Arbuckle has one sincere mourner, one mourner whose love and faith no reports can shake. That mourner is Luke, Fatty's old bulldog. Luke usually goes with Fatty on long trips, but the comedian didn't take him to San Francisco with him.

This is the longest time that the comedian and Luke have been separated. And out at Fatty's house, Luke sits, disconsolate at the door, waiting for the familiar step and the well-known voice. He doesn't eat. He waits.

Whatever befalls Fatty, Luke will not forget.

Apparently, since Roscoe had been away from home for one day longer than he had been the week before, Luke had gone on a hunger strike, waiting for Roscoe to return.

Luke had been reading the newspapers, right?

Another headline promised OTHER ILLEGAL ACTS CHARGED TO FILM STAR and then suggested that Arbuckle may have attended Hollywood "drink and drug orgies."

And there was more. A headline asserted, SECOND GIRL ESCAPES FATE OF MISS RAPPE, but was actually about Lowell Sherman luring a model into his room after Virginia was moved to room 1227.

An article in a Flagstaff paper was headlined FATTY ARBUCKLE TREATS WIFE ROUGH IN ARIZONA and alleged that, more than 12 years earlier, not only did he beat Minta, giving her two black eyes, but he also abandoned her with no money at the train station in Benson, Arizona, where she was rescued by the good people of Bisbee. The single source listed for this was "word received here today," although not once in any interview or in her own memoirs did Minta ever make the claim that Roscoe was physically abusive.

But why let the truth get in the way of a good story?

Oddly, in the many newspaper reports that followed Roscoe's arrest all of them shunned the word "rape." They had policies against using that word, which is probably why they tossed around the word "orgy" so much, which seems much worse, but apparently, there weren't any rules against that. The word, which had not been used by either police or prosecutors, had first appeared in print on September 11 – DYING GIRL LAID BLAME ON COMEDIAN: SO CHARGES WOMAN AT BEDSIDE OF ORGY VICTIM IN STATEMENT TO S.F. POLICE. Soon after, there was an orgy of "orgy" headlines across the nation. The September 5 party – originally just an informal gathering – was called an "orgy," the incident at Mishawum Manor, which Roscoe did not attend, was called an "orgy," and there were many stories about the assumed prevalence of "Hollywood orgies" that must be taking place.

A headline in Tuesday's *Baltimore Sun* was typical – ARBUCKLE AFFAIR NO SURPRISE AFTER ORGIES OF FILM COLONY. On Wednesday, the *San Francisco Examiner* wrote about Roscoe: "Tales of his sickening orgies have spread from one coast to the other. Everybody who knows anything about him or his kind ought to know what a 'party' given by him would mean."

Most "orgy" headlines promised a lot more than they delivered when it came to scandalous content, but an article published in the *Philadelphia Evening Public Ledger* was an exception. On page two – next to two large photos of Virginia and an article titled "Arbuckle Party Drank Forty Quarts" – was a piece called "Hollywood Orgies Exposed by Police," which purported to blow the lid off a group called the "Live Hundred," which was made up of Hollywood stars and executives, including, allegedly, Fatty Arbuckle. The greatest detail was offered about an "orgy" that was reportedly attended by witnesses in the Arbuckle case, during which "the host spent $20,000 for decorations" alone. There was no way to know what the host – "a prominent male actor of the screen," spent on booze and refreshments but:

> *From without, as the group sat down at the long table in the "grotto," the watchers [detectives] saw a maid push a wheeled tea tray in after extensive indulgence by all in drinks. On the tray was an assortment of needles, opium pipes, morphine, cocaine, heroin, and opium. Each guest hilariously helped himself or herself to liberal does of drugs and selected needles or pipes as the individual desire demanded.*

With the party in full swing, a cocaine-snorting actress announced, "I want the most beautiful man here. I am his!"

This was presumably supposed to kick off the "orgy" part of the night, but detectives interrupted by beating on the door. By the time it was opened, all the evidence had been destroyed or concealed, and the host had escaped.

A headline in the *Denver Post* on Thursday promised another salacious piece of fiction under a ludicrous headline that read: NARCOTICS NEEDLES TURNED TAME PARTY AT HOLLYWOOD INTO ASTOUNDING SUCCESS.

Sure, they did.

Suddenly, every Hollywood rumor, scandal, and tall tale was dragged into the papers, no matter how ridiculous they were. A United Press story, which ran on the front pages of numerous newspapers on Monday, linked Virginia's death with six other Hollywood scandals, including Charlie Chaplin's divorce on grounds of cruelty, the Mishawum Manor "orgy," and the accidental fatal poisoning of Olive Thomas, who mistakenly drank a solution of mercury bichloride in September 1920.

A September 13 editorial in the *Los Angeles Times* announced that Roscoe had killed Virginia but still offered:

> *For three or four years, the smart set in the movies has been traveling at a furious pace. Their marital infidelities have clogged the pages of the divorce records. They have taken supreme delight in flinging their money from the windows. However moderate might be the pictures they produced, in real life the machine was always*

This film publicity shot became a favorite for scandal-skewed newspaper stories since it portrayed Roscoe surrounded by women – and in his bathrobe

running on high. Now one of the fastest of the furious set has driven his machine into the ditch.

The Times trusts that the example will prove a salutary warning to others who have been going at a similar pace, for Arbuckle is not the only cinema star who has given mixed parties at which the host received the guests clad only in a bathrobe and pajamas.

The constant harping about the "Labor Day Orgy" attended by those in and around the movie industry – which was linked to other such "orgies" and "scandals" – helped politicians and preachers paint Hollywood as a modern-day Babylon. The attention and abuse -- even though it was mostly incorrect, far-fetched, or simply fantasy – rocked the movie business and had repercussions for decades to come.

But the most damage that first week was to the reputation of Roscoe Arbuckle. He had gone from a beloved icon to, at best, a degenerate, and, at worst, a rapist and killer. His size and weight, which had previously shown him to be jolly, fun-loving fat man, suddenly became the symbol of carnal desires and an inability to control his libido.

On Tuesday, the *Denver Post* printed a front-page artist's illustration of Roscoe behind bars and appearing twice as heavy as his 266 pounds and twice his age of 34. The next day, the same paper published an article entitled "Arbuckle's Fat Is to Blame for His Trouble,

Declares Famous Psychoanalyst." In the piece, the "psychoanalyst" stated that "the hundred too many pounds rolling over the film comedian's body is so much moral weakness and potential crime."

Got it. If you're overweight, you must be a criminal, too.

The *Dayton Daily News* piled on in an editorial: "Arbuckle is a gross, common, bestial, drunken individual, and it is perfectly apparent that he has never deserved the patronage he has received. This is not his first escapade. Filled up with liquor, his low bestiality asserts itself in treating a woman like a grizzly bear would a calf."

Before the Labor Day weekend mess, Roscoe had been revered as a working-class entertainer who'd seen tough times and who'd become wealthy because he was talented and worked hard. Now, he was a lucky-to-be-rich creep who lived outside of society's norms.

Obviously, jealousy fueled some of this reaction. An editorial in the *Atlanta Constitution* entitled "Ruined by Wealth" claimed, "Arbuckle, made suddenly famous because his grotesque figure and comical antics before the camera was amusing to the movie-going world, accumulated money so rapidly that his most difficult problem was to spend it as fast as it came up."

The photos that accompanied the stories about Roscoe portrayed him in two ways. He was shown to be either unsmiling and pensive, as if troubled by what he'd done, or as his Fatty character – the overgrown, mischievous, somewhat lecherous boy in an undersized bowler hat.

In contrast, the press never got tired of publishing glamor shots of a smiling Virginia Rappe, where she was frequently called "the best dressed girl of the movies." Most of those photos were at least five years old, emphasizing her youth and beauty. Full pages were often devoted to photo montages with titles like "Once in Happy Repose" and "Beautiful, Laughing Virginia Rappe in Film Scenes." Often, dour or ridiculous photos of Roscoe were inserted near photos of Virginia, as if he was lurking nearby and interrupting her carefree life.

Perhaps the most shameless of these was plastered across the front page of Thursday's *San Francisco Examiner*. It showed a spiderweb, spun by an illustrator's pen, ensnaring a series of photos. At the center was an arachnid Roscoe with two bottles of liquor while around him was his prey – the seven female guests at his Labor Day party, including Virginia. The image was called "They Walked Into His Parlor," and the caption began, "Caught in the web spun lightly at an afternoon party a week ago, the eight persons shown in the above photographic cartoon today find the mealies still sticking to them."

DIED AFTER WILD PARTY

The *New York American* stuck with this theme. In a piece called "Hope of Fame Lured Actress to Her Death," it asserted that the "lure of something better in her motion picture career, possibly the stardom she had craved for years but never hat attained, was the snare in which Roscoe Arbuckle, charged with her murder, enticed Virginia Rappe into his net."

Except for statements from his relatives, friends, co-workers, and the loyalty of his dog, as well as biographical sketches that described his improbably rise to stardom, nearly all the press that first week cast Roscoe in a negative light and, for the most part, presumed his guilt. He was the entitled movie star who ignored the limits of polite society, was forever seeking the next thrill, was openly disdainful of his marriage, and a slavering beast named "Fatty."

Virginia was painted as the stylish but innocent beauty lured into his lair, engaged to be married, always smiling, and now tragically dead. Her age was invariably given as 25, even though she had turned 30 on September 5 – only four years younger than Roscoe.

Roscoe's attorneys seemed to be facing an unwinnable case. Even the prospects of choosing an impartial jury seemed impossible thanks to the endless barrage of lurid news coverage from local newspapers.

The lawyers had their work cut out for them.

WHILE THE ODDS SEEMED STACKED AGAINST ROSCOE, THOSE who loved him were determined to do what they could to help.

"Roscoe Arbuckle is just a great big, lovable, pleasure-loving, overgrown boy whose success and prosperity have been a little too much for him, but he is not guilty of the hideous charge made against him in

Minta remained loyal and supportive to her estranged husband.

San Francisco," the always supportive Minta Durfee told the press while preparing for a five-day train trip to San Francisco.

She had been vacationing on Martha's Vineyard with her mother and hadn't learned about her husband's arrest until she received a telegram from her sister on Sunday night. The next day, she and her mother returned to New York City to find reporters camped out in the lobby of her apartment building.

By Tuesday, Minta was ready to talk. "I am going to him because I think it is my duty to be near him. I want to help him in any way I can," she told the newsmen.

Speculation was swirling about the Arbuckle marriage. That same day, the *New York Times* reported the "rumor" that they couple had recently separated.

Minta, who asked to be named in print as "Mrs. Arbuckle" to show her support for Roscoe, clarified the situation: "Five years ago, we agreed to disagree, and I received a separation maintenance. A reconciliation? That depends on whether I find that my place is with him and whether he finds that he is ready to return to the life we led when we were married, when I was his inspiration. All I know now is that I am going to a friend who needs every bit of help he can get."

ON TUESDAY MORNING, THE CORONER'S INQUEST CONTINUED and Mrs. Bambina Maude Delmont took the stand as the star witness. She was wearing black, like a mourner – or a villain.

In the newspaper photo that appeared of her that day, her head is titled up, chin lifted, as if in defiance, and a black hat sits atop her graying black hair. Light-colored eyes glared from under tired lids and a frown tugged downward at the corners of her thin, tight lips. Despite the rigid appearance of an unhappy librarian, she was described as a "an exceedingly nervous witness" who took frequent drinks of water. This might have been because of Roscoe's presence in the room. He stared at her during her testimony, looking away only to whisper to one of his attorneys.

Maude told a story that agreed with her affidavit and previous statements – more or less. There were some important modifications, though. The big one was that Roscoe did not take hold of Virginia, and he did not drag her into the bedroom.

Her account was punctuated by Virginia saying, "I am hurt! I am dying! He did it!" The *he*, she said, was Roscoe Arbuckle. As she testified, "Right from the start, Virginia accused Roscoe – she always called him that – but she didn't want anyone to tell Lehrman about it." In that way, Maude served up the crucial accusation from Virginia's lips and placed Roscoe there to hear the dying woman and not deny it.

Even so, her account was erratic. Coroner Leland frequently cautioned her to "consider your statements well." He admitted that he might have been leading her with his questions and once after an affirmative answer from her, he noted, "Sometimes people go to sleep and just say 'yes.'"

Oddly, Maude replied, "I'm not asleep, for I had a little hypodermic before I came here and I'm all right." There was no mention about what was in that hypodermic.

When asked why she had been wearing a pair of Lowell Sherman's pajamas at the party, Maude said that she'd become warm while dancing. As for her Prohibition violation, she didn't seem to care, confessing to drinking from her own pint of whiskey on the Saturday ride from Los Angeles. At the time, it was legal to consume liquor in your own home or at a private residence where you were an invited guest, but it was illegal to transport it. She admitted to drinking gin and orange juice at the party and claimed that Virginia had three orange blossoms herself. As for Virginia's accused murderer, she said, "It impressed me that Arbuckle was more intoxicated than anyone else in the party. He was just a little gone. He showed it in his eyes and by being very talkative. He was not staggering or anything of that sort."

But Maude couldn't have been a good judge of anyone else's state of mind that day after, by her own admission under oath, also consumed "eight or ten" whiskeys at the party.

The coroner asked, "How do you know what happened if you had so many drinks of whiskey?"

Maude had the nerve to reply, "My memory is very good."

The two nurses, Jean Jameson and Vera Cumberland, were two presumably impartial witnesses who had been with the Virginia during her illness before her death. Although Nurse Jameson testified that Virginia claimed she "had been suffering for six weeks with internal trouble," Vera Cumberland said, "The patient admitted to me that her relations with Arbuckle in the room had not been proper." Virginia had hinted to her that she'd slept with Roscoe, but she made no mention of rape or if him hurting her in any way.

Both corroborated one element of Maude's testimony, recalling that Virginia had expressed anxiety about Henry Lehman hearing of the events in 1219, indicating that she still had strong feelings for him. The testimony of the two nurses barely got the attention of the press.

When Al Semnacher testified, he explained that he had not been at the party during the events in question and hadn't returned until around the time the assistant manager was called. When he next saw Virginia, she was naked on the bed. According to him, she wasn't much of a drinker, saying that he had seen her have one or two drinks and get dizzy. He then reiterated his odd reasoning for taking her torn clothing, which was introduced as evidence: "I thought the shirtwaist would make a nice dust cloth for my car."

When he visited Virginia on the day after Labor Day, she supposedly told him, "Roscoe hurt me."

Salesman Ira Fortlouis – who'd been kicked out of the party before Virginia became ill – wasn't much of a witness and spent little time in front of the jury.

Because Alice Blake and Zey Prevost hadn't testified, the jury wasn't able to deliberate, and the coroner once again complained about the prosecution. The district attorney's office assured the coroner the two women would be there to testify the next day.

Once again, Roscoe was escorted out of the room and led asway to his cell, ignoring the barrage of reporters' questions and the hazy explosions of camera flash powder.

Some of those reporters managed to witness the confrontation that

Al Semnacher

occurred when Al Semnacher stopped to say goodbye to Maude Delmont. She asked why he hadn't brought Virginia's "aunt" to the inquest from Los Angeles, and he replied that he wasn't aware that Kate Hardebeck was without money – suggesting she could pay her own way – and he added that he'd left for San Franciso in the middle of the night.

Growing agitated, Maude asked, "Well, what am I to do about my bills at the St. Francis? They come to about $250."

"I'm sure I don't know," Al replied.

"Well, if you were a man, you'd pay them. And why am I still holding the bag?"

"Why, Maude, you know the only bag you're holding is that little bag in your hand."

Outraged, Maude shrieked and swung the bag viciously at Al's face but missed. "You dirty dog! Get out of here!" she screamed at him as she was subdued by a nearby police officer.

As Al left the room, he shook his head and remarked," Why should I pay her bills? I'm under no obligations to her."

But Maude's bill did get paid. A short time later, presumably at her request, Henry Lehrman wired her the money to cover her stay at the St. Francis.

AFTER THE PROMISES MADE TO THE CORONER ABOUT THE TWO missing witnesses, District Attorney Brady got busy working on his strategy. He knew after her coroner's inquest testimony that Maude Delmont wasn't going to fare well under cross-examination in a criminal trial. That meant that the two previously unknown chorus girls who dreamed of showbiz success and answered to stage names had become much more important. If Zey Prevost and Alice Blake – friends with no one at the party except each other – backed up Delmont's version of events, then Brady believed a murder conviction was likely. The problem was that Prevost refused to tell the grand jury what she told detectives on one occasion and prosecutors on another – that Virginia had said, "I'm dying. I'm dying. He killed me." She now claimed she'd been frightened and confused when originally questioned.

Accompanied by her mother, Zey Prevost was escorted to the Hall of Justice by the police. Meanwhile, Alice was brought in by a family friend who claimed she'd gone into hiding to protect her wealthy Oakland family from the embarrassment.

Separately, prosecutors worked to get both showgirls to sign statements that backed up Maude's charge that Virginia had said, in Roscoe's presence, "He did it" – a less precise accusation than "He

MINSTER, MASS., WEDNESDAY, SEPTEMBER 14, 1921.   TEN PAGES   TWO CENTS.

EADERS
MBLE IN
IN TODAY

INDICTMENT OF MANSLAUGHTER
PLACED AGAINST ARBUCKLE

PROPOSALS OF LLOYD GEORGE
UNANIMOUSLY APPROVED TODAY

T WILL
ER MATTER

More Out of Work
In 1914 Than Now
Says Sec. Davis

Two Charges Voted Against Star Movie Comedian—Prosecution On Murder Complaint, Already Under Way, Will Not Be Stopped—Indictment Goes Direct to Superior Court—Warrant for Arbuckle's Arrest Expected Friday.

(By the Associated Press)

SAN FRANCISCO, Sept. 14.—Two charges today had been placed against Roscoe (Fatty) Arbuckle, movie star comedian in connection with the death of Miss Virginia

killed me." Both eventually signed. Zey's new recollection claimed, "He hurt me, he hurt me. I am dying. I am dying. I am dying."

Brady called the grand jury back into session at 8:00 P.M. on Tuesday and produced three witnesses – Zey Prevost, Alice Blake, and Grace Halston, the nurse at the first autopsy. The chorus girls backed up Maude's version of events, though they were still hesitant about the details. Zey had given the grand jury a different account the day before so it's not really clear if her changing her story this time around really helped the prosecution.

The grand jury's decision came during the early morning hours of Wednesday. In the death of Virginia Rappe, Roscoe Arbuckle should be indicted for involuntary manslaughter – a killing committed without premeditation and with a maximum penalty of 10 years in prison.

But this wasn't enough for Brady. He still had Maude's first-degree murder complaint ready to proceed in police court and he was hopeful that the coroner's inquest would bolster it by recommending a murder trial.

LATER THAT MORNING, ROSCOE WAS GETTING DRESSED IN HIS cell when he heard the news from a guard that he had been indicted for manslaughter by the grand jury.

Roscoe merely looked at the guard. He said nothing but he did tell his cellmate, Martin, that he hadn't slept well. Moments later, the duo's breakfast was delivered, along with Roscoe's usual stack of letters and telegrams.

DISTRICT ATTORNEY MATTHEW BRADY WASN'T HAVING IT.

"I protest this in the name of the state against these girls being called," he said. "For them to testify will be detrimental to the case of the state."

D.A. Brady with Alice Blake

The girls he was referring to were Alice Blake and Zey Prevost, who were now household names, and Brady didn't want the defense to have a record of their inquest testimony, which could reveal possible discrepancies.

Brady spoke again, "I repeat that there are but two people who know exactly what took place in that hotel room. One of them is dead. The body of Virginia Rappe, lying in the morgue, cannot speak. The other one is Roscoe Arbuckle, and he is in this room. Call him if you want the facts."

Roscoe's attorney, Frank Dominguez, rose from his seat at the counsel's table to forcefully assert that Roscoe was within his rights not to testify.

Coroner Leland deliberated with the jury in his chamber and announced they did not need to hear from the two young women. Instead, Dr. Strange and Dr. Ophuls returned to the stand and testified again about their autopsies. Ophuls stated that only violence of "some force" could have caused Virginia's bladder rupture. When asked to elaborate on a violent cause, he replied, "Finger pressure."

The coroner's jury began deliberating at noon. As they filed out, Roscoe tried to light a cigarette, but his hands were shaking too badly. The jury returned three and a half hours later, and Roscoe leaned forward to listen to the verdict being read by the coroner. He trembled a little when his name was mentioned two times.

After briefly stating the particulars, the verdict read:

Said rupture was caused by the application of some force which, from the evidence submitted, we believe was applied by one Roscoe Arbuckle, and the undersigned jurors, therefore, charge the said Roscoe Arbuckle with the crime of manslaughter. We recommend that the District Attorney of the City and County of San Francisco, in conjunction with the Grand Jury, the Chief of Police, and Federal Prohibition officials, take steps to prevent a recurrence of affairs similar to the one in which this young woman lost her life, so that San

Francisco shall not be made the rendezvous of the debauchee and gangster.

That's the verdict that made it into the newspapers and was splashed across front pages all over the country, but it wasn't the only verdict that came out of the jury room that day.

There was another that went unreported at the time, a statement written by a dissenting juror named Ben Boas. He wrote the following:

I, the undersigned juror, find that the said Virginia Rappe came to her death from peritonitis caused by a ruptured bladder. Said rupture was caused by the application of some force, and from the evidence submitted I am unable to determine who was responsible for the application of said force.

But no one cared. This wasn't scandalous, salacious, or exciting. No – instead it was level-headed, honest, and followed the law. There was no solid evidence at this point that Roscoe Arbuckle had done anything other than make bad choices.

But that, of course, didn't sell newspapers.

FOLLOWING THE SHOCKING NEWS OF ROSCOE'S INDICTMENT, his legal team's priority became getting him out from behind bars on bail.

While Roscoe had been locked up in the city jail, his $34,000 customized Pierce-Arrow was parked in an alley behind the Hall of Justice. It was visited daily by scores of curiosity-seekers and became the city's newest tourist attraction. Prohibition agents had been threatening to seize it, if they could prove liquor had been transported in it, but so far, hadn't had any luck.

Something similar was happening in Los Angeles, as locals and tourists alike came to see Roscoe's West Adams mansion, loitering on the sidewalks and blocking the street.

Roscoe's net worth at the time was estimated at between $500,000 and $1 million. The press had trumpeted his extravagant free-spending habits, estimating that he'd spent at least $100,000 on cars and thousands more "just having a good time." The amount he could liquidate into cash was around $200,000.

After his arrest, a furniture company in L.A. filed a lien against him, claiming that Roscoe owed $6,500 for 25 pieces of furniture. Two days later, an interior decorator filed an attachment against all known Arbuckle property, claiming the actor owed $11,400 for decoration of his house and grounds.

Roscoe had made purchases on credit because retailers and contractors offered him deals to win his implied endorsement, but now that his name hurt their reputation more than it helped, they started calling in the debts. He had managed his money badly and the man with the "million-dollar contract" had less in the bank then he should have – and it didn't help that his outrageously expensive lawyers were gobbling up what was left.

But pricey or not, those lawyers were having a hard time getting their client out of jail. The grand jury's manslaughter indictment was presented on Thursday, bail was set at $5,000, and the legal team handed over a cashier's check in exchange for their client's freedom.

But Roscoe remained locked up. He spent another night in jail, waiting for the hearing on the murder charge in police court on Friday morning. It seemed a formality – surely it would be dismissed in favor of the manslaughter charge endorsed by both the grand jury and the coroner's inquest. The defense team was so confident of their client's release that they booked a car for him on the Saturday train to Los Angeles.

But they didn't know D.A. Matthew Brady – or about Henry Lehrman's need for revenge.

On Thursday, Brady held a long, private conference with Police Chief O'Brien and Captain of Detectives Matheson. He was being pressured by women's clubs in the city, and he'd received a telegram from Henry Lehrman, which was conveniently released to the public. It read:

For the sake of God and justice to men, don't let justice be cheated. It brought tears of rage to my eyes when I read your speech that influence, and wealth are brought into play to bar justice. I cried because you told the truth in spite of the pressure of gold to stifle it. You are convinced from the facts and I from knowledge that Arbuckle killed Virginia Rappe. Now, don't let them cheat justice, for God's sake, for he is guilty. I held court with the facts in my conscience and convicted him.

A massive crowd overwhelmed the Hall of Justice on Friday morning in hopes of getting a seat for Roscoe's arraignment. Thousands pushed their way toward the building's entrance from both sides of the street. A so-called "army of special police" was enlisted to help keep order inside and outside.

Thanks to an agreement that Brady made with the local women's clubs, the hearing was held in a women's court, which didn't allow male spectators so women could more openly testify in rape and other emotionally sensitive cases. The only men allowed inside were court personnel, attorneys, and reporters, which meant the 156 available seats in the courtroom were occupied by women dressed in black and fortified with sandwiches. They had been seated hours before the proceedings began,

With the trial being held in women's court, the spectators were overwhelmingly female

while the courtroom's doors were still locked against the crowds outside.

To the disappointment of those crowding the sidewalks outside and corridors inside, Roscoe was brought from his cells to Police Judge Sylvain Lazarus's chamber by way of an interior passageway. He remained there with his attorneys and Lou Anger while other cases were adjudicated.

Eventually, the clerk read, "The next case if number five on the continued list your honor – the state of California against Roscoe Arbuckle, murder."

As the courtroom fell into a hushed silence, the seated women craned their necks to see the accused walk into the room and stand in front of the judge. He shifted nervously, never looking back at the audience behind him.

Brady confidently announced, "The people are ready to proceed on murder charges." His words were followed by a few quiet gasps and murmurs from the spectators. Roscoe stared at the floor and bit his lip.

In a decision that – according to Brady – came just before Friday's arraignment, he ignored the grand jury's manslaughter complaint and the manslaughter recommendation from the coroner's inquest and instead proceeded on the original murder charge. Whether because of pressure from voters – especially women, who had earned the right to vote in 1920 – his desire to defend Virginia's honor, his own reckless pride, or a combination of all of them, Brady refused to budge. He told the judge that he was ready to begin the preliminary hearing without delay.

Roscoe was stunned and so were his attorneys. There was no evidence to uphold such a charge, but Brady was determined to prosecute Roscoe for murder. No one could change his mind.

Frank Dominguez immediately asked for a delay of 12 days. Brady countered with six. Judge Lazarus agreed with Brady and set a court date for the following Thursday, September 22, at 1:00 P.M.

After getting his way, Brady smugly remarked, "We want to be courteous to everyone, even if they come from Los Angeles." The barb was met with applause from the women in the courtroom.

When the hearing was over, Brady issued a written statement:

The District Attorney's office, from the time that the facts became known, has always been firmly of the opinion that the correct charge involved in the Arbuckle case was murder. It is the sole province of the trial jury to determine, after the evidence has been taken, in the event it should find the defendant guilty, whether the verdict should be one of murder, manslaughter, or any other crime comprehended in the charge, and also to fix the degree thereof.

And so, Roscoe remained a resident at the San Francisco City Jail. Feeling defeated, he was led away from the photographers and the glaring women in black and back into the judge's chambers.

He nervously smoked a cigarette and spoke with his attorneys before guards ushered him back to his cell, which would remain his home for an indefinite amount of time.

WHILE ROSCOE ARBUCKLE WAS BEING CHARGED WITH HER murder, Virginia Rappe was lying in repose in a parlor at the Halsted & Company funeral home in San Francisco.

Thousands of mourners – almost all of whom only knew her through recent newspaper accounts – shuffled past her. She was dressed in "slumbering robes" of silver cloth and draped with cream-colored silks that made "veils that a bride could wear." A newspaper account described her: "On the beautiful face there is a peaceful expression, and the lips are smiling with unearthly knowledge."

The room was infused with the smell of roses, chrysanthemums, and funeral wreathes – some compliments of Virginia's old friends Sidi Spreckels, most from strangers, many with cards identifying the sender as a "sympathetic mother."

Maude Delmont attended and, predictably, collapsed in dramatic anguish.

The most impressive floral display of 1,000 pink lilies was from Henry Lehrman. There was a ribbon attached with gold letters that read "To My Brave Sweetheart, From Henry." He paid all the funeral bills and, via telegram, instructed the undertaker to whisper "Henry loves you" in Virginia's ear before he closed the casket lid.

Virginia was lying in repose in a San Francisco funeral parlor in while Roscoe was in court being charged with her murder

Late that night, while Roscoe was trying to sleep in his jail cell, Virginia's body, encased in a metal casket, was loaded onto a Southern Pacific train bound for Los Angeles from San Francisco.

It was the same trip, on the same train, that she'd made five years earlier when she was first seeking her fame and fortune in Hollywood.

TWELVE

HERE IT WAS – PROOF THAT AMERICA HAD TURNED ITS BACK ON Fatty Arbuckle. It was right there in black in white, painted on the front pages of newspapers across the country on September 18, 1921.

An angry mob of more than 150 men had mobbed a movie theater in a small Wyoming town, firing guns at the screen, which was filled with the smiling face of Roscoe Arbuckle. They stormed into the projection room, ripped the reels from the machine, carried the film out into the street, and set the nitrate ribbons on fire.

The next day, a headline that proclaimed WYOMING MOB SHOOTS UP FATTY showed up in papers from one side of the country to the other. Editors couldn't resist a story of good guys with guns blazing saving society from America's greatest villain.

There was one small problem, though – it was a lie.

The story had been concocted by the theater's manager to drum up publicity. A small retraction was printed four days later, buried in back pages, if papers bothered to run it at all.

Adolph Zukor wrote to William Randolph Hearst, who was not just a newspaper tycoon but also the owner of a movie production company, asking him to tone down his paper's coverage of the Arbuckle case. Hearst gave him a curt reply: "Will do the best I can but it is difficult to keep news out of the newspaper. I agree that certain kinds of publicity are detrimental to moving pictures but the people who get into the courts and coroners are responsible. The newspapers are no more responsible than the courts."

Needless to say, the coverage wasn't toned down.

ROSCOE'S SECOND WEEK OF CAPTIVITY AT THE JAIL WAS MUCH the same as his first – he sat behind bars on a wooden bench, slept on a wooden bunk, chatted with his cellmate, Fred Martin, and others on the block. He smoked, he worried, and he read his endless stack of letters and telegrams.

The majority of the mail was supportive, but some letters were downright unnerving. His wife, Minta, later wrote, "Some of the mail that came to us was unbelievable. There were threats against Roscoe's life and against mine. Some wrote and said that Roscoe had torn down the moral fiber of the country, that he was a monster, that he deserved to hang."

He was visited by his brothers, Arthur, who lived in San Francisco, and Harry, who lived in Fresno. They huddled together for 20 minutes and while no one overheard the conversation, Roscoe was seen smiling broadly.

It was the first time Fred Martin had seen his cellmate smile since Roscoe had been indicted.

WHILE ROSCOE WAS WAITING IN HIS JAIL CELL, DISTRICT Attorney Brady and Assistant D.A.'s U'Ren and Golden were visiting the twelfth-floor suite at the Hotel St. Francis where the Labor Day party had been held. They were accompanied by their three main witnesses – Maude Delmont, Alice Blake, and Zey Prevost.

The women were instructed to arrange the furniture in 1219, 1220, and 1221 as it had been on Labor Day. The rooms had been cleaned by a maid and then, just two days prior, checked for fingerprints, which seemed pointless after nearly three weeks.

But Brady had insisted. He also examined marks on the wall and on the small table between the two beds in 1219. He listened, from 1220, to the volume of voices in 1219 with the door closed.

He said he was there just to "get the lay of the land."

ON THE SUNDAY MORNING AFTER ROSCOE'S INDICTMENT, church ministers across the nation again railed against the funny fat man and his sinful ways. There was no presumption of innocence for the Hollywood star, whose occupation alone was enough to imply that he was guilty of murder. Even if he wasn't, they said, he was a married man in a hotel room cavorting with showgirls, consuming the devil's liquor, and pursuing extramarital sex.

There was one notable exception to the religious assaults, and it was delivered by America's most famous evangelist, Billy Sunday, whose daughter-in-law, Mae Taube, had been at the Labor Day party. As Sunday told his audience, "I feel sorry for Fatty Arbuckle and do not see how any court in the land could convict the fallen idol for murder or manslaughter."

He blamed liquor for Virginia's death and called for greater funding for Prohibition enforcement. "The girl died," he admitted, "but I believe her death was caused by an accident and not by Roscoe Arbuckle."

He finished on a cautionary note, invoking an image of Babylon that would later become widely shared. In so doing, he previewed what would eventually be a key strategy for the defense – tarnishing the victim. Billy Sunday announced, "The party of Arbuckle's was just a case of a modern Belshazzar entertaining. Fatty fell for whiskey and wild women."

Billy Sunday

ON THE SAME DAY AS BILLY SUNDAY'S SERMON, VIRGINIA'S BODY was placed on display again, this time at the Strother and Dayton funeral parlor on Hollywood Boulevard. Thousands of people milled past her silver casket, looking down at her "angelic face." She was shrouded in white silk and her casket was filled with white roses.

Among the assortment of flowers that surrounded the casket was a bouquet of roses from Maude Delmont with a note that read: "To Virginia" You know I love you as though you were my sister." Keep in mind, that she knew Virginia for only a few days and most of that time, the dead woman had been delirious from pain and in and out of consciousness.

And just like at the San Francisco visitation a few days earlier, there was an overwhelming display of lilies from Henry Lehrman to his "brave sweetheart." In this era before commercial airline travel, though, Henry stayed in New York City.

On Monday morning, Virginia's funeral was held at Strother and Dayton's and for the first two hours, the chapel was filled with mostly female curiosity-seekers. The police were then enlisted to clear the pews and lock the doors, only allowing intimate friends inside. The police held off the growing crowd on the street outside.

Among those admitted were actress Mildred Harris – the teenage ex-wife of Charlie Chaplin – Al Semnacher, and Virginia's adopted "aunt and uncle," Kate and Joseph Hardebeck. The six pallbearers

Virginia's casket being removed from the hearse at her funeral in Los Angeles. She was buried at Hollywood Memorial Park – but she'd never rest there in peace

were made up of directors Al Herman, David Kirkland, and Normal Taurog, who was a friend of Henry Lehrman and oversaw Lehrman's requests for the burial and funeral. There as also actor Frank Coleman, who appeared in three movies with Virginia; actor, writer, and director Larry Semon; and little-known actor Oliver Hardy, who went on to form one of cinema's most beloved comedy duos with Stan Laurel.

They carried Virginia in her flower-covered coffin through the parted crowd to a white hearse that was parked on Hollywood Boulevard. Followed by a procession of automobiles, the hearse traveled only a mile to Hollywood Memorial Park – now Hollywood Forever Cemetery.

They passed dozens of automobiles that were clogging the entrance of the cemetery and were parked on the sides of the roads in the cemetery itself. The mob that walked over graves and clustered around the burial site was estimated to be at least 1,500 people.

The plot where Virginia was buried belonged to Henry Lehrman. His secretary had been buried there two years earlier. It was only four blocks from the home that Virginia had shared with the Hardebecks when she came to Hollywood five years earlier.

A hush fell over the crowd as the words of a brief ceremony were spoken. And then, in the quiet that followed, Virginia Rappe was buried on a gentle slope beside a lily pond.

There, she would rest for all time – but she wouldn't do so in peace.

WHILE A GRAVE WAS BEING DUG FOR VIRGINIA AT HOLLYWOOD Memorial Park, Frank Dominguez was in Los Angeles doing some digging of his own. However, the dirt that he was uncovering was on the prosecution's star witness, Maude Delmont.

Maude herself remained in San Francisco, claiming to have been mentally and physically overwhelmed by her role in the affair. From her bed at the Plaza Hotel – where she was being cared for by a nurse and guarded by a police officer – she told the press, "I'm ready for the defense anytime. All I have to do at the trial is to tell the truth. And all the Fatty Arbuckles and Frank Dominguezes in the world won't be able to shake me. Virginia Rappe was a good girl. Any suggestion to the contrary is a lie and a defamation."

In an earlier interview, she'd admitted her testimony at the coroner's inquest was "somewhat inaccurate," blaming that on illness and medication, which was presumably the self-administered "hypodermic" she mentioned at the time. She said that she planned to "alter" her testimony at the manslaughter trial and shore up her story to "greatly benefit the prosecution's case."

What? That's not how testimony is supposed to work – not if it's the truth anyway.

On the Monday of Virginia's funeral, Minta Durfee and her mother, Flora, arrived at the Hall of Justice in San Francisco. So that Roscoe's defense team could coach them not to speak to the press, Milton Cohen and Charles Brennan met their train in Sacramento, after which a press release from Minta about her husband's innocence was given to reporters.

When the two women reached the jail, along with Roscoe's brother, Arthur, they were allowed to meet with Roscoe in the visitor's area. He embraced his wife and then the four of them spent the next 30 minutes together.

Minta traveled to San Francisco with her mother, Flora, so both women could show support for Roscoe

ON TUESDAY, THE GRAND JURY RECONVENED TO DEAL WITH TWO questions that had been raised – was the initial autopsy of Virginia legal? And did the defense tamper with a prosecution witness?

The first question required testimony from Dr. Melville Rumwell and the second forced them to delve into the allegation that party guest Joyce "Dollie" Clark has said, "There is money in the Arbuckle case and I'm going to get some of it." She and two men had allegedly plotted to collect money from the defense by suggesting that Dollie could impeach the testimony of her friend, Zey Prevost. The two men had visited Milton Cohen and asked what Dollie should say under oath.

Cohen's reply: "Tell the truth."

The grand jury took no action on either question.

The following day, at the request of San Francisco D.A. Brady, a Los Angeles grand jury questioned Al Semnacher about something he hadn't previously shared. Al said that on the morning after the Labor Day party, Roscoe claimed he had "forcibly applied a piece of ice to Miss Rappe's body."

Newspaper coverage of this claim varied wildly. On the hysterical side was this glaring headline: DECLARES ARBUCKLE TOLD OF USING FOREIGN SUBSTANCE IN ATTACK ON MISS RAPPE. That one would lead to a dozen or so false claims over the years, naming that "foreign substance" as everything from ice to Coca-Cola and champagne bottles.

Brady investigated this alleged statement by Al Semnacher further by questioning Fred Fishback and Ira Fortlouis. Lowell Sherman was subpoenaed while on a train headed for New York City. A process server – and a knot of eager reporters – were waiting for him when he stepped off the train at Grand Central Station, only to learn that he'd given them the slip by getting off the train at an earlier stop.

After he was located the next day in his Manhattan apartment, he gave a statement to the New York D.A. that supported the defense, and he agreed to return to San Francisco for the preliminary hearing on Roscoe's murder charge. But he never did. He later gave a deposition swearing that Roscoe was never alone in a room with Virginia – a definitive and false statement that ultimately clashed with the strategies of both the defense and the prosecution.

He was trying to minimize his connection to the scandal, and it worked. His movie career thrived, but only until 1934, when he died from pneumonia at only 46.

ON WEDNESDAY, 11 DAYS AFTER ROSCOE'S ARREST, PARAMOUNT Studios invoked a non-performance clause in his contract to stop all payments to Roscoe Arbuckle.

The next day, Universal became the first studio to add a morality clause into their contracts, permitting them to stop paying the salaries of "actors or actresses who forfeit the respect of the public."

Universal's attorneys stated that although the studio had no relationship with the accused murderer, the clause was a "direct result of the Arbuckle case in San Francisco."

THE PRELIMINARY HEARING TO DETERMINE IF THE STATE HAD sufficient evidence to bring Roscoe to trial for murder began on Thursday, September 22.

That day, an editorial published in the San *Francisco Bulletin* was syndicated across the country. Skewed predictably against Roscoe, it called him "a fiendish monster" who "perpetrated a foul crime in the St. Francis Hotel" during a "drunken orgy." It went on to say:

From the details at hand, the attack appears to have been savage without qualification. The veritable giant, one that has been described as a mountain of lecherous flesh, hurled himself upon a frail woman and fought with her after the manner of a mad elephant. But for that final avalanche of lard, the woman named have saved at least her life, for she seems to have struggled until the last vestige of her clothing had been torn to tatters...

We know that a fiendish crime has been committed and that one of the principals in that crime is a man suddenly raised from obscurity and a difficulty in earning his living into the spotlight of the world and an affluence greater than many kings. Petted by the public and showered with riches, he lost all sense of decency and came to the belief that he was above the moral code and could write whatever code he chose. He lived a law unto himself, flaunting his newfound wealth and spending it all with recklessness of immoral and bestial ignorance. Like the most brutal of the feudal barons, he believed that he could command whatever was necessary to satisfy his savage passions.

Not surprisingly, with such allegations making the rounds in the newspapers, it looked as though it would be difficult to find an impartial jury anywhere in the region.

But for now, it was only a preliminary hearing that was taking place and crowds of women began showing up at the Hall of Justice at 8:00 A.M., even though the hearing wouldn't start for another five hours. The *Los Angeles Times* described the scene: "Men are being excluded everywhere, shoved forcibly out through thick ranks of women, laughed at, snickered at, jeered at. It is a no man's land."

Hundreds of women, most dressed in their Sunday best and fortified with box lunches, crowded into the hallways and stairways outside the women's court of Judge Sylvain Lazarus – the same room and judge as at the arraignment one week earlier.

Judge Sylvain Lazarus

Police officers cleared the courtroom at noon, much to the irritation of those who already managed to get seated. The doors were reopened a short time later and hordes of women streamed inside and crowded into the available seats. After all of them were filled, another 500 women remained in the hall. Officers parted the sea of women with great difficulty so that Roscoe, his wife, mother-in-law, and defense team could pass through.

Judge Lazarus would decide whether the murder charge would proceed, but before he ruled, both the prosecution and defense would call witnesses, cross-examine them, and introduce evidence.

With Assistant D.A. U'Ren asking the questions, the prosecution called three witnesses the first day – Dr. Shelby Strange, Dr. William Ophuls, and nurse Grace Halston. They testified to the ruptured bladder, the newness of the injury, and the injury's probably cause, which Ophuls stated was "some force from outside." Photographs of the bruises on Virginia's arms were placed into evidence. Frank Dominguez decided against cross-examining any of them.

Al Semnacher was the only witness the following day. The prosecutors gave him the task of telling the story of the Labor Day party, but he gave up details of drinking and dancing with such reluctance that the D.A. declared him a hostile witness.

The session finished after three contentious hours, with Al still on the stand and yet to deliver his bombshell. That went off the following day, when the crowded courtroom of mostly concerned mothers heard a lot more than they'd bargained for when they pushed and shoved their way into their courtroom seats. To their shock, all the vague stories about a "foreign substance" suddenly became clear.

Assistant D.A. Golden asked Al Semnacher about what he'd heard on the morning after the party. "Did Arbuckle say anything at that time about a piece of ice?" he asked.

"He did," Al replied.

"What did he say?"

"He told us that he had placed a piece of ice on Miss Rappe."

"On?" Golden asked him.

"No," Al answered.

"Well?"

Al's response was not printed in the newspapers, but he said that Roscoe claimed to have placed the ice *inside* Virginia. A collective gasp was heard in the courtroom as the women realized what he meant. Roscoe, his face red, stared at his fidgeting fingers. Behind him, Minta also looked down, fussing with a long string of amber beads that she wore around her neck. She then reached up and patted her husband on the shoulder.

Golden pressed his witness. "Exactly what did Arbuckle say?"

Al glanced up at the room of mostly women who were staring at him. "I don't want to say his words."

Golden insisted, "They are important."

When Al hesitated again, Golden told him to whisper it to the court reporter. He did so and then the words were written on a note, which was passed to the prosecution and the defense.

Roscoe allegedly said he had placed the ice in Virginia's "snatch" – her vagina.

Al Semnacher never uttered the word in court, but Golden had no qualms about saying "snatch," and he did so again and again, using it like a weapon that he could strike his hostile witness with. He also used it to destroy Roscoe's reputation, as if to say that any man who could use such a crude profanity about a woman as she lay during in a nearby hotel room was capable of anything – including rape and murder.

A correspondent for the syndicated United Press described the testimony: "Arbuckle's time in court today was only ninety minutes, but he heard Al Semnacher, his friend, and Miss Rappe's former manager, charge that when Virginia was lying nude on one of Arbuckle's twin beds, the big baby-faced comedian had tortured her indescribably."

Of course, Semnacher was not Roscoe's friend and wasn't Virginia's manager and, more importantly, the ice incident wasn't presented in court as "torture," but as a bad joke by a heartless celebrity. Under questioning from Golden, Semnacher said that Roscoe made no explanation for inserting ice into her vagina and stated that when he said it, the listeners laughed. He wouldn't name those who laughed, which likely means he was one of them.

Regardless, the United Press account of his testimony gave birth to headlines like WITNESS TESTFIES ARBUCKLE CONFESSED HE TORTURED ACTRESS.

When Golden was finished with his questions, Frank Dominguez got Al to admit that he had never witnessed any improper conduct by Roscoe toward any of the women at the party. He agreed that Roscoe had behaved like a gentleman that day, which prompted an objection by Golden, who questioned whether the "snatch" remark was gentlemanly. Dominguez objected to the comment and while it was sustained, the damage was done. Calling the defendant a "gentleman" wasn't going to make anyone forget about the obscene comment.

Dominguez went on the attack in the next court session. First, he livened up what should have been the mundane questioning of hotel doctor Arthur Beardslee by asking him if his visits to room 1227 – where Virgina lay ill with Maude Delmont watching over her – if Maude was "under the influence of alcohol or morphine" or if he ever saw her "taking a white powder." The prosecution objected loudly, but to no avail.

This turned out to be a warm-up for the frontal assault that Dominguez launched on Al Semnacher when he was called back to the stand that afternoon. The attorney first established that Al was not Virginia's manager, despite him being called that in the press. Semnacher said he'd been misquoted and confessed that he'd only known her well for about six weeks. Dominguez also got him to admit that Roscoe may have said he placed the ice on Virginia's "snatch," not in it. Dominguez was less successful implying there was something questionable about Semnacher occupying a room at the Palace Hotel that connected with the room of Virginia and Maude.

After that, the defense attorney really got down to business, first with some minor shots at Maude's character, then with the introduction of a new character – Early Lynn, a minor movie actor. Maude had supposedly tried to extort money from Lynn's father in exchange for her keeping silent about having sex with Lynn and a resulting pregnancy. Golden objected and Judge Lazarus ruled that the defense was not allowed to go beyond the murder case at hand.

But Dominguez explained the relevance of this new information. He told the judge, "If we can, we will show that Semnacher, in conversation with Mrs. Delmont and someone else, plotted that

Virginia Rappe's torn clothing should be taken to Los Angeles, there to extort blackmail from Arbuckle. If we can show that Semnacher was aware of the circumstance that we expect to show connecting Mrs. Delmont and Earl Lynn, of Los Angeles, we will then establish the intimate relations existing between Semnacher and Mrs. Delmont. We will show, moreover, that Earl Lynn is not the only individual to be mentioned in this connection."

Judge Lazarus wasn't convinced. "I am not going to try the character of every witness appearing here."

But it was too late for Al Semnacher. At his own request, the question of him conspiring to blackmail Roscoe was promptly brought before the grand jury. He testified as the only witness. The grand jury took no action and when it was over, Semnacher told reporters he was going to bring a civil suit against Dominguez for defamation of character.

He never did – and likely for very good reason.

The question of why Virginia's torn shirt and undergarments were found in Al's possession has never been satisfactorily answered. At the preliminary hearing, he said he was only joking about using the underwear to dust his car but never explained why he'd kept them. It's very possible that Al and Maude – who kept Virginia's other clothing – saw the possibility in enlisting Virginia in a conspiracy to blackmail Roscoe with the promise they'd keep events out of the press and not report them to the police. The clothing could have been used as possible evidence of an assault. When Virginia died and the authorities became involved, the blackmail scheme collapsed.

But that didn't mean there wasn't another scheme that was still in the works – or at least someone who was desperately trying to clean up the mess left behind from one.

The preliminary hearing was beginning to reveal just how deeply Maude Delmont was involved in the criminal case. To those who believed that Roscoe was guilty, she was an avenging angel and to those who believed him wrongly accused, she was a conspiring con artist.

What was known about her life before September 1921 was that she had been born in New Mexico in 1882. Her parents, Mr. and Mrs. Winfield Scott, were both from Indiana. She had a younger sister. At some point before 1910, she married a man named Delmont but by the time of the 1910 census, she was divorced and lived in a New York hotel. No occupation was listed.

On November 27, 1912, she remarried in Los Angeles to John C. Hopper, a Canadian farmer and military veteran. They separated on

March 1, 1914, and Maude was granted a divorce on grounds of nonsupport.

Like Frank Dominguez, reporters in 1921 dug for dirt about her past, but didn't find much. A wire story reported that she had lived in Wichita, Kansas, for a while under an assumed name. The *Los Angeles Times* reported that she had been ordered by authorities to leave Catalina Island in 1919: "She conducted a beauty parlor in the dance pavilion. She left without contesting the official warning. Her baggage was held some time on the island until certain debts were paid, island officials say."

According to the 1920 census, she rented a home in Los Angeles with her sister, a nurse. She reported her occupation as a corset saleswoman. It's likely she owned a small corset business with her next-door neighbor, a divorced 41-year-old mother who listed the same occupation on the census form.

Maude married again on February 26, 1921. Her new husband, Cassius Clay Woods, was a publicist. Both were divorced, lived in Los Angeles, and were 38 years old.

But there was much about Maude that remained a mystery. Why did she take the trip to San Francisco with Semnacher when she'd only been married six months? What did she think they'd been doing during the trip? And why did she claim to be the close friend of a woman she'd only known for a few days?

Maude Delmont was an enigma.

THE FIFTH AND FINAL DAY OF THE PRELIMINARY HEARING WAS September 27. Alice Blake and Zey Prevost testified, both recalling, with minor variations, that after Virginia moaned, "I'm dying," Roscoe told her to be quiet or "I'll throw you out the window."

Zey confirmed parts of the ice story. According to her, Roscoe said to Virginia about the application of ice, "That'll bring you to" – which might indicate that he intended it as a remedy for her pain and semi-conscious state. It could also be interpreted as a crude joke, but that seems less likely considering Virginia's behavior at the time.

The prosecution then brought in a surprise witness, a nervous and stout woman in a blue dress named Josephine Keza. She

Josephine Keza

was a maid at the Hotel St. Francis. She explained in heavily accented English that on Labor Day she had been in the twelfth-floor hallway when she heard a woman scream behind the door of room 1219 and then say, "No! No! Oh my god!" A man's voice followed saying, "Shut up!" Dominguez probed her story and tried to trip her up on cross-examination but didn't get very far.

After that, the prosecution rested.

The defense team was shocked. Dominguez leapt to his feet. "Do you mean to say that the prosecution in this case is not going to call Mrs. Maude Delmont to the stand? She is the principal witness. She swore to the complaint. In the interest of truth and justice, I appeal to you, Mr. District Attorney, not to deny this defense the right to cross-examining this witness."

Brady merely sneered at him. "Put her on the stand yourself."

"She is your witness," Dominguez insisted. "I have no desire to be responsible for her testimony. I appeal to you in the interest of fair play and justice to put her on the stand. I never knew of a case in the jurisprudence of California where a complaining witness has not been placed on the stand. I know you do not want to put her on the stand. And I'll tell you, the only reason you will not call her is because you know that the moment you give me the opportunity to cross-examine her, I'll impeach every word of her testimony."

Judge Lazarus was also surprised at the failure to bring Maude before the court. He warned Brady, "You are traveling very close to a line which might necessitate me dismissing these proceedings."

But Brady refused to call her, which led to the defense resting without calling a single witness. Court was adjourned for the day and the participants and spectators filed out in silence, as though stunned by the final minutes of the day.

The following afternoon, September 28, Judge Lazarus announced he would deliver his decision. But first, he said, "the court will indulge in a little discussion." He blamed the Hotel St. Francis and all of society for allowing "this orgy" to take place. He said, "It is of such common occurrence that it was given no attention until something happened, until the climax made it notorious."

As for the prosecution's case, he said Arbuckle's action with the ice was regrettable – if true – but had no connection to murder. He added, "Some of the witnesses were absolutely worthless, especially Semnacher, who occupied two days' time. The only witness in the entire case who gave any direct testimony bearing on the guilt or innocence of Arbuckle was the nervous chambermaid, Josphine Keza." And yet the judge also dismissed the voices the maid overheard as perhaps something that could also have been said within the bounds of consensual sex.

Finally, he concluded, "The question for me to decide from the merest outline of evidence, this skeletonized description of what occurred in those apartments on Labor Day, is whether I am justified in holding the defendant for murder. And I don't think I am justified in sending him to trial on this grievous charge under the circumstances. Therefore, I hold him for trial on the charge of manslaughter."

These words were greeted with applause from the mostly female audience while Roscoe embraced his wife and hugged and kissed his mother-in-law. When court was adjourned, a dozen women – who'd previously assumed Roscoe was a brutal killer – came forward to shake his hand and to congratulate him. He accepted their well wishes with watery eyes. As he, Minta, and Flora were ushered into the judge's chambers, Minta started to collapse, and Roscoe held her up, quieting her and wiping away her tears with great affection. His mother-in-law smoothed back Roscoe's hair and the women in the courtroom who witnessed the incident responded with tears of their own.

The $5,000 cashier's check that had been submitted nearly two weeks earlier for Roscoe's bail was finally accepted. Roscoe was finally a free man, even if it was only temporary. He returned to his cell and said goodbye to Fred Martin and others as he stuffed his clothing into a suitcase.

Newsmen crowded the cell, snapping photographs with bright flashes of brilliant light. One of them called out, "Roll a cigarette with one hand while we take the next snap!"

Roscoe just shook his head. "I can't. It's the other Arbuckle that does that."

When he left the Hall of Justice with his family and his lawyers, women on both sides of the street cheered for him. An accusation of murder that had transformed into manslaughter had apparently caused the feelings of the women of San Francisco to change toward Fatty Arbuckle.

But was that all there was to it? Probably not. Just as Roscoe's celebrity created a wave of negative press, it helped him, too. Some fans could never shake the image of him they'd seen onscreen. They felt like they knew Fatty – sure, he was silly, crude, and even committed crimes in his films, but no one stayed hurt for long. He certainly wasn't a rapist or a killer.

One crying woman who waited in the hall outside the courtroom to see him as he passed by said, "I've only seen him on the screen, and

Minta, Roscoe, and Flora Durfee

I wanted to see him in real life." Based on the reaction of the women in the courtroom after the judge tossed out the murder charge, there was obviously more ladies like her in the courtroom than it initially seemed.

As for the mothers who came to see justice done for Virginia, there is no tally of how many of them, if any, who cheered or otherwise approved of the judge's decision. However, most of them had come to the courthouse to make certain that justice was served, so perhaps those who witnessed the hearing agreed with Judge Lazarus that the case for trying Roscoe for murder had not been made.

Another factor in the softening of feelings toward Roscoe was the daily presence of Minta and her mother. The wife, who was also a celebrity, had traveled across the country to stand by her man, even though they lived separately. And Flora – a mother just like so many of the women in the courtroom – was standing by him, too. In a women's court where all the lawyers were men, where the judge was a man, the reporters were men, and all the spectators were women, the presence of two other women visibly supporting Roscoe and proclaiming his innocence spoke volumes.

The newspapers reported Minta's reactions as closely as they reported what Roscoe said and did. Her photos ran regularly during the hearing, highlighting her choice of dress, necklace, and hat, crowding out the photos of another fashionable woman – Virginia Rappe.

But while the feelings of many of the women following the case had changed about Roscoe, the feelings of D.A. Brady had not. That evening, he issued a statement that declared that if Roscoe "were unknown and unimportant, he would have been held for murder."

In reality, though, it was much more likely that an unknown man would never have been charged with murder at all. Not only had the grand jury and the coroner's inquest already favored a manslaughter charge, but there was barely any evidence for manslaughter, let alone murder. The witnesses were sketchy, there was no physical evidence against Roscoe, and no one could agree for sure on what killed Virginia.

The only reason the case hadn't already been dismissed was because of Roscoe's celebrity – and because Virginia's death happened within the jurisdiction of a district attorney who had a desperate need for fame, notoriety, and higher office.

ON FRIDAY NIGHT, ROSCOE RETURNED TO HIS WEST ADAMS mansion for the first time in three weeks and found himself the guest of honor at a homecoming party thrown in his honor.

Limousines pulled up outside, delivering friends in the movie business. Behind closed doors, Roscoe was finally able to smile. As Minta later wrote, "He has seen his fair-weather friends fall away from him, and he has learned the value of his true friends."

It was the last day of September and his first party since the ill-fated bash on Labor Day. No liquor was served this time.

"Half the people there whispered and tiptoed around, and the others laughed too loud," Buster Keaton would remember. "What could you say to the poor bastard?"

As Roscoe shook hands, accepted hugs and kisses on the cheek along with the congratulations, he kept a smile on his face. Inside, though, small whispers reminded him that the trial was still ahead of him, and his days of freedom and happiness might be numbered.

THIRTEEN

JUST OVER THREE WEEKS AFTER THE DEATH OF VIRGINIA RAPPE, the *Los Angeles Times* published a letter that was written on October 3, 1921. The letter read:

Now that the wave of insanity, for it was nothing less (nor more) in regard to the Arbuckle case has passed over, it would seem that disappointment is to be the daily portion of those who, blind to the fact that no evidence is forthcoming, merely hoped for the downfall of Roscoe Arbuckle for no reason but that he was a successful screen star.

I couldn't have put it better myself, but this was, in 1921, still the sentiment of the minority. It was growing, though, especially in Los Angeles, which depended on people like Roscoe for its image and for the success of the biggest industry in town. That's best illustrated in an editorial that appeared in *Moving Picture World* on October 1. It read: "Enclosed in the following space is our idea what should be said by everybody in the motion picture business about the Arbuckle Case from now forth until the entire matter is settled."

The rest of the page was blank.

But Roscoe wasn't generating work for anyone now – including himself. His banishment from the movies was so complete that one of his films had been pulled from a screening at Sing Sing prison and all future Fatty films were banned from being shown there.

I'm not sure it gets much worse than that.

Roscoe probably felt the same. On October 1, 1921, he wrote a letter to Joseph Schenck, asking Schenck and Zukor to have faith and confidence in him. He wrote to him:

I have done no wrong, my heart is clean, and my conscience is clear and when it is over I have the guts to come back and make good. I know they have tied up in me at present and irrespective of whether we ever do business together again, I will come out of this affair clean and vindicated so that they can realize on their tremendous investment.

I am not asking for sympathy or forgiveness. I have done no wrong, but I do want you and the ones financially as well as personally interested to know that I am innocent, a victim of circumstance, the only one of prominence in the party and therefore I had to be the goat.

What – if anything – Schneck wrote as a reply to the man who'd helped make him rich is unknown.

WHILE IN LOS ANGELES, ROSCOE WAS FOLLOWED EVERYWHERE by San Francisco detectives, but he made their job very easy because the man who once rarely spent an evening at home now rarely left it.

Patrolled by a newly hired security company, the West Adams mansion had been transformed into a bunker, fortified against a world that had largely turned against him. At all hours of the night and day, people slowed down in front to honk and cheer for Fatty – or to hurl insults or an occasional rock.

The only bright spot was that Minta, for the first time, was living there with him. They slept in separate bedrooms but only, Minta said, because she believed Roscoe was self-conscious. She remembered, "Neither of us wanted to speak about what happened in that suite at the St. Francis. And yet we both knew we couldn't avoid the issue. It was what had brought us both together and allowed me to come home with him. We had to live together for the sake of the public. We had to show everyone that we were a loving man and wife, even though there was that long separation."

ON OCTOBER 7, ROSCOE WAS FORMERLY ARRAIGNED FOR manslaughter. Frank Dominguez wasn't present for the proceedings. The official store was that he's quit as chief counsel because the trial was going to take up too much of his time and because Roscoe would be better served by a San Francisco attorney.

However, the decision was likely made by Schenck and Zukor, who were unhappy with Dominguez's strategy at the preliminary hearing, especially his failure to call Roscoe and Maude Delmont to the stand. They felt their star should have been cleared and his movies

Gavin McNab making a point at the defense counsel table to Milton Cohen, Roscoe Arbuckle, Charles Brennan, and Joseph McInerney

returned to the screen, so Dominguez was out, and Gavin McNab was in.

McNab was not only a San Francisco native and moved in the city's highest political circles, but he also had experience with celebrities after representing Mary Pickford in her divorce and boxer Jack Dempsey for draft evasion the year before. McNab brought the case to one of his law partners, Nat Schmulowitz, and another local lawyer, Joseph McInerney, was also brought on board. The defense team also included Roscoe's regular attorney, Milt Cohen, and his original San Francisco lawyer, Charles Brennan.

Assistant D.A. U'Ren referred to them as "a million-dollar array of counsel – a description that fit.

ON THE SAME DAY THAT MCNAB TOOK OVER THE CASE, A STORY appeared in Chicago that claimed Virginia Rappe had a daughter there. Supposedly, the father vanished before the girl was born and Virginia had moved away soon after the birth, leaving her daughter – and a fistful of cash -- with foster parents.

The story had only one source -- which should have raised alarms – a Chicago-based traveling salesman named John Bates, who had written to officials in Los Angeles and San Francisco, trying to learn the value of Virginia's estate. It was, by the way, about $800 in cash and some stocks and bonds.

Bates estimated that the daughter was now eight or nine years old and while he claimed not to know her whereabouts, he was confident he could find her. He said that if Virginia's estate was of any value, he intended to "see that her daughter receives the benefit of it."

No such daughter was ever located but it opened a can of worms with others in Chicago claiming to have more sensational stories about Virginia's teen years and young adulthood. Eager to hear them, attorney Charles Brennan soon boarded a train going east.

Meanwhile, the prosecution was following leads of its own. Matthew Brady went to Los Angeles twice in October on fact-finding tours of the seamier side of Hollywood. When the second trip ended, the *Los Angeles Times* lambasted the San Francisco prosecutor with an article entitled "Ho, Hum, Wild Parties Tame," which laughed about how the parties he'd been looking for, "where hypodermic needles were passed around by pasty-faced party guests on a tray" were just knitting bees. The editor wrote: "Where, of where (in a loud despairing wail) is the reputed wickedness of Los Angeles?"

Then, on October 11, Roscoe was back in the news – sort of. The headline read DEAD MOVIE MAN IN ARBUCKLE CASE. Al Stein, an assistant director who worked with Fred Fishback, died at 26 after a night of drinking. Newspapers played up notes found in Stein's L.A. apartment that were made by Fred and allegedly had something to do with the Arbuckle case. In death, Stein was a potential witness and possible murder victim but in reality, he was neither of those things. He'd died from alcohol poisoning, a common occurrence with all the bad booze going around during Prohibition and he'd known nothing about the case.

But why let the truth get in the way of a good story?

Leaving out Al Stein, though, liquor was part of the case against Roscoe. The Prohibition violations at the Labor Day party were being investigated along with the manslaughter charges. Roscoe was a high-profile lawbreaker, flaunting the liquor laws, and the feds were determined to punish him.

On September 30, Gobey's Grill, the restaurant that had provided alcohol for the party, was raided. The manager and three employees were arrested but the shelves where $40,000 in high-end booze was supposed to be sitting were empty. Gobey's had been tipped off, so the feds went after Jack Lawrence, the deliveryman who'd taken the liquor from the restaurant to the party. He'd skipped town when the restaurant was tipped off but was tracked down in Oregon and returned to San Francisco. He pleaded guilty and was fined $250.

After being arraigned for manslaughter, Roscoe was charged with violating the Volstead Act and posted a $500 bond. It seemed like a long way to go just to make an example of a celebrity who bought

Edward O. Heinrich, the man dubbed "America's Sherlock Holmes," who played an important – and controversial – role in Roscoe's trials

some bootleg liquor but, like D.A. Brady, the Prohibition agents in San Francisco were trying to make some headlines by going after an easy target.

MAKING A LOT OF EFFORT FOR VERY LITTLE RETURN SEEMED TO be a theme for San Francisco officials in the Arbuckle case. That seems clear when we look at the involvement of Edward O. Heinrich in the proceedings. He was the most respected scientist involved with forensic investigation in the early 1920s. Often called "America's Sherlock Holmes," he developed techniques for fingerprinting and the testing of hair and blood samples after obtaining a chemistry degree. He later consulted on numerous criminal investigations and was even appointed chief of police in Alameda, California.

In 1919, he accepted a post as criminal expert to the city of San Francisco, as well as a position as a chemistry professor at Berkeley. In his lab in Oakland, he studied and practiced, working to achieve expertise in all fields of criminal science. Just before the Arbuckle case, he investigated the August kidnapping and murder of a priest and helped to prove the guilt of the man who found the body by connecting him, via microscopic details, to beach sand and a tent cord on and near the corpse. It became a landmark forensics case.

Heinrich was determined to find forensic evidence in the Arbuckle case. Do you recall the earlier mention of the search for fingerprint evidence in room 1219 weeks after Virginia's death? That was Heinrich and he didn't enter the room until 11 days after the Labor Day party and after it had been cleaned.

Regardless, he visited the room three times and compared hairs that he found there with hair from Virginia's head. He also searched for fiber that matched her clothing and even had the doors to the room taken to his laboratory, searching for clues that were invisible to the naked eye.

But again, it was a tremendous amount of effort that would prove nothing in a court of law. Had Virginia been in the room? Yes, everyone admitted that. Finding her hair or particles of fabric that matched her clothing – if it could be done after nearly two weeks -- just proved something everyone already knew.

But it looked good in the newspapers that the prosecution had made the effort. It was pointless busy work, but it made a good story.

ON NOVEMBER 12, TWO DAYS BEFORE JURY SELECTION BEGAN, Roscoe moved into what would be his home for the duration of the trial – the Palace Hotel where Virginia Rappe had stayed over Labor Day weekend.

He spoke to reporters after checking in: "I'm certainly glad my trial starts Monday morning. You may think it's funny that I'm so eager to go before a judge and jury and take a chance of lounging in the penitentiary for ten years. But if you'd gone through what I have – the loss of friends, the shame, the stories, the rumors about me, the attitude of the American public, the sermons of ministers, to say nothing of the loss of money – you'd be glad to get it over with, too."

Although the Nineteenth Amendment, which guaranteed women's right to vote nationwide, was ratified in 1920, women had served on juries in California since 1911. It was repeatedly challenged but was finally codified in state law in 1917. Even so, traditionalists – or misogynists, if you prefer – balked at members of the "fairer sex" being taken from their household duties to hear salacious testimony, being sequestered with male strangers, and passing judgement on men. They considered women to be too emotional and irrational to decided matters of life, death, and imprisonment.

And so, this made the possible inclusion of women on the Arbuckle jury national news. When the pool of 66 potential jurors included 13 women, headlines appeared like WOMEN MAY TRY ARBUCKLE. But most newsmen scoffed at this. One even predicted, "When the jury is finally completed, there will be no women let upon it."

He was wrong. Over four days, a jury of seven men and five women was selected, along with one male alternate. While the occupations of the men varied from confectionery owner to explosives expert, four of the women were listed as "wives" and the fifth was a "spinster."

Before opening statements an overly emotional juror admitted to having formed the opinion that Roscoe was innocent and had to be removed.

Roscoe's first trial began on November 18, 1921

The emotional juror was a man.

After he was excused, the alternate took his place on the jury and a new alternate was selected. That twelfth juror and one of the five women were going to have a profound impact on the life of Roscoe Arbuckle.

THE TRIAL OPENED ON NOVEMBER 18 WITH ASSISTANT D.A. LEO Friedman, replacing Isadore Golden, taking the stage with a long opening statement. The defense chose to delay its opening statement until after the prosecution presented its case.

The first witnesses for the state were Dr. Shelby Strange and Dr. William Ophuls, who discussed the two autopsies – again. The defense scored points by getting Strange to admit that Virginia's bruises may have been caused after death and by getting Ophuls to say that a bladder could rupture without pressure being applied to it, as the state claimed.

Another riveting witness introduced architectural drawings of the hotel rooms.

On the second day, after nurse Grace Halston testified, defense lawyer McNab asked Dr. Arthur Beardslee, "Did Mrs. Delmont give you what was purported to be the history of the case? What was the history she gave you?"

D.A. Brady objected, and Judge Harold Louderback sustained the motion.

McNab pressed on: "Did Mrs. Delmont or Miss Rappe intimate to you that Mr. Arbuckle was responsible for her condition?"

"Objection!" Brady exclaimed.

Again, the judge sustained his objection.

Assistant D.A. Milton U'Ren labeled the question "poison," which led to a verbal battle between the prosecution and the defense. The defense was trying to get comments by Virginia into evidence because Delmont had supposedly heard her make a statement to the hotel detective that they said absolved Arbuckle. Further, Maude supposedly told Dr. Beardslee that Roscoe had attacked Virginia, only to have Virginia contradict her. The state called all of this hearsay.

Judge Harold Louderback, a 40-year-old San Francisco native, graduate of Harvard Law, and in the middle of his first year as a Superior Court judge, repeatedly sustained the prosecution's objections about Virginia's alleged statements.

Judge Harold Louderback

On the third day, the state called Dr. H. Edward Castle, who had briefly attended Virginia at Wakefield sanitarium, and the head of the facility, Dr. W. Francis Wakefield. Both testified that Virginia was bruised before her death.

They were followed by Zey Prevost and Alice Blake, the state's star witnesses. After the preliminary hearing the two reluctant celebrities had been placed in protective custody at the house of the D.A. clerk's mother. While Alice's wealthy family eventually got her released, Zey had spent the last seven weeks under a sort-of house arrest in someone else's house. The defense made a big deal of this and at one point, McNab made a retort to the prosecution, "I don't know what she was doing when she was in your private prison."

On the stand, Zey recounted how Virginia entered room 1219 and "Mr. Arbuckle followed her and closed the door." She said that a half hour later, Maude Delmont kicked at the door several times and demanded, "Open the door. I want to speak to Virginia." Zey stated that a red-faced Roscoe opened the door, fumbling with his robe but said nothing as he strolled into 1220. When Maude and Zey entered 1219, they found Virginia on the bed, fully clothed, but moaning and writing in pain.

"Did she say anything at this time?" D.A. Friedman asked.

Zey nodded. "Yes, she said 'I'm dying. I am going to die.' She then began tearing at her waist."

She explained that she and Maude had then removed Virginia's clothing for a cold bath, after which Fred Fishback, who had just returned to the suite after scouting his filming location, carried Virginia back to the bed.

Friedman asked, "After the bath, did she say anything?"

"Yes, she said, '"He hurt me.'"

It was at that moment that the crucial statement the prosecution had counted on during the preliminary hearing fell apart. "I'm dying" was no longer linked directly with 'He hurt me," which meant that the latter could have been referring to Fred carrying Virginia to the bed.

Friedman, undoubtedly knowing what had just happened, quickly moved on. "Did the defendant say anything?"

Zey nodded again. "Yes, he said, 'Aw, shut up. I'll throw her out the window if she doesn't stop yelling.'" Sahe also recounted Roscoe applying ice to Virginia's "abdominal region" and saying, "That will make her come to."

While Roscoe's comment about throwing Virginia out the window was certainly rude – he had been drinking all day, after all – the incident with the ice was now being shown in a whole new light.

During cross-examination, McNab hammered all this home, highlighting the inconsistencies of Zey's varying recollections and suggested that D.A. Brady had pressured the young woman to sign a statement with the words "He killed me."

Alice Blake turned out to be a supporting player when compared to Zey Prevost's starring role on the stand. She testified briefly before she was excused until the prosecution could produce a suppressed statement she'd made to a detective.

After Kate Hardebeck testified about Virginia's good health, the state called Jess Norgaard, a 62-year-old security guard who'd worked at Henry Lehrman's studio was Roscoe was there making *The Hayseed* and *The Garage*. He claimed that in August 1919, when he walked into a studio office to get his hat, Roscoe asked him for the key to Virginia's dressing room. When the guard refused, Roscoe said it was for a joke and offered him a "big roll of money" in exchange for the key.

When he heard Norgaard claim this on the stand, Roscoe laughed so loudly that the bailiff had to call for order. This never happened.

When Alice Blake returned to the stand the next day, her statement to a detective was introduced. Apparently, she'd told the detective that Virginia only said, "I'm dying." On the stand, she recalled that Virginia later said, "He hurt me." However, this was not in her original statement.

It would have been better for the prosecution if they hadn't tracked down the statement because McNab pounced during cross-examination. He asked her if her memory of the incident was clearer when she spoke to the detective than it was now. Alice admitted that it was. Now "I'm dying" wasn't just separated from "He hurt me" – it seemed the second statement was never said at all.

Al Semnacher was on the witness stand after Alice was dismissed. He told of seeing Virginia in pain, tearing at her clothing and claiming she was dying. He said the morning after Labor Day everyone merely thought Virginia was drunk, and Roscoe told the ice story. Again, when it came to the ice, Semnacher wrote but did not speak the word "snatch." Under cross-examination, he admitted that he had seen Virginia tear off her clothes "two or three times" when drinking on previous occasions.

After a silly demonstration by Virginia's personal trainer on how to use a medicine ball, which illustrated her good health, the state brought back what it believed was its most effective witness from the preliminary hearing – hotel maid Josephine Keza.

The judge hadn't been won over by her story in the hearing and at the trial, the reason was clear, or perhaps the defense was better prepared for her story. She offered a theatrical retelling of hearing a woman screaming behind the closed door of room 1219, adding the woman's voice saying "No! No! Oh my god!" followed by a man saying, "Shut up!"

But Keza had supposedly been in and out of the suite throughout Labor Day, sometimes hiding in closets, other times listening at keyholes, and under cross-examination, the details of the day flowed into one debauched party. "Oh, what an afternoon!" she exclaimed to laughter, playing to the audience. This statement was stricken from the record.

Her account had grown wilder since the preliminary

The hallway to Room 1221 at the St. Francis Hotel

hearing. She claimed that she'd seen Lowell Sherman sneaking out of a room with a woman, both dressed only in their underwear, and spotted another underdressed man chasing a lingerie-clad woman down the hall. She also said that Virginia screamed on and off for an unlikely two hours, and that multiple men – not just Roscoe – had told her to shut up.

It was an entertaining story – although an improbable one – that was eaten up by the spectators and by the press, who now had more material to flesh out the "orgy" part of the weekend.

The state saved its only direct evidence for a dramatic – albeit pointless – conclusion. "America's Sherlock Holmes," Edward O. Heinrich, finally got his starring moment when he brought the door leading from 1219 to the hallway into the courtroom. He explained that he'd found fingerprints on it that matched both Roscoe and Virginia, aligned in a way he stated showed that Roscoe had pressed Virginia's hand against the door. He said this indicated she might have been trying to leave, and he prevented her exit.

If McNab didn't object to this bit of speculation, which concluded the state's case, he certainly should have.

IF YOU'VE FINISHED READING ABOUT THE PROSECUTION'S CASE, you might have noticed that a name was missing from their witness list. It was the same witness missing from the preliminary hearing roster – Bambina Maude Delmont.

Maude had been subpoenaed for the trial and she even attended as a spectator, but she didn't testify. The press was as baffled by this as the legal buffs who were closely following the proceedings. As one newsmen wrote, she "hovered behind the scenes of the Arbuckle trial, remaining a mysterious figure in the case."

And she was destined to remain mysterious, but the reason was no mystery. The defense had expended much of its resources investigating Maude's past and in addition to the Earl Lynn extortion charge, they uncovered numerous instances of fraid, unpaid debts, and petty crimes. They were prepoared to present Maude as a con artist whose latest and greatest victim was Rocoe Arbuckle.

Brady couldn't risk putting her on the stand. He knew the defense would dredge up her past – a past that he knew all about. In fact, he was aware of an investigation that had started in late September and on the first day of testimony in the Arbuckle trial, a formal complaint was filed against her. Brady delayed the matter in case he needed Maude to take the stand but quickly decided against that.

When the Arbuckle trial ended, the complaint led to Maude's arrest, and she was charged with bigamy. After separating from John Hopper in 1914, she had never finalized their divorce before marrying Cassius Wood seven years later. When she entered a guilty plea on December 10, she was sentenced to one year's probation, which made front-page news across the country.

It's impossible not to wonder if Roscoe would have been arrested at all if the authorities had spent as much time looking into the credibility of the complaining witness as they did trying to make headlines by taking down a celebrity.

"THE STATE HAS MISERABLY FAILED TO PROVE ITS CASE!"

Those were the first words of Gavin McNab's opening statement when the defense began its case. Judge Louderback struck this assertion from the record, but he's made his point. When the judge asked him to simply state what he intended to prove, he used the next 30 minutes to say that he'd prove the innocence of Roscoe Arbuckle.

Until the start of the defense case, much of the press coverage of the trial focused on Roscoe's reaction to the testimony he heard from the stand. *The Los Angeles Times* repeatedly interrupted its coverage of the testimony by describing Roscoe's nervous habits. Among the descriptions were:

Arbuckle dug into his pocket, extracted a gold pencil and began to play with it, his eyes gazing downward.

Arbuckle took an open letter from his pocket and began to scribble on it.

Arbuckle turned the envelope over and scribbled some more.

Arbuckle's eyes dropped and he ceased scribbling.

Arbuckle wrinkled his brown and squinted at Friedman.

Arbuckle was busily engaged tearing paper into tiny bits.

Often, reporters said that he looked disinterested, but it was all an act. When Zey Prevost spoke about him applying ice to Virginia, he seemed to be purposely distracting himself – and some of the reporters, too: "Arbuckle balanced his chair on two legs, leaned over and took a thumb tack from the *Times'* section of the press table. Arbuckle stuck his thumb with the tack, winced, and then the noon recess was declared."

While every one of Roscoe's twitches and tics made news, so did every article of clothing worn by Minta Durfee. She and her mother sat behind Roscoe, sometimes joined by his brother, Arthur, and the daily outfit of the estranged but loyal wife got a lot of ink. On the second day of prosecution testimony, the San Francisco Examiner noted, "There was but one feature of importance to yesterday's proceedings – Mrs. Minta Durfee Arbuckle wore her black velvet hat."

But Minta's fashion choices – and Roscoe's habits -- took a backseat to the witnesses on the stand as the defense's case began in earnest. McNab's first witness was George Glennon, the former house detective at the St. Francis, to whom Virginia allegedly made a statement absolving Roscoe of guilt. The state objected, calling it hearsay. The judge agreed and Glennon was excused. McNab tried again on another day to get Glennon on the record, but he failed again.

The next witness was an elderly St. Francis maid, Kate Brennan, who testified that she had dusted and thoroughly polished the door of room 1219 before Heinrich had checked it for fingerprints.

Another witness, a guest in room 1218, stated that she was in her room all Labor Day and heard no screaming or moaning.

A San Francisco film producer named R.C. Harper testified that he had in the hallway outside of the twelfth-floor suite for 35 minutes starting between 2:30 and 2:45 P.M. and stated that he never heard anyone screaming and he also never saw Josephine Keza. According to his story, he'd come to the hotel with a business proposal for Roscoe but wasn't able to work up the nerve to knock on his door. He decided to wait and possibly catch him in the hallway instead but gave up on this plan after about a half hour.

The story was a little hard to believe since it conveniently occurred during the time that was most crucial to the defense's case, but the prosecution couldn't shake him, even after D.A. Friedman asked him, "Is it not an insult to one's intelligence to ask us to swallow a story like this?" The prosecutor implied that Harper, who worked at the edges of the movie business, was trying to ingratiate himself with some insiders, but Harper stuck by his story.

The next morning, the jury, judge, attorneys, and defendant went to the Hotel St. Francis and took a brief tour of the three rooms in question on the top floor. The furniture and furnishings were arranged as closely as possible to how they were on Labor Day. Reporters said that Roscoe never spoke but "appeared thoughtful" as he walked through the connected rooms.

Back in the courtroom, the defense called Fred Fishback, who testified that Virginia was tearing at her clothes on the bed in 1219 when he returned to the party. He said, "She was making a noise, but

WOMEN WITNESSES IN ARBUCKLE CASE

I don't know whether it was moaning or screaming or what sort of noise it was."

He demonstrated to the court how he had lifted her into, and then had taken her out of, the cold bath, which could have caused the bruises on her body. Fred also said that Virginia didn't seem to be in pain, a claim the state challenged on cross-examination by introducing an unsigned statement that Fred made to the contrary. He claimed he'd been misquoted in the statement.

Dr. Olav Kaarboe supported Fred's story by testifying that, as the first doctor to examine Virginia, he also said that Virginia didn't seem to be in pain.

Dr. Asa W. Collins testified that a spontaneous rupture of a bladder was possible if it was distended, but when cross-examined, he admitted such ruptures were rare and that he had never treated a patient who'd suffered one.

The next day was Thanksgiving and Roscoe, Minta, and Flora feasted on turkey stuffed with oysters at the home of Roscoe's brother, Arthur, while the jurors walked in the cold rain to a restaurant. None of them saw their families on the holiday. They were sequestered during the trial at the Hotel Manx, unable to read newspapers, with their incoming mail being censored of any mention of Roscoe, Virginia, or the trial. Their only entertainment was the occasional group trip to a movie theater or restaurant, always under the close eye of four deputy sheriffs.

On Friday, Dr. Melville Rumwell took the stand to testify about this treatment of Virginia before her death. He said that she was unable to recall what caused her injury. Three weeks earlier, Dr. Rumwell had been arrested for the misdemeanor crime of performing an unauthorized autopsy on Virginia and was subsequently fined $500.

Most of the other defense witnesses that day and the next could be separated into two categories – doctors who stated that distended bladders could rupture on their own and people who had previously seen Virginia intoxicated and could testify that she'd complained of abdominal pain, acted strangely, and tore off her clothing.

Irene Morgan was one of these witnesses. She was a nurse and housekeeper employed by Virginia when she lived with Henry Lehrman and she said that Virginia had frequent bouts of abdominal pain and ripped off her clothes when drunk.

Minnie Neighbors, the wife of a retired Los Angeles policeman, also took the stand and described encountering Virginia while she was suffering from terrible stomach pains at a spa the month before her death.

Harry Barker had dated Virginia in Chicago from 1910 to 1915 and claimed he'd seen her "all doubled up and tearing at her clothes" on several occasions. His testimony was damaged a bit when he denied under cross-examination that he had been engaged to Virginia, and she had broken things off with him. Three days later, a rebuttal witness claimed to have witnessed Virginia breaking off the engagement.

Florence Bates, who worked as a clerk at Mandel Brothers department store in Chicago in 1913, testified that during a two-week fashion exhibit in which Virginia was a model, she was in terrible pain and publicly tore off expensive clothing three times.

Film actor Philo McCullough testified about Virginia bringing her own gin to a party at his home in Hollywood and, after becoming drunk, loudly removed her stockings and her blouse.

The defense spent a lot of time emphasizing Virginia's habit of stripping in public, hoping to tarnish her character, but it did more to bolster the idea that she had some sort of prior medical condition. This behavior did little to answer the question of Roscoe's guilt or innocence. The state and the defense already agreed that Virginia was clothed while alone with Roscoe in 1219. It was only afterward, when others were present, that she started to undress.

Philo McCullough

The defense next called Edward O. Heinrich back to the stand so McNab could beat him up over his testimony and reputation. This included a mocking jab at him for referring to himself as "Sherlock Holmes." After slapping him around a little, the defense called Ignatius McCarthy to the stand. He was a former investigator for the U.S. Department of Labor, and he claimed the fingerprints on the door of room 1219 were forgeries, which was how they survived the door being cleaned by the housekeeping staff over the next two weeks. He raised a good point, but the prosecution managed to successfully challenge his credentials as a fingerprint expert.

After that, the defense only had one witness left on their list -- the only living person who could testify with firsthand knowledge about what happened behind the door of room 1219 on Labor Day afternoon.

ROSCOE ARBUCKLE TOOK THE STAND AT 10:35 A.M. ON MONDAY, November 28, 1921. After he was sworn in, he settled into the wooden witness chair and those who had been out in the hall chatting and smoking after Ignatius McCarthy's was cut short, hurried back into the courtroom. No one wanted to miss the big show.

McNab began guiding Roscoe through the story of how he came to be at the booze party – other than that he'd been the one who threw it – attended by Virginia Rappe and other women, none of whom he'd invited. His wife and mother-in-law smiled at him, and he slowly grew more at ease as he revealed what occurred that afternoon. McNab then guided him out of room 1220 and into 1219 and

Jury Hearing "Fatty" Arbuckle Manslaughter Case

what follows is Roscoe's version of what happened in the room he shared with Fred Fishback:

> When I walked into 1219, I closed and locked the door, and I went straight to the bathroom and found Miss Rappe on the floor in front of the toilet, holding her stomach and moving around on the floor. She had been vomiting. I saw it in the bowl and there was the odor of it. When I opened the door, the door struck her and I had to slide in this way [he stood up to show how he turned to the side] to get in, to get by her and get hold of her. Then I closed the door and picked her up. When I picked her up, I held her, and she vomited again. I held her under the waist, like that [he stood up again to show what he meant], and by the forehead, to keep her hair back off her face so she could vomit. When she finished, I put the seat down. Then I sat her down on it. She was gasping and had a hard time getting her breath. Later, I asked her, "Is there anything I can do for you?" She said, "No, just leave me lie on the bed." Before that I had given her two glasses of water.

He then recounted how he had helped her to lie down on the single bed. He lifted her feet off the floor and left her lying there as he returned to the bathroom. He continued:

I came back into 1219 in about, well, I was there about two or three minutes, and I found Miss Rappe between the two beds rolling about on the floor and holding her stomach and crying and moaning, and I tried to pick her up, and I couldn't get hold of her. I couldn't get alongside of her to pick her up, so I pulled her into a sitting position [on his own double bed]. She turned on her left side and started to groan, and I immediately went out of 1219 to find Mrs. Delmont.

He claimed that he wasn't able to find Maude right away, which contradicted with the story told by Zey Prevost, who claimed Maude had been kicking at the door of 1219. When he found her, Maude and Zey went into 1219. Roscoe followed them.

Miss Rappe was sitting on the bed, tearing her clothes. She pulled her dress up, tore her stockings. She had a black lace garter, and she tore the lace off the garter. And Mr. Fishback came in about that time and asked the girls to stop tearing her clothes. And I went over to her, and she was tearing the sleeve of her dress, and she had just one sleeve hanging by a few shreds – I don't know which one it was – and I said, "All right, if you want that off, I'll take it off for you." And I pulled it off for her. Then I went out of the room.

He returned to room 1219 a short time later and now he found that Virginia was naked on the single bed.

I went in there, and Mrs. Delmont was rubbing her with some ice. She had a lot of ice in a towel or a napkin or something and had it on the back of her neck, and she had another piece of ice and was rubbing Miss Rappe with it, massaging her. There was a piece of ice lying on Miss Rappe's body. I picked it up and said, "What's this doing

What Happened Behind That Door

ROSCOE (FATTY) ARBUCKLE

here?" Delmont says, "Leave it here. I know how to take care of Virginia." I put it back on Miss Rappe where I picked it up, and I started to cover Miss Rappe up, to pull the spread down from underneath her so I could cover her with it, and Mrs. Delmont told me to get out of the room and leave her alone, and I told Mrs. Delmont to shut up or I would throw her out the window, and I went out of the room.

This statement had negated the salacious business with the ice and, in confirming one of the more incriminating comments attributed to him, contended that he was not threatening to throw Virginia out the window but that his anger was directed at Maude, the accuser who had not and would not be appearing at the trial to dispute Roscoe's testimony. Some have expressed the feeling that because Virginia was naked at the time, Maude ordering him out of the room seemed appropriate and that his remark to her was undeserved. However, Roscoe had been trying to cover Virginia up. She was lying on top of the bedspread, and he'd been trying to get it out from under her so he could cover her up when Maude snapped at him. It's understandable that he snapped back.

Roscoe continued:

Mrs. Taube came in and telephoned the hotel manager. I told Mrs. Delmont that the manager was coming up. Mr. Boyle, the manager, then came in. Mrs. Delmont and I put a bathrobe on Miss Rappe. We then took her around to room 1227. Mr. Boyle opened the door. I carried her part of the way. She seemed to have no life in her. I asked Mr. Boyle to boost her up in the middle. He took her out of my arms and into 1227.

McNab asked him, "Was the door of 1219 to the hallway unlocked all day?"

"As far as I know it was," Roscoe replied. He replied to other questions from McNab that established that the window in the room was open and that he had opened the curtains himself.

McNab asked, "During the time you were in 1219, do you hear Miss Rappe say, 'You hurt me?'"

"No, sir, I heard nothing that could be understood," Roscoe answered.

"The next day, or any other time, did you talk with Mr. Semnacher regarding a piece of ice?"

"No, sir."

"While in 1219 with Miss Rappe, did you ever at any time place your hand over Miss Rappe's on the bedroom door?"

"No, sir."

"Have you ever had a conversation with Kess Norgaard at a Culver City studio regarding the keep to Miss Rappe's dressing room at the studio?"

"No, sir."

Then, after ensuring that his client had nothing more to add, McNab, with a wave of his hand, defiantly said to the prosecution, "Cross-examine the witness."

Assistant D.A. Friedman would be the one grilling Roscoe on the stand. D.A. Brady frequently whispered strategy and suggestions to him as the cross-examination progressed. When answering Friedman's questions, Roscoe again recounted the start of the party. Liquor consumption was highlighted, as was the boozy noon meal that Roscoe called "breakfast for some, lunch for others." Then the prosecutor steered Roscoe into room 1219. "At 3:00 P.M., you decided to go into room 1219 and get dressed. What was the first thing you did?" he asked.

"I locked the door," Roscoe answered.

And on that note, Judge Louderback halted the testimony for the noon lunch recess. Dramatically, a female deputy coroner carried in a specimen that would be used as a prosecution exhibit when the questioning continued – the ruptured bladder of Virginia Rappe.

After lunch, Friedman hounded Roscoe on the timeline of occurrences in 1219, trying to shake him free of his claim that he was alone with Virginia for no more than 10 minutes. But Roscoe stayed firm, refusing to be rattled. He even elicited a big laugh from the courtroom observers when he answered how he knew the clock on the mantlepiece in 1220 was accurate. "Well, everything else in the hotel is pretty good. I suppose their clocks ought to be all right."

After failing to poke holes in Roscoe's story, Friedman finished by trying to dismantle the picture the defense had painted of Roscoe as someone who tried to help the ailing Virginia. "Did you tell the hotel manager what caused Miss Rappe's sickness?" the D.A. asked.

Roscoe shook his head. "No. How should I know what caused her sickness?"

"You didn't tell anybody you found her in the bathroom?"

"Nobody asked me," Roscoe shrugged.

"You didn't tell anybody you found her between the beds?"

"Nobody I asked, I'm telling you."

"You never said anything to anybody except that Miss Rappe was sick?"

"Nope."

"Did you tell the doctor what caused Miss Rappe's illness?"

Roscoe let out an exasperated noise. "No! How could I tell him what I didn't know?"

Friedman then established that Roscoe had only told his version of what happened in 1219 to his attorneys – trying to make this look like he had something to hide instead of it being one of the few smart decisions he made, especially after the way he was being portrayed to the public.

Roscoe spent four hours on the witness stand before being dismissed. Some of his answers seemed unlikely – like claiming that he was unaware of the women coming to the party and put the blame for buying alcohol on Fred Fishback – while some seemed crude, like his cavalier attitude toward Virginia's nudity, but he had reframed the events in 1219 from assault to assistance. Holding back the hair of a sick person – someone not a relative or even a close friend – so they didn't vomit into it seemed an act of kindness.

In those four hours, a new image of Roscoe Arbuckle had been created for the public and the press. It was an image that could compete with that of the spoiled Hollywood playboy who raped and fatally injured an innocent young woman. He was now seen, his attorneys hoped, as a man alone in a bathroom aiding and comforting a sick woman at the lowest moment of her life.

AFTER ROSCOE FINISHED HIS TESTIMONY AND OVER THE prosecution's objection, the deposition of Dr. Maurice Rosenberg was read into the official record. The physician had been interviewed by defense attorney Brennan and had treated Virginia in Chicago in 1913 for cystitis, a chronic inflammation of the bladder. This was not a curable illness at the time, only one that could be treated, and it was his opinion that she would have continued to suffer from it throughout her life.

After the deposition was read, the defense rested its case.

The next day, the state began calling rebuttal witnesses. It speaks volumes that they never tried to impeach Roscoe's testimony. The only witness who could do that was Maude Delmont – who had a different version of events about what occurred in 1219 – but they couldn't risk putting her on the stand. So, instead, they refocused on Virginia's health.

Catherine Fox – whose real name was Dot Nelson – of Chicago claimed to have known Virginia for 22 years but never knew her to be in pain, tear her clothes, or drink alcohol. After Assistant D.A. U'Ren questioned Fox for two hours, the defense only asked her one question.

"Were you with Maude Bambina Delmont yesterday?" McNab asked her.

"Yes, I was with her all afternoon," she replied.

"That's all," smirked McNab with a gesture that dismissed everything the woman had just told the jury.

Other witnesses testified to Virginia's good physical health and included the former assistant manager of the Hollywood Hotel, where Virginia lived; a psychiatrist who treated her; a chauffeur, a nurse, a director, and a cameraman. A magazine publisher testified to the bad reputation of R.C Harper – the hallway lurker – casting doubt on his story.

Harry Boyle stated that 1219 had not been occupied since Roscoe checked out and while this turned out to be untrue, during the trial, it gave a small amount of credence to Edward Heinrich's forensic investigation – even though it ignored the fact that the room had been cleaned at least once after the party ended.

A clerk at the spa where Minnie Neighbors said she'd encountered Virginia in pain said she didn't remember Virginia and then produced the spa's register, which didn't include her name. Kate Hardebeck returned to the stand to say that Virginia had not been away in August, when she was supposed to be at the spa. Before the day was over, D.A. Brady had Minnie arrested for perjury. The case against her, however, was later dismissed by a judge.

However, the next day, the defense called an attendant at the spa who remembered renting a bathing cap to Virginia and speaking to Minnie Neighbors about her. McNab then recalled the spa clerk and proved that her memory of guests was far from perfect.

The state then countered by introducing the spa's swimwear rental book, which didn't include Virginia's name. The story of the spa had become an entire subplot of its own.

And it wasn't the only one. And even more thrilling story revolved around witness Irene Morgan, who testified to Virgini's frequent fits of agony and her habit of public stripping. The state attempted to impeach her by proving she lied under oath when she claimed to have served as a Canadian military nurse during World War I. After she was recalled to the stand and grilled by the prosecution, D.A. U'Ren threatened to investigate further and hit her with a perjury charge.

But during the defense's closing statement, Milton Cohen broke the shocking news that Irene had been poisoned by a "tall, gray-haired official-looking man" she claimed to have seen in the courtroom the day before and who followed her to a dance hall. Incredibly, when he offered her two pieces of candy, she accepted them. After she ate them, though, she became very dizzy and the man allegedly said to her, "Go to hell. You're done for. You've made others suffer – now suffer yourself!" Irene was later found unconscious in her hotel room and the hotel doctor deduced that he had been poisoned with opiates.

It was a silly story, and one suspiciously timed to avoid that perjury charge, but in his closing statement, McNab called her "a heroine, wounded in battle."

D.A. Brady could hardly restrain himself and sarcastically promised to enlist the entire police force to find the perpetrator of the dastardly crime.

The final witnesses in the trial were three physicians who had been appointed by the court to examine Virginia's bladder – the one in the jar that had been brought into the courtroom before Roscoe's testimony. The panel found that Virginia suffered from a lingering case of cystitis, just as Dr. Rosenberg had diagnosed in 1913. The panel's findings were somewhat ambiguous, though. They failed to determine how long she suffered from the ailment or the severity of her symptoms and were unable to say with certainty that cystitis predisposed her bladder to rupture.

The panel did refute the defense theory that she may have had a partial tear prior to the deadly rupture, but the confirmation that she had abdominal pains and a bladder disease that dated back at least eight years was considered good news for the defense.

ASSISTANT D.A. LEO FRIEDMAN TOOK THE STAGE WHEN THE prosecution began its closing statements. "At the expiration of 13 days, it devolves upon the people to present facts against Arbuckle," he said solemnly. "We are here to try Roscoe Arbuckle – not Roscoe Arbuckle the comedian, not Roscoe Arbuckle the hero of a thousand laughs, not Roscoe Arbuckle the nationally-known figure, but Roscoe Arbuckle the man."

As he spoke, he contrasted the story of what occurred in the twelfth-floor suite as told by prosecution witnesses – especially Zey Prevost, who saw Roscoe followed Virginia into 1219 and Maude Delmont kicking at the door -- with the benign story told by Roscoe. He explained that none of the doctors who testified had ever seen a case in which injuries similar to Virginia's developed with the application of an external force. He pointed to the physical evidence like Virginia's bruises and Roscoe's fingerprints over Virginia's on the door. He claimed ridiculously, "That fact alone is sufficient to say Arbuckle is guilty."

Friedman laid out the state's theory of what caused Virginia's bladder to rupture, contending that Roscoe had followed Virginia into 1219, closed, and locked the door. Virginia was standing near the bathroom. She tried to get away from him, rushing to the door that led to the hallway. He pulled her away from that door and threw her on the double bed. He then threw himself on top of her, planning to sexually assault her, but when his heavy body met hers, her distended bladder ruptured, and she fainted due to the sudden loss of blood pressure caused by the rupture. Roscoe then successfully revived her, he claimed.

Keep in mind that attorneys are usually given a lot of leeway when it comes to opening and closing statements because, in this case, Friedman was clearly testifying since few of the "facts" in his theory had been gleaned from witnesses during testimony. This is the theory the prosecution *wanted* the jury to accept, but they hadn't proved it during the trial.

After presenting his own, Friedman ridiculed the various theories put forward by the defense: "The theory that the rupture may have been caused by dipping the girl in a tub of cold water was a defense theory until Dr. Franklin Shields pulled the plug and let that theory go into the sewer. The theory that the rupture may have been caused by vomiting. Where in this entire case, other than the defendant's testimony, has been shown evidence that Miss Rappe was vomiting? The theory that falling off a bed may have caused it, contained only in the defendant's story. A theory here and a theory there with the evident purpose of confusing the minds of the jurors. Fact by fact has been brought her to refute all these theories."

Friedman became animated as he lambasted Roscoe, who was sitting at the defense table, gazing downward and fidgeting with his tie. Seated behind her husband, Minta was holding a small bouquet of violets in one hand and smelling salts in the other. The prosecutor waved his arms around as he raised his voice: "The big, kind-hearted comedian who has made the whole world laugh – did he say, 'Get a doctor for the suffering girl?' No, he said, 'Shut up, or I'll throw you out the window!' He was not content to stop at throwing her out the window. He attempted to make sport with her body by placing ice on her. This man then and there proved himself guilty of this offence. That act shows you the mental makeup of Roscoe Arbuckle. I say there was a struggle in 1219. Roscoe Arbuckle tried and succeeded in keeping her there. I leave it to you what was the purpose of his attack upon her. The rupture that caused her death was caused by no other manner than by the assault Roscoe Arbuckle made upon her!"

Gavin McNab began the defense's closing by bolstering their allegedly poisoned witness Irene Morgan – then supposedly clinging to life – against the state's attacks on her character, dramatically taking the side of the injured woman.

He also noted the absence of the complaining witness: "It is not mercy that keeps Mrs. Delmont out of the case, because you witnessed the venom with which our case has been attacked."

One by one, he dismissed the testimony of various prosecution witnesses. He recalled Semnacher's damning allegation that Roscoe placed ice in Virginia's vagina but mistakenly referred to it as "a collateral incident," which endorsed the prosecution's version of what happened to the ice. It's not what he meant, but it's what went into the record.

Using clocks as props, he plotted out the timeline established by witnesses and asked when an attack could have occurred. He compared Heinrich's fingerprint evidence to a belief in witchcraft. He asked why the healthy, athletic woman presented by the prosecution couldn't even bother to shout for help if she was being assaulted. By reading their conflicted statements and testimony, he questioned the veracity of the stories told by Zey Prevost and Alice Blake. He pointed out how D.A. Brady had placed them under house arrest to make sure they gave the evidence he wanted at trial, taking away their liberty, he said, "the same way the state might do to an innocent man."

McNab stated there were many ways that Virginia's bladder could have ruptured before or after Roscoe entered room 1219. His strongest theories were that the trauma was caused by the strain of violent vomiting, a fall in the bathroom, or off the bed.

He summarized: "The prosecution has painted Arbuckle as a monster, and yet we see him carrying Miss Rappe in his own arms to a place of comfort. He was in the room alone with Miss Rappe but ten minutes, and during that time there was no outcry or sound of a struggle. I gather these facts from prosecution evidence. The scientific men we produced said there were many ways in which Miss Rappe could have suffered her fatal injury. Surely the jury must admit there were many ways also rather than the one pointed out by the prosecution."

McNab then managed to squeeze a tear from his eye – and from the eye of at least one juror – as he concluded: "Since Christ said, 'Suffer the little children to come unto me,' the instinct of little children has always gone out to good men, never to bad, and Arbuckle has been crucified here by speech but not by evidence. This man, who has sweetened human existence by the laughter of millions and millions of innocent children, comes before you with the simple story of a frank, open-hearted, big American and submits the facts of this case to your hands."

McNab then gripped his client by the shoulder, looked at him with compassion, and took his seat at the defense table.

The defense was finished, but the state still had the final word. Milton U'Ren conjured up a tortured biblical connection of his own as he spoke: "He came up here and the word was sent out by his friend Fishback that Fatty was in town, and the people poured into his quarters, food was spread, drinks were served, and this modern Belshazzar sat upon his throne and was surrounded by his lords and their ladies, and they went on with the music, feasting, wine, liquor, song, and dancing. The great Belshazzar saw the handwriting on the wall and quaked as it was interpreted. The modern King Belshazzar has also seen the handwriting on the wall. The king is dead, and his kingdom is divided. He will never make the world laugh again."

U'Ren spent another hour summarizing the state's case again, placing great emphasis on the fingerprints, which the prosecution had a theory about, but had no real evidence that made it true.

He repeatedly countered McNab's use of innocent children, presenting Roscoe as a deceiver of young people because he hid his "rotten nature." U'Ren looked at the famous fat man and sneered: "Oh, if the children of America could have seen Roscoe Arbuckle put ice in the private parts of Virginia Rappe, how they and their mothers would have laughed with glee!"

He shook his head, pretending to be terribly sad as he finished: "We ask you to do your duty so that when you return to your families, you can take them to your breasts, and we ask you to do your duty so that when you take your children upon your knees that you will know that you have done what you could to protect them from the defendant and from all the other Arbuckles in the world, not existing and yet to come. And ask you to do your duty so that this man and all the Arbuckles of the world will know that the motherhood of America is not their plaything."

AFTER FINAL INSTRUCTIONS FROM JUDGE LOUDERBACK, THE case was turned over to the jury at 4:15 P.M. on Friday, December 2.

While the seven men and five women deliberated behind a closed door, Roscoe was in the courtroom, pacing around and chatting with his attorneys and reporters. Minta sat nervously between the comforting wives of Arthur Arbuckle and Milt Cohen. The jury took a break for dinner and then returned to their deliberations when they were finished. Bailiffs were called into the jury room several times, which always started a flurry of whispers among the observers, but they returned each time with no verdict.

Finally, at 11:00 P.M., court was adjourned for the day. Rumors spread that the jury was deadlocked 11 to one for acquittal, but it was later learned that early ballots had been nine to three for acquittal – or more accurately, eight to three with one juror refusing to vote. Word leaked that the holdout was a woman and the image of that lone female juror, standing firm for Roscoe's guilt took hold over the weekend with headlines like WOMAN VOTES ACTOR GUILTY SAYS REPORT, which appeared on the front page of the *San Francisco Examiner*.

The jury continued deliberating on Saturday. The women who packed the courtroom saw Roscoe joking with reporters, attorneys, and bailiffs, chatting with the alternate juror, smoking, eating, reading newspapers, and even performing magic tricks.

Hours dragged on. The jury adjourned for the second night at 10:37 P.M. and Judge Louderback ordered them back at 10:00 the next morning.

The sequestered jurors had been kept away from newspapers during the trial, so they had no way of knowing that their names, addresses, and occupations had been appearing in the papers they couldn't read. There was even a group photo of them in the jury box that had been printed.

Curiously, one person hid when that photo was taken. She'd ducked so that it revealed only the top of her black hat. As the jury remained deadlocked on Saturday, that juror – Helen Hubbard, the 46-year-old wife of an attorney – became famous as the "lone holdout."

On Sunday morning, the jury was deliberating again while Roscoe played hide-and-seek with a child in the hallway. Then, at noon, nearly 44 hours after the trial went to the jury, the members of that jury announced they were hopelessly deadlocked. The tally of the final ballot was 10 to 2 for acquittal.

Helen Hubbard – the "lone holdout" – ducked her head during the jury photograph

Mrs. Hubbard had been joined in her protest against Roscoe's innocence by a 54-year-old candy shop owner named Thomas Kilkenny, the former alternate juror who had only been seated after one of the original jurors admitted that he believed Roscoe was innocent.

"We had some wild times in the jury room," one of the 10 said of the heated attempts to convince the two stubborn jurors to agree with the rest of them.

"We felt the case had not been sufficiently proved," another said. "Some of the jurors believed Arbuckle was innocent, others believed that not enough proof had been presented to warrant a conviction.

The jury foreman, sales manager August Fritze, released a statement that read in part:

The ten members of the jury who voted on the last ballot for acquittal felt that they voted on the evidence – fully considering it all. One of the two minority refused to consider the evidence from the beginning and said at the opening of the proceedings that she would cast her ballot and would not change it until hell froze over. The other was fluctuating, sometimes casting a blank ballot, sometimes voting for the defense and sometimes for the prosecution.

Kilkenny, the "fluctuating" juror, never spoke to the press and quickly faded into history. It was reported that he voted with Helen Hubbard in an effort to win her confidence and then convince her to change her vote to one for acquittal, but that doesn't make much sense. Most likely, he just wasn't the great story that Hubbard was. She captured the attention of the press, mostly just because she was a woman and portrayed as having an ax to grind against Arbuckle because of his treatment of Virginia Rappe.

Mrs. Hubbard granted one interview to two female reporters from the *San Francisco Chronicle* and the *Examiner*. Because she was married to an attorney, she expressed surprise at being allowed to serve on the jury. She felt that she didn't need to read through the over 1,300 pages of trial transcripts nor review the evidence in the jury room – she'd already heard it all in the courtroom.

"It was the matter of fingerprints purely in the final analysis that decided me," she said. "Arbuckle failed to convince me with his story absolutely. Once on a jury I would vote my own husband guilty if I really believed him to be that in my heart, and nothing could shake me once that belief was established in my mind."

I'm sure her husband was reassured when he read this.

But it wasn't Roscoe that Mrs. Hubbard saved her harshest criticism for – that was August Fritze and the other men on the jury, whom she accused of verbal abuse in trying to get her to change her vote. She complained, "There is no place for the woman on the jury. Any woman is a fool to even get on one if she can possibly get out of serving. I'd rather die than go through it again. The general attitude and language of the men is offensive to a woman."

Of course, most newspaper editors – who were men – agreed with her about women serving on juries, writing that the indignities to which female jurors were subjected were cruel. "As an editor for the *San Francisco Chronicle* noted, "Certainly a woman's mind and body are less well equipped to withstand strains to which they are put in cases of this character."

An editor from the *Chicago Tribune* also chimed in: "It is a firm presumption that the cause of exact justice was injured by the presence of women on the Arbuckle jury. A woman might have to overcome her aversion for a man charged with immorality before she could get anywhere near the issue of whether he was guilty of manslaughter."

Not surprisingly, the men had missed the point. It wasn't the presence of women on the jury that was the problem. It was the presence of one woman, who had her mind made up before the trial even began and refused to ever consider the idea that the story being spun by the prosecutors and newspapers trying to make headlines might not be true.

The Women's Vigilant Committee – a group that worked for women's rights in San Francisco and had made sure that its members were in the courtroom each day of the trial – praised Mrs. Hubbard's independence. They also chastised Roscoe saying, "Regardless of the guilt or innocence of this defendant, this committee wish he had shown more humility at the end of his trial. He admitted that he had staged a drinking and dancing party."

They also missed the point. Humble or not humble, the "drinking and dancing party" wasn't the reason that Roscoe Arbuckle had been on trial.

WHEN ROSCOE HEARD THE NEWS OF THE JURY'S INDECISION, HE rolled another cigarette. Minta dabbed away tears. And when the date of January 9 was agreed upon for a new trial, he lit the cigarette, inhaled, and then exhaled a dejected cloud of smoke.

Assistant D.A. U'Ren stepped toward the defense and extended a hand to McNab. "I just want to congratulate your client on his gameness."

Roscoe, standing next to McNab, snorted, "I'm game because my conscience is clear, much clearer than yours, U'Ren."

Afterward, as Roscoe and his attorneys drafted a statement for the press, Minta stood with her mother and friends outside the Hall of Justice. "The poor boy," she sighed. "Now he'll have to go through it all again."

The statement from Roscoe read:

While this is not a legal acquittal, through a technicality of the law, I feel it is a moral one. But for one woman on the jury of thirteen, who refused to allow her fellow jurors to discuss the evidence or to reason with her, and who would give no explanation for her attitude, my trial would have resulted in an immediate acquittal.

This statement was released before Helen Hubbard had granted an interview, which explains the remark about her lack of "explanation for her attitude."

After the organized propaganda designed to make the securing of an impartial jury and impossibility and to prevent my obtaining a fair trial, I feel grateful for this message from the juror to the American people. This comes, too, after the jury had heard only part of the facts. The effect of the District Attorney succeeded in excluding from the evidence statements made by Miss Rappe to people of high character, statements completely exonerating me.

The undisputed and uncontradicted testimony established that my only connection with this sad affair was one of a merciful service, and the fact that ordinary human kindness should have brought upon me this tragedy seems a cruel wrong. I sought to bring joy and gladness and merriment into the world, and why this great misfortune should have fallen upon me is a mystery that only God can reveal.

I have always rested my cause in a profound belief in divine justice and in the confidence of the great heart and fairness of the American people. I want to thank the multitudes from all over the world who have telegraphed and written me in my sorrow and expressed their utmost confidence in my innocence, and I assure them no act of mine ever has or ever shall cause them to regret their faith in me.

Now, as Minta said sadly on the front steps of the Hall of Justice, Roscoe had to do it all over again.

FOURTEEN

DURING THE MONTH BETWEEN THE END OF THE FIRST TRIAL AND the start of the second, Roscoe stayed mostly out of sight in his West Adams mansion, living with a wife that wasn't so estranged anymore.

He'd granted an interview with the press soon after his return from San Francisco: "This case has put quite a crimp in my pocketbook. I resent the damage that it done to me because I know I am innocent."

He later told a reporter that he was "broke" As a result of the first trial and his lack income, leaving out that he's bought Minta a diamond and emerald brooch and a $1,000 jeweled purse for Christmas. Roscoe had never handled his finances very well but there were estimates that the first trial cost him $35,000 and that his loss of work during that time cost him at least $100,000.

Both of those figures later turned out to be too low.

Roscoe also told reporters that he had sworn off alcohol and that he and Minta were reunited for good. He told the press, "My wife has proven that she is the one woman in the world for me, and I intend to keep her – if she will let me, and I think she will."

But those interviews were only the first stops on Roscoe's "redemption tour." The last two issues of *Movie Weekly* in 1921 featured Roscoe on the covers. The first included a piece called "The True Story of My Husband" by Minta Durfee Arbuckle. The second followed a week later and featured a story from Roscoe called "The True Story About Myself."

Minta's story, which was surely composed by or with the defense team, intended to answer pressing questions about her marriage. It began with, "As surely as God is above me, and I believe in him sincerely, I know that Roscoe Arbuckle did not do the thing which he has been made to stand trial.

While Roscoe was not eager to speak to the press after the first trial, Minta offered a lengthy defense of him to "Movie Weekly." Roscoe followed with a defense of his own.

She addressed the motives of his accusers by saying that Roscoe had told her that he'd complained about the actions of some of those in attendance, telling them they were going too far. She noted that, "Perhaps that very thing around a spirit of revenge that was responsible for the charges made against him." She also said that with her husband's reputation for generosity and his poor money management that he'd attracted "people who were after him for what they could get."

This, of course, led to her to commend about Maude Delmont, who she said was "really the only one to accuse Mr. Arbuckle directly" and her story must have been so flimsy that the prosecution refused to put her on the stand.

Minta also said that whenever she saw the name Virginia Rappe involved in the case, she knew immediately that "my husband was being made a victim of circumstance." But she added, "I do not want to say anything against her."

Minta even had an excuse for Roscoe wearing his pajamas at the party. This doesn't seem so unusual today – when people unfortunately wear their pajamas to the grocery store – but at that time, it was considered very improper. She said that shortly before the trip to San Francisco, Roscoe had been accidentally burned by muriatic acid, which was then used in various stain removers for clothing. Minta didn't say where he'd been burned but did say it was covered with a heavy bandage. Loose pajamas and a robe – which covered him in thick material from neck to ankles, by the way -- were more comfortable to wear.

And this led her to discuss his feelings of unease about his body and size, especially around women. She wrote, "I do not want the women of the country to know that in spite of all the insinuations and ugly stories that have been circulated since things began, Roscoe Arbuckle is the most modest of men. I never remember a single action or a single word that, by the farthest stretch of the imagination, could be called even immodest, to say nothing of vulgar or lewd."

Minta even offered a hint about their sex life: "It is an actual fact that in all the years I have been his wife, I have never seen him when he was not clothed."

She then attempted to explain why she didn't believe the stories the newspapers were spreading about him: "All his life Roscoe has been embarrassed by his size. He has believed that women could not like a fat man, and for that reason he has hesitated even more than might be natural about developing friendships among women. He is not the type of man who caresses a woman. If he likes a girl, he will tease her or give her presents or generally be nice to her, but he will never think of putting his hands on her. In fact, he carries it so far that it is almost an obsession."

The "damage control" article from Roscoe took a different approach, focusing primarily on the events that happened in room 1219 on Labor Day. It clung to the tale he'd told in court about finding and assisting an ailing Virginia Rappe. The narrative was straightforward and saved most of the passion in his writing to present himself as a victim of his accusers, prosecutors, reporters, and the fans who had turned against him.

He stated that he couldn't understand how he'd been dragged into a murder trial. He wrote: "Whatever motive inspired the people who accused me, it was not knowledge that I had done the thing they

say I did. It seems almost impossible to me that anyone could be so cruel; and malicious as to make such terrible charges against a man without the most positive proof to support those charges, and yet this is what happened."

He also said that the claims he had been infatuated with Virginia Rappe and had been trying to "get her" for years were absurd. He wrote, "I knew her for several years. We had worked at the same studios, and I had met her in other places, but that was absolutely all."

He had been pursuing Virginia or anything other women because, he made it clear, he still loved his wife. He added, "One really good thing has come out of all this trouble. It has been the means of reuniting my wife and myself after five years of separation. We are happy to be together again, and we have discovered that the things that kept us apart were very unimportant after all."

He concluded the article by bemoaning his "great misfortune" but he'd add to the statements that he'd made in writing when he spoke with reporters in the hallways outside the courtroom at the Hall of Justice, just before the second trial began.

The statement appeared in newspapers:

It's not prison I'm afraid of. It's not the loss of fame and fortune. It is the loss of regard; the loss of affection, the fact that the kids may think I am guilty that hurts me. Guilty? The law says a man is not guilty until he is proven so. But, my friend, let the man once arrested and charged with a crime; let his name go broadcast in those first, cruel stories, regardless of fact, and he is branded guilty... I have suffered. All I ask in repayment of the wrong done me is that the world which once loved me now withhold its judgement and give me a chance to prove before another jury that I am innocent.

JURY SELECTION FOR THE SECOND TRIAL BEGAN ON JANUARY 11, 1922, in Judge Louderback's courtroom.

It proved much more difficult in the second manslaughter trial, because so many people had formed an opinion based on the overwhelming coverage of the original trial. A jury pool of 79 men and women were exhausted before the defense and the prosecution were able to agree on a panel of 11 men and one woman and two alternates – a man and a woman – to serve in the second trial. The jury would again be sequestered in a hotel.

District Attorney Brady had shifted gears with the second prosecution, basing it on the grand jury's manslaughter indictment

Thanks to the publicity that surrounded the events, indictment, and first trial, it was much more difficult to choose a jury for Roscoe's second trial

rather than the police court charge sworn by Maude Delmont. He hoped this would help him to sidestep criticism by not calling her to the stand. As the state began its case, a familiar parade of witnesses took the stand – Al Semnacher, Harry Boyle, Jess Norgaard, Josephine Keza, Dr. W. Francis Wakefield, and Dr. Arthur Beardslee. He used them to reconstruct the events before, during, and after Labor Day.

The state's star witnesses remained showgirls Alice Blake and Zey Prevost, but neither was as strong as she'd been the first time around. Alice, in particular, was the very definition of a reluctant witness, speaking so softly in the court's morning session that all her testimony had to be reread after the lunch break. She recalled seeing Virginia and then Roscoe enter room 1219, Maude demanding entrance, and Virginia saying, "He hurt me, he hurt me. I'm dying," but on the important point of Roscoe being in the room when Virginia made this assertion, Alice couldn't remember. "I don't recall," became her common, whispered reply to numerous questions she'd answered previously.

In the newspaper, an image of Alice was printed and below it was a caption headed with HER MEMORY GONE. Below it, the rest of the caption read, "This is Alice Blake, who now, on the second trial of Fatty Arbuckle, forgets everything that happened at the famous party."

Zey Prevost was even less helpful for the prosecution. On the stand, she recanted her testimony from the first trial and the grand jury and police court hearings. She now said she never heard Virginia say, "He hurt me." When Assistant D.A. Friedman pressed her on previous statements under oath, she answered, "I did not remember. I'm telling the truth now."

To Roscoe's attorney, McNab, she explained that Brady's team wanted her to sign an affidavit saying that Virginia said, "I'm dying. He killed me," and when she refused, she was locked in a cell and threatened with jail time before she finally signed it. She told the jury, "I told Mr. U'Ren that I didn't remember Virginia saying anything of the kind, but that if he said that she said it, it was all right."

D.A. Brady asked the court to declare Zey a hostile witness so that the state could impeach her, but the motion was denied. The next day, the *New York Times* led with: "The case against Roscoe "Fatty" Arbuckle seemingly went to pieces today with the examination of Miss Zey Prevost, a show girl, who had been one of the state's star witnesses."

Rumors that Brady would drop the case in the wake of her testimony were denied, but two days after she testified, the state called the clerk who took her original statement to the stand. The defense objected and it was sustained.

When Edward Heinrich returned with the hallway door to room 1219 and explained the science of fingerprints, McNab against jabbed at him for calling himself "Sherlock Holmes" and got him to admit that fingerprints could be planted.

Warden Woolard from the "Los Angeles Times," who broke the news of Virginia's death to Roscoe

Warden Woolard, the *Los Angeles Times* reporter who broke the news of Virginia's death to Roscoe, testified that the actor denied having hurt her but admitted he "pushed her down on the bed to keep her quiet" when she was in pain. Because of the contradictions between Woolard's account and what Roscoe said on September 9 – saying he was never alone with Virginia – and his testimony from the first trial, the state had Roscoe's entire testimony read into the record. This triggered the defense to announce with a shrug that they no longer needed to call Roscoe to the stand.

When the defense opened, they brought in two experts to contradict the testimony of Heinrich, which they hadn't been able to do in the first trial. The experts were Adolph Juel and Milton Carlson, and the state immediately challenged their credentials. The wrangling over Juel's credentials went on for more than an hour, despite the fact that he was employed as a fingerprint expert by the San Francisco Police Department and had testified in prior cases for the same district attorney's office that was now objected to him. Eventually, both Juel and Carlson were allowed to take the stand, expressing doubts that the prints on the door were those of Roscoe and Virginia.

Fred Fishback returned as a defense witness and while being cross-examined, he forgot some of the answers that he'd previously given.

An employee of Henry Lehrman's studio disputed Jesse Norgaard's claim that Roscoe tried to get the key to Virginia's dressing room.

Dr. Rosenberg's statement about treating Virginia in Chicago was read into evidence again, and other doctors testified that distended bladders could spontaneously rupture. As in the first trial, the defense tried unsuccessfully to get the St. Francis hotel detective's recollection of a conversation with Virginia into the record.

When the maid Kate Brennan returned to speak about thoroughly cleaning the room before Heinrich's examination, she became embroiled in a new legal subplot. The state petitioned to have all her testimony stricken from the record by presenting evidence that she spent 1909 to 1920 locked in an asylum because of mental illness that was never cured. The judge denied the request, but this allowed arguments about Brennan's mental faculties.

The defense claimed it wanted to call Irene Morgan, famous for her alleged poisoning, but had failed to locate her after three weeks of searching. They did recall Florence Bates, who retold the story of an agonized Virginia violently tearing her clothes off in a Chicago department store in 1913.

There were also new witnesses called to speak about Virginia's past, including a screenwriter named Eugene Presbrey who stated that Virginia went into convulsions at the Hollywood Hotel in March 1917 after drinking two glasses of wine.

A café owner named J.M. Covington said that Virginia and Henry Lehrman argued in his establishment in May 1918 and that after drinking liquor, the actress went outside "tearing her clothes and shrieking in pain."

Helen Barrie testified to being at a party on April 22, 1921, at the home of a film director, and that after a few drinks "Miss Rappe threw herself down on a divan and tore at her clothing."

Annie Portwell, resident of the Selma ranch where Al Semnacher, Maude Delmont, and Virginia stopped on their way to San Francisco, testified, "We were out riding in my car when Miss Rappe said, 'Please stop the car if you do not want me to die.' She left the car all doubled up and drank a quantity of dark-colored liquor from a gin bottle. She said it was herb tea." The bottle was introduced into evidence.

The last witness called by the defense was the state's leading attack dog, Assistant D.A. Milton U'Ren, but the questions he was asked only pertained to what U'Ren knew about the fingerprints on the door to room 1219.

When the defense finished its case, the state began calling rebuttal witnesses. Two fingerprint experts affirmed the prints on the door belonged to Roscoe and Virginia.

An asylum superintendent confirmed that Kate Brennan had been an inmate.

A doctor claimed that the rupture of Virginia's bladder could have occurred unrelated to the chronic condition she had.

Kate Hardebeck said that the liquid in the bottle Annie Portwell had testified about was indeed tea, and she spoke again about Virginia's "excellence of health" – a claim that was damaged when the defense got her to admit that Virginia had been treated by a doctor.

The state called the assistant manager of the Mandel Brothers department store in Chicago, who presented employment records showing that Virginia and Florence Bates didn't work at the store when Virginia suddenly disrobed there in 1913. When recalled to the stand, Florence denied that the signature on a 1910 employment application was her own, but the state countered with a handwriting expert who said that it was.

And with that – wrangling over a 12-year-old signature on a Chicago department store employment form – the second Roscoe Arbuckle manslaughter trial sputtered to an end. Even before that, there had been empty seats in the courtroom for the rerun of what had previously been the toughest ticket in town to get.

Things were so anticlimactic this time around that, on Saturday, Judge Louderback even delayed the trial so he could conduct a wedding.

Most of the disinterest came because there seemed to be no promise of fresh scandal. There were no new details and no shocking evidence that was going to lead to the movie star ending up in prison. Newspapers highlighted the weaknesses in the prosecution's case and predicted that Roscoe would be acquitted.

The defense seemed in a hurry to be finished and offered no counter to the state's rebuttal testimony. There was nothing left to do but present the closing arguments.

Those presentations began on Monday with Assistant D.A. U'Ren taking the stage. He began by attacking Roscoe's testimony from the first trial and by pointing fingers at the defense for the testimony of Alice Blake and Zey Prevost, claiming they'd been coached by McNab and his associates. He then cut to the essence of what occurred behind the locked door to room 1219: "The ailment which the defense says resulted in Miss Virginia Rappe's death was of years' standing. It is strange that it should have reached its fatal climax while she was alone in a locked room with Arbuckle. The prosecution has blasted part of the truth out of the lips of Zey Prevost and Alice Blake. What the whole truth is, it is for you to determine. Virginia Rappe entered Arbuckle's room, a well and vigorous girl. A few minutes later, she was in a death agony."

U'Ren spoke for 96 minutes and was followed by a 15-minute recess, during which the defense conferred. "Whatever you do is all right," Roscoe said, lighting a cigarette as he walked away from his attorneys. When court was gaveled back into session, the defense team whispered with Roscoe again before McNab stood and addressed the judge: "If the court please, we have decided that it is unnecessary for us it make an argument. We feel the case is so simple that argument on it would but weary the jurors. We therefore submit it without argument."

Shocked murmurs spread through the courtroom and D.A. Brady was visibly distressed. This strategy cut off the state's rebuttal, for which it had surely saved its strongest arguments, but it also left nothing for the jury to consider aside from McNab's brief statement of confidence.

After instructions from the judge, the case went to the jury at 3:42 P.M. on Wednesday, February 1. Minta sobbed as the jurors left the courtroom.

Two hours later, the jury returned to the courtroom and the participants and spectators rushed back in, anticipating a verdict but instead, they wanted to have the testimony of the eavesdropping housekeeper Josephine Keza read again.

They were back again at 9:30 P.M. but there was still no verdict. They wanted Judge Louderback to reread his instructions to them.

The jury deliberated until 11:00 P.M. before retiring for the night. With absolutely no evidence to base it on, the *Chicago Tribune* claimed on its front page the next day: JURY QUITS FOR THE NIGHT, 11 TO 1 FOR ARBUCKLE. A little suspense was needed for a trial that didn't have much of it to share.

D.A. Brady knew that, too. He told the press when the jury retired for the night: "This is the end. No matter what this jury does, this is final. I'm through with this case for good," he said.

FIFTEEN

ROSCOE ARBUCKLE DIDN'T KNOW IT THEN BUT ON THE SAME day the jury began deliberating his fate, something occurred in Los Angeles was going to overshadow his second trial and move his story to a smaller section of each newspaper's front page.

No one would know what happened until the following morning, February 2, when an African American valet and cook named Henry Peavey entered the home of his employer, director William Desmond Taylor. The bungalow was one of eight homes crowded around a courtyard in the fashionable Westlake District near downtown Los Angeles.

When Peavey found Taylor's lifeless body on the floor, he shrieked, backed out of the house, and yelled for the landlord. He rushed in, accompanied by several neighbors. At first, it was assumed that he died of natural causes – until someone discovered that he'd been shot in the back by a .38-caliber revolver.

Taylor's murder was just about to become a sensation – and it's never been solved. It managed put Fatty Arbuckle's story on the back burner thanks to the entire Hollywood "cast of killers" linked to his death. Depending on what rumor you heard, the murderer might have been an actress who had killed him in a jealous rage, the mother of a child star who was angry that Taylor had

William Desmond Taylor

deflowered her daughter, the husband of a woman Taylor had elevated to stardom in exchange for sex, and even a butler with whom the director was supposedly having a homosexual affair.

Taylor soon proved to be an enigma, which made the gossip spread even faster. As the police began investigating his death, they began uncovering the director's man secrets, which linked him to two of Hollywood's sweetheart screen stars.

There would be many questions, but very few answers, mostly thanks to Paramount Studios executives, who tampered with the crime scene and stayed involved in the police investigation to ensure that anything too damaging slipped through the cracks.

No one wanted another Roscoe Arbuckle-style scandal.

But Paramount couldn't control everything and soon, whispers of sex, drugs, famous actresses began spreading through Hollywood and finding their way into the newspapers. Once again, just like it was with Fatty Arbuckle, the public found itself stunned, horrified, and fascinated by the lurid stories that surrounded the murdered director.

Taylor as a young man, when he was still William Deane-Tanner and had just arrived in America.

TAYLOR WAS BORN WILLIAM CUNNINGHAM DEANE-TANNER IN April 1872, just south of Dublin in Ireland. He was the second of four children born to a British army officer and his Irish society wife. His father ran the household like a military barracks and father and son quarreled often.

When William was 15 years old, he left home and went to England. By 1890, using the name Cunningham Deane, he began performing on the stage. When his father learned his son was engaged in something as disreputable as acting, he sent William to America and enrolled him at Runnymede, a school in Kansas that turned troublesome and wealthy young men into respectable farmers. William was happy to be on his own, but he hated that he was stuck in a university for farmers. As luck would have it, though, the school went bankrupt 18 months after his arrival. Now free to do as he pleased, he decided not to go home. He was going to stay in America.

William went to New York and began earning a living doing manual labor, selling magazines, gambling, and finally, opening a successful little restaurant. But he'd never gotten the acting bug out of his system. In 1895, he returned to the stage. After a few small parts on Broadway, he began touring with actress Fanny Davenport, until her death in 1898 ended that job.

By then, William had met Ethel "Effie" Hamilton, a pretty young chorus girl from a wealthy family. They were married in December 1901 and the following year, their daughter, Ethel Daisy, was born. Effie never returned to the stage and William decided to take up a new line of work to support his family. With a $25,000 loan that he acquired from his in-laws, he bought two eastside Manhattan antique stores and became a great success. He and his wife and daughter moved into a fashionable home in suburban Larchmont, dined in the finest restaurants, and shopped in all the best stores.

In 1908, though, everything fell apart. There was gossip that several vintage items sold in his shops were fake and customers began demanding refunds and a fraud investigation. Worse, an expected inheritance from Effie's uncle never materialized after the elderly uncle married, then died, leaving everything to his new wife. William began drinking heavily and then it was discovered that he had taken a summer trip to the Adirondacks with a woman who was not his wife.

When his father-in-law called in his loans and his wife's attorney emptied his bank accounts, William fled New York after emptying the register in one of the antique stores of $600. He never went back. In 1912, Effie's divorce was final. She later remarried and never saw her ex-husband again.

Initially, William only ran as far as New Jersey. But he gave himself a new name – William Desmond Taylor – and joined a mediocre acting troupe. After the group disbanded, Taylor went west, doing factory work in Chicago, and then gold mining in Colorado and the Yukon. He drank hard, went through a string of women, and seemed destined for a blue-collar but colorful existence.

But he still couldn't shake off the lure of the theater. In San Francisco, he managed to get a

Filmmaker Thomas Ince, who gave Taylor his first break in the movie business.

Taylor was involved with a young, married actress Neva Gerber

leading role in a show and was discovered by filmmaker Thomas Ince. He talked Taylor into coming to Hollywood and appearing in silent pictures.

Taylor worked for Ince for a time and then in 1914, started appearing in movies for Vitagraph. As a side note, when the movie was shown in New York, Taylor's daughter, Ethel Daisy, happened to see it and found her long-lost father.

With film roles few and far between, Taylor began to realize that he was never going to be a star. He was in his mid-40's and nothing special on the screen. He decided that he would try working behind the camera as a director instead.

He was working for the Balboa Amusement Producing Company in Long Beach when he met and fell in love with leading lady Neva Gerber. Unfortunately, Neva was 20 years old, married, had a child, and a much older husband who refused to divorce her. She got involved with Taylor anyway, but the romance soon soured.

Neva learned that Taylor suffered from terrible bouts of depression. Sometimes, after completing a new picture, he left on trips to Northern California and was always vague about where he was going and what he was doing there. Later, when Neva was finally single again, she decided that the troubled director was not exactly "marriage material." However, the two remained close friends.

After Pallas Pictures was bought out, Taylor found himself at Paramount, where he finally found great success.

Taylor's career began to thrive and in the middle 1910s, he switched studios again. Taylor was brought to Pallas Pictures by Julia Crawford Ivers, a screenwriter, producer, and director. When Pallas was bought out by Paramount, Julia and Taylor often worked together and maintained a close friendship, even though Julia wanted it to be something more. For whatever reason, romance never blossomed between them.

At Paramount, Taylor became very successful, directing a steady stream of major pictures. But then in 1917, he asked for time off from the studio to join the Canadian Army and serve in World War I. By August 1918, he was based in Nova Scotia for military training and then shipped out to England. Although the war was over by the time he arrived, the filmmaker asked to be stationed in France until his discharge. By the spring of 1919, he had risen to the rank of major.

Taylor in uniform during World War I, when he served in the Canadian Army

Taylor returned to Hollywood later that year and got right back to work for Paramount. One of his first major films was *Anne of Green Gables*, starring child actress Mary Miles Minter.

He was named to the position of president for the Motion Pictures Directors Association and settled into an affluent Hollywood life. He moved from the Los Angeles Athletic Club to one of eight bungalows that made up Alvarado Court. Popular among movie insiders, others who lived at Alvarado Court included comedy actor Douglas MacLean, and his wife, who were members of Taylor's social circle.

Taylor hired staff to run his household, including Edward F. Sands as a combination secretary, valet, and cook, and Earl Tiffany, who often worked as his driver.

During the spring of 1921, Taylor had surgery and went abroad in June to recover. While he was away, he loaned out his bungalow to playwright Edward Knoblock in exchange for the writer's London apartment. To make sure that his guest was comfortable, Taylor

The valet, cook, and secretary who betrayed Taylor's trust, Edward Sands

Two of the women in Taylor's life – Mabel Normand (Left), who was a close friend, and Mary Miles Minter (Right), who was in love with the much-older director – much to her mother's disapproval.

foolishly left a signed blank check for Edward Sands to use in case of an emergency. While his employer was away, Sands not only cashed the check in the amount of $5,000, but he also forged several smaller checks from Taylor's accounts. A week before Taylor returned home, Sands vanished. When he arrived home, Taylor discovered that, in addition to the missing funds, Sands had also stolen much of his wardrobe, some jewelry, many personal items, and an automobile, which was later found wrecked. Taylor filed a report with the police and then, a few months later, he received a letter from Sands, half-heartedly apologizing for what he had done. The note also contained two pawn tickets for diamond cuff links that had been given to the director as a gift. Sand's job at Taylor's home was taken over by Henry Peavey.

The diamond cuff links had been a gift from a mutual friend of Roscoe Arbuckle's – Mabel Normand. By then, Mabel had signed with Samuel Goldwyn to make feature films and had also developed an alcohol and cocaine habit, as evidenced by her stay in a New York sanitarium in late 1920 for a "nervous breakdown." But she and Taylor were close friends, and the director was sympathetic to her drug problem. He tried to keep her off drugs and keep her away from the

Taylor's home at Alvarado Court and (Right) his
valet and cook, Henry Peavy, who discovered
Taylor's body on the morning of February 2.

dealers who were feeding her dangerous
and -- if the public found out -- scandalous habit.

Another woman in Taylor's complicated life was Mary Miles
Minter, who by 1922 was 19 years old. Taylor had directed Mary in three
features, and the young girl had fallen deeply in love with him. Under
the watchful eye of her controlling stage mother, Charlotte Selby, Mary
saw Taylor as both a father figure and a dashing hero. She fantasized
about marrying him and she continually pursued him, despite his
efforts to dissuade her.

On the night of February 1, 1922, Taylor spent the evening at his
home, working on his income taxes from the previous year at his desk
in the living room. Henry Peavey later told the police that he
summoned Taylor to dinner at around 6:30 P.M.

The director was eating when he received a telephone call. He
was still engaged in this conversation – no one knows who was on the
line with him – when Mabel Normand stopped by to pick up two
books that Taylor had recently purchased for her. Mabel was an avid
reader, and the pair often got together to discuss the books they were
reading.

Peavey opened the door for Mabel at the same time Taylor hung
up the telephone. Henry then mixed two cocktails for the pair.

At 7:30, Peavey left for the evening and on his way out, he stopped
to chat with Mabel's driver for a few minutes. When he left the house,
Taylor and Mabel were sitting on the sofa, talking and sipping their
drinks. Mabel later said that she left the bungalow a little before 8:00
P.M. Taylor walked her to the car, leaving the front door open behind

Taylor's Alvarado Court neighbor, Edna Purviance

him. She waved as her driver pulled away from the curb and Taylor returned to the house.

Four hours later, at almost precisely midnight, actress Edna Purviance, who also lived in Alvarado Court, returned home and noticed all the lights were still on at Taylor's home. She thought of stopping for a nightcap but then decided it was too late for a visit.

No one saw Taylor again until Henry Peavey found his body the next morning.

As the news spread around Alvarado Court, several residents hurried to Taylor's house and rushed inside, which hopelessly contaminated the crime scene.

When Taylor's new driver. Howard Fellows, arrived he telephoned his brother, Harry, an assistant director who worked with Taylor at Paramount. Harry contacted Charles Eyton, Paramount's general manager, and gave him the bad news. Eyton immediately ordered Harry, Julia Crawford Ivers and her son, James, who was Taylor's cinematographer, to go directly to Taylor's bungalow. He instructed them to remove anything that might damage the director's reputation, which, of course, could make the studio look bad – like the Arbuckle case had done.

At this point, no one had called the police.

Julia, James, and Harry hurried to the bungalow and gathered up anything they could find that might make Taylor look bad. They took letters written to Taylor from Mabel Normand, Mary Miles Minter, and Neva Gerber, as well as notes from Ethel Daisy to her father. They also removed all bootleg liquor from the house. It was all stashed in Harry's car.

Finally, they called the police.

Once detectives arrived, they began questioning the staff and the neighbors. Shortly after that, Paramount boss Charles Eyton arrived. The police greeted him and didn't stop him from going into the house to look around. They didn't ask him any questions when he came out and never checked to see if he'd moved anything or had taken anything from the crime scene.

The next to arrive were the deputy coroner and his assistant and it was only then that it was discovered that Taylor had been shot in the back. This was a surprise to everyone at the scene, prompting a call to the LAPD's homicide squad.

Why was everyone so surprised? The first officers at the scene believed that Taylor had died of a stomach hemorrhage. They came to this conclusion because a "doctor" had earlier been in the neighborhood, allegedly making a house call, and came by to see

The room where Taylor's body was found. It wasn't until the police arrived that it was discovered that he'd been shot to death

what all the excitement was about. Without turning the body over, the doctor offered his snap diagnosis. The police made a note of it but failed to obtain the man's name. The physician – if he really was one -- left the scene and was never heard from again.

A horde of reporters descended on Alvarado Court and a flurry of wild accusations, rumors, crazy theories, and outright lies began appearing in the press. As with the Arbuckle scandal, the reporters weren't about to let the story get derailed by the truth.

Rumors, gossip, and newspaper stories – which were all about the same since no one really knew anything -- insisted the killer had to be the missing Edward Sands, a theory that was eventually dismissed.

For a time, journalists also theorized that Henry Peavey was the culprit. Since he was African American and a homosexual, he was an easy target. On the day after the murder, Taylor had been scheduled to appear in court on Peavey's behalf in a sexual misconduct allegation. Because of this, it was hinted by the media that Taylor might also have been gay and that this might have something to do with his murder. Peavey was eventually cleared by the police but rumors of Taylor being a homosexual –or at least bisexual – have never gone away.

With rumors and innuendo running rampant, it was hard to tell what was fiction and what was fact. Taylor's closest neighbors, the MacLeans, told the police that their maid heard someone in the alley between their house and Taylor's after 7:00 on the night of the murder.

L.A. District Attorney Thomas Woolwine, who had close ties to the major players in the movie industry

Later, when Mrs. MacLean heard a noise that sounded like a car backfiring, she had looked outside and saw a person leave Taylor's bungalow and walk calmly away. She described this person as a "roughly dressed man," wearing a cap and a scarf.

However, this lead went nowhere. It was discovered that a friend had borrowed Taylor's car for the evening and had returned it to his house that night. After parking it in the garage, he went to the door, but when he got no reply, he left. The police believed that he was the figure seen by Mrs. MacLean that night.

The investigation was further muddled by L.A. District Attorney Thomas Woolwine, who had close ties to the major players in the movie industry. One newspaper accused the district attorney of "erecting a barricade of silence between the searchers for truth and the truth itself."

Everything about the investigation was poorly handled, even purposely hamstrung, to try and protect Taylor and the studio. It also

Mary Miles Minster (Left) and the note that she wrote to Taylor (Left), which was discovered by investigators and became a scandal

EXTRA EVENING HERALD **LATEST NEWS**

LOS ANGELES

The Evening Herald Grows Just Like Los Angeles

VOL. XLVII. THURSDAY, FEBRUARY 2, 1922 THREE CENTS NO. 80

MYSTERY GUNMAN KILLS
FILM DIRECTOR TAYLOR

28 KILLED AS BLAST WRECKS MINE, IS REPORT

52 Cardinals Meet to Name New Pontiff

Arbuckle Jurors Still Held Up

REVENGE MOTIVE IN SLAYING IS BELIEF; HUNT EX-EMPLOYE

didn't help that some of the witnesses withheld information to protect their own reputations – no one wanted to be another Roscoe Arbuckle. That included Mabel Normand, who downplayed her friendship with Taylor and was deliberately vague about her cocaine habit and Taylor's efforts to help her stay clean.

But nothing, of course, hurt the investigation as much as the newspapers did. In a rush for lurid headlines, journalists were quick to report the discovery of Mary Miles Winter's monogrammed pink "lingerie" at Taylor's house. The young actress denied that she'd left any undergarments there and the "lingerie" turned out to be a monogrammed handkerchief that she had once loaned him.

But stories about lingerie suggested to the public that the supposedly innocent Mary and the much-older director were having a clandestine romance. This rumor was bolstered by a note that was discovered tucked inside a book from Taylor's well-stocked library.

On the stationary were the initials M.M.M. The letter read:

Dearest, I love you. I love you. I love you.
XXXXXXXXXXXXXX
Yours always, Mary

When Mary was questioned about this, she admitted, "I did love William Desmond Taylor, I loved him deeply and tenderly, with all of the admiration that a young girl gives to a man with the poise and position of Mr. Taylor."

She portrayed it as the love a young woman would show toward a father, but Taylor's closest friends knew that Mary been head-over-heels about him for a long time. Taylor had tried to discourage the crush and there is nothing that suggests their relationship was ever sexual.

But that didn't stop the rumors, and Mary didn't help to discourage them. At Taylor's crowded funeral, Mary approached the director's casket and kissed his corpse full on the lips. She then caused a stir in the room as she loudly announced that the corpse had spoken to her. "He whispered something to me," she said, "it sounded like 'I shall love you always, Mary!'"

The scandal had already damaged her career, but this bit of theatrics made sure it never recovered.

The coroner's inquest was held on February 4, 1922, and lasted less than an hour. Not all the witnesses on hand were called to testify. The coroner's jury quickly concluded that the director's death had been caused by a gunshot wound "by some person or persons unknown to this jury."

Charlotte Shelby, the mother of Mary Miles Minter, was one of the many suspects that emerged in Taylor's murder

Reporters weren't impressed and many suggested that the poorly managed murder investigation was nothing more than a series of contrivances used to silence any potential scandals. An article in the *Chicago Tribune* stated: "Twenty people are said to be under suspicion. Twenty thousand theories of the crime are being aired, but there has not been one arrest and not one clue. It is believed that movie interests would spend a million not to catch the murderer, to prevent the real truth from coming out."

Worried about this perception, Paramount executives established a special committee that, it was announced, would help the press establish the facts of the case. In reality, though, it had been created to get everyone to forget about the case as quickly as possible. A few reporters who didn't bow to pressure from the special committee claimed to be intimidated by the Los Angeles police.

The case was never officially resolved and as the years passed, bits of truth continued to emerge, lost among the stories, rumors, and Hollywood legends. Speculation included the idea that Taylor was murdered by a hired killer who was working for one of the drug dealers servicing Mabel Normand.

Friends of Taylor claimed he had appealed to the U.S. Attorney a short time before his death to try and combat a narcotics ring that was selling cocaine to Normand. A dozen known addicts and dealers were questioned and detectives even traveled to Folsom Prison to question two convicts that the warden implicated in Taylor's murder. One of them said that the other had killed the director at the urging of "a well-known actress" who resented Taylor for interfering with her dope supply. After more investigation, however, detectives became convinced the convicts were lying in hopes of getting transferred to a minimum-security facility.

But it is true that the most popular murder theories have involved Mabel Normand and Mary Miles Minter, one or the other of whom were said to have murdered Taylor during a lover's spat. Another bit of guesswork suggests the killer was Mary's manipulative mother, who was also a jealous rival for the director's love.

Mabel's career weas damaged by the Taylor scandal, as well as by another incident that occurred shortly afterward involving her chauffeur and the murder of a Hollywood playboy. She made a few additional films but by then, her drug abuse had ruined her health. She died in 1930 from tuberculosis and pneumonia.

Mary Miles Minter retired permanently from the screen in 1924. She spent the next few decades feuding with her overbearing mother who finally died, leaving Mary in peace, in 1957. Mary died a recluse in 1984.

The deaths of those rumored to be involved in the murder didn't end the speculation or the odd stories that still circulate about the case more than a century later.

District Attorney Woolwine, the man who probably knew more about the case than anyone else, resigned due to poor health and died soon after.

In 1926, his successor, Asa Keyes, re-opened the Taylor case and announced that an arrest was imminent. But the arrest never happened. Why? Keyes claimed that vital evidence, kept in a locked cabinet in his office, "mysterious vanished." The case went cold once again. Keyes later died after going to prison for accepting a bribe in a million-dollar oil scandal.

In 1929, the mystery was resurrected again when F.W. Richardson, a former California governor, stated that back in 1926 he had received "positive information" that a "certain top screen actress" had killed Taylor, but he was unable to do anything about it because of the corrupt conditions that existed in the L.APD at the time. Richardson implied that the film industry had bribed officials to "bury the investigation." But nothing ever came of Richardson's startling announcement.

In 1943, a man arrested on federal narcotics charges in Indiana offered to name William Desmond Taylor's killer in return for immunity. The government refused to make the deal, and the man remained silent and died of pneumonia in the prison hospital.

At that point, the case had become so cold that it was largely forgotten. From time to time, writers, reporters, and retired cops have come forward and claimed the killer was known to the authorities at the time, but no one could do anything about it. Some have spoken mysteriously of an "actress" or an "actor" who was involved, but no definitive proof has ever been offered.

BUT IN 1922, IT WAS BIG NEWS AND THE SCANDAL GENERATED hundreds of newspaper stories and outraged editorials about the dangers and depravity of Hollywood. Calls for censorship increased, and front-page stories about the ever-widening mystery of Taylor's murder snagged much of the outrage and attention that had been focused on Roscoe Arbuckle.

Roscoe and Taylor had been acquaintances. They both worked for Paramount and had attended the same social and business events for years. While the jury was deliberating on February 2, a reporter broke the news to Roscoe that the director had been murdered.

"Taylor was the best fellow on the lot," Roscoe said, his eyes watering. "He was beloved by everybody, and his loss is a shock. I cannot understand why anyone would wish to murder him as he is the last man in the world to make an enemy."

Sadly, the same thing might have once been said about Roscoe Arbuckle himself.

AT 10:00 A.M. ON THE MORNING THAT TAYLOR'S BODY WAS found, the jury began its second day of deliberation in the manslaughter case. Shortly before noon, the jury asked for the trial transcript, followed by more silence.

Throughout the day, Roscoe was seen pacing the corridor outside the courtroom, smoking, chatting with reporters, or talking to Minta. In a front-page story titled, "Arbuckle Abandons Hope," the *Los Angeles Times* claimed he had given up on a verdict.

ARBUCKLE JURY FAILS TC AGREE; DISCHARGED

for Acquittal of Film Comedian—Woma
kle Willing to Rest Ca
onfidence of Fairness
Out 41 Hours—Retrial D

41 hours of deliberation th
er tried Roscoe Arbuckle on a
Virginia Rap

Deliberation was cut short that evening when one of the jurors became sick. Also, that evening, Maude Delmont, under probation for bigamy and presumably having legally untangled herself from her previous marriages, announced her engagement to a vaudeville actor. They were in Lincoln, Nebraska, where she was said to be "attending to business matter." The engagement made news across the country.

At 1:30 A.M. on Friday, February 3, the jurors returned to the courtroom and the audience scrambled to fill the seats in the courtroom before the proceedings were called to order. More than 44 hours after getting the case, the jury was hopelessly deadlocked. The first 10 ballots had been nine to three. The last four were ten to two.

But the reports had been wrong – the majority had not been for acquittal. Ultimately, 10 of the 12 jurors had voted Roscoe guilty of manslaughter.

Roscoe was shocked, as were his attorneys and the prosecution. A buzz of surprised muttering filled the courtroom. Minta loudly burst into tears.

The two men who had voted for acquittal on all 14 ballots, declined to speak with reporters. Other jurors said plenty, revealing that the defense's crucial mistake had been when they overconfidently declined making a final argument.

One said, "the jurors believed that the defense's failure to argue was due to fear of Prosecutor Friedman, whose argument was cut off by the defense action."

Another juror told the press: "The defense presented a very weak case. Its failure to argue the case counted greatly against it. The fact that Arbuckle did not take the stand had no effect on us."

That may have been true, but a third juror said, "From the reading of Arbuckle's testimony at the last trial, the majority of the jury believed that his story was contradictory."

There's no doubt that their observations were correct. Guilty or not guilty, Roscoe should have taken the stand in the second trial to answer the contradictions and to present himself as a believable witness. Without making a closing argument, the defense also failed to argue what the state had highlighted as the problems with Roscoe's story.

It was a big mistake, but McNab tried to make the best of things by using some creative math to focus on the votes and adding in the two alternate jurors, who both said they would have voted for acquittal. It seemed like a more palatable loss when he recalled those who'd voted for acquittal in the first trial.

D.A. Brady wasn't buying it: "Had the majority of the jury been in favor of an acquittal, I would have asked for a dismissal. As the jury stood ten for conviction and two for acquittal, it is manifestly my duty to try this case again."

Roscoe claimed that he wasn't as discouraged by a third trial as he undoubtedly was. He told the press, "In this life, you've got to take a punch now and then. I am ready to go to trial again. I feel sure that I shall be able to prove my innocence of this charge at another trial."

But the punches Roscoe had taken – too hard and too many of them – had taken a toll on him that he wasn't yet ready to admit.

✒IXTEEN

ROSCOE ARBUCKLE'S THIRD MANSLAUGHTER TRIAL WAS scheduled for March 16, but before it could begin, there were signs that this would not be like the first two trials.

Just four days after the second trial ended, a newspaper story quoted a Chicago attorney named Albert Sabath, who, acting on behalf of the defense, had acquired a deposition from a new witness who could testify about Virginia Rappe's past. Sabath told a reporter, "The vote of ten to two for conviction by the last jury ended the defense policy of shielding Miss Rappe. It appears almost impossible to free Arbuckle and at the same time street the testimony clear of the facts about Miss Rappe's condition. We must show the kind of life which she had led."

And that wasn't all. Not surprisingly, Zey Prevost had vanished again after the second trial. Unwilling to testify a third time, she skipped town and on February 14, was reportedly checked into a hotel in New Orleans. She checked in under the name Zabelle Elruy, with no given address, and while denying to newspaper reporters that she was Zey Prevost, she claimed she was leaving soon for Cuba. New of her presence leaked and soon, detectives were at the hotel with authority from San Francisco to arrest her. But while the cops were waiting in the lobby, Zey tied together bed sheets and escaped out of her third-floor window to a courtyard below.

It seemed like a smart thing to do for Zey. She had been held for seven weeks in a stranger's house before the first Arbuckle trial, impeached in the second trial, repeatedly ridiculed in the press, and faced a possible perjury charge from the San Francisco district attorney. Climbing out of a window seemed the most rational thing for her to do if it meant dodging those staked out in the lobby – both the reporters and the policemen who wanted to extradite her back to San Francisco for yet another trial. She vanished again and the search for the prosecutions sort-of star witness continued, stretching now all the way to Cuba.

Zey's biggest fear was that potential perjury charge. The prosecution knew that the earlier perjury charge – the one against Minnie Neighbors – had effectively eliminated one defense witness and had potentially frightened away others. So even though the charge against her had been dismissed, they brought another. Before jury selection in the third trial, a grand jury indicted both Minnie and Florence Bates for perjury. Ultimately, neither woman was tried, but neither woman testified again.

D.A. Brady's "dirty trick" perjury charge had worked. With what had become a volatile case, no one – telling the truth or not – wanted to take the chance.

It was purported that Henry Lehrman was in San Francisco at the start of the third trial, meeting with the prosecution, and possibly preparing to take the stand and defend the honor of his "fiancée." But if this was true, he never appeared in the courtroom as a witness or a spectator. Three days before the trial ended, Lehrman – who was still allegedly grieving for Virginia – announced his engagement to a 19-year-old Ziegfeld Follies dancer. They were married 17 days later and then divorced 20 volatile months later.

ON MARCH 16, AFTER QUESTIONING A POOL OF 51 PEOPLE, A jury of eight men and four women was seated for the third trial. Once again, Judge Louderback ordered them to be sequestered in a hotel during the trial. But then, soon after opening statements began, the state tried to remove juror Edward Brown because the grocer had twice been prosecuted for violating pure food laws and could be prejudiced against the district attorney. But the judge blamed the D.A. for not striking him from the jury and because Brown had already been sworn in, he stayed. He even served as the jury foreman, which must have had Brady steaming.

The prosecution called five doctors, including Ophuls, Wakefield, and Beardslee, to discuss Virginia's condition before and after her death. But the defense was determined not to merely repeat the previous two trials for a new audience. During cross-examination, they delved into the health of Virginia's bladder and urethra to get the doctors to admit that an inflammation in the former may have caused a constricting of the latter, and that a resulting inability to urinate may have caused her bladder, which was predisposed to become distended, to rupture.

TWELVE TO DECIDE COMEDIAN'S FATE

The jury chosen for Roscoe's thirds manslaughter trial

The still reluctant witness, Alice Blake, recounted her version of events for the sixth time and her memory was still hazy, and under cross-examination, she burst into tears. The defense scored points when Alice could remember seeing Virginia and Roscoe enter room 1219 nor Virginia subsequently saying, "He hurt me." She also said that the pair were in the room alone for no more than 15 minutes.

Alice's fellow "star witness," Zey Prevost, was found again in New Orleans – she'd never gone to Cuba – and was arrested. She sent a telegram to Brady that read, "If you want me to appear as witness in the Arbuckle case wire me ticket and I will come immediately." Brady sent the money, but Zey then claimed she became sick just before the train's departure and didn't know when she would be well enough to travel. She never recovered – until the trial ended, that is.

Nurse Grace Halston testified again and, after strong defense objections, described in detail the bruises she had seen on Virginia's body. A police photographer then presented photos of the bruises. When one photo showing Virginia's lifeless face was presented, Roscoe looked away.

Friday, March 24, was Roscoe's 35th birthday, which he spent in the courtroom listening to Zey Prevost's previous testimony being read into record and other prosecution witnesses retelling their stories from earlier trials – Dr. Rumwell and Dr. Strange on Virginia's autopsies, Dr. Castle on Virginia's medical treatment at Wakefield Sanitarium, and the always crowd-pleasing housekeeper Josephine Keza, who under defense cross-examination suddenly announced, "I don't think I'll answer any more questions." This, of course, got a big laugh.

Roscoe received birthday telegrams and presents from fans and, during recesses, well-wishes from many of the spectators in the courtroom.

One of the presents he received was a fancy checkbook from an unknown admirer. Roscoe quipped, "I don't see why I should be sent a checkbook. I haven't money enough anymore even to make out one check, much less a whole book."

This was obviously meant as a joke but on Sunday, the headline ARBUCKLE IS BROKE appeared on front pages across the country.

The state continued to bring back witnesses from the earlier trials, like Warden Woolard, fingerprint examiner Edward Heinrich, Kate Hardebeck, and studio security guard Jess Norgaard. When the defense brought up Norgaard's recent arrest for escaping from a prison chain gang in 1918 – he'd been arrested for selling booze to soldiers – the prosecution objected, calling McNab a "shyster." When McNab replied with a similar insult, Judge Louderback told both sides they were close to being held in contempt.

The prosecution's case continued to follow the same pattern as the second trial, although it was a bit more contentious since the defense could more easily challenge the weaknesses of the witnesses they had come to know. Even so, it seemed the state planned to rely on its nearly winning strategy of weeks earlier, but then D.A. Brady produced a surprise final witness – one that no one had heard of before. Her name was Virginia Breig, and she was a secretary at the Wakefield Sanitarium.

She had a story that was potentially devastating to Roscoe.

Breig claimed that she had visited Virginia on the day she died. "She asked me about the amount of the bill that would be due," the secretary said of the feeble Virginia. "She said that she did not see why she would pay the bill as Arbuckle was response for her being there. I told her that if Arbuckle or anyone else should pay the account after she left, the money paid by her would be returned. She replied that she was not going to leave, that she was going to die. Then I asked her why she thought she was going to die. It was then that she told me the details of the party."

And this was the clincher. According to Breig, the dying young woman said, "Arbuckle took me by the arm and threw me on the bed and put his weight on me, and after that I do not know what happened."

Brady finally had what he needed – a witness that heard Virgina say that Roscoe committed a specific act that could have caused her bladder to burst.

McNab was immediately out of his seat. He asked if Breig had telephoned Arbuckle asking him to pay Virginia's bill, with the threat that if he didn't, she would tell her story to the district attorney. Breig denied this.

He asked why she had kept this story to herself until that Monday – six and a half months after Virginia's death. She said she wanted to avoid the notoriety and had been summoned to testify only two days earlier.

McNab moved to have Virginia's alleged deathbed accusation, as told by Virginia Brieg, stricken from the record as hearsay, but the judge denied the motion.

WHEN THE DEFENSE'S PROMISED DESTRUCTION OF VIRGINIA'S character began, it turned out to be less than advertised. The defense did win some early headlines, though, when Chicago nurse Virginia Warren stated that Virginia gave birth to a premature baby during bladder trauma in 1910. But then she stumbled during cross-examination when her nursing credentials were challenged because she'd changed her name and couldn't remember what name she'd used on her license.

Most of another day was filled reading a deposition from Chicago medical personnel about a younger Virginia's bladder and abdominal pains. The state managed to get one of the depositions struck from the record when the doctor was uncertain if the girl he remembered was Virginia.

But the most damning deposition was that of Josephine Rafferty, who was probably the "surprise witness" that Albert Sabath was talking about when he spoke of showing the kind of life which Virginia led.

In the deposition, Rafferty said:

I first saw Virginia Rappe in February 1908 in my home. I had studied medicine for three years and was a midwife. At that time, Virginia Rappe, then 16, was about to become a mother. Between that time and 1910, Virginia was about to become a mother on four other occasions. I attended her on each occasion. The first time she was very ill. On the next three occasions, I attended her six weeks each time. The first time she was ill a baby was born. Miss Rappe, throughout my attendance of her, was a sufferer from bladder trouble.

If you've read between the lines in this statement, then you understand what was happening at Mrs. Rafferty's house. Virginia had given birth to a premature infant when she was 16 – as recalled by the nurse, Mrs. Warren – but she had returned to see Mrs. Rafferty four more times when she was pregnant, but those pregnancies ended by the six-week mark.

Mrs. Rafferty, the midwife, also performed abortions, which was illegal in Illinois at the time. But the operations being illegal didn't mean that didn't happen and often, under less than sterile conditions.

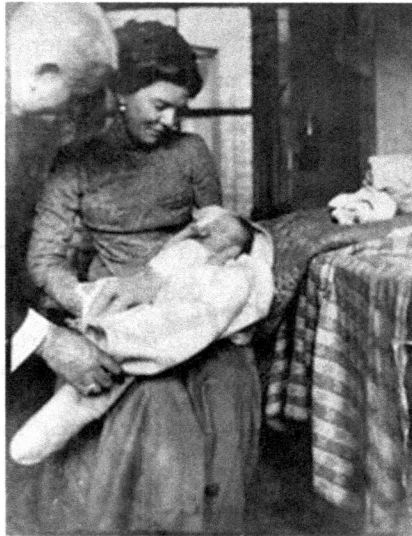

Midwife Josephine Rafferty testified that Virginia had been pregnant at 16 and had returned to her on four occasions for abortions.

Because Rafferty was not called to the stand, the state couldn't cross-examine her, but prosecutors would take shots at her in the closing statements. Friedman treated her with disdain as he stated that "according to her own testimony and the testimony of Mrs. Warren, she was conducting nothing but a house of abortion."

Jess Norgaard's character, still stinging by the defense bringing attention to his recent arrest, took up most of one day when a justice of the peace testified that he could speak to Norgaard's morals but not his integrity, which then caused the trial to veer off into legal quicksand as a dozen authorities and a dictionary were quoted so the prosecution and the defense could try and define "integrity."

Are you surprised to learn that neither side was sure what the word meant?

A screenwriter and two actors took the stand and all recounted Virginia's inability to consume alcohol without experiencing serious pains and tearing off her clothes.

A woman named Helen Whitehurst testified that when she and Virginia were friends in Chicago in 1913, Virginia two similar public attacks at cafes and one at a political campaign dinner.

Two doctors took the stand to explain why the symptoms that Virgina suffered from indicated chronic bladder problems.

Fred Fishback was back, too. This time, though, he couldn't recall much of anything that happened. A headline reads FISHBACK LOSES MEMORY ON THE STAND. He also lost his name a short time later. In the wake of the scandal, he began directing using the name Fred Hibbard – but not for long. He died of lung cancer in 1925 at the age of 30.

The defense had learned from its mistakes in the second trial and the attorneys put Roscoe on the stand at 10:45 A.M. on April 5. He was smiling as he eased his way sideways into the witness box and sat down. Word was out that Roscoe was again taking the stand, which made the trial the toughest show to get into that day. The courtroom was packed for the first time during the third trial, though the press described female audience members as "less enthusiastic" than they were the first time around.

Roscoe retold the story of finding Virginia in the bathroom of 1219 and trying to help her. Asked if Virginia said anything to him, he replied, "Miss Rappe never said a word while I was in the room. She moaned and groaned."

He admitted that he had known Virginia for several years but said he knew none of the other guests at the Labor Day party, other than the friends who traveled from Los Angeles with him. He added that he had never met Jesse Norgaard, who claimed he'd asked for a key to Virginia's dressing room.

Roscoe also denied placing ice on – or inside of -- Virginia and denied placing his hand over hers on the 1219 door. "I was not near that door for the whole time I was in the hotel, except when Miss Rappe was carried from the room," he said, referring to when he carried her part of the way to room 1227.

Roscoe's modest purple bathrobe, which the defense sarcastically referred to as "wicked" – a word stricken after the state objected – was placed into evidence by the defense team.

During the rebuttal, the prosecution brought in a doctor who testified that bladders didn't spontaneously rupture. They also brought in people – friends from Chicago, the Hollywood Hotel manager, a driver she employed – who claimed she was healthy during various times in her life.

Kate Hardebeck testified again that Virginia was mostly in great health, though the state likely regretted calling her when she said Virginia was treated for an unnamed ailment in 1921 and a doctor had advised her to have an operation. She did say, though, that she wasn't aware of Virginia ever being pregnant.

The defense tried to lessen the state's rebuttal by calling Virginia's former boyfriend Harry Barker, who repeated his story of seeing her in pain and tearing off her clothing in Chicago.

They also called a doctor, Charles Barnes, who stated that he had operated on Virginia in Chicago in 1909 for a bladder abscess. A woman claimed to hear Kate Hardebeck saying that Virginia had been ill, and two chauffeurs said Virginia's former driver told them his employer once had an attack in his car.

WHEN PROSECUTOR MILTON U'REN BEGAN HIS CLOSING statements in the third trial, he trotted back out the biblical story of the King Belshazzar, the handwriting on the wall, and the fall of kingdom and death. And while he didn't stick with the religious theme, he did end the first part of his opening by announcing dramatically, "Roscoe Arbuckle's kingdom is ended! He has been weighed in the balances and found wanting! God has finished his kingdom!"

But he returned to reality by focusing on the inconsistencies in Roscoe's story, arguing about the unlikeliness of events behind the locked door of room 1219 happening the way he said they did. He also pointed out how his story was kept secret until the first trial, when he seemingly tailored it to counter the state's witnesses.

U'Ren highlighted how Virginia had seemed fine before spending time in room 1219 with Roscoe, and he returned to the incident with the ice. U'Ren attacked him with that, saying, "Oh, if the mothers of the children of America could have seen Roscoe Arbuckle making such sport of the poor, sick, senseless body of Virginia Rappe! The moral leper made the world laugh? Thank god, he will never make it laugh again!"

Again, avoiding the big mistake of the second trial, the defense delivered a closing statement. Gavin McNab first reiterated the length of Virginia's history of bladder illness and highlighted the medical testimony about bladder ruptures.

And then things got emotional.

When not quoting scripture, he built back the previously damaged reputations of defense witnesses while tearing down the expertise and impartiality of the prosecution witnesses. The object of his greatest scorn was the Wakefield Sanitarium secretary, Virginia Brieg. He pointed out the absurdity of Virginia sharing her deathbed accusation with a "sordid bill collector" only to have that accusation remain secret until the third trial. He also accused Brieg of trying unsuccessfully to extort the defense and then sell out to the prosecution for the cost of a hospital bill.

In conclusion, McNab widened his argument beyond the freedom of his client: "If, through the extraordinary attention to his case, the vile, hideous, and barbarous practices that have prevailed in criminal processes in San Francisco, unknown to the public, are no longer possible, and unfortunates, that are being railroaded to the penitentiary without offense against the law, will have fair trials hereafter, then this prosecution will have served a good purpose and Arbuckle will be repaid."

The prosecution, of course, got the last word, delivered by Milton Friedman, who said as he began, "Mr. McNab, who is so quick to invoke the scriptures, who so gladly calls down the Ten Commandments to his aid, forgets that there is one which reads 'Thou shalt not kill,' He also beautifully eulogizes womanhood, then blasts and damns every woman appeared in this case, including his own witnesses."

Friedman criticized the claim that the state had coached Alice Blake and Zey Prevost, and he belittled much of the medical testimony, saying it made no difference why Virginia's bladder was distended. He argued that Virginia was too young for multiple pregnancies in and before 1908, even though she wasn't – she turned 17 that year. But mostly he again spelled out the state's version of what happened in room 1219, stating it was the only logical explanation for why Virginia's life ended.

Roscoe Arbuckle, he said, forced Virginia onto the bed, "three his weight upon her, her bladder ruptured, and she passed into a state of unconsciousness. With do not claim – with all the talk of disarranging clothes – we do not claim that he consummated his purpose. We claim that he attempted to accomplish a purpose, to fulfill a desire, and that his attempt resulted in the death of this girl."

THE JUDGE'S INSTRUCTIONS WERE GIVEN TO THE JURY AND THEY filed out of the room. There were no predictions made this time. There was no talk of them making them the correct decision – or any decision at all. After two deadlocks – each with a larger vote count in opposite directions – no one could be confident about anything.

The third jury left the courtroom at 5:10 P.M. on Wednesday, April 12 – and at 5:15 P.M., a knock was heard from the same door they had left through. To the astonishment of everyone in the courtroom, the jury had reached a verdict. An announcement was made and spectators who had left for a break rushed back in, refilling the seats and standing where they could. As the bailiff took a folded paper on which the verdict was written from foreman Edward Brown, Judge Louderback warned the audience about outbursts.

The judge looked at the paper, folded it, and asked the foreman of the jury had reached its verdict.

"We have, your honor," Brown replied.

"And how do you find the defendant on the charge of manslaughter?" the judge asked.

Brown answered that the jury found the defendant, "Not guilty."

Roscoe let out a huge sigh and Minta began to sob quietly. After the judge gaveled the case to a close and retired to his chambers, the audience erupted into a cheer. People stood on their chairs and pressed against the railing, hoping to see Roscoe as he hurried to the jury box. He shook hands with the jurors, who crowded around him, patted him on the back, and affirmed their belief in his innocence as some of them dabbed away tears.

Then Roscoe, his attorneys, and the jurors pushed through the swarming, congratulating crowd and entered the jury room. A statement was then read for the benefit of the press. It had been signed by each of the 12 jurors and the two alternates. As camera flashes exploded, foreman Edward Brown read it aloud:

Acquittal is not enough for Roscoe Arbuckle.

We feel that a great injustice has been done him. We feel also that it was only our plain duty to give him this exoneration, under the evidence, for their was not the slightest proof adduced to connect him in any way with the commission of this crime. He was manly throughout the case, and told a straightforward story on the witness stand, which we all believed. The happening at the hotel was an unfortunate affair for which Arbuckle, so the evidence shows, was in no way responsible.

We wish him success, and hope that the American people will take the judgement of fourteen men and women who have sat listening for thirty-ones days to the evidence that Roscoe Arbuckle is entirely innocent and free from all blame.

While technically acquittal merely meant that the state did not prove Roscoe guilty beyond a reasonable doubt, this unusual post-trial statement went much further than that – declaring Roscoe "entirely innocent and free from all blame," and it asked the American people to believe it.

The jury hadn't had time to draft the document during their few minutes in the jury room, so it was likely written before the verdict. While many believe it was likely written by Roscoe's attorneys or

EXONERATED OF MANSLAUGHTER

Roscoe Arbuckle and Virginia Rappe.

It took a mixed jury less than one minute to arrive at a verdict of not guilty, and five more minutes to reduce it to paper, in the third trial of Roscoe Arbuckle, charged with the death of Miss Virginia Rappe.

possibly movie producers hoping to revive his career, there's no evidence of that. All we do know is that all the jurors signed it and stood behind it.

District Attorney Brady issued his own statement, saying, "I am an American citizen, and I take off my hat to the verdict of an American jury. The district attorney's office had done what it deemed to be its duty in this case, nothing more or less. And I intend to always do my duty as I see it."

Brady never ran for higher office, as was expected. Perhaps three trials and a loss took the steam out of his plans, no one knows. Regardless, he remained San Francisco D.A. until he was defeated in 1943 by future California governor Pat Brown.

Brady's comments seemed tailored for the voting public, but Roscoe's post-trial comments were made for his former fans and for moviegoers, whose verdict he awaited next.

His statement read:

This is the most solemn moment of my life. My innocence of the hideous charges preferred against me has been proven by a jury of the best men and women of San Francisco – fourteen in all – rendering a verdict immediately after the trial. For this vindication, I am truly grateful to God and my fellow men and women. My life has been devoted to the production of clean pictures for the happiness of children. I shall try to enlarge my field of usefulness so that my art shall have a wider service. It is the duty of all me to use the lessons that have been given tot hem by experience and misfortune for the benefit of all – to make themselves more useful to humanity. This I shall do. I can only repay the trust, confidence, and loyalty bestowed

Roscoe had every reason to celebrate after being acquitted in his third trial because he believed that life could finally go back to normal and he could quickly restart his career – but nothing went like he believed it would.

upon me during my trouble by millions of men and women throughout the world by rendering service in justification of their faith.

He also spoke to the press about his weight gain during the trials and his future in the movies. He told reporters, "I am going to take a good rest and get rid of some of this surplus flesh. I must get back into physical shape before I even think of pictures. Then I will be able to go on with my work, if the public wants me. If the public doesn't want me, I'll take my medicine. But, after the quick vindication I received, I am sure the American people will be fair and just. I believe I am due for a comeback."

On the night of the verdict, Jesse Lansky from Paramount said, "Our contract with Arbuckle expired at the time of the trouble. Whether or not this contract will be renewed will depend on the public. The public makes or breaks all stars. If the public receives favorably the Arbuckle pictures we have on hand, one of which will be released at once, then we will be ready to consider the matter of a future contract."

Roscoe didn't escape all legal consequences from the affair. He offered a guilty plea to a federal charge of the unlawful possession

As well known as the face of the man in the moon

of alcohol and was fined the maximum of $500. It was an amount that wouldn't have been of any consequence eight months earlier but now, the trial expenses – attorney fees, investigation fees, hotel and travel bills – couple with the loss of income had devastated his bank accounts. It was reported that his defense for the three trials cost more than $110,000, not including the attorney bills. The inclusion of those fees is believed to have ballooned the cost of his eventual acquittal to more than $750,000.

When Roscoe returned to his Los Angeles home on April 15, he refused an opportunity to speak to paying audiences from a theater stage, telling reporters, "I do not wish to capitalize on my good fortune so soon after achieving it. I will return to my profession when I consider it proper to do so."

And his films were soon back on screens.

Crazy to Marry and *Gasoline Gus* – both of which had barely played the previous August – were released once again and did strong business. *Skirt Shy* and *Freight Prepaid* had never been seen by American audiences and Paramount was anxious to get them in front of fans.

But the public began weighing in even before Fatty made it back into local theaters. In the days immediately after the acquittal, a battle began between censors and their foes, between those who believed in Roscoe's innocence and those who remained certain of his guilt – if not for manslaughter than for the sort of behavior that callously led to a young woman's death.

On the evening of April 18, six days after Roscoe's acquittal, all Paramount films featuring Fatty Arbuckle were effectively banned from American theaters.

It was the first decision announced by a man who would lead an organization that was going to change movie history forever. That man's name was Will H. Hays, and he was going to do his best to end the career of Roscoe Arbuckle once and for all.

⌁EVENTEEN

FOR AS LONG AS THERE HAVE BEEN MOVIES, THERE HAS BEEN someone who didn't want you to see them – or at least the parts of the film they didn't approve of.

In 1896, one of the first publicly screened films – Edison's 47-second *The Kiss*, which includes a man and woman kissing – sparked newspaper editorials called for police suppression of films.

In 1906, investigations into the allegedly negative social influence on the working class began, led by some of the same people who teamed up to push for Prohibition laws. They were the Christian fundamentalists, the progressive reformers, and the racist nativists and they were the first to conspire to regulate motion pictures. They condemned the movies just as they condemned the evils of liquor in American.

The Chicago City Council passed the nation's first motion picture censorship law in November 1907. It prohibited "immoral or obscene" movies and required the city's police department to issue a permit for every film shown. The law had to be enforced soon after it was passed because the portrayal of movie bandits was said to promote crime.

Other cities, like San Francisco and Los Angeles, followed Chicago's lead and created their own censorship committee, and between 1911 and 1916, state boards were established in Pennsylvania, Ohio, Kansas, and Maryland. The censorship rules were extreme. For example, in Pennsylvania, it was forbidden for a film to portray "expectant maternity." This wasn't just a pregnant woman – films couldn't even show someone knitting baby clothes.

After New York City closed all nickelodeons for two days in December 1908 and then barred all children under 16 from movie theaters unless accompanied by an adult, exhibitors were forced to fight back. First, they enlisted "surrogate parents" to escort kids into theaters and then they formed the National Board of Censorship of Motion Pictures to find inappropriate films before they were banned. The unfortunate name of the organization was changed in 1915 to the National Board of Review of Motion Pictures and by then had spread to over 250 local groups across the country. They reviewed nearly every film America produced, classifying them as "passed," "passed with changes as specified," or "condemned." Using the board's ratings, the movie industry hoped to avoid censors, but whenever a film didn't land a passing grade, censors flagged those films and forced producers to cut the objectionable material.

D.W. Griffith's landmark 1915 film *The Birth of a Nation* was frequently banned – although usually with good reason. The NAACP challenged its screenings because of its depiction of African Americans and was outlawed by communities who feared it would spark a race riot. When the producers protested a ban in Ohio, the case made it all the way to the U.S. Supreme Court, which issued a unanimous decision that compared films to "the theater, circus, and all other shows and spectacles." Films were "a business pure and simple, originated and conducted for profit" and so, were not shielded from censorship by the First Amendment. That wouldn't change until May 1952.

In 1916, the studios formed the National Association of the Motion Picture Industry, which lobbied for legal protections for movies. In March 1921, it issued "Thirteen Points" that the industry promised to avoid, including "suggestive bedroom and bathroom scenes" and scenes "that tend to weaken the authority of the law." The association's efforts at averting film censorship were mostly unsuccessful, as were those of the National Board of Review of Motion Pictures, which lost influence as critics accused it of whitewashing objectionable content.

After a flood of news coverage and a long but ultimately failed effort by the movie industry to prevent it, a fifth state established a censorship board in May 1921 – the most populous one, New York. Governor Nathan Miller said he signed the bill because it was the "only way to remedy what everyone conceded had grown to be a very great evil."

Dozens of other states followed New York's lead as conservatives in their legislatures introduced similar laws. The fervor against unregulated films continued to build in 1921 – and then it exploded.

In the days after Roscoe Arbuckle's arrest on September 10, all his films were pulled from every theater nationwide. As the home of the often-rebellious film industry, Los Angeles usually did all it could to protect their biggest business but occasionally, when movies brought shame, it seemed necessary to punish the offender. On September 14, 1921, the city council held a "public welfare" meeting to discuss ratcheting up the regulation of films.

The discussion at the meeting became heated with local ministers demanding the implementation of stricter film censorship. But their demands were tempered by the president of the Motion Picture Directors Association, William Desmond Taylor. At that point, he still had four and a half months to live. At the meeting, Taylor spoke up, "I have listened with amazement to the charges of these ministers that we are debauching the morals of the youth of this city. I know that the great majority of directors are building plays that are clean. We have pledged ourselves not to put anything into pictures that will hurt the morals of any youth."

Thew following day, Taylor issued a widely distributed statement that was entitled "The Nonsense of Censorship." It read, in part:

> *Censorship of motion pictures is a menace to the very principles of the Constitution of the United States of America. How strong a grasp it has obtained over the constitutional rights of America may be seen in the fact that nearly one-third of the total population of this country may now see only such motion pictures as some commission has decided they may see.*

The censorship battle was fought in city council meetings and on editorial pages and it continued for over a month before Los Angeles' attempt to censor movies failed on October 21.

From the perspective of the movie industry, however, the censorship problem was larger than the possibility that a city council might ban a single title or demand that a scene be cut out. It was the overall effect on ticket sales caused by bringing attention to the alleged evils of movies.

That's why the studio's greatest concern after September 10 was not censors – it was the perception, fueled by preachers and politicians, that the industry itself was uncensored. Hollywood followed no rules, pursued wealth and pleasure and failed to heed the constraints of common decency.

And this wasn't completely inaccurate. Hollywood had been plagued by drug overdoses, suicides, and scandals. There were constant demands for Hollywood to be "cleaned up" and this was before the Arbuckle affair. Roscoe wasn't the entire problem, it's just that his scandal got the most attention.

With the relentless press coverage in the weeks that followed Roscoe's arrest, the opinion grew that Hollywood was the center of immorality and was capable – thanks to its products and the statue of its stars – of infecting all of America with this disease.

Public outcry about "immorality" in Hollywood convinced the studios they needed to act fast to show they shared the concerns of the public. This led to the creation of the Motion Pictures Producers and Distributors Association – which became the MPAA in 1945 – an industry trade and lobby organization.

It would be led by a man who became the public face of Hollywood censorship and whose name would be attached to a code that changed American films for decades.

Will Hays

WILLIAM HARRISON HAYS WAS BORN IN NOVEMBER 1879, IN THE farming community of Sullivan in southwestern Indiana. His father was an attorney, Presbyterian elder, and Republican. His son followed in his footsteps, joining his father's law firm after college, representing railroads, coal companies, and other corporations. A skilled speaker with a passion for politics, he rose through the party ranks to become Indiana's Republican party chairman, even while continuing to live in Sullivan with his wife and a son, who was born in 1915.

Hays had what some might kindly call a "memorable" face – huge ears, bird-like nose, and a scramble of uneven teeth – and it was one that would become a gift to newspaper cartoonists. He was short, very thin, and while Roscoe Arbuckle claimed to be too fat to serve during World War I, Hays would turn out to be too frail. By then, he was the chairman of the Republican National Committee, a position to which the Progressive wing of the party had elevated him to in February 1918. In an era during which candidates were handpicked from movers and shakers behind the scenes, party chairman was seen as just a short step away from a Senate seat or a governor's mansion, but for now, he was sleeping on trains and in hotels as he crisscrossed the country working to elect other Republicans.

Hays expertly built alliances, and he capitalized on the fact that his party had regained the House and the Senate from the Democrats, thanks to an unpopular war. Then in 1920, his candidate, Warren G. Harding, won the presidency in a landslide. Harding appointed Hays to the cabinet position of Postmaster General in his administration. This

Hays became the U.S. Postmaster General in the cabinet of President Warren G. Harding

was, until the post office was reformed in 1970, one of the most important positions in the cabinet. In addition to overseeing mail delivery, the postmaster wielded most of the party's patronage, appointing supporters to postal service management positions. Hays moved to Washington, D.C. for his new job, although his son and his wife, who suffered from "lifelong frailty" stayed home in Indiana.

Hays came to the position with several postal services reforms in mind. In a luncheon speech to the American Newspaper Publishers Association, he announced, "First, it is no part of the primary business of the Post Office Department to act as a censor of the press. This should not and will not be." Soon after, he granted second-class mail status to a socialist magazine, stating that the previous administration had forced it to use a more expensive service as a form of censorship. It was the first of several radical publications to which he gave a mail status that had previously been denied.

Hays brought the skills he'd learned as party chairman to the White House. He was an excellent organizer, deal maker, and publicist and had connections in cities and towns nationwide – the same communities that were now launching film censorship boards. As the possibility of federal film censorship loomed, Hays made an unusual champion to stand against it. He was a teetotaler and a Presbyterian church goer from rural Indiana. His background was nothing like those of the major film studio heads, all of whom were Jewish and immigrants. Even so, when disaster struck just after Labor Day 1921, it was to Will Hays that those studio heads turned.

A letter was drafted to enlist Hays to the cause of minimizing the repercussions of the Arbuckle affair. It was signed by dozens of studio executives, including Adolph Zukor and Jesse Lasky, and it was hand-delivered to him on December 8. Although word leaked that he was considering the offer, he remained silent on the subject until he accepted it on January 14, 1922, just before testimony began in the second Arbuckle trial.

The announcement made front-page news, and Hays was christened the "Judge Landis of the movies," comparing him to the first commissioner of major league baseball, who'd been appointed in November 1920 to restore faith in the national pastime after the 1919 "Black Sox" bribery scandal.

But why would the 42-year-old political operative with his own aspirations for higher office give up a presidential cabinet position after just one year to involve himself in censorship fights, the Arbuckle trials, and an industry being hammered with accusations of drug-fueled orgies? The answer to that was the $100,000 annual salary that came with the job. He's made only $12,000 as the postmaster general. Even the president only made $75,000.

Hays was welcomed to Hollywood at the Directors Club banquet, convinced he was going to fix the public image problems caused by the Roscoe Arbuckle trial and the scandal by the murder of William Desmond Taylor

Hays stayed on as postmaster general until March 4 – a month after the William Desmond Taylor murder damaged Hollywood's reputation even more. He became the new head of the Motion Picture Producers and Distributors of America and after devoting a month to studying the movie industry, he outlined how he hoped to modernize it and clean up its tarnished image.

He told the press, "As to censorship I think that will be the least of our troubles. The matter of censorship will take care of itself when our objects as to the pictures are accomplished."

In other words, Hollywood didn't need states and cities to create censorship boards to point out the problems with their films. Hollywood was going to take care of those problems on its own.

What could go wrong?

FOR DECADES, IT WAS ASSUMED THAT WILL HAYS ALONE DECIDED to ban Roscoe Arbuckle from the movies on April 18 – a week after Roscoe's acquittal and a month after Hays started his new job. But after Hays died in 1954, his memoirs were published and while only three of the book's 600 pages mention Roscoe, whom Hays never met, Hays put the blame for Roscoe's banishment on someone else – Joseph Schenck and Adolph Zukor. Hays claimed the two men came to see him after the third trial and asked him to ban Roscoe from working in the movie industry. Hays said that Zukor insisted on it, even though Paramount had two unreleased

Hays quickly became a controversial figure in Hollywood

Fatty Arbuckle movies and two that had been barely released.

Hays wrote:

With hundreds of thousands of dollars tied up in completed but unreleased films, Zukor decided to make a sacrifice rather than bring further discredit on the industry or give the slightest added impetus to public outrage. So far as he was concerned, the outrage was very real. Arbuckle had let him down – he had let the whole industry down no less than his fans – and Zukor was prepared to take the loss.

That's the best possible spin anyone could put on Zukor's demand that Roscoe been banned from films. Over the course of three trials, Paramount had likely become resigned to writing off any further box office grosses from Fatty's films. Then came the protests, scathing editorials, and censorship calls when they released *Gasoline Gus* and *Crazy to Marry* after the acquittal.

During the trials, Roscoe was rarely associated with the studio but now, with his movies returning to theaters, he was a Paramount star again. Zukor did the math and decided that Paramount had more to lose in the long term by continuing its association with Fatty, who was hatred by most of the country, than it had to gain in the short term from those who still loved him or forgave him. The studio wanted a clean slate – even if its top executives were too cowardly to take the blame for it.

Hays wrote that he asked Zukor to issue the statement on Roscoe's ban, but Zukor refused, saying that if it came from the Association, it would show that the Association meant business.

Hays, never an expert at spinning, took on the task while Zukor hid behind him. He was blacklisting Roscoe from Hollywood, but rather than face any public backlash, he secretly passed the job to Will Hays, who dutifully did as he was told.

For the Paramount president, it was a win-win. He could rid himself of Arbuckle and let Hays take the blame. As a bonus, Hays would get the credit, giving the appearance that the new MPPDA was serious about cleaning up Hollywood.

But was that all there was to it?

As we're discover in the pages that remain, the Roscoe Arbuckle and Virginia Rappe story has generated more legends and conspiracy than possibly any other Hollywood scandal. Zukor's second-hand banishment of Roscoe is just one of the many oddities that have been pointed out by those who have searched for answers about what really happened in room 1219.

It's been speculated that Roscoe's ban from films was engineered by Adolph Zukor – not for fear of losing money because of the scandal but for revenge

It's always been accepted that profit was Zukor's primary reason for banishing Roscoe but there are stories that say it was really revenge. Zukor allegedly resented Roscoe for his hefty salary and the freedom he enjoyed when making his films. No matter what direction Zukor gave him, Roscoe continued to do whatever he wanted – like deciding to goi out of town over Labor Day weekend instead of taking part in the parade and film screenings that he'd been ordered to attend.

It's been claimed that Zukor made a mysterious payment to the re-election fund of San Francisco District Attorney Matthew Brady on November 14, 1921. It was assumed to be a bribe to control the outcome of the case – although not in Roscoe's favor. The damage had been done and Zukor wanted Roscoe to get what was coming to him.

It's even been theorized that Zukor, angry over Roscoe defying his order and eager to teach him a lesson, had masterminded the Hotel St. Francis party to get his star in trouble with the Prohibition authorities. Zukor could then bail Roscoe out and smooth things over and have him under the studio's thumb.

But the party, planned only to get Roscoe in trouble and make him look bad, went wildly out of control.

And it was all Adolph Zukor's fault – if you believe this rumor anyway.

WITH THE ARBUCKLE BAN IN PLACE, HAYS WENT TO WORK fighting against official censorship. He convinced several states – and the federal government – to abandon their plans for film censorship boards and used his finely honed political skills to form a public relations committee within the MPPDA to which organizations could voice complaints about the studios.

He also instituted the "Formula" in 1924. It was a strategy to use in reviewing the outlines of every movie in preproduction. In keeping with its mysterious title, the Formula was vague, until a list of 11 "Don'ts" (nudity, profanity, mixed races) and 25 "Be Carefuls" (brutality, crime, treason) was adopted in 1927. The Hays Office – as the MPPDA became known, claimed to reject 125 proposed films over the next five years, but submission was voluntary and any outline that was rejected could become a movie without any consequences.

Hays became a celebrity in his own right, regularly making newspaper headlines for everything from establishing a movie copyright bureau to unionizing film production labor to leasing the most expensive apartment in New York City. More than anyone else, he was the face of the movie business – characterized as the "czar of the movies." Reporters never got tired of presenting, if not mocking, him as a paragon of virtue, even as he became entangled in political scandals like the Teapot Dome – a bribery case involving President Harding's secretary of the interior.

In the greatest contrast to his public image, Hays lived apart from his family for over a decade until divorcing his wife in 1929 and winning custody of their son. He remarried in 1930.

By then, silent films had given way to the talkies, and the new spoken dialogue greatly increased the odds of offensive content in films. Demand grew for federal film censorship and hays began facing renewed criticism from religious groups. Meanwhile, civil liberties organizations sought ways to repeal the censorship laws that already existed. If this is added to the financial instability of the industry, suffering from the Depression and proposed antitrust legislation, it becomes clear why Hays was receptive to the Motion Picture Production Code.

The Code was outlined by Martin J. Quigley, the publisher of a Chicago-based motion picture trade newspaper, who wanted a plan that not only included a list of what should be banned from movies but also contained a moral system that movies should help to promote – a system specifically based on Catholic theology. He recruited Father Daniel Lord, a Jesuit priest and instructor at the Catholic St. Louis University, to write such a code and on March 31, 1930, Hays adopted it formally as the Motion Picture Production Code, or the "Hays Code" as it became commonly known.

The Code had three general principles:

1. No picture shall be produced that will lower the moral standards of those who see it.

2. Correct standards of life, subject only to the requirements of drama and entertainment, shall be presented.

3. Law, natural or human, shall not be ridiculed, nor shall sympathy be created for its violation.

This was vague enough to dance around, but the devil was in the details. There were 21 "Particular Applications" that spelled out numerous topics to avoid. Nudity and "suggestive dances" were prohibited. Religion could not be ridiculed. Illegal drugs were forbidden, and alcohol could only be featured when required by plot. Certain types of crime (like arson or safe cracking) could not be shown. No reference could be made to sexual perversion (i.e. homosexuality) and childbirth could not be depicted. The language

section banned various offensive words and phrases and adultery and illicit sex, although recognized as sometimes necessary to the plot, could not be explicit or justified and were not supposed to be presented as an attractive option.

The Code was officially adopted on March 31, 1930. Both scripts and finished films were to be submitted to the Hays Office for approval.

For a few years, though, Hollywood got away with ignoring the code. The studios continued to produce racier films because the Code, like previous efforts at self-censorship, lacked enforcement. Gangsters, monsters, risqué humor, and nudity ruled in what's now regarded as a high point in

movie history dubbed "Pre-Code Hollywood," a brief period before the Code was enforced.

But it wasn't meant to last.

In response to movies like *Baby Face* with Barbara Stanwyck and just about anything with Mae West, Martin Quigley and Joseph I. Breen, the Los Angeles-based assistant of Will Hays, conspired to use the Catholic Church to exert pressure on the Hollywood studios. They helped spearhead the creation of the Catholic Legion of Decency, as well as boycotts and blacklists of the movies throughout the country.

In 1934, an amendment to the code was passed that forced all films to obtain a certificate of approval before they could be released. The studios were forced into going along with the Code for the next three decades.

By the late 1950s, the studios were facing threats from television and foreign films, which couldn't be regulated. Hollywood began to push the envelope with new productions and after studios were forced to give up ownership of theaters due to violations of the antitrust laws, independent art houses began to appear that would play films that did not have certificates of approval. Finally, when boycotts from religious groups no longer guaranteed a film would fail, the Code was weakened further and was finally abandoned in November 1968, when a ratings system that still exists today finally replaced it.

Will Hays had stepped down as head of the MPPDA in 1945 and while he stuck around as a consultant for the next five years, he retired to a life of luxury in New York. Though he rarely returned to Indiana, he died there in March 1954 at age 74.

Before and after his death, Hays was lambasted as the great censor of the movies. There is no doubt that the Hays Code altered the history of American films. It forced writers to temper their dialog, made actors afraid to speak some of that dialog, and frightened producers away from topics that may have been turned into great movies if it hadn't existed.

The Code was certainly a form of censorship, but it was probably necessary to combat a more direct form of it. Government censors continued to function, but they rarely contemplated banning anything that had been given the Production Code's seal of approval.

The Code undoubtedly went too far and lasted too long, but, despite popular belief, it was not the result of the personal morality of Will Hays. His overwhelming motive was to simply protect the business of making movies – and this motive affected no one as much as it did Roscoe Arbuckle.

EIGHTEEN

Fatty Arbuckle was a movie "goat." While he escaped conviction in court, he was crucified by public sentiment which demanded that somebody be made to pay for the loose lives of too many of the movie stars. It was just Arbuckle's misfortune that the choice fell upon him. It might have been anyone of a number of others no better than he. A little more than usual vulgarity and an accident directed selection of Arbuckle, so he is paying for all.
- Newspaper editorial, November 22, 1922

ROSCOE ARBUCKLE WAS HEARTBROKEN.

His greatest hope over the last seven months had been, once cleared of the charges against him, he could go back to work doing what he loved – making movies.

But that wasn't be. When he discovered that he had been blacklisted from Hollywood, the hope drained out of him. Minta later wrote that the light that had always been in eyes was gone. Her husband sat for hours, silently petting Luke. She often heard him say to the dog, "Well, boy, do you know the future? I am sure I don't.

He was deeply in debt. He had deeded his West Adams mansion to Joseph Schenck as security to pay for the trials, so he and Minta became tenants when they returned to live there. He sold his Pierce-Arrow and the other luxury cars, and he still owed his trial attorneys at least $100,000, and likely more. He needed his Hollywood paychecks just to get him out of debt, so his unexpected banishment by Will Hays caught him off guard and left him reeling. Five days after he received the news, he issued a response:

The question of the release of my pictures is entirely within the jurisdiction of the Famous Players-Lasky Corporation, owners of these pictures, who are undoubtedly working in harmony with Mr. Will Hays. I shall do everything possible to cooperate with the leaders of the industry. In the meantime, I shall prove to the world by my conduct that I am entitled to an opportunity to earn my living in the only profession I am equipped to follow and shall patiently and hopefully await the final opinion of the American public, in whose sense of fair play I have never lost confidence.

But the most vocal segment of the American public in the wake of the Hays announcement was not interested in "fair play" toward Roscoe, who they considered the living, breathing symbol of Hollywood depravity. Soon after he released this statement, the California Congress of Women and Parents voted in support of banning his films. A similar resolution was passed by the San Francisco Federation of Women's Clubs.

So much for a "not guilty" verdict.

IN THE DAYS AND WEEKS THAT FOLLOWED, ROSCOE DECLINED offers to appear on the vaudeville stage and instead, tried to return to films. He wrote a short comedy script, "The Vision," for Buster Keaton and sold it to Joseph Schneck. Roscoe was even supposed to direct it, but the movie never got made.

When *Photoplay* editor James Quirk wrote Roscoe a letter of encouragement, Arbuckle wrote back, again stating his case but also strategizing: "You can be of real service to me by writing Mr. Hays, asking him to lift the ban and telling him that my innocence of the charges placed against me in San Francisco justifies your request."

Quirk did what he could to help and wrote the letter to Hays. So did others, including representatives from American theater owners, who asked for Roscoe's reinstatement.

But, of course, there were also those who didn't feel that Hays had done enough. Senator Henry Lee Myers denounced Roscoe on the floor of the U.S. Senate – a place filled with upstanding citizens – and used him as an argument for film censorship, saying, "At Hollywood, California, is a colony of these people, where debauchery, riotous living, drunkenness, ribaldry, dissipation, free love, seem to be conspicuous."

In June, Minta left that "colony" and moved to New York to live with her sister. Roscoe denied that his wife had left him and claimed

Although Roscoe and Buster remained close friends, both of them (especially Roscoe) wished for better days

she'd return when he was able to support himself again. She wouldn't but Roscoe likely wasn't ready to face that truth just yet.

Roscoe continued to live in the West Adams mansion with Lou Anger and his wife, renting it from Joe Schneck. He spent most of his time at home, feeling sorry for himself. Al St. John later remembered his uncle sitting alone for hours in a car in the garage of a house he no longer owned, starting out through the windshield and never moving.

At his friend Buster Keaton's insistence, Roscoe often visited Comique and helped Buster with his latest comedy short. But there were simply too many hours in a day to fill. The man who'd sworn off booze forever started drinking again.

Roscoe remained generous with his money, even when he owed much more than he had. Besides Buster, his closest friend was matinee star and notorious womanizer, Lew Cody, who later recalled, "Once when we were both pretty broke, I had a chance to go to New York to work. I managed to borrow enough to buy a ticket. Just before the train pulled out, Roscoe came aboard and after he'd said goodbye, he handed me an envelope. 'Don't open this until after the train starts,' he said. 'It's just a letter telling you what a lousy actor I think you are.'

When I opened the envelope, two $100 bil.ls dropped out. He'd borrowed the money here, there, and everywhere. That's the kind of pal Fatty was."

Roscoe also managed to find the cash for a trout-fishing vacation in Vancouver, British Columbia, and in August, he sailed from San Francisco for the Orient, returning to the places he'd last seen a decade before. His attorney, Milt Cohen, accompanied him on the trip.

Roscoe spoke to reporters in San Francisco before the ship departed: "I need a rest and intend to take it easy and, at the same time, see some other parts of the world. I'll come back to the United States in due time and then will be my opportunity to decide what I'm going to do. It's entirely up to the people – the people who see the movies and who used to be, and I think, will be, my friends, whether I return to the screen or not. Maybe I'll get back to making comedies, but I don't know. San Francisco doesn't make me feel very funny and I can't say right now."

Roscoe's original plan was to also visit the Middle East and Europe, but after he slipped and fell on some steps and badly cut his hand, he ended up making it no farther than Japan. An infection set in, requiring surgery in Tokyo and generating a lot of front-page stories. Though he was greeted warmly in Japan, the injury had drained his enthusiasm, so he ended the trip and sailed back across the Pacific.

His time in the Orient, he later said, convinced him that California was a good place to live.

ROSCOE WAS NOT THE ONLY HOLLYWOOD STAR IN TROUBLE.

A gloom had settled over the movie industry during Roscoe's trials and during the investigation into William Desmond Taylor's murder, but the darkness was felt more at Paramount than anywhere else. The studio -- where Roscoe had been the top actor and Taylor one of the top directors – was dealt a double blow and was scrambling to recover.

Then came the next blow.

Milt Cohen (Left) with Roscoe at his first criminal trial. The men remained friends when it was over

Wallace Reid

After Roscoe was arrested, Wallace Reid stepped in as Paramount's biggest star. The tall, athletic actor with dashing good looks was elevated to leading roles, but Reid had a secret. Back in 1919, he had been injured working on a film and Jesse Lasky had sent the studio doctor to see him. The movie star was soon addicted to morphine.

Although he was strung out, Reid worked at a breakneck pace, starring in physically demanding roles for Paramount, seven each year in the first three years of the 1920s. He also began drinking heavily and sometimes the crew had to literally prop him up to get the shots they needed. His habit became widely known in Hollywood circles but in the wake of Roscoe Arbuckle's troubles, no one was talking. Finally, in September 1922, things became so bad that Reid's wife admitted him to a Hollywood sanitarium for treatment.

But soon, Hollywood's worst-kept secret broke on newspaper front pages. WALLACE REID CRITICALLY ILL, "DOPE" BLAMED blared one headline. In Los Angeles to meet with studio executives, Will Hays visited Reid in a padded room at the sanitarium. Hays said that the former movie heartthrob, then weighing only 130 pounds, was recovering. But Hays was wrong, and Reid died just one month after the visit on January 18, 1923.

Roscoe Arbuckle wasn't working, but at least he wasn't dead – so far.

AS SHOCKING AS IT HAD BEEN FOR WILL HAYS TO BLACKLIST Roscoe, it was even more stunning when he suddenly decided to remove the ban eight months later. On December 20, 1922, Roscoe received what he called an early Christmas present when Hays made a public statement about his decision:

Every man in the right way and at the proper time is entitled to his chance to make good. It is apparent that Roscoe Arbuckle's conduct since his trouble merits that chance. So far as I am concerned, there will be no suggestion now that he should not have his opportunity to go to work in his profession. In our effort to develop a complete cooperation and confidence within the industry, I hope we can start this New Year with no yesterdays. "Live and let live" is not enough; we will try to live and help live.

In his memoirs, Hays claimed he reinstated Roscoe only after long deliberation but, in fact, the April 18 ban had been vague, merely stating that at Hay's request, Paramount had "canceled all showings and all bookings of Arbuckle films." That said, with Paramount shelving two unreleased Fatty features, the implication was clear – don't work with Roscoe Arbuckle.

The December 20 statement, though, wasn't vague at all. It was clear – Roscoe's films were again welcome in theaters and producers were free to put him back to work.

Hays had been pressured to drop the ban by theater owners, who were eager to start screening Fatty films again; from studios other than Paramount, who worried about the Hays Office hampering their profits; from newspaper editors; and from letter-writing members of the public. It's also likely that Hays had heard from enough sympathetic industry people while in Los Angeles that he decided it was the smart thing to do. With the trials long over and Arbuckle's association with Paramount now in the past, Zukor and the other executives had gotten what they wanted from the ban and likely had no concerns about their former star going to work for someone else.

But Hays had no idea what was coming for him.

He later admitted, "It seemed a relatively commonplace decision to me, and I anticipated no such excitement as ensued. But for the next three months it became a *cause célèbre* as newspaper editorials and civic leagues presented me with every public building in the country, brick by brick."

Those bricks – lots of them – began to be thrown at Hays within hours of his announcement, but first, there was excitement. Roscoe rushed into Joe Schneck's office at 10:00 A.M. that morning, looking for confirmation of what he'd heard from reporters. He was so overcome with emotion that he was shaking and stammering so badly that it took Schneck a moment to understand what he was saying. But what he'd heard was true – the ban had been lifted.

A brief statement was drafted and handed out to the press: "Mr. Hays had made his decision. It is my intention in every way to live up to what Mr. Hays expects of me."

It was a simple, carefully considered statement. It contained no expressions of triumph. It was simply a grateful-sounding collection of words from a man who was then more excited than he'd been in a very long time.

Joseph Schneck also made a statement to reporters: "I cannot say just now how soon we can get a picture for him or what kind of pictures he will make. Stories do not come out of thin air, and we must have something suitable to him, something in his character. I have received many telegrams today from all parts of the country congratulating me and Arbuckle. People have been saying nice things over the phone. I believe the American public is just, and that it has come to realize that Arbuckle should be back on the screen."

However, as Schenck was speaking to reporters, Roscoe's enemies were lining up on the other side of the battlefield, intent on making sure that he never worked again.

Roscoe's friend, Joe Schneck, who remained loyal to the comedian through his legal problems.

On the same day that Will Hays welcomed Roscoe back into the good graces of Hollywood, the Los Angeles Federation of Women's Clubs was holding an emergency meeting and passing a motion calling for Roscoe to never appear in another film.

The Illinois Motion Picture Association promptly announced that Fatty Arbuckle films would not be shown in any of its theaters.

He wasn't welcome on Michigan movies screens either.

There would be no Arbuckle movies in Boston, Indianapolis, Chicago, and on and on it went. In many cases, cities and towns merely reasserted the bans that had been in place since shortly after his arrest.

Protesting telegrams deluged Will Hays. They came from religious groups, schools, women's clubs, teacher unions, and more.

Two days after its hasty statement, the Illinois theater owner's organization reversed it, deciding to let Roscoe's films be shown – but only if the public wanted to see them. The same "let the people decide" edict was accepted in New York and California.

The Motion Picture Directors Association, which under the late William Desmond Taylor had been opposed to censorship of any kind, held a long emergency meeting and, after a heated debate, passed a controversial resolution that didn't mention Roscoe but stated "that under no circumstance should any person or persons who by their actions have proven a menace to the well-being of our industry be tolerated or excused."

Responding to pressure from women's clubs, the mayor of Los Angeles vowed to keep Roscoe off the movie screens in the city. He sent a protest telegram to Will Hays, as did many other politicians. On December 23, Hays responded with telegrams of his own, claiming that he was not reinstating Arbuckle but would not stand in the way of him making a living. Even though he'd taken a small step backward, this small surrender pleased no one.

And that included Roscoe Arbuckle, who released another statement, which appeared in newspapers on Christmas morning. It began with, "All I ask is the rights of an American citizen – American fair play," and then rehashed his acquittal and argued that those "who are unjustly, untruthfully, maliciously, and venomously attacking me are refusing to abide by the established law of the land" as well as "A higher law." Roscoe, who'd never been religious before but knew that it was religious groups who were leading the attack on him, quoted scripture and accused his critics of ignoring the spirit of the Bible. He pointed to Christ forgiving the penitent thief and asked if modern Christianity was about charity or was a "thing of only teeth and claws." It was, he concluded, an antithesis to the "spirit of Christmas" that America's churches refused to forgive him – an innocent man.

But Roscoe's sermonizing fell on deaf ears. On the day after Christmas, the San Francisco Federation of Women's Clubs – who had made such a strong showing at Roscoe's trials – met to urge Hays to restore Arbuckle's banishment to make an example "of those who brazenly violate the moral code of a Christian nation."

Roscoe did have some allies in his fight, however. Theatrical producer Arthur Hammerstein offered Paramount $1 million for the two never-released feature films as well as for *Gasoline Gus*, which had only been out for a short time. When that was refused, he offered to exhibit the features for only 10 percent of the profits because he was

so confident they'd be successful he'd still make money. Paramount refused to budge.

During the last week of 1922, Roscoe traveled to San Francisco and there, his former defense attorney Gavin McNab and a group of financiers organized a company to fund Fatty films in Los Angeles. McNab was able to secure $100,000 for productions and Roscoe went to work on a script for a two-reel comedy, *Handy Andy.*

Debate over Roscoe returning to films continued in the new year. Hays met with both religious and civic leaders and found himself disagreeing with their demands that he advise producers against releasing Fatty movies. After some consideration, Hays issued his "final statement," saying that he was leaving what happened to Roscoe Arbuckle to the public, Roscoe's employers, and Roscoe himself. Hays was washing his hands of anything else to do with the decision.

Perhaps things would have been different if Roscoe had never been banned. He might have been able to weather the initial outrage, keep his head down, and let the outrage burn itself out, and then smooth things over with the popularity of some new Fatty features. Instead, his own studio turned on him and then fanned the flames. He escaped punishment from the law only to receive it from the movie industry, then, by reversing the ban eight months later, it looked like the industry suddenly condoned the "booze-fueled orgy" that he hadn't committed, making people mad all over again. It looked like Roscoe was just taking a little time off before he reclaimed his stardom like nothing had happened.

If it had just been about one man, even one as famous as Roscoe, that presumptive return would have never created the uproar it did. This was about more than that. It was American's first real instance of someone being "canceled" – the first real battle in the culture war. Society was changing fast – too fast for many people – and Hollywood, with its drugs, sex, illegal liquor, disrespect for authority, and loose morals, was at the forefront of this change.

Or so the preachers said. And so, the newspapers said – louder and more often once Wallace Reid's drug addiction became common knowledge. Movies themselves were a new and powerful force, soaring to prominence in only the last decade, and people were still coming to terms with the technology that allowed Fatty to ogle a young woman on thousands of screens at the same time.

And that's why so many were outraged by the idea that the man who represented the worst of Hollywood immorality could so easily be allowed back onto those screens again.

THE EVENTS THAT FILLED ROSCOE WITH HOPE ON DECEMBER 20 now sent him into the depths of despair in the weeks that followed when he realized his dreams of returning to the life that he once knew had been dashed. An article in January portrayed Roscoe as deeply depressed. He had moved out of his West Adams mansion, his home at the height of his fame and fortune and now lived in "a little obscure cabin in Hollywood" with his loyal dog, Luke. "I just want to work and make people laugh – and to eat," Roscoe said.

The article ran on January 10 – the same day that he began acting in *Handy Andy*. It was never released and likely never finished.

At some point, he decided that being in front of the camera wasn't going to work – not yet anyway. He ducked behind the camera instead. On January 31, it was announced that he had signed to direct five shorts for Reel Comedies, a company that Joe Schneck had incorporated the day

a Paramount Picture

before. Among those who backed the venture were Lou Anger, Buster Keaton, and Gavin McNab.

Roscoe may not have had money or fame anymore, but he still had friends, which says a lot, in my opinion, about the true character of the man.

The announcement about the comedies was accompanied by a statement from Roscoe. He said that directing was "a good chance to make good in the right way." He added that he was done with acting.

A reporter who interviewed him on several occasions during this time later recalled, "He was very bitter over what he believed was injustice, which financially and professionally ruined him. I had never seen a more hopeless man."

But Roscoe did appear in a film in 1923 – and, shockingly, for Paramount. James Cruze, director of five of his Paramount features, made *Hollywood*, a comedy film about the struggle to find success in the movie industry. It was loaded with cameos by celebrities, including Charlie Chaplin, Douglas Fairbanks, and Mary Pickford – but one uncredited bit part stole the show. When the naïve heroine joins a casting cattle call, an unrevealed overweight man steps aside to give his place to the nervous wannabe. After she strikes out, the man steps up to the casting director's window, only to have that window slammed in his face. He stares at the CLOSED sign on the window and then the camera reveals his identity – Roscoe Arbuckle.

The movie played with no notable protests. In fact, Roscoe's appearance was applauded at screenings – including in San Francisco – two years after that fateful Labor Day.

IN THE END, ROSCOE RECEIVED NO CREDIT FOR HIS WORK writing, directing, and producing those shorts for Reel Comedies. It was decided that attaching his name to them was a bad idea and increased the potential for protests.

His unacknowledged efforts began in February 1923 with *Easter Bonnets*, which allowed to finally cast the now 23-year-old actress Doris Deane, whom he'd met on his way home by steamship on Labor Day 1921. The next five shorts starred Edwin "Poodles" Hanneford, a circus clown known for his horse-riding tricks.

Work on the films kept Roscoe occupied and provided him with a creative outlet, even if it didn't bring him the joy that he'd experienced as a movie star. He also needed the money that acting provided if he was ever going to pay down his many debts.

In May, he signed on for a four-week stint at the glitzy Marigold Gardens cabaret club in Chicago. He told jokes, danced, and sang. When Roscoe was a vaudevillian and started acting in the movies in 1909, he was accused of "slumming it." Now he'd gone in full circle – he was a former movie star from glamorous Hollywood returning to the fading vaudeville stage. The money was good – a guaranteed $2,500 a week and more if tickets sales were strong – but most of what he made went straight to the IRS, to which he owed $30,.000 in back taxes.

On June 4, his first night at Marigold Gardens, the crowd first saw him on a movie screen, running toward the camera, getting larger and larger, and then the real man burst through the paper screen and onto the stage. The resulting applause lasted for 15 minutes.

"This is the first smile I've had a in a long, long time," he told the audience.

The show's producer later recalled that night: "A little girl strolled over to present him with a rose. The comedian went down on his knees and with tears streaming down his face, he kissed the child in gratitude. The entire audience, including myself, was in tears."

That producer admitted that he had friends planted in the audience on opening night to generate applause in case the crowd was cold, but the ringers were never needed.

The show was popular because people wanted to see Fatty – it wasn't because the show was good. Trying to transfer some of his slapstick antics to the stage was not exactly an artistic success. "The people have been very kind," Roscoe said. "They have come out to see me and they have been extremely generous in their applause. In return, I have done my best to amuse them with a poor act."

And "poor act" may have been an understatement. It included Roscoe in a ballerina dress and the return of the infamous Keystone custard pies. And not shying away from misogynistic humor, one song included the lines, "Our women are lead and fat, and some are good-looking, but the only use we have for them is when they do our cooking."

After his stint in Chicago, Roscoe took the show to Atlantic City, where he began pulling in $6,000 a week. Interestingly, Minta was set to perform at a competing club, where she was being billed as "Mrs. Fatty Arbuckle." This angered the owner of the club that had hired Mr. Arbuckle, and he tried to forbid him from seeing Mrs. Arbuckle when she was in town. Then the club owner tried to get Roscoe to sue his wife for using his name. Roscoe was flummoxed by the request. He told reporters, "She stood by me in my time of trouble. Sue her? I'll be at the train when she arrives with a bouquet of roses!" And he was.

The couple had remained close friends but there was no chance of reviving their marriage. On November 2, 1923, Minta filed for divorce in Providence, Rhode Island. It was, at that time, the "Reno of the East," known for its relatively easy divorces.

In a letter from Roscoe to Minta dated November 18, it's clear that he'd been regularly sending her money, as ordered by their separation agreement. The tone of the note was affectionate toward his soon-to-be ex-wife and her family, and it also revealed the private humor shared by the couple – the kind that could never appear in Roscoe's films.

Early in the letter, he explained why he had "been busier than a dog with turpentine in his ass," saying "I have been thrown in at the last minute to direct Buster's next picture and have been very busy trying to get the story ready."

When he closed, he wrote:

Well, kid, don't get discouraged, keep a stiff upper lip. That's the only thing of mine that's stiff. I think somebody put salt peter in my coffee. Kisses and flowers, will write soon.

Dingle-tit Roscoe

BUSTER KEATON'S THIRD FEATURE, *SHERLOCK JR.*, WAS RELEASED in April 1924 and it was his first project where he alone was credited as the director. Today, this film is regarded as one of the greatest films of the silent era. In the surreal comedy, Buster plays a movie projectionist who dreams that he climbs into a film he's projecting and becomes part of its storyline. The action and stunts come at a breakneck speed, and it offers astonishing special effects for the 1920s.

It remains an amazing film, even for those who have an aversion to silent movies.

And the original co-director of this masterpiece? It was Buster's close friend and mentor, Roscoe Arbuckle.

Buster Keaton later wrote:

We were about to start Sherlock Jr. *in 1924 when I decided that I must do something for my pal, Roscoe... Roscoe was down in the dumps and broke. I suggested to Lou Anger that we give Roscoe a job directing* Sherlock Jr. *Lou said it could be arranged, but that we better get him to use some other name. I suggested "Will B. Good," but this was considered too facetious, so we changed it to "Will B. Goodrich."*

The experiment was a failure. Roscoe was irritable, impatient, and snapped at everyone in the company. He had my leading lady, Kathryn McGuire, in tears dozens of times a day. One day, after Roscoe went home, the gang of us sat around trying to figure out what to do next. It was obvious that we couldn't make the picture with a man directing whose self-confidence was gone, whose nerves were shot.

Knowing a little about what went on behind the scenes of the film may explain what was happening with Roscoe at the time. Even though he'd do just about anything to work again, the need for him to use a pseudonym was probably nerve-rattling. If you recall that "William Goodrich" was the name of Roscoe's father, who abandoned him twice as a child, then his lack of self-confidence can also be explained.

Also, in one of the scenes that Roscoe directed with Kathryn McGuire, she is abducted by her butler and is taken to a shack, where the implication is the butler is just about to rape her. Directing this scene had to have been stressful for Roscoe, as he would have likely felt that everyone was watching him.

He lasted just three weeks as co-director of the film before his best friend fired him. "He hadn't recovered from those trials," Buster

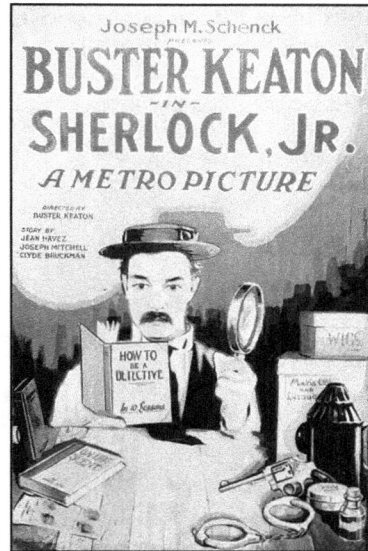

said later. "It just changed his disposition. In other words, it made a nervous wreck out of him."

Roscoe's love interest – actress Doris Deane

ROSCOE MIGHT NOT HAVE DIRECTED *SHERLOCK JR.* BUT HE DID write and direct four comedy shorts in 1924. All of them starred Al St. John, who was credited as writer and director in his uncle's place.

All of them also featured Roscoe's new – and long-delayed – love interest, Doris Deane. She was 13 years younger than Roscoe and born Doris Biddle in Wisconsin in 1900. She was the only child of parents who seemed to have a hard time staying in one place. In 1910, the family rented a house in Iowa, where her father worked in a saloon, but by the time Doris was in high school, they lived in Butte, Montana, which was then copper-mining boomtown. After that, they moved to Southern California.

It was there when Doris, then 19 and using her new name, landed her first film role. She was a tall, thin brunette with dimples and an easy smile. She dreamed of being a movie star and things suddenly seemed to be looking up for her when she met Roscoe on that steamship in 1921. One week earlier, her second film, *The Shark Master*, was released by Universal. She had a major part in it but only two smaller roles followed for her before Roscoe began casting her in comedy shorts in 1923.

Doris was then best-known for the publicity she got in December 1922 when rumors spread about her engagement to Jack Dempsey, the world's heavyweight boxing champion. Chummy photos appeared of them in the sport pages, but the rumor was never confirmed or denied – until she ended up marrying another heavyweight instead.

BY THE SUMMER OF 1924, ROSCOE WAS FEELING MUCH MORE like himself. He'd been working steadily – usually under other names – and paying down his debt. He also had a new love interest, which was helpful in lifting his mood, as well as a new car -- a fire-engine red McFarlan Knickerbocker Cabriolet with FATTY license plates.

In June 1924, Roscoe returned to Alexander Pantages' vaudeville company, which he had first traveled with 20 years earlier, when he was still a teenager. He had been hired to perform a comic monologue as the show's star attraction.

At his first show at the Pantages Theatre in San Francisco, he was greeted by a standing ovation that lasted for 11 minutes. Even D.A. Brady backed off his criticisms of Roscoe, saying that three trials were "the only way an accused man could be cleared of a horrible charge" and "I would father build up than tear down and help than hurt, and Arbuckle has been condemned and hurt enough."

Roscoe told reporters: "San Francisco's reception of me is, I think, just evidence of the American fair play spirit that never dies – given time. I've had my dose of foul play. Now it's fair play."

When asked if he thought his films would now be released, he had a quick reply: "I hope not. They would be old stuff now. I want to make new comedies. Better pictures. I'm more serious now than I was in the old days." He exercised daily, and he claimed to have lost 20 pounds in the previous three weeks, all part of his effort to get in shape for his return to the screen.

But it wasn't all good times and applause. In some communities where he played, censors fought to keep him off stage just as they had movie screens. In Kansas City, Missouri, as a resolution was being read before the city council that would ban him from local theaters, Roscoe walked into the council chambers and asked to speak. He asked the council for a "chance to live a clean, decent life and pay my debts." After the council peppered him with questions, the resolution was defeated.

When his appearances in Quincy, Illinois, were protested by a local minister, Roscoe asked to speak at the minister's church about how his life had changed since the infamous party. The preacher refused but he shut up after that, and the Quincy shows ended up drawing large crowds.

In Cleveland, Roscoe headlined a bill that included a local singing, dancing, and comedy duo. One of the performers,

In Cleveland, Roscoe met a young song, dance, and comedy man and liked him so much that he helped get his career started. His name was Lester Hope – and he soon became famous as Bob Hope.

Lester Hope, impressed Roscoe so much that he recommended him to a vaudeville producer and helped him kickstart his career. Lester later changed his name to Bob and became one of the most famous entertainers in history.

As Roscoe traveled from one show to the next, he spoke with reporters, theater owners, and the public, talking about how he planned to return to Los Angeles when his tour was over so he could appear in a new movie. He also noted that he'd sworn off women and booze. None of those things, including the movie role, were true. However, this had become his practiced storyline over the previous two years – that returning to the screen was all about his reform. If people believed he was a changed man, why couldn't they accept his again as a comedic film character?

Whenever he appeared on stage, he obtained the permission of the theater manager before spending a few minutes of the show talking "personally to motion picture fans and if possible, obtain consensus of opinion regarding my return to my life work – motion pictures."

During those "few minutes" on a theater's stage, Roscoe would tell his appreciative audience, "I don't claim to be an angel." He' say this just before reading them the third trial jury's statement about his innocence. When finished, he added, "I was a young fellow whose head had been turned around by success. I had plenty of money and there were plenty of fair-weather friends to say 'yes' to me. I was simply led into bad company – and for that I already have paid dearly."

This was a different spin from the strategy he'd used during the trials. When he testified, he claimed that he had been an "angel," coming to Virginia's aid when she became sick. Now he said he'd been taken down the wrong path, blaming his connection to the tragedy on his playboy lifestyle. As to him being a "young fellow" in September 1921? He'd been 34 years old.

But his new version of events didn't always work. His tour through the Pacific Northwest turned out to be a bust. By unanimous vote, the city council in Portland, Oregon, banned him from performing. When the censorship board blocked him from taking the stage in Tacoma, Washington, Roscoe and the theater tried to get a court injunction to stop the board. It failed twice, once on appeal to federal court. After that, he returned to Los Angeles and performed at the Pantages Theatre there.

THE UPS AND DOWNS OF ROSCOE'S CAREER CONTINUED DURING 1924 and into early 1925. Then, on May 16, 1925, Roscoe and Doris Deane were married at her mother's home. Buster Keaton was the best man and Buster's wife, Natalie Talmadge, was the maid of honor. Jospeh Schenck, who was by now chairman of United Artists, and Lou Anger were among the 35 guests. After the ceremony, hundreds attended a reception at Buster and Natalie's new Beverly Hills home. A short time later, the newlyweds moved into a nearby house they rented from Schenck, but not until after they returned from a honeymoon at a location reportedly "hidden away in the country."

Doris and Roscoe were married in May 1925. Buster Keaton was the best man and his wife, Norma, was the maid of honor.

The press, predictably, had a field day with their coverage of the nuptials. Most of the stories were congratulatory, while others were cautious, but there was one headline that read DORIS IS DARING.

Shortly after the wedding, one of the guests, producer Roland West, gave Roscoe a very welcome gift – a contract worth $100,000 to direct 10 two-reel comedies.

The press made a big deal out of the new contract, but it was essentially what Roscoe was already doing, directing low-budget shorts at a time when everyone really wanted features. He had already made 13 shorts for Reel Comedies, the last seven starring his nephew, and his name had appeared on none of them. The new comedies starred either Johnny Arthur or Lupino Lane, former vaudeville performers who went on to busy but lackluster film careers. Even though the new contract got a lot of publicity, when the shorts were released "William Goodrich" was credited, not Roscoe.

But "William Goodrich" did become a very prolific director. For Roscoe, the clock had been turned back to when he was doing the anonymous movie work of 15 years earlier, doing chores for paychecks. Charlie Chaplin and Buster Keaton were now winning great acclaim with their innovative feature films, while Roscoe was toiling away on forgettable shorts starring second-string talent.

Usually it was second-string talent, but not always. For one short called *The Iron Mule*, which was a spoof of John Ford's railroad epic

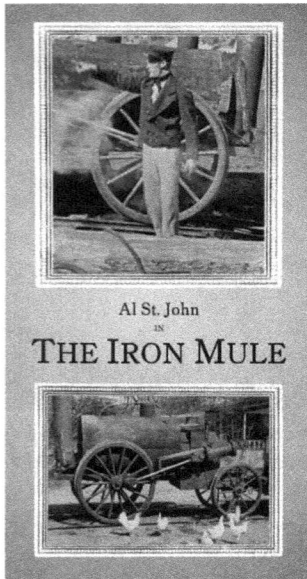

Al St. John
IN
THE IRON MULE

The Iron Horse, Buster Keaton allowed his friend to use the exact replica of the steam engine that had been built for Keaton's feature *Our Hospitality*. Buster also appeared in the short as a Native American. He was uncredited and virtually unrecognizable.

The roles were reversed a few months later when Roscoe appeared in drag for Buster's 1925 feature, *Go West*. As Buster's character tries to stop a cattle stampede through Los Angeles, Roscoe plays a frightened mother in a department store with rotund actress Babe London playing his daughter. Neither role was credited, and it was hard for audiences to miss Fatty in a dress.

But the cameo was more than just another practical joke between Buster and Roscoe. As Babe London remembered, "It was their way of thumbing their noses at the people who had decreed that Roscoe could not appear on the screen."

BUSTER WASN'T THE ONLY MOVIE INDUSTRY FRIEND WHO STUCK by Roscoe. The Masquers, an all-male social club of mostly Actors, was founded in May 1925 as a sort of West Coast version of the famous Friars Club. Roscoe was made an official member by October of that year. Other early members included Buster, Joe Schenck, Tom Mix, and Lionel Barrymore. Others who later joined included Henry Fonda, Frank Sinatra, Humphrey Bogart, and others.

At the time Roscoe became a member, it had been four years since the Los Angeles Athletic Club had kicked him out, so being voted into another exclusive club by his peers was very satisfying for him.

But he also found out that some things hadn't changed. A week or so after being voted in, the Masquers were supposed to perform a comedy revue at Hollywood High School. After receiving protests, though, the school demanded that Roscoe be dropped from the cast. The Masquers stood by their newest member, however. They canceled the high school show and rented the Philharmonic Auditorium instead, where the revue played to a packed house of movie professionals. Roscoe's appearance in the first sketch caused a long ovation, and when it faded and some faint booing was heard, the applause began again.

In December 1925, Hollywood heavyweights Cecil B. DeMille, Charlie Chaplin, and every studio head were among the 600 gathered for a banquet in honor of Sid Grauman – the man he'd worked for as a teenager, singing illustrated songs on a vaudeville bill.

Writer Rupert Hughes, the master of ceremonies, introduced some of the notables at the event and when he came to Roscoe, he asked him to stand. "Here is the sad spectacle of a man being punished by so-called democracy!" Hughes cried out as Roscoe bowed his head. "A man who was acquitted of a trumped-up charge by three American juries! But our militant 'good people' arose to crucify, to persecute an innocent man! They dragged him, down from the topmost pinnacle of being the clean and funny comedian he was and made of him the world's most tragic figure!" The applause that followed was thunderous, much louder for Roscoe than anyone else.

But that applause couldn't help but ring a little hollow. Here was Hollywood showing its love to a man that Hollywood had placed on the blacklist.

IT'S IMPOSSIBLE FOR US TO KNOW HOW OFTEN ROSCOE thought about – or how much he could forget about – the events at the Hotel St. Francis that came to define his life, but at least there were many good times, too.

A front-page article in February 1926 called "Fatty Arbuckle Does Comeback!" showed him as a happily married man, making $2,000 a week as a director, and living in Beverly Hills with his wife and two servants. A photograph accompanied the story and showed Roscoe and Doris with their St. Bernard dog. Luke, sadly, had recently died. The article noted that he'd erased a large part of his debt and planned to have the remainder paid off within three years. He was quoted as saying, "With my wife and my new work, I have found happiness."

In March, Roscoe and Doris, along with friends Buster and Natalie, drove to Yosemite National Park in Roscoe's new convertible Lincoln Phaeton. When

Roscoe's beloved dog, Luke, passed away in 1926.

Roscoe and Doris were often photographed as a happily married couple but what people saw in the movie magazines was later revealed to be fiction

they arrived, Roscoe disregarded orders not to use an automobile entrance that was still under construction so, in retaliation, the road crew blocked the entrance, making it impossible for them to exit the park. They had to hire a train to ship themselves and the car out. It seemed like a plot from one of their old Comique shorts with the merry pranksters one-upping the officials with no sense of humor. A headline appeared in the wake of the incident: MOVIE STARS ESCAPE FROM PARK PRISON.

Lew Cody also remained one of Roscoe's pals and often traveled with him on his adventures, especially those that included alcohol. At 3:00 A.M. on September 17, 1926, Lew and another of Roscoe's friends, Mabel Normand, got drunk and then got married.

By then, Mabel's health was in decline, and her career was almost over. She appeared in her final comedy shorts in 1927 and died of tuberculosis in 1930 at the age of only 37.

ROSCOE'S FIRST ATTEMPT AT DIRECTING A FEATURE – WHEN HE tried to work on *Sherlock Jr.* for his friend, Buster – failed badly. But his second chance came in 1926 from an unlikely source: William Randolph Hearst, who'd made a fortune using Roscoe's name to sell papers five years before. Hearst, although he had never divorced the wife he'd married in 1903, lived openly with his mistress, actress Marion Davies, who was 34 years younger than he was. Hearst had created a production company, Cosmopolitan, just for casting Marion as the star of comedies and costume dramas, burning his way through a large group of directors in the process. Most directors didn't want to work for him, but "William Goodrich" wasn't that choosy, and Roscoe signed on to make a romantic comedy called *The Red Mill*.

From the start, the tyrannical Hearst was anxious about getting the results he wanted from Roscoe, so he assigned MGM director King Vidor to oversee the production. Actress Colleen More recalled, "The intrigues on the set of *The Red Mill* would have made a good thriller. Everyone was aware they were being watched. Arbuckle watched Marion, Vidor watched Arbuckle, and Mr. Hearst watched all three of them. Roscoe had a nice way of making everyone on the set feel relaxed. He was very workmanlike and had no problems communicating what he wanted his cast to do."

The Red Mill turned out to be a flop, which caused Hearst to hire a new director for Marion's next vanity project. But even if the film made no money, it looked great and that may have been what lead Roscoe's old home studio of Paramount to give him another shot. He was hired to direct *Special Delivery*, a comedy feature starring theater legend Eddie Cantor, whose vocal talents didn't translate to silent films. Cantor plays a mailman who is pitted against a suave man – played by a then-little-known William Powell – for the affections of a young woman. The final chase is well-staged, funny, and exciting, proving the directorial skills of "William Goodrich."

Unfortunately, though, the public was no more interest in a

funny mailman than they were in a comedy starring William Heart's girlfriend and Roscoe never worked for Paramount again.

ROSCOE WAS BACK ON NEWSPAPER FRONT PAGES ON MARCH 15, 1927, when he reportedly signed a deal worth $2.5 million over five years to direct and perform in feature films financed by Abe Carlos, who had formerly been with Fox Studios.

Finally, six years after his arrest, Roscoe would again star on the silver screen. Doris would be acting opposite her husband in the films and the first was going to begin production in Germany on October 1.

In the meantime, Roscoe set out on what was billed as his final vaudeville tour – a farewell to the stage before getting back in front of the camera. A Los Angeles review noted the large ovations for him before and after his set but wished that his act or "quips and wisecracks" had focused less on his "misfortunes" and "hard luck."

Roscoe had been down for so long it was going to take some time for him to adjust to the fact that maybe things were going to start looking up. But as it turned out, he was wise to take everything with a grain of salt. As a wise man once said, "a pessimist is always pleasantly surprised."

After the spring vaudeville tour, Roscoe starred in a Broadway revival of the farce, *Baby Mine*. Humphrey Bogart had a supporting role. Roscoe's opening night ovations were strong, but he was awkward on stage. "Mr. Arbuckle is not much of an actor," said one review. It didn't help the show when between acts, its star broke character to speak to the audience about his troubled attempts to return to movies and his impending comeback. *Baby Mine* closed after only 12 performances – another of Roscoe's "misfortunes."

And there were others. Once when he appeared on a New York vaudeville stage, the National Educational Association protested. A lien was placed on his accounts because he'd failed to pay all his 1926 taxes. Minta – to whom he still owed a percentage of his earnings as stated in their divorce decree – sued him for unpaid money based on what the tax filings listed as his income the previous year. Worst of all, the reported October 1 start date of his new film had come and gone.

Roscoe had no choice but to continue his theatrical appearances into 1928. They were still being advertised as "his last vaudeville tour prior to re-entering the movies" but as time passed, his return to film seemed more like a longshot with every day that went by.

Delegations of ministers in Clarksburg, West Virginia, protested Roscoe's appearance at a theater there. He was banned from the stage in Minneapolis because it was feared he "might corrupt public morals." A performance in Waterloo, Iowa, was canceled at the last minute due to protests. And then finally, the movie deal, which would revive his career and rescue his finances, was canceled without explanation.

The growing list of negatives in his life tended to drown out the positive events, like a Kansas City, Missouri, theater showing a Fatty comedy he'd made with Keystone in April 1928 "in defiance of the Hays organization." The morality czar of the movies was now so tarnished by the Teapot Dome Scandal that Senator James A. Reed quipped in a presidential campaign speech, "I have never paraded as a reformer, but I propose that the motion picture industry remove Will Hays and put back Fatty Arbuckle." The crowd laughed, roared, and applauded in agreement.

Weirdly, a French crowd had a different response to Roscoe. He traveled first to Cherbourg and then Paris to perform a comedy show at the prestigious Empire music hall. When he'd embarked on the trip, he'd told a reporter, "Some of my old films have been shown abroad successfully and, on my trip here some years ago, I met with every courtesy."

Not this time. The crowd was so hostile toward his act that theater officials had to summon the police because they feared a riot. Sthe stage manager turned off the lights for eight minutes, "hoping the audience would cool off." They never did and the show was canceled, plus news of the disastrous "riot" was heavily reported in America.

Roscoe's love life wasn't going much better. In May 1928, Roscoe – who had spent the previous 12 months in hotels and on trains and steamships – returned to Los Angeles and moved into the Hollywood Hotel, which had once been the home of Hollywood hopeful, Virginia Rappe. After three years of marriage, he and Doris had separated. As Roscoe put it to a friend, "We haven't got along happily for some time, and if I've got to be lonesome, I might as well be lonesome here."

The marriage between Roscoe and Doris only lasted three years and ended with a litany of accusations and complaints

When Doris filed for divorce in August 1928, she made an explosive charge, claiming that the couple had attended a party in April 1926 at the home of a "prominent resident" of Hollywood where Roscoe became "terribly intoxicated" and forcibly tried to get physical with a female guest. Allegedly, the screaming woman was rescued by Doris and others.

Was it true? Almost undoubtedly, it wasn't. The accusation was never brought to court and aside from a smattering of headlines like ANOTHER WILD PARTY FOR FATTY ARBUCKLE, the press showed almost no interest in the story. Made public more than two years after the incident allegedly occurred, the unsubstantiated charge was merely an attempt by Doris to paint her husband in the worst possible light. She sought $750 a month in alimony and claimed Roscoe had been "vicious, morose, and nagging" during their marriage. The divorce was delayed, and the unhappy marriage continued a little longer.

Actress Viola Dana remembered Roscoe being verbally abusive toward Doris on occasion. She later recalled, "Roscoe was an easy man to like, if you let him be in charge. After that third trial, he believed that everyone was going to let bygones be bygones. But that isn't the way things work in the movie industry, even if people like you. He took all his frustrations, person and professional, out on poor Doris until she couldn't take it anymore."

NO ONE WILL EVER KNOW WHAT MADE ROSCOE DECIDE TO open his own nightclub.

Maybe it was a way to get the party started again, a way for a middle-aged has-been to return to the glory days before Prohibition when his nights were filled with drinking, dancing, and eating. His world then had been a blur of pretty starlets, boxing matches, poker games, steak dinners, and lots of booze. He had his famous friends, none of whom were as famous as he was, and everyone knew him

Roscoe's ill-fated Plantation Club Cafe

and wanted to be his pal. On sleepless nights at the Hollywood Hotel, he dreamed and talked about going back to those glory days until, at last, he bought that nightclub.

He called it Roscoe Arbuckle's Plantation Café. Launched under different ownership in the summer of 1922, the café, with its row of eight Corinthian columns and bright white façade, resembled a southern mansion, as did buildings at MGM and Culver Studios, both located nearby. The club was in Culver City, a city within the city of Los Angeles that had little enthusiasm for Prohibition.

Culver City's main street, Washington Boulevard, was lined with nightclubs and flashing signs – Ford's Castle, Doo Doo Inn, Kit Kat Club, Monkey Farm, and Lyon's Den – and thousands came nightly for live jazz from future legends like Lionel Hampton and Lawrence Brown.

They also came for dancing, gambling, prostitution, and booze. Much of the liquor was brewed in the backyards of nearby houses, which added another boost to the local economy and ensured that Culver City cops and officials kept looking the other way.

The hottest joint on the Washington Boulevard strip was Sebastian's Cotton Club, but the Plantation Café already had a reputation as an upscale destination, thanks to its quality jazz groups, comedy revues, and actors who often appeared as masters of ceremonies. However, the Plantation Club seemed to be the spot that saw the greatest number of liquor raids. Most were for show, although arrests were often made, booze seized, and fines were levied and paid so the Plantation Club could open back up the next night.

Inside the Plantation Club Cafe

Vaudeville comedian Jack Pearl often performed at Roscoe's club

Frequent appearances by Roscoe's pal and cowboy star Tom Mix always pleased the customers at the club

By the time Roscoe and his fellow investors bought the club in July 1928, it's shine had faded a bit. Roscoe was determined to change that. On opening night, August 2, the foyer was jammed with floral tributes, including a giant likeness of Roscoe from Mabel Normand. Celebrities dined on the $10-a-plate dinner ($130 today) and after a handful of cabaret acts, Roscoe, Buster, Al St. John, Tom Mix, and vaudeville comedian Jack Pearl performed a series of slapstick antics, including a custard pie toss.

One article reported about the night: "Every screen star of note now in Hollywood was present with ears pinned back and hair well larded. And if their hosannas are a criterion, the future of Arbuckle as a restaurateur is assured."

The newly revived club was a hit from the start, selling out each night to "a strange crowd of big-time movie stars, would-be stars, and tourists." Jazz greats played the Plantation Cafe, but

Roscoe was the biggest attraction in his own club. He also inspired its new theme – fat farmers. The waiters, hat check girls, and parking attendants were all large and, in keeping with the theme of plantation workers and, as a callback to Roscoe's own country bumpkin character, they all wore bib overalls.

The month after the club opened, Britain's Prince George, a notorious playboy, was in Los Angeles and was partying with a young actress. His first stop had been at the estate of Hollywood power couple Douglas Fairbanks and Mary Pickford and then went on to Gloria Swanson's house. At some point during the early morning hours, his entourage, which now included a number of celebrities, arrived at the Plantation and persuaded Roscoe to keep the place open. The shindig ended at the club at 5:00 A.M. but the party moved back to Gloria Swanson's.

Roscoe, of course, went along with them. This was the life he wanted – Hollywood royalty and a party that seemed like it would never end. It was the lifestyle he'd sworn off six years before when what he wanted most was a return to movie stardom. Now that his return to films had been denied, though, he embraced the party lifestyle more openly than ever.

Two days before Christmas in 1928, the Plantation was raided, and 10 men, not including Roscoe, were arrested for Prohibition violations. It was business as usual, but it was the first raid that had occurred since Roscoe owned the place.

In January 1929, the club was cited after neighbors complained about the noise. Roscoe ignored the order to keep things quiet until the Culver City mayor visited and threatened to close the club. Then in May, a fight broke out at the club and when the police arrived to disperse the brawlers, they turned on the cops and the incident turned into a riot. One policeman was critically injured in the resulting mess.

The riot wasn't great for publicity, but it might have survived if it hadn't been for what happened next – the stock market crash of October 1929 and the subsequent Depression.

Roscoe sold his share of the club in 1930 and soon after, the Plantation Café closed for good.

NINETEEN

ROSCOE'S RESURRECTED DIRECTORIAL CAREER CRASHED AND burned before it even got a chance to start again. After the failure of two features, he went back to what he knew would pay the bills – vaudeville. He spent the next three years on the stage and greeting guests at the Plantation Club while it lasted.

Meanwhile, without him, the movie industry started to talk.

Since the start of films, actors had been rendered mute, and their silence was a peculiar part of the cinema that everyone accepted as normal. Silence limited the films but also gave actors and directors a variety of different ways to express themselves. Some complexities of storytelling and character-building were lost but silent films in the 1920s developed a way to compensate for anything that a viewer might miss without sound. In fact, many were critical of sound films, claiming that taking away the silence would destroy their art, just like destroying a painting or a sculpture.

But audiences weren't as attached to silent films as the critics were. From almost the start, inventors had tried to make moving pictures talk. In 1895, two years after unveiling his viewing-box Kinetoscope, Thomas Edison introduced the Kinetophone, which added sounds using a phonograph player. Viewers listened to music and effects with earphones as they looked into the cabinet, watching moving pictures that were out of synch with the recording. Only 45 such machines were sold, and film projectors soon made the viewing boxes obsolete.

Other inventors tried to synchronize projected films with phonograph records. Competing systems with names like Chronophone, Synchroscope, and the Cameraphone. Edison even unveiled one in 1913, but none of them caught on.

Others took a different route. In 1901, German physics professor Ernst Ruhmer created a Photographophone, which played back sounds recorded as waves on film strips. The volume was controlled by increasing or decreasing the amount of light used during playback.

A former Edison employee named Eugene Lauste made the greatest advances in recording, projection, and amplification of sound and picture on film. He secured the patent for his system in 1907 – and then shot America's first sound film in 1911. He worked to improve the technology, but World War I and a lack of financing killed the project.

In 1919, Lee de Forest patented an improved method for recording sound and moving images on film simultaneously. He commercially screened 18 short sound movies in New York City on April 13, 1923 – and the "talking picture" industry was born.

The major studios weren't interested yet but in 1924, a small animation company began using de Forest's system for sing-a-long cartoons, but after his financing fell through, his company declared bankruptcy. The sound patents were sold to Fox Film Corporation, and Fox released *Sunrise* on October 23, 1927, with the first feature-length sound-on-film soundtrack. Still, those sounds were only music and effects. The dialogue was still subtitled.

Around the same time, a struggling Warner Brothers utilized the sound-on-a disc system from Bell Telephone Company, which Warners dubbed Vitaphone. Their first use of them connecting a phonograph record soundtrack with a motion picture was *Don Juan*, released in August 1926. Again, the characters stayed silent while the synchronized soundtrack played music and effects.

Sound-on-disc movies were cheaper to make than sound-on-film productions and had superior audio but getting them synched to the film was a continuous challenge, as was the delivery of the necessary discs, which wore out quickly, often skipped, and were easy to scratch or break. Thanks to this, a coalition of studios – that didn't include Warners and Fox – agreed to a standard sound-on-film technology in early 1927.

The Vitaphone projector

But it was Warner's sound-on-disc system that launched the "talking pictures" phenomenon when *The Jazz Singer*, starring Al Jolson, was released on October 6, 1927. Though most of the audio was a score recorded separately and most of the "talking" was singing, Jolson's songs and some of the dialogues were recorded live on set – the first time for any feature film.

It was a huge success that changed Hollywood forever.

Well, it would eventually change everything. At first, even the sound-on-film studios were hesitant to produce their own talkies. With the addition of audio, movies became a new medium, with new problems and new expenses.

Dialogue became a screenwriter's priority. It couldn't be an afterthought added to an intertitle as an afterthought anymore. Delivering those audible words became the crucial function of actors, many of whom, by the late 1920s, had never spoken a line heard by an audience. Directors were restrained by the need to record with microphones and cameramen were hampered by bulkier cameras, which had to be padded to quiet the hum that might be heard on the soundtrack. Studios had to invest in audio equipment and hire people to operate it. Theaters had to purchase and install sound systems. And the list went on.

Fighting the inevitable, there was a brilliant burst of creativity in silent films in 1927 and 1928, but they turned out to be the final attempts to save a dying format.

"Talking pictures" became all the rage and even the hesitant studios gave in to progress and by the end of February 1929, all the major studios had released at one sound feature. The last entirely silent feature came out that August.

The art and industry of D.W. Griffith and Mack Sennett, along with the comic stylings of Buster Keaton, Mabel Normand, and Roscoe "Fatty" Arbuckle were now a part of the past.

Hollywood was heading toward the future.

AFTER ENDING UP ON THE VAUDEVILLE STAGE AGAIN – PLUS THE arrival of talking pictures -- Roscoe must have felt the movies had left him behind for good. But in November 1929, it was announced that he was going to be starring in a new talking feature directed by the always-loyal James Cruze, who had directed Roscoe's final four features before Labor Day 1921 and had slipped him into 1923's *Hollywood*. Cruze had started his own production company, and he was going to put his old pal back to work.

Right away, reporters mused about the numerous protests that had accompanied other announcements about Roscoe returning to the movies. "Now Hollywood wonders – and expects soon to learn – whether the passing of years as softened these opinions," one wrote.

They hadn't softened and the Cruze-directed film was never produced.

Instead, Roscoe made the best of a bad situation, returning to the business he loved by writing uncredited gags for comedy sound shorts for RKO. Later that years, "William Goodrich" also started directing comedy shorts for performers whose names have been forgotten over the years.

Over the next two years, "Goodrich" directed – and frequently wrote – 27 talking shorts for Educational Films and made five more for RKO in his spare time. It was the Keystone pace of approximately one movie every three weeks. In two of the RKO shorts, Roscoe took a shot at the incident that led to his banishment. In both *That's My Line* and *Beach Pajamas*, a scheming female traps an innocent salesman by putting him in a compromising position.

One of those 27 films starred another Hollywood outcast, Louise Brooks, who had once been a Paramount star and a flapper icon. At the height of her career, though, she snubbed the studio and went to Europe, where she starred in the sexually charged *Pandora's Box* in 1929. She starred in the ninth film on the list; *Windy Riley Goes to Hollywood* in 1931 and later recalled: "He made no attempt to direct

Louise Brooks

this picture. He sat in his chair like a man dead. He had been very nice and sweetly dead since the scandal that ruined his career. But it was such an amazing thing for me to come to make this broken-down picture, and to find my director was the great Roscoe Arbuckle. Oh, I thought he was magnificent in films."

Windy Riley Goes to Hollywood was one of seven of Roscoe's new shorts with *Hollywood* in the title, and each typically focused on a young starlet trying to break into the movie business. Two of them starred a teenage Betty Grable, who became a major star in the 1940s. The *Hollywood* films allowed Roscoe to poke fun at the studios that prevented him from appearing onscreen. *Windy Riley* is an awful film and was immediately followed by another movie with the same theme, so it's easy to believe what Louise Brooks believed – that Roscoe was just there for the paycheck.

But if you watch a film that he made one year later called *Bridge Wives*, starring Al St. John as the neglected husband of a woman addicted to the national craze for playing bridge, Roscoe was very creative. The soundtrack used a radio that can neither be turned off nor destroyed, using original camera angles, and expertly captured Al's maniacal acting. Maybe the clever script and that fact that he was working with his nephew inspired him, but Roscoe managed to hide the small budget of the film with quick pacing and originality that's helped it age well. It's much better than most early sound films.

It makes you wonder what Roscoe could have accomplished if he'd had more money, more time, and longer stories. But that wasn't in the cards, and he directed his final movie, *Niagara Falls*, in the summer of 1932.

SOME OF ROSCOE'S LATER FILMS USED THE DRAMA OF married life as the inspiration for the comedy – and that's no surprise. He likely had a pretty bleak view of it after two failed marriages. In September 1929, Doris filed a second divorce complaint, but this time made no mention of another wild party. Instead, she claimed desertion and cruelty: "He left me and went to a Hollywood hotel. I called him and asked him to come back, but he wouldn't. He said he was through."

The marriage, though, was not officially dead for another 13 months. Around the time of the divorce, Roscoe met his next wife. Like the first two, Addie McPhail was a young actress.

Born in 1905, Addie spent her early childhood in Kentucky before her family relocated to Chicago. Now a teenager, she began entering singing competitions and usually won. In 1922, the week after she turned 17, she married a musician and a daughter, Marilyn, was born. The couple soon split up, though, and in 1925, Addie moved with her family to Los Angeles and quickly landed her first movie role.

Addie McPhail

The pretty young woman with dark hair, a dimpled smile, and striking jawline, Addie signed with a low-budget company and was featured prominently in two series of comedy shorts and in smaller roles in several features. "I was a stranger in Hollywood, so it was only my appearance that opened doors, although they never opened very wide.," she later said. She continued to work steadily, but real stardom managed to elude her. In 1930, she was living in a Hollywood apartment with her father and her daughter.

Roscoe claimed he fell in love with Addie, who was 18 years younger, when he saw her in two films in 1930. He cast her in the shorts he made for Educational. Addie later recalled, "I had feelings for Roscoe, but we worked together for several months at the studio before we even had lunch together."

Once their relationship began, Roscoe cast her in more films, including *Beach Pajamas*, which was mentioned earlier. He also began taking her out on the town. They dined at the Brown Derby and went dancing at the Ambassador Hotel and in the rooftop garden on top of the Roosevelt Hotel. Roscoe turned 44 in 1931 and most of the other partiers at Hollywood hot spots were the new stars of the talkies and were, like Addie, much younger than he was, but Roscoe still lived the high life.

Roscoe still spent plenty of cash on food and drinks for himself and his friends – as well as the "friends" that tagged along in his entourage. He still had a flashy car, and he still went out to the nightclubs. He was then living in an apartment a block from the heart of the Sunset Strip in what is today West Hollywood. Back then, this area was unincorporated, which made it immune from Los Angeles police raids.

For Addie, for whom acting had just brought in a modest income, she was now thrust in the spotlight of Hollywood gossip columns, VIP areas of exclusive clubs, reserved restaurant tables, and black-tie events.

The largest of those events was held on November 7, 1931, when a massive number of film notables gathered in the ballroom at the Biltmore Hotel for the opening of the movie industry's social season – Great Depression all but forgotten.

Roscoe and Addie

Dinner was served at 10:00 P.M. and dancing ended around dawn. A highlight "was the dancing of the serpentine by all the guests, during which Roscoe Arbuckle became the drummer in the orchestra in an impromptu display of jazz-band talent."

As for exclusive clubs, none was more exclusive than the Embassy Club, an opulent spot in Hollywood with a glass-enclosed rooftop lounge. The 300 members included Charlie Chaplin, Sid Grauman, Gloria Swanson, and Roscoe Arbuckle, and only members and their guests were allowed to enter. The Embassy was a place for celebrities to eat, drink, and dance in private. No tourists allowed.

On September 19, 1931, Roscoe was at the club with a screenwriter and two unidentified women, one of whom was likely Addie. When they left at 2:00 A.M., a police officer refused to let Roscoe drive because he thought he was intoxicated. Roscoe smashed a bottle of liquor that had been in his car and quipped, "There goes the evidence." He later claimed he had no idea where the bottle came from, saying, "I thought someone was playing a practical joke on me and, when the officer addressed me, I threw it out merely as a precaution."

At the police station, Roscoe and the screenwriter both passed sobriety tests and Roscoe good-naturedly insisted the officer take the test, too. He did and passed. The whole incident was shrugged off after Roscoe paid a $10 fine for breaking the bottle.

ALTHOUGH ROSCOE WAS STILL INTENT ON ENJOYING HIS extended adolescence, he still found himself unhappy. In the March 1931 issue of *Photoplay*, an article about him appeared under the title, "Just Let Me Work." It summarized his struggle against censorship and his attempts to clear his name and reclaim his place in front of the camera. One section read: "For years, his name and the news of the fight were good copy. But then, inevitably, came the indifference that is worse in Fatty's profession than the most rabid condemnation. Fatty was left to be forgotten."

The article concluded by allowing Roscoe to make another argument for his return:

All I want is to be allowed to work in my field. It isn't for the money. I'm not broke. My conscience is clear; my heart is clean.... People have the right to their opinions. The people who oppose me have the right to theirs. I have the right to mine – which is that I've suffered enough and have been humiliated enough. I want to go back to the screen. I think I can entertain and gladden the people that see me. All I want is that. If I do get back, it will be grand. If I don't – well, okay.

Two months later, *Motion Picture Classic* published a piece called "Isn't Fatty Arbuckle Punished Enough?" It stated that one recent plan for Roscoe's return had been deterred by protests from women's groups but still, the article tried to rally its readers: "Statisticians have figured out a life sentence in prison is commuted on an average of 10 years. Isn't a decade a long sentence for any man to serve? Hasn't Fatty suffered enough? Is he to be forever denied a chance to stage a comeback?"

Meanwhile, James Quirk from *Photoplay* went on a radio program and asked listeners for their opinions about Roscoe's possible return to films. Over 3,000 letters poured into the magazine, overwhelmingly in favor of Roscoe. Among the letter writers was D.A. Matthew Brady, who stated again, "Arbuckle should be allowed to make his own living in his own way."

A third fan magazine, *Motion Picture*, also chimed in with two articles – "Doesn't Fatty Arbuckle Deserve a Break?" and "The Fans Want Fatty Arbuckle Back on the Screen."

But Roscoe's hopes had been dashed too many times already for him to believe these new attempts would succeed where others had failed in the past. Even so, in June 1931, likely hoping for some sympathy, he told a reporter, "I have no desire to return as an actor. In the dark hours of my life, it was a consolation to know that I had given happiness to millions of people. There doesn't seem to be much chance of happiness for me. No man can live and be happy without work, and all I want to do is to be permitted to use whatever talents and training I have in the writing and direction of pictures under my own name."

Roscoe and Addie on their wedding day, posing with guest, Jimmy Durante

ROSCOE CONTINUED TO EARN MOST OF HIS MONEY ON THE stage. He embarked on a vaudeville tour of eastern Canada with fiancée Addie as his female lead. She recalled later that he was warmly received, even in the larger cities, and ran into very little opposition.

In early May 1932, he was booked for six weeks in and around New York City. The Palace Theater on Broadway advertised his show with a sign about the marquee with his name in giant letters. Below were six additional names, including Milton Berle. Roscoe also took part in a vaudeville benefit show at the Metropolitan Opera, where Berle, who often performed in drag, was "master or mistress of ceremonies."

While their vaudeville tour was hopscotching cities in the east, Addie and Roscoe decided to get married. The wedding took place at 2:30 A.M. on June 21 in Erie, Pennsylvania, after a court reporter and a justice of the peace were roused from their beds.

A month later, when the couple was back in New York and performing at a vaudeville house in Brooklyn, Roscoe was contacted by his agent, Joe Rivkin, and told that Warner Brothers wanted him to star in a new sound short. Filming was going to take place at the Vitaphone studio in Brooklyn. Addie remembered, "Roscoe felt like he had been given his life back. It was the call he had been waiting 11 years for."

He signed the contract in New York City on July 27. A photo of that moment, with his new wife and a studio executive watching, was titled "Star Emerging from Eclipse." A story from the Associated Press noted, "Frankly gambling on Fatty's chance for success, the producers decided to risk just one picture. If the Arbuckle box office power of the past is apparent, Fatty will be on a high road to the most spectacular comeback in film history."

"It's kind of like home to me, you know – pictures," Roscoe told a reporter, and he explained that comedy styles were always changing. "You got to adapt," he said, but quickly added, "But I can promise they'll be good, clean, wholesome pictures. Broad comedy, with something for the children."

That promise had to be made – clean and wholesome. The event that had driven him from theaters nearly 11 years earlier was never far from his mind – and he knew it was never far from the minds of most people when they thought of him either.

Roscoe added, "They got all the money I had. II ended up a quarter of a million dollars in debt. I've paid it back in vaudeville. Did they cram it down my throat? Plenty…"

"They" were the people who had made him out to be a monster – the prosecutors, the press, the censors, and the protestors. Then, as if to answer the question before it was asked, Roscoe said, "I never did anything. I've got a clear conscience and a clean heart."

TWENTY

ROSCOE'S FIRST SOUND FILM WAS RELEASED IN NOVEMBER 1932. Titled *Hey, Pop!* it was not only his starring role in over 11 years, but it was also the first time that most of his fans heard him speak. He'd never appeared in anything other than a silent film.

Warner Brothers had been careful about everything connected to the film. They had returned Roscoe to his customary onscreen get-up – oversized pants and undersized bowler hat – and frequent secondary costume of a dress, and as slapstick plot and gags that were reminiscent of the two-reelers he made in the 1910s. The only addition was dialogue and Roscoe handled that like a champ.

Shorts like *Hey, Pop!* always played ahead of feature attractions and typically weren't advertised on marquees or in newspapers. Thanks to this, Roscoe's comeback created little controversy and while it garnered some positive reviews, it mostly went unnoticed.

There was by now a new generation of movie stars and movie fans. The transition from silence to sound proved to be a clear line between the present and the past. Silent comedians and their sight gags had been placed in the dustbin of movie history.

Buster Keaton was one of the few silent stars to make it into the new era unscathed. With sound, he also returned to making comedy shorts, appearing in 26 of them between 1934 and 1941. He went on to have roles in feature films, plays, and television programs until his death in 1966 at the age of 70.

Roscoe ended up making three comedy shorts for Warner Brothers, all in the last five months of 1932 and each shot in less than a week at Brooklyn's Vitaphone studio. The second of these, *Buzzin'*

Around, featured Al St. John and a swarm of animated bees and became the last of 63 films with uncle and nephew.

A third film, *How've You Bean?* had Roscoe mishandling some Mexican jumping beans. Like the bees in the second film, the beans were animated. Thanks to the rise of Mickey Mouse, short comedy was increasingly animated. And slapstick, which had gone from vaudeville to silent films to sound films during Roscoe's lifetime, it now found a new and lasting home in cartoons.

IN LATE 1932, NEW YORK GOSSIP COLUMNS FREQUENTLY reported on the after-hours activities of Roscoe and his young, attractive wife. They appeared in all the right night spots and danced at such legendary joints as the Cotton Club, Onyx Club, and Roseland Ballroom.

A suite at Manhattan's elegant Park Central Hotel became home for Roscoe, Addie, Addie's then eight-year-old daughter, Marilyn, and their maid. Roscoe never had a child of his own, but he loved kids, and they loved playing with him. For the first time since he'd lived with Minta's family in the early 1910s, there was a child in his home, and he went out of his way to spoil and dote on the little girl.

In early 1933, the family of three returned to Los Angeles on vacation. When it was over, they boarded a train and returned to the east. It was the last time that Roscoe saw California – a place that he once loved so much.

During Mardi Gras week in March 1933, he and Addie played a weeklong vaudeville engagement to packed houses in New Orleans.

In April, he was back at Vitaphone Studios, starring in a comedy short called *Close Relations*, which featured Shemp Howard of Three Stooges fame. He also made two others – *Tomalio* and *In the Dough* – and had no love interest in any of the shorts, avoiding any association with the scandal of Labor Day 1921.

Roscoe's final film, *In the Dough*, was a reminder of more innocent times. Its spirited pie fight hearkens back to Roscoe's Keystone

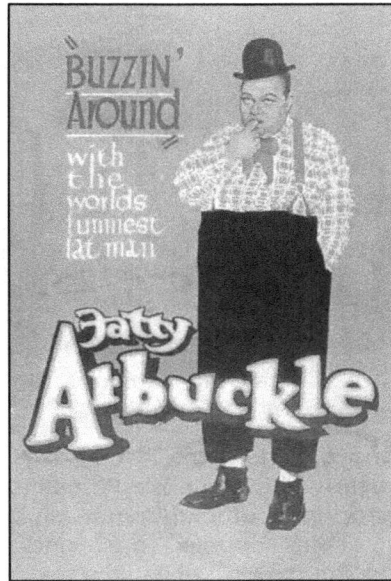

A scene from Roscoe's final film, "In the Dough"

days, when every scene had the potential to turn into a custard battle and Fatty's fame was getting bigger by the day. Production on the short began on June 22 and wrapped on the afternoon of June 28.

That evening, Roscoe and Addie belatedly celebrated their one-year anniversary at Billy La Hiff's Tavern, a popular hangout for Broadway and film notables in midtown Manhattan. Booze was served at the tavern with a wink at Prohibition, which was on that summer evening nearing its official demise on December 5.

The couple ate and ordered cocktails. Addie played backgammon, while Roscoe chatted with friends, including former world boxing champ Johnny Dundee. Roscoe had tickets to the world heavyweight championship fight the following evening at the Madison Square Garden Bowl, a 72,000-seat outdoor arena in Queens. Roscoe and his agent, Joe Rivkin, discussed his Midwest vaudeville tour, which was scheduled to start in four days and about Warner Brothers' plans to produce eight additional Fatty shorts. A feature film was even a possibility.

It seems perfect that the last full day of Roscoe's life was spent with him acting in a film and then going out on the town, eating, drinking, and socializing with friends – those were the things that made him happiest.

Roscoe told Joe Rivkin that night, "I've made my comeback. There are lots of stars not doing as well as I am right now."

Roscoe and Addie had planned to go to a nightclub after supper, but he felt unusually tired and wanted to go home. Since her husband rarely passed up the chance to keep the party going, Addie knew he wasn't feeling well. At around 11:30 P.M., he and Addie took a cab seven blocks back to their suite at the Park Central Hotel. Roscoe was in bed by 12:30 A.M.

At some point during the early morning hours of June 29, 1933, Roscoe Arbuckle died from a heart attack in his sleep. He was only 46 years old.

Roscoe's funeral in New York. His final services were held at the Fresh Bond Crematory in Queen. Addie later scattered his ashes on the beach in Santa Monica – a place he'd always loved

ROSCOE'S BODY, DRESSED IN A GRAY SUIT, WHITE SHIRT, AND dark bow tie, was laid in a casket in the ornate Gold Room of Frank E. Campbell's Funeral Church on Manhattan's Upper West Side. As many as 1,000 mourners and curious onlookers filed past his body on June 29 and 30.

Campbell's had a reputation for discreetly and securely handling the funeral needs of the rich and famous, dating back to 1926, when they handled the services of Rudolph Valentino.

Funeral services were conducted by officers of an Elks Lodge – Roscoe was an Elk – at 1:00 P.M. on Saturday, July 1. At least 300 people attended, and honorary pallbearers included Billy La Hiff, Joe Rivkin, Ray McCarey – director of Roscoe's last three movies – and comic actor Bert Lahr, who later played the Cowardly Lion in *The Wizard of Oz*. Because only two days elapsed between his death and his funeral, Roscoe's friends in California didn't have time to make it across the country by train. Buster Keaton, Charlie Chaplin, and Joe Schneck were among those who sent flowers.

An Elks official said in the eulogy: "We think of his love of children and how he brought a surcease of sorrow to those in pain. There is nothing in the world like laughter, and so we may say that he made the world laugh. And now that the end has come, we know he will be judged by the good he has done."

After the service, a sobbing Addie, wearing all white, followed the flower-covered casket outside to the hearse, while the police pushed back a crowd of at least 500 of the morbid curious. She followed the hearse in a chauffeur-driven car to Fresh Pond Crematory in Queens. Later that day, Addie, Marilyn, and their maid returned to Los Angeles.

Within weeks of his death, Roscoe's brothers, Harry and Clyde, contested his will, claiming they had the right to over $100,000 in stocks and bonds. In July 1934, though, a New York court ruled that the assets in Roscoe's estate totaled only $2,00. Minus debts, Addie was awarded $396.

Addie only appeared in a few more films in the years that followed. The parts were always small. She later remarried and lived in Los Angeles until her death at age 97 in 2003.

On September 6, 1934, Roscoe's ashes were shipped to Addie in Los Angeles. Alone, she stood out on the end of a pier and committed the ashes to the pacific Ocean off Santa Monica – the waters in which Roscoe had loved to swim on those happy days two decades earlier when his fame and fortune were just starting to grow.

And when Roscoe could have never imagined the highs and lows that his life would reach in the years ahead.

ROSCOE'S OBITUARIES MOSTLY FOCUSED ON THE LOW POINTS of his life and career. The *Los Angeles Times* was particularly unkind. The obituary read:

Died. Roscoe Conkling ("Fatty") Arbuckle, 46, globular old-time cineactor; of a heart attack; in Manhattan. Although acquitted of manslaughter after the death of one Virginia Rappe eleven years ago, the malodorous evidence brought out at the trial dropped him to obscurity; resulted in the appointment of President Harding's Postmaster General Will H. Hays as public apologist for Hollywood.

Some obituary writers used Roscoe to tell a cautionary tale:

Instead of being the innocent and jovial bystander he so amusingly depicted, Arbuckle was disclosed as a weakling who couldn't stand prosperity and who, under the influence of intoxicants, became a coarse vulgarian. But now there can only be a feeling of pity for Fatty Arbuckle – a man who muffed a wonder opportunity in life. Young people should be able to learn something from a study of his life – it is as important to know the road to avoid as the road to take.

Others told a tragic story:

Arbuckle got a rough deal in life. He was yanked from the heights and shot to the depths so that I sometimes wonder how he managed to survive the ordeal. And for what? For doing something that happens in every city, in every state, in every hotel on every day of the year. For staging a drunken party. But Arbuckle got the rap that most partygoers are fortunate enough to miss. In his case, a sick girl died. And the holier-than-thous swooped down upon the man with such vengeance that they deprived him of his livelihood for many years.

Will Rogers

Will Rogers, as only he could do it, poetically echoed that sentiment by saying, "Those who demanded their pound of flesh finally received their satisfaction. Fatty Arbuckle accommodated 'em by dying, and from a broken heart."

His heart may have literally broken, but Roscoe was happier than he'd been in over a decade. He was married again – this time happily – and had a stepdaughter that he adored. He was working onstage and acting in films. He was no longer burdened by overwhelming debts and was optimistic about his future for the first time in a very long time.

But June 29, 1933, may have been as good as it would ever get. His comeback may have continued, and he may have been able to make some more comedy shorts but judging by the careers of most other silent stars, it likely would have faded away in a few years, and it almost certainly would have never reached the heights that he enjoyed before Labor Day 1921.

Or perhaps I'm wrong. Maybe Roscoe would have ended up like Buster Keaton, becoming a film legend and managing to keep his career going for decades to come.

Maybe, or maybe not.

One thing we can say for sure is that Roscoe's final films continued to play after he was gone – and some of them are still around today. Just as the people who saw them in theaters in the mid-1930s, we can still watch him fall, get in trouble with the cops, win over the pretty girl, and throw custard pies.

And we can laugh, just like his audience used to do, and like them, we can forget about his trials and his troubles for a while and forget, just as they did, about the reality of our own lives.

Roscoe Arbuckle was a man who deserved better. He may not have been perfect, but his life was ruined thanks to lies, greed, and the need that so many people so desperately have to want to chip away at the pedestals on which we place others, only so we can watch them fall.

TWENTY-ONE

LET ME START THE FINAL CHAPTER OF THIS BOOK ABOUT THE RISE and fall of Roscoe Arbuckle by saying up front that no one knows what truly happened in room 1219 at the Hotel St. Francis on Labor Day 1921.

I'll reiterate one line from the preceding paragraph – no one knows. No one will ever know. Only two people ever knew. One of them died a few days later and the other was charged with her death, went on trial three times, and died himself in 1933.

But since no one ever knew what truly happened, it seems unfair that Roscoe Arbuckle was ever arrested or charged at all. The accusations against him were made by a woman who never testified at his trials and the newspapers whipped the public into such a frenzy that prosecutors had no choice but to try and punish him, not once but three times.

In the decades that followed the events of Labor Day 1921, the story faded until only a handful of unfortunate descriptions of those events remained, like "tried for the rape death of actress," "scandal-plagued," thrown out of Hollywood." And there were the more vivid and salacious details that hung on whenever the name "Fatty Arbuckle" were mentioned, things like ice, champagne bottles, Coca-Cola bottles, and description of Fatty being "well-endowed."

Legends, lore, myth, and mythology.

The true story of Roscoe Arbuckle has been lost over time. It's become forgotten, misremembered, confused, and so filled with anecdotes that have defamed both Roscoe and Virginia Rappe in ways that it becomes no surprise to learn that both of their ghosts are rumored to still linger behind – but we'll come back to that.

So, what really happened that afternoon in room 1219?

As I said, no one knows for sure but there are plenty of theories – some of which make more sense than others – and there are also plenty of legends and lies that need to be dispelled so that we can get to the heart of the matter.

WHILE MANY WERE CRITICAL OF ROSCOE'S LIFE AND ALLEGED crimes when he died, he had his defenders, too. And many of them continued to protect him in the decades after his death.

Dashiell Hammett

One of them was Dashiell Hammett, the author of such hard-boiled classics like *The Maltese Falcon* and *The Thin Man*, but before he wrote about private detectives, he was one. In January 1922, he was 27 years old and a transplant from the East to San Francisco. At the time of Roscoe's first trial, he was nearing the end of his six-year employment with the Pinkerton National Detective Agency. The Pinkertons had been hired by the defense team to find evidence and locate witnesses to assist with their case. Hammett was one of those investigators.

His assessment of Roscoe's case was worthy of a detective novel and conspiratorial enough that it could have only been untangled by someone like Sam Spade. Hammett said, "The whole thing was a frame-up, arranged by some corrupt local newspaper boys. Arbuckle was good copy, so they set him up for a fall."

One of Roscoe's greatest postmortem defenders was celebrity journalist Adela Rogers St. John. In 1950, she wrote a piece called "The Arbuckle Tragedy" for the *American Weekly*, a magazine that was widely circulated as a newspaper supplement. In it, she quoted her male housekeeper, who said that he had also cleaned for Virginia Rappe until the day the naked actress ran outside, shouting for help, and claiming that the housekeeper had attacked her.

"The neighbors said whenever she got a few drinks in her she did that," the unnamed housekeeper told her. Adela alleged that she had confirmed this was with the unnamed neighbors.

She also framed the story so that it appeared that Roscoe had been easily acquitted by not mentioned the first two trials at all.

Instead, she simply noted that "the jury acquitted him in less than a minute."

In 1957, movie power broker Donald Crisp claimed that Roscoe was framed: "He was no more guilty of killing that girl than the man in the moon. He wasn't even in San Francisco. Her dead body was discovered at three in the afternoon. He didn't get to San Francisco until that evening." Yes, it's hard to take this story seriously since it's so... wrong, but if nothing else, it showed how easy it was to rewrite the entire story.

There were well-meaning people trying to defend Roscoe – no matter how badly they were doing it – but their attempts to come to his rescue only kept the scandals and rumors alive and did

Adela Rogers St. John

nothing to help preserve the knowledge of his talent and humor.

In 1949, a public opinion poll of the top 15 funniest comedians of all time, Charlie Chaplin was the only silent star to make the list at number 15. Roscoe did get a few votes, though, as did Buster Keaton and Harold Lloyd, although Bob Hope came out on top. That same year, in a cover story in *Life* Magazine called "Comedy's Greatest Era," respected critic James Agee championed slapstick of the silent era. Only one sentence of the 16-page article was dedicated to Roscoe, mentioning his talent without mentioning the scandal. Then, in separate and lengthy tributes, "the four most eminent masters" were named – Charlie Chaplin, Buster Keaton, Harold Lloyd, and Harry Langdon.

Roscoe had been written out of the history of silent comedies, even though he had a profound effect on at least two of the men who made the list.

But there were exceptions. Bob Hope, who never forgot his early debt to the banished star, often spoke about the joy of watching Roscoe at work.

Roscoe was also one of the original 1,158 people chosen by the motion picture selection committee for the Hollywood Walk of Fame. These initial sidewalk stars were laid without ceremony in 1960 and 1961, and Roscoe's inclusion sparked no protests.

In a funny sidenote, Charlie Chaplin was rejected from the first round of sidewalk stars because of his liberal politics. Roscoe's

inclusion and Charlie's rejection prompted one Hollywood observe to quip, "It's apparently all right to rape and murder, but it's not all right to be a pinko." Charlie got his star in 1972.

Beyond those exceptions, Fatty footage was included in the 1960 feature documentary about silent film slapstick called *When Comedy was King*, and its 1961 sequel, *Days of Thrills and Laughter*. His scenes are all celebrations of his artistry and are without any mention of controversy.

THE BOOK✒

THE FIRST BOOK THAT ATTEMPTED TO TELL THE STORY OF Roscoe's case didn't come out until 41 years after his arrest. The absence of Arbuckle books was in sharp contrast to the number of book announcements made by his ex-wives.

The first, announced by Doris Deane, came in 1935 and was to be a biography and possible film. Neither happened.

Minta Durfee

Four years later came the news that Minta Durfee had written a play about her former husband titled "The Clown Speaks." It never appeared but in 1951, she said she was writing a book of the same name. By 1955, the title had been changed to "My Clown Cried." In 1971, a news item claimed the book was finished and that "Bob Hope was interested in buying the movie rights." The book was never published, although sections of her manuscript can be found today in the Margaret Herrick Library of the Academy of Motion Picture Arts and Sciences.

In 1960, a lengthy United Syndicate article focused on Roscoe's trials. Most of what it had to say can be summarized in one line from the piece: "The, in 1921, Funny Fatty became involved in a sordid sex affair and all the people who loved him suddenly and mercilessly decided to hate him." Just how sordid that alleged "sex affair" was rumored to have been remained a whispered rumor for decades after its occurrence. It wasn't even published in underground "tell-all" books like *The Sins of Hollywood*. By the early 1960s, though, these rumors started to find new life in print.

And that's when things really started to get wild.

IN 1952, *CONFIDENTIAL* MAGAZINE WAS LAUNCHED BY ROBERT Harrison. Its slogan was "Tell the Facts and Name the Names," though facts were hard to find in its pages and names were usually attached to nothing more rumor and innuendo. Mostly by emphasizing gossip and celebrity sexuality, the circulation numbers for *Confidential* quickly soared to over three and a half million people. The huge success of the magazine spawned more than a dozen imitators and the newsstands filled with racks of garish colored rags with shocking headlines that screamed for attention. After being hit by a score of libel suits, the magazine was eventually tamed by the studios in 1958, and Harrison sold it.

Roscoe's scandal had faded so far into history by the time *Confidential* began its six-year run that it was never featured in its pages, but later coverage of the case owes a debt to what *Confidential* achieved by blazing a trail so that future publishers could delve into all kinds of Hollywood sex scandals – including Roscoe Arbuckle's.

The book appeared in 1962. Just inside the front cover was a screaming, caps locked description of what was inside:

HERE IS THE SHOCKING, SOMETIMES SORDID, AND ALWAYS FASCINATING STORY OF ONE OF THE MOST FAMOUS CRIMINAL TRIALS OF ALL TIME – THE FATTY ARBUCKLE CASE.

The cover itself featured Roscoe's giant, frowning face, carefully blocking the view of the unclothed parts of a pretty brunette who is lounging next to a bottle of liquor. Erven though it hadn't been "one of the most famous criminal trials of all time," it still deserved better than *The Fatty Arbuckle Case*, a paperback written by Leo Guild, whom in 2007, on the tenth anniversary of his death, was dubbed by a newspaper "the Worst Pulp Novelist Ever."

Guild was once a columnist for the *Hollywood Reporter*, and over a long career, he churned out a lot of less than inspiring material, including gambling how-to books, horror novels, joke books, and dozens of sexploitation titles. He also called himself a celebrity biographer, writing books about Josephine Baker, Farryl Zanuck, and Liberace. The latter book, *The Loves of Liberace*, was published in 1956 and was an attempt to portray the flamboyant pianist as the ultimate ladies' man.

If that doesn't put the credibility of his Fatty Arbuckle book into question, I'm not sure what would.

In *The Fatty Arbuckle Case*, Guild wrote, "These are the rumors, the facts and the theories, sifted and arranged in what seems to this author to be the most reasonable and probably recreation of that fateful day." But don't be fooled by what seems to be a logical-sounding introduction because in his version of events, Roscoe and Maude Delmont conspired in Los Angeles to get Virginia to the party so he could have sex with her. The party livened up when Maude stripped to only her panties for the amusement of all and compared her bare breasts with those of an unnamed and equally topless showgirl. Soon after that, Virginia went willingly with Roscoe into room 2019.

With regard to what followed, Guild hedged his bet. The most "sane explanation," he reported, is that Roscoe and Virginia had sex and "by force or roughness, Virginia's bladder was broken." But he also wrote, "One rumor was that the drunken Arbuckle had ravaged her with a Coke bottle. Another said he used a jagged stick of ice."

And there it was in print, almost three decades after Roscoe's death, the now-legendary supposition – he ruptured Virginia's bladder while raping her with a bottle.

The broader rumor was that Roscoe had been too drunk to achieve an erection and substituted another item for his penis, most often identified as a Coco-Cola bottle. Of course, not only is there no evidence of this but there is no way to puncture a bladder in that way without doing serious damage to the vaginal wall. There is no evidence that Roscoe had any contact with her vagina, and no such contact was ever alleged in court – other than his application of ice. Virginia was clothed while he was alone with her in 1219, but 30 years later, the persistent myth took root and began to grow.

And this wasn't a myth relegated to just cheap paperbacks. The following year, Charles Beaumont, who was best known as a scriptwriter for *The Twilight Zone*, revisited the case in a book of essays. Though he made it clear that he believed Roscoe got a raw deal, he still dished some dirt: "Three versions of the incident were in office and alley circulation – Arbuckle had raped the girl, killing her with thrusts of his presumably enormous penis; he had used a Coca-Cola bottle or a dildo; he had impaled her with a broom handle. Most people devotedly believed all three stories."

As it turns out, though, the bottle rumor had grown from whispers to legend even earlier than 1962 – just not in the United States. Leo Guild apparently expanded on a version of the story that appeared in another lurid book, which he probably consulted in its original French-language edition when he wrote his book.

However, Guild's book would be largely forgotten when the English translation of that earlier book was released a few years later – creating a version of what happened in room 1219 that would have a greater impact on the public's perception of the case than anything before or since.

BORN KENNETH ANGLEMYER IN LOS ANGELES IN 1930, KENNETH Anger – as he came to be known – made his first film appearance in *A Midsummer Night's Dream* when he was four years old. Later in his career, he danced with Shirley Temple, and in 1947, he completed his first experimental film at age 17, using his parent's home movie camera.

His avant-garde films, which explored the occult and sex, generated both praise and protest and made Anger a minor celebrity in the cinema underground, but not much money. In the 1960s, Anger became involved with bands like The Rolling Stones and Led Zeppelin – as well as Charlie Manson protégé Bobby Beausoleil – when they began delving into Satanic themes and the works of occultist Aleister Crowley, but in 1950, when he moved to Paris, he was broke.

A few years later, he started collecting stories of movie industry depravity and influenced by magazines like *Confidential*, he wrote a photo-heavy book of scandals called *Hollywood Babylone*. It was published in French in 1959. Soon after, an item in American newspapers read, "Vacationers returning from Europe are smuggling in a book called *Hollywood Babylone*, written entirely in French but apparently well worth translating."

Marvin Miller, an American publisher who specialized in quick knockoffs of successful sex-themed European books, contacted Anger and encouraged him to translate his book into English. Anger finished two-thirds of the translation, but Miller took care of the other third, ramped up the vulgar content, and added stories of his own without informing Anger.

Hollywood Babylon was released in 1964, and despite being sold in a plain brown wrapper like the pornography of the era, it was stocked in mainstream bookstores and advertised in newspapers. It's been estimated that this "bootleg" version sold as many as two million copies, but none of the profits were earned by its author. Miller also turned the book into a sexploitation "documentary" with low-budget recreations of tawdry scenes, including the 1921 Labor Day party.

Anger sued Miller, demanding over $500,000 in royalties and damages, and eventually won a settlement, which he never collected from the publisher, who had vanished with the cash.

But Anger now knew just how much demand there was for his book, so updated the text and it was released again in 1975. The legit edition of *Hollywood Babylon* was also a success, and Anger even took the show on the road, reading theatrically from the text and screening appropriately inappropriate silent film clips.

I won't lie – this was my first introduction to the Roscoe Arbuckle story, along with a lot of other stories from old Hollywood. It wouldn't be until years later that I learned how many lies the book contained, but by then, I had been immersed in the 305 pages of scandals, sins, lurid images, and shockingly gory crime scene photos for longer than I'd care to admit. The book was essentially a compendium of all the ways that fame and fortune weren't all they were cracked up to be - - murder, drug addiction, sexual dysfunction, public humiliation, suicide, depression, and more.

The book memorialized long-gone stars but always through rumors, innuendo, and lies. Lillian and Dorothy Gish were remembered not as pioneering female stars in early Hollywood, but as possible lovers. Clara Bow is commemorated not as a leading actress of the 1920s or as the original flapper but as a nymphomaniac who had sex with the entire USC football team in one night. Charlie Chaplin wasn't in the spotlight for his comic genius but for the much younger women he romanced and married. And thanks to this book, generations know nothing of Roscoe Arbuckle's comedic talents, but they were certain that he'd once killed an actress by raping her with a bottle.

The third chapter of *Hollywood Babylon*, titled "Fat Man Out," is devoted to Roscoe. From its first line about Mack Sennett discovering "plumber's helper" Arbuckle "when he came to unclog the comedy producer's drain," the chapter is overflowing with bad information. Roscoe supposedly stripped with the prostitutes at "Mishawn [sic] Manor" and Virginia worked in minor roles at Keystone, where she "did her fair share of sleeping around and gave half the company crabs. The epidemic so shocked Sennett that he closed his studio and had it fumigated."

None of that happened.

Anger then tells a lively – albeit completely false – version of the Labor Day party. Maude Delmont (who is misidentified with a photo of Minta Durfee) is Roscoe's "friend" whom, as in Leo Guild's book, he enlists to bring Virginia to San Francisco. Anger offers no opinion about what occurred behind the closed doors of 1219 and instead used italics and ellipses to spread the rumors:

"Hollywood Babylon" took advantage of the Arbuckle scandal by spreading numerous lies about what happened in 1921.

Even some of the photos were fake, including this one, which was alleged to be Room 1219 in the wake of the party. It wasn't – it was just a photo for the book

"As headlines screamed, the rumors flew of a *hideously unnatural rape*: Arbuckle, enraged at his drunken impotence, had ravaged Virginia with a Coca-Cola bottle, *or* a champagne bottle, then had repeated the act with a jagged piece of ice... *or*, wasn't it common knowledge that Arbuckle was *exceptionally well endowed?*... *or*, was it just a question of 266-pounds-too-much of Fatty flattening Virginia in a *flying leap?*"

It's clear which rumor Anger likes best when, in reference to Roscoe's acquittal, he highlights "the lack of specific evidence (such as a bloody bottle)," as if the theory of the bottle had been introduced in court. And at the end of the chapter, he mentions the 1931 incident outside the Embassy Club -- when Roscoe tossed out a bottle that was evidence of illegal drinking – and asks, "Was he thinking of another bottle that went sailing out the 12th floor window of the Hotel St. Francis on Labor Day 1921?"

The myth of "Fatty's bottle party" spread like a virus. A 1971 book called *Fatty* by Gerald Fine featured a scene where a drunk Maude Delmont private tells D.A. Matthew Brady about walking into 1219 just after Roscoe was alone there with Virginia: "She was all beat up and bruised... lying on the floor between the two beds. There was a coke bottle on the floor. Fatty shoved it up her cunt, the son of a bitch... She said that when she wouldn't give in that he used the coke bottle to force her open. Then she said when he took the bottle out, he mounted her." Brady dismissed Maude's story because "she had been bought or had some powerful hatred for Fatty."

The book was labeled a "novel," probably because of scenes like that one, but it's mostly sympathetic to Roscoe.

The same can't be said for the 1974 memoir of silent-era screenwriter Anita Loos, which was titled *Kiss Hollywood Goodbye*. She stated that Roscoe caused Virginia's death "when she tried to fight off his unorthodox lovemaking."

In 1994, an article in *Newsweek* that was tied to the arrest of O.J. Simpson for double murder, concocted facts and cruel Arbuckle quotes to make him look guilty, and it ran another of Kenneth Anger's rumors: "Arbuckle had told others that he had jabbed a large, jagged piece of ice into her vagina. Three days later, she died from a ruptured bladder, having been literally raped to death."

An article in London's *Independent* called "When Apes Put Men to Shame" chose a third Anger rumor to print in 1998: Hollywood has always had its share of call-girl scandals. In 1921, American actor Fatty Arbuckle was charged with crushing to death a starlet during an orgy in San Francisco."

One of the most blatantly false descriptions of the alleged assault appeared in a 1993 volume of the *Journal of Popular Culture*, written by legendary TV host Steve Allen:

The popular comedian Fatty Arbuckle, in the 1920s, never worked again in the motion picture business after his arrest in conjunction with an incident in which a prostitute died, apparently because Arbuckle, in a sexual context, had inserted in the poor woman's body a Coca-Cola bottle, which broke and cut her internally, after which she bled to death. If such a thing were to happen today, I would not be surprised if Arbuckle ended up doing a TV commercial for Pepsi.

AS THE REFERENCES TO "CALL-GIRL SCANDALS" AND A "prostitute" show, Virginia Rappe's reputation has also been tarnished by history – the same way the defense team in Roscoe's third trial attempted to do.

Adela Rogers St. John doubled down on her previous remarks in her 1978 book, *Love, Laughter and Tears*. She placed all the blame for Virginia's death on Virginia: "During this vacation, an extra girl named Virginia Rappe got some alcohol in her system, stripped off her clothes, and plunged Fatty and Hollywood into our first major scandal."

The other main critic of Virginia Rappe was Roscoe's former wife, Minta Durfee. Although her manuscript was never published, her remembrances interested other writers, and she readily granted interviews for their books. Minta – who never remarried and appeared in small roles in over two dozen movies and TV shows from the mid-1930s to the early 1970s – lived modestly in Los Angeles until her death in 1975 at age 85, so she was always willing to talk about the people she had long outlived.

Minta's interviews appeared in many books, including Kevin Brownlow's history of silent film, *The Parade's Gone By*, from 1968. In that interview, she said that Virginia "was suffering from several diseases," one of which resulted in Mack Sennett fumigating Keystone – where Virginia never worked.

Her interviews influenced *Fatty* by Gerald Fine as well as Stuart Oderman's 1994 biography, *Roscoe "Fatty" Arbuckle*. In that book, Minta is quoted as saying, "Virginia Rappe was one of those poor young girls who came to Hollywood looking for a career and who wound up being used more in the dressing room or in some executive's office than in front of the camera. At Sennett's, she spread syphilis all over the studio, and Mr. Sennett had to have the place fumigated."

Somehow, Minta had inflated Kenneth Anger's anecdote, turning crabs into syphilis, as if a venereal disease could be "fumigated" by an exterminator. There is no evidence that Virginia ever suffered from either crabs or syphilis. And again, Virginia never worked at Keystone, so even if she had, she couldn't have "spread it all over the studio."

She made that first claim in 1969 and then returned to the topic in 1973, when she told an interviewer, "Mr. Sennett had to close the studio down for several days while he had everything repainted and fumigated" because Virginia had "spread syphilis all over the studio." Apparently, painters were also part of the Keystone healthcare system.

That interview was published as a chapter in 1975's *You Must Remember This*, and it's filled with inaccuracies: "Our lawyers proved with medical records that Virginia died of cystitis, an inflammation of the bladder. She had such a severe case that she had to use a catheter to eliminate. Her sphincter muscle wouldn't work."

And that wasn't all the bad information that she shared. At this point, it's likely that Minta no longer knew what was true and what was false since she'd been confusing the two to make Roscoe look good and those who opposed him look bad for decades.

She said that Maude Delmont "had 72 affidavits out against her for being a professional correspondent, a woman that's found in bed with a husband when a photographer bursts into the room and takes a picture. That was when they had these set-up divorces and the only grounds for divorce was adultery. Maude Delmont had gone to the well too often, she'd made it into a racket, and so the cops were down on her. When the cops found out that Maude Delmont had been at the party at the Hotel St. Francis, she must have made a deal with the district attorney. They'd forget about the 72 affidavits if she'd frame Roscoe."

There were a lot of rumors about Maude, especially about her relationship with Earl Lynn, the minor actor whose father Maude allegedly tried to blackmail to keep rumors about her and his son out of the papers. There were, however, no affidavits as Minta claimed.

Interestingly, though, while there are no records of Maude being part of an operation to help obtain divorces, there is a belief that this was the reason she came to San Francisco with Al Semnacher. He had been estranged from his wife for nearly a year and had run into trouble getting things finalized. He'd known Maude for years and if the stories about her side hustle were true, it's possibly the reason he brought her along for the ride.

Minta also talked about William Randolph Hearst, the "dreadful, dreadful old man" who attacked Roscoe relentlessly in the newspapers because, as she put it, he wanted revenge against Hollywood for not making his mistress Marion Davies a star. In truth, Marion appeared in 29 films between 1918 and 1929, so he had no reason for a vendetta against Hollywood in 1921. Also, Minta failed to mention that Roscoe had directed one of those 29 films.

She also blamed Will Hays for Roscoe's downfall: "This awful Will Hays, who was the censor in our business, instead of standing up like a man and declaring Roscoe absolutely guiltless, was absolutely ruthless. I've never seen a man in all my lifetime that looked more like a rat dressed up in men's clothing than Will Hays."

She was partially right about this. Hays banished Roscoe from the business, but he reinstated him eight months later.

She was also correct when she said that Hayes looked like a rat.

But let's get back to Virginia Rappe. In most accounts of the case, she ends up as a minor supporting player in her own tragedy. She's called a showgirl, an extra, and a slut if not an actual prostitute. A 1994

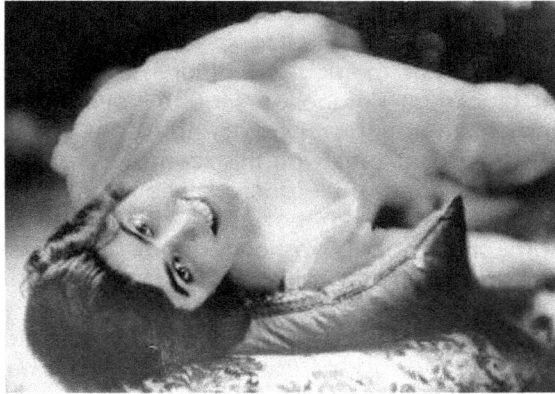

Virginia Rappe and Roscoe Arbuckle have one thing in common – both of their reputations have been destroyed over the years. The words of the attorneys in the three manslaughter trials were tame compared to the books and articles written about both of them since

Associated Press story even claimed that Roscoe hired the "notorious" Maude Delmont "to supply party girls," one of whom was Virginia, who had been fired by Mack Sennett "after she allegedly infected several actors with a venereal disease. An alcoholic, she drifted in the Hollywood lowlife."

I probably don't need to remind you – if you read the chapter about Virginia early in this book – that none of this was true.

The first full-length biography of Roscoe Arbuckle was published in 1976 by David Yallop. It was titled *The Day the Laughter Stopped: The True Story of Fatty Arbuckle* and in it, readers are once again treated to the story of Virginia's venereal disease forcing a fumigation at Keystone studios. It also includes a statement from Dr. Melville Rumwell, concluding that Virginia had gonorrhea, although Dr. Rumwell never said this at any of the three trials, not did any other doctor who examined her before or after her death.

In addition, none of the medical experts, witnesses, or attorneys ever mentioned that Virginia hit Roscoe up for "a great deal of money" at the Labor Day party because "she was pregnant, and she was sick. She needed money to have an abortion, and she wanted to have the abortion as soon as possible."

Explaining the lack of evidence, the author conveniently suggests Dr. Rumwell performed an illegal autopsy to cover up the illegal abortion he'd performed on the dying Virginia. He then blames the bladder tear on either a spontaneous rupture or a catheter used to treat a prior medical condition. He also pins an unspecified scheme to blackmail Roscoe on Maude Delmont and suggests that Virginia may have been involved, trying to get money for her abortion.

The problems with this scenario are many, not the least of which was that none of the doctors who examined Virginia – before or after she died – found that she was pregnant. Even if she had been, someone would have noticed that she'd recently had an abortion. It's safe to say that Virginia was not pregnant at the time of the Labor Day party.

The next book on the subject came out in 1991. Titled *Frame-Up! The Untold Story of Roscoe "Fatty" Arbuckle*, it was written by Andy Edmonds and relies on Minta Durfee as a primary source. The author explains that he was introduced to her in 1976 by a mutual friend, although Minta died in September 1975. This may just be a mistake, though, since there are several other dates, names, and events that are incorrect in the book.

Minta offered another impression of Virginia: "I couldn't stand the girl. She was sweet enough, naïve, but had no morals whatsoever. She'd sleep with any man who asked her. In fact, Mack Sennett had to shut down the studio twice because of her... because she was spreading lice and some sort of venereal disease. She was a sad case."

Edmonds notes that Virginia, who had had "at least five abortions by the time she was sixteen" and a bay at seventeen that was placed in a foster home, wasn't just in San Francisco for an abortion – though the procedure, performed by Dr. Rumwell before the party "accounted for the tenderness of her abdomen." In room 1220, Virginia supposedly tickled Roscoe, who then reflexively and accidentally, kneed her in the abdomen. In pain, she ran into 1219, and her bladder ruptured. Roscoe found her in the bathroom, as he explained.

It's a far-fetched version of the party, but the author's theory of how it all came about touches on some of the rumors that have existed in Hollywood since the 1920s.

In the book, he claims that Adolph Zukor designed a frame-up, and Fred Fishback pulled it off. He doesn't explain how all the pieces were arranged but somehow Fred brought together "a nightgown salesman, an actress who was known to strip, and a woman who would take compromising photos and say anything in court for the right price."

This seems like a stretch, but the rest of it doesn't. His theory was that Zukor wanted to obtain comprising photos of Roscoe to use against him in contract negotiations. The plan failed – or worked too well, depending on how you look at it – when the actress who was known to strip died.

It's still a bit far-fetched but I've certainly heard of stranger things that have occurred in Hollywood over the last century. It was briefly mentioned earlier that Zukor had been looking for a way to control Roscoe after he skipped out on the parade and screenings that he'd been ordered to attend that weekend. Was this part of that plan? Probably not, but based on the ruthlessness of Hollywood's studio heads, it's at least a possibility.

BEYOND THE BOOK✒

THERE HAS NEVER BEEN A MOVIE ABOUT ROSCOE ARBUCKLE.

It's strange that nothing has been made, for the big screen or the small one, since interest in him has ebbed and flowed since the 1930s.

Minta Durfee first optioned the film rights to her version of the story in 1957, which was the same year that a TV network announced it was planning a film about Roscoe. At the time and for almost a decade after, Jackie Gleason was the first choice for the role.

John Belushi was considered for the lead in a big-screen film but then he died in 1982. John Candy began doing research to play Roscoe in 1993, but he died the following year. And then in the sort of coincidence that sounds like a curse, Chris Farley met with screenwriter David Mamet in January 1997 to plan an Arbuckle biopic that he would star in. Farley died that December, which seems to have killed off any plans for a film – at least for now.

The closest thing to a Fatty movie that's ever been made was *The Wild Party*, a Merchant Ivory production from 1975. The film starred James Coco as "Jolly Grimm," an aging silent film star who stages an orgy in the 1920s and ends up killing his mistress (Raquel Welch) and her actor boyfriend. The movie probably would have really confused the facts of the real 1921 "wild party" if anyone had seen it. The movie bombed at the box office.

The underrated and underappreciated 2022 film, *Babylon*, was inspired by not only real-life characters from silent era Hollywood, but many of the events that gave the movie industry its sordid reputation at the time.

In the film, Roscoe is referenced through the character of Orville Pickwick, a popular, overweight actor who engages in lewd behavior at the party that opens the film. I'm not going to go into detail about what happens next but the portrayal of the character's interactions with a young woman and the subsequent use of a bottle, is obviously meant to draw parallels with Virginia's death and the scandal that impacted Roscoe's life and the image of Hollywood.

But Roscoe's story did make it to television in the 1990s, although never as a full-length film. There was an episode about the Arbuckle case on the syndicated series *Hollywood Babylon*, based officially but loosely on Anger's book; on an episode of *Mysteries and Scandals*; and on *Biography* in an episode called "Fatty Arbuckle: Betrayed by Hollywood."

In 2020, HBO rebooted the old TV show *Perry Mason* for the small screen, starring Matthew Rhys as the title character, who starts out as a private detective before becoming an attorney. In the first episode, Perry is hired to tail a movie star named Chubby Carmichael who is being investigated for violating the morals clause in his contract. When Chubby spots Perry taking photos of him having sex with a young starlet, the corpulent comedy actor chases the detective down the street while in the nude. As a final nod to the legend of Roscoe Arbuckle, the character he inspires in the episode is portrayed as being "exceptionally well endowed," to use the description by Kenneth Anger.

Despite these recent references to Roscoe, most Americans who recognize the name Fatty Arbuckle today know it only as a punch line to a dirty joke, even if they're clueless about the setup. They've heard that he raped someone with a bottle, but they're unsure of who he was or why he mattered. They recognize his name from *The Simpsons*, when Krusty the Clown asks," What has Fatty Arbuckle done that I haven't done?"

And in almost every case, popular culture offers only one answer to Krusty's question, usually saying that he was charged with puncturing the bladder of a "naïve young actress" during "forced sex with a bottle." The stories often claim that he died "after falling into alcoholism and lurid obscurity."

If it's possible to be both lurid and obscure, that's only happened to him in the years since his death.

Becoming a movie star offers a person the ability to stay forever young. They are captured in moving images that will be seen by generations long after they die. Roscoe achieved this kind of immortality, but this isn't the only kind. Always, it seems, whenever there's a celebrity scandal that involves sex or violence, he returns, just briefly, to the news. He also gets mentioned when there are battles over censorship or when there is a sensational celebrity trial or the tragic death of a Hollywood actress.

Over the years, his name was invoked during the paternity suits against Charlie Chaplin in 1943, the 1947 Elizabeth "Black Dahlia" murder, the 1962 suicide of Marilyn Monroe, the 1969 murder of Sharon Tate by the Manson Family, the 1988 Rob Lowe sex tape scandal, the arrests of Hugh Grant and Pee-Wee Herman, O.J. Simpson's arrest, the Clinton impeachment, Michael Jackson's molestation trial, Janet Jackson's wardrobe malfunction, and dozens of other times when murders and scandals rocked the country.

Fatty is forever the life of the party, forever a defendant and forever a villain or a victim or both, always remembered – when he is remembered – for his devastating fall from grace.

LABOR DAY 1921 REVI**/**ITED

TAKING THE READER BACK TO NOT ONLY THE START OF THIS chapter but the start of this book, we should revisit what we do know happened in room 1219 on Labor Day 1921. Perhaps by taking one final look, we can tell ourselves that while we'll never know for certain what occurred in that room, we can form an opinion that will allow us to sleep a little easier at night – assuming that any of us are losing sleep over a scandal from more than a century ago.

GETTING INTO ROOM 1219

WE'LL BEGIN WITH WHAT OCCURRED IN ROOM 1220 PRIOR TO the events that happened when Virginia and Roscoe were alone together in room 1219.

At trial, the state and the defense agreed that Virginia had been at the party in room 1220 for three hours, drinking orange blossoms, talking, and dancing, when she tried to enter the bathroom in room 1221 just before 3:00 P.M. The door was locked, and the bathroom was occupied by Maude Delmont and Lowell Sherman. Virginia then passed back through room 1220 and entered room 1219. There was no indication that Virginia was sick or distressed at that point.

At this point, the prosecution claimed that Roscoe watched her enter 1219 and he followed her. The defense, though, said that Roscoe was unaware that Virginia went his room and that he only entered 1219 – and locked the door to 1220 – so that he could change out of his pajamas and into a suit before taking Mae Taube for her promised car ride.

In truth, either version of this story could have been true. It seems unlikely that Roscoe would have missed Virginia walking from one door to the other, but he may have been distracted by the others at the party or may have been facing one of the room's two outer walls and missed her entirely.

IN⁄IDE ROOM 1219

THERE ARE TWO CONFLICTING VERSIONS OF WHAT CAUSED Virginia's injury in room 1219. During the third trial, both sides presented a closing argument, using information gathered from the preliminary hearings and the previous two trials.

The prosecution's version of events led with Roscoe following Virginia into the room. They maintained she did not enter the bathroom because Roscoe stopped her, then blocked her return to room 1220. Based on the door fingerprints, they started that Virginia tried to flee through the hallway door to the room, but Roscoe stopped her.

According to the closing statements, "When the defendant forced her toward the bed, Virginia Rappe was in the most perfect condition to have her bladder ruptured if any force was applied to her. All that was necessary was a distended bladder."

The state and the defense agreed that Virginia had a distended bladder at this point, but whether the condition was caused by her cystitis (a condition confirmed by a panel of doctors during the first trial), her ingestion of orange juice and gin (both liquids are more diuretic than water), or something else that was immaterial because it didn't explain how the bladder burst. The state claimed the rupture had nothing to do with cystitis (which may not have been true) and that spontaneous bladder ruptures are rare (true). Because of this, they contended that an external force caused her bladder to rupture.

The prosecution's explanation for the rupture was that Roscoe "threw his weight upon her" and that Virginia passed out from shock and pain. They claimed that Roscoe then revived her using ice and at that point, he opened the door to room 1220.

Because the state didn't claim that Roscoe's attempt at sexual assault went beyond throwing her on the bed, they did not have to present any physical evidence of those actions beyond the rumpled sheets reported by witnesses, which could have happened for a wide variety of reasons.

The defense challenged the state's account using hair and fingerprints at the scene, as well as the prosecution's suggested timeline.

Hairs thought to match Virginia's were found by the state's forensic expert Edward Heinrich – America's "Sherlock Holmes" – between the two beds and in the bathroom. The defense stated that this validated their story. How else could Virginia's hair gotten into the bathroom? She had to have gone in there.

The defense also strongly challenged the state's claim that the two handprints on the hallway door showed that Roscoe placed his hand over Virginia's to prevent her escape.

The handprints were hotly debated in each trial and were largely responsible for one of the jurors holding out for a guilty verdict in the first trial. Modern forensic experts have determined that the state's theory about the dual prints would not hold up in criminal court today. Fingerprints cannot be dated, let alone time to the same moment, to prove that one hand was pressing on the other.

The defense also argued about the timeline, claiming there was insufficient time – approximately 10 minutes – for everything to have occurred the way the prosecution claimed. This is a flawed argument, though. If Roscoe had committed the acts he was accused of, it could have happened in much less than 10 minutes.

The main way that the defense countered the state's version of events was by telling a very different story using the only surviving person who knew for certain what occurred in 1219.

According to Roscoe, "I closed and locked the door, and I went straight to the bathroom and found Miss Rappe on the floor in front of the toilet, holding her stomach and moving around on the floor. She had been vomiting."

The defense then suggested two ways that Virginia's bladder could have ruptured – spontaneously or by some external force.

After suggesting that her bladder had been weakened by many years of cystitis and overextended by hours of drinking without urinating, they proposed that the violent action of her abdominal muscles caused by vomiting caused the rupture of her overextended bladder. While spontaneous bladder ruptures are rare, when they do occur, they usually happen after alcohol consumption, which both fills the bladder and, by dulling the nerve impulses, reduces the feeling of needing to empty it. A chronic case of cystitis could also have weakened the bladder walls, making her more susceptible to the rupture. Still, a spontaneous rupture would have required some kind of stress. Vomiting could qualify, but only if Roscoe's story was true. There was no other witness to the vomiting and no physical evidence of it.

So, if the rupture was not spontaneous, what could have caused it? The defense conjectured that Virginia could have struck the side of the door when she entered the bathroom, or she could have fallen and struck her abdomen on the toilet or the tub. Or the rupture could have occurred after Roscoe initially tried to help her. According to his testimony, he lifted her from the floor and put her on the toilet seat, then helped her get to the smaller bed in the room. After he assumed she was resting, he went into the bathroom and when he came back out, he found she had fallen on the floor.

The defense stated, "We do not know exactly how she got on the floor, but it is not unreasonable to suppose that, suffering from a spasm of the bladder while lying on the bed, writhing in pain, she fell off the bed onto the floor." It was then conjectured, based on medical opinions, that Virginia could have fallen on her abdomen or other parts of the body which "might produce sufficient force to rupture an overextended bladder."

It seems unlikely that Virginia could have bumped into the bathroom door with enough force to cause the rupture, unless she was stumbling drunk. If she was inebriated enough to collide with a door, no one noticed it. Falling in the bathroom is less unlikely, but still improbable, especially since Roscoe never mentioned it. His testimony regarding the time they were both in the bathroom emphasized her nausea, though he did say she was "holding her stomach" and that after he assisted her, she was "gasping and had a hard time getting her breath." He implied that she was in greater pain in the bedroom later: "I found Miss Rappe between two beds rolling about on the floor and holding her stomach and crying and moaning."

I feel the greatest possibility of a fall causing the rupture was when she fell off the bed and onto the floor, but we'll come back to that soon.

WHAT HAPPENED NEXT

The prosecution challenged the defense's account by questioning Roscoe's immediate actions in assisting Virginia and his comments – or lack of comments – about those actions soon after and then days later.

Roscoe was asked, after finding Virginia sick in the bathroom, why he didn't immediately seek assistance. He replied that he thought Virginia was merely sick to her stomach from drinking too much, so his actions were appropriate.

He was further asked why Roscoe never told anyone at the party, nor the hotel's assistant manager, Harry Boyle, nor the first doctors summoned, Dr. Olav Kaarboe, that he found Virginia in the bathroom, nauseous, that he helped her to the bed and that she had likely fallen off the bed. He told no one what occurred in 1219 on that first day. "Is that the way an innocent man would act?" the prosecution asked.

The state was right; it did seem suspicious – but only if Roscoe thought Virginia was seriously injured. By his account, he did not. Neither did anyone else at the party, not Dr. Kaarboe, who attended to her that evening. All assumed she'd just had too much to drink and that she'd sleep it off. Based on that, it wasn't surprising to anyone, including Roscoe, that Virginia had vomited and fallen. In fact, it would have been unkind for Roscoe to bring up what happened and embarrass the young woman.

The prosecution, of course, made much of the fact that not only did Roscoe not speak up at the time of the incident but that on September 9, soon after learning of Virginia's death, he gave a different story than the one he later gave under oath.

His delay in telling his second version of events may have been a strategy to come up with an appropriate story for the criminal trial. However, it's also possible that he may have wanted to tell the authorities and preliminary juries about assisting an ill Virginia but was cautioned not to do so by his attorneys since it was a story that was filled with more potential problems than his original "I-was-never-alone-with-her" deflection.

Either way, he was exercising his right to remain silent, as instructed by his first defense attorney, Frank Dominguez, and his silence cannot be used to say whether he was truthful or not.

The most significant thing about his second version of events was that it was very different from the first version – which was completely untrue. This makes Roscoe look much less credible -- even if the initial lies were the quickest way he could think of to hopefully dodge bad publicity. If that was the case, it doesn't necessarily mean the second, more detailed and complicated, story is untrue, but if he was lying from the start, you can't help but wonder if he ever told the whole truth at all.

ACCOUNTS OF WHAT OCCURRED AFTER ROSCOE UNLOCKED THE door to 1219 were disputed by both sides. The state claimed that Roscoe only opened the door after Maude Delmont repeatedly kicked it, demanding entry. Roscoe insisted that he opened the door without being asked so that he could find Maude, who was not located right away.

Since Maude never testified in the criminal trials – and the statements from Alice Blake and Zey Prevost changed several times – it's impossible to know the truth. While Roscoe had a greater motivation to lie, he and Virginia had been behind a locked door for a relatively short amount of time, and no cries or other noises were heard from Virginia that would have provoked Maude's alleged door-kicking.

AFTER THE DOOR WAS UNLOCKED, MAUDE DELMONT, ZEY Prevost, and Alice Blake entered room 1219 to find Virginia on the double bed in great pain and barely conscious.

The state and the defense agreed that the women moved Virginia to the single bed because the double bed was wet, and when Virginia began tearing at her clothing, they helped her remove them. Roscoe came back into the room, followed by Fred Fishback, who had just returned to the hotel. Roscoe helped Virginia remove her arm from one sleeve of her dress because she was ripping it. Then, he left the room again.

With assistance from Zey and Maude, Fred carried the naked Virginia into the bathroom for a cold bath, meant to ease her pain. Afterward, he carried Virginia back to the single bed.

No one could agree on what happened next.

When Roscoe came back into room 1219, the state claimed that Virginia said, "He hurt me," to which Roscoe replied, "Aw, shut up. I'll throw her out the window if she doesn't stop yelling." When ice was used to comfort the naked woman, Roscoe inserted an ice cube into her vagina, saying, "That will make her come to."

The defense told a different story. They said that when Roscoe returned to room 1219, Maude was rubbing the naked Virginia with ice. There was piece of ice on or near her vagina. Roscoe picked it up and asked, "What's this doing here?" Maude answered, "Leave it here. I know how to take care of Virginia." He put it back and started to cover Virginia with a sheet, but Maude told him to leave. Arbuckle replied, "Shut up, or I'll throw you out the window."

These were two of the most notorious parts of the case – the ice incident and the "throw her out the window" comment. Neither version reflects well on Roscoe but since Maude Delmont never testified, there was only her friend, Al Semnacher, who was left to testify that he heard Roscoe make a crude comment about the ice the next day. I'm not convinced his version of events can be trusted, but then again, everything connected to the ice remains in question. I think it's possible that Roscoe did make some kind of comment about the ice – it fit his sense of humor – but the defense wanted to downplay it as much as they could since it made the funny man seem much coarser than what his fans saw in the movies.

While anything to do with the ice makes Roscoe look disrespectful and sexist, it seems unlikely that he would have made such a comment if he really had attempted to sexually assault her. That would bring unwanted attention to him. The "throw her out the window" comment, if it was made about Virginia – which I doubt – could be taken as a crass comment and yet, it wasn't the kind of comment that a man trying to hide his guilt would make.

AFTER THE ALLEGED ICE INCIDENT, BOTH SIDES AGREED THAT Roscoe and Maude put a bathrobe on Virginia. Soon after, Mae Taube arrived and called the front desk. Assistant manager Harry Boyle came up to the suite. From Boyle, Roscoe secured room 1227, just down the hall, and he carried Virginia most of the way there before handing her to Boyle, who took her to the bed. Boyle called the hotel doctor, Dr. Kaarboe, who attended to Virginia in 1227. His diagnosis was that she drank too much alcohol and needed to sleep it off.

Down the hall in 1220, the party continued. There, Boyle told Roscoe that a doctor had seen Virginia and concluded there was nothing wrong. Boyle left. Roscoe took Mae for the promised ride in his Pierce-Arrow while others arrived at the party. Maude and the hotel detective finished off the gin and orange juice. Roscoe returned to the party and that evening, went out for dinner and dancing. He never checked on Virginia or even asked about her. Like everyone else, he assumed she was sleeping off the liquor she'd consumed. The next time he heard about her was four days later when he learned that she was dead.

The state tried to portray Roscoe continuing the party while Virginia was dying as "criminal callousness," but if that was true, then everyone who was there, including Maude Delmont and Al Semnacher, should have been arrested. They all assumed that Virginia was merely drunk and since the doctor had told them nothing else was wrong with her, it was a valid assumption. Roscoe's actions were not inappropriate. A guilty man would have been more concerned about Virginia's and might have wanted to know what she was saying to others, but Roscoe didn't think about her again. He made this point later when talking to reporters saying, "To show how serious we thought it was, I and the other men danced in the hotel that night."

AFTER THE PARTY

NO MATTER WHAT YOU MIGHT BELIEVE ABOUT THE TRUTHFULNESS of Roscoe's story, the material that the state presented failed to show that Roscoe acted in a criminal way. Even if he had done some – or all – of the things the prosecution claimed he did, they couldn't prove it. There were no witnesses to what happened in room 1219 and no one could prove what caused Virginia's death.

Reasonable doubt in a nutshell.

If Roscoe had been guilty of causing Virginia's death, it's curious that in the four days she lived after the party that she never implicated Roscoe in the sort of assault the state alleged. She never said she tried to escape through room 1219's other door, where the handprints were supposedly so obvious. She was never heard screaming or calling for help.

Even Virginia Breig, the Wakefield secretary, who suddenly materialized only for the third trial, did not claim Virginia said that Roscoe acted without consent. She allegedly said, "Arbuckle took me by the arm and threw men on one bed and put his weight on me, and after that I do not know what happened."

Was this an act of violence or an act of mutual passion? The maid, Josephine Keza, claimed she overhead a woman saying "No, no, oh my god," and a man saying, "Shut up." But even if this is true – and questions about that remain – this did not necessarily indicate a crime. The judge at the preliminary hearing suggested these words could simply have indicated the "shifting boundaries of passion."

That's probably not an argument that would work these days, but as you might imagine, consent is defined a little differently today than it was in the 1920s.

Over the two days that Virginia was in room 1227, she was treated by three nurses – Jean Jameson, Vera Cumberland, and Martha Hamilton. There women were sober, medical professionals, with whom Virginia, after sustaining her injury, may have been inclined to talk with candidly. They had no biases toward either the prosecution or the defense. Martha Hamilton testified to hearing nothing specific about the cause of the injury. Jean Jameson and Vera Cumberland testified at the coroner's inquest, and both presented accounts that differed from what both the state and the defense claimed happened in 1219, so neither side called them at the criminal trials. Because of that, their coroner's inquest testimony was never highlighted by the press.

According to Jean Jameson: "Mis Rappe told me that relations with her sweetheart were responsible for the ailment from which she weas suffering. She was very anxious that the party and what had occurred there be kept from Henry Lehrman, who she said was her sweetheart. As she expressed it, he would throw her down if he found out. She said she had been suffering for six weeks from internal trouble. She frequently asked me, 'What could have broken inside of me?' She asked me several times to determine if she had been assaulted. She said she was unconscious."

Vera Cumberland stated: "The patient admitted to me that her relations with Arbuckle in the room had not been proper. She did not say whether her actions had been voluntary or involuntary. She said that she had been living with Henry Lehrman for some time and that several months ago she and Lehrman had had a quarrel and that he had gone to New York. She was very anxious that what happened be kept for him."

Virginia Told Her the Story

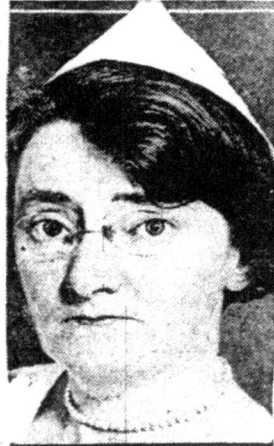

Mrs. Jean Jameson

Mrs. Jean Jameson, nurse in charge of Miss Virginia Rappe when the motion picture actress died in San Francisco, and to whom she related details of the alleged attack, for which Roscoe Arbuckle faces murder trial. Mrs. Jameson is regarded as an important witness.

It is unclear what Virginia meant in Nurse Jameson's account when she brought up "relations with her sweetheart," but she likely thought the pain was emanating from her uterus, not her bladder, and may have believed it was caused by previous sexual relations with Lehrman, or she wanted the nurse to think that. It's also possible that she feared it was the sign of a venereal disease, even though it's more likely it was pain from her cystitis.

The account from Nurse Cumberland is more telling. Virginia admitted that she and Roscoe had improper relations, which likely meant kissing and caressing since both remained clothed. The fact that she didn't say those relations were involuntary suggests they were more likely consensual.

It's interesting that both accounts emphasize her being anxious about keeping her behavior at the party from the volatile Henry Lehrman. If Virginia had been attacked, she would almost certainly have wanted Lehrman to know that anything that occurred was not her fault. Instead, feeling guilty about her behavior, she wanted to make sure he knew nothing about the party at all.

LABOR DAY 1921:
WHAT I THINK HAPPENED

ADMITTING ONCE MORE THAT WE WILL NEVER KNOW FOR certain what occurred in room 1219 on Labor Day, this is what I think most likely occurred during the party.

Roscoe and Virginia had been seated together, chatting in room 1220. He was in his pajamas and purple robe, and she was in her jade skirt and blouse. They were flirting. Both were unattached. Virginia was split from Henry Lehrman and Roscoe and Minta had been separated for a long time. If anything happened, they were two consenting adults.

Virginia had been drinking for hours and tried to use the bathroom in 1221. I think it's possible that she needed to vomit. I think most readers can agree that we have known people – or maybe you are one of those people – who throws up during a party and then goes right back to drinking. I think that it's also clear from testimony that Virginia sometimes had a strange reaction to alcohol. We have no idea how she was feeling at that moment, but we do know that she needed to use a bathroom. When she couldn't get into the bathroom in 1221 – because Maude and Lowell were presumably having sex there – Virginia went to room 1219 to use the bathroom there.

Roscoe followed her into the room and locked the door behind her. I believe that his story about assisting her while she was getting sick was true, but I don't believe, at that point, that she was in the kind of pain she'd later be suffering from.

When the pair left the bathroom, I believe they began to kiss. They may have pressed against the hallway door, leaving handprints there. Things became passionate and kissing and embracing, Roscoe guided her to the double bed, and she laid down on it. He pressed himself on top of her and then, when his weight settled on her abdomen, her distended bladder – which had been ravaged by her chronic cystitis for years – suddenly ruptured.

The searing pain caused Virginia to black out. Her loss of consciousness, mentioned in one way or another by virtually everyone who spoke to her later, may seem like an unlikely or convenient coincidence, but as doctors pointed out, the loss of consciousness immediately after the rupture of a distended bladder is a common occurrence because of the resulting drop in blood pressure.

Roscoe used water (frozen or not) when he attempted to revive her, which was why the bed was wet. Moments later, whether it was kicked or not, he opened the locked door.

Having blacked out when her bladder ruptured, Virginia was not only in terrible pain but had no idea what had happened to her. She would naturally question whether something had been done to her while she was unconscious to cause the pain she was feeling -- "She asked me several times to determine if she had been assaulted."

Further, the actions that she could remember were ones that she didn't want anyone beyond the nurses she confided in to know. She especially wanted to keep it from Henry Lehrman – "The patient admitted to me that her relations with Arbuckle had not been proper."

Virginia died from the ruptured bladder, although no one could ever prove what caused it to happen, but I think this version of events makes the most sense.

I think Virginia's death was an accident. It was caused by a chronic illness that had been doing damage to her bladder for many years, and it had reached a point where it was going to rupture. Roscoe's weight on top of her abdomen caused I to happen. He didn't do it on purpose, and he had no idea it was happening and honestly, it may not have been Roscoe's weight that caused it to happen. It might have occurred with anyone who was with Virginia. The rupture could have happened at any time if the pressure and position occurred in just the right way.

SO, WHAT HAPPENED THAT LED TO CRIMINAL CHARGES AGAINST ROSCOE? I believe there were two people responsible for the police involvement in the case and Roscoe's subsequent arrest and trials.

Those two people were Maude Delmont and Roscoe Arbuckle himself.

I don't believe that Maude Delmont was involved in some vast conspiracy when she threw herself into caring for Virginia and then went to the police with her many claims of Roscoe's wrongdoing. I think Maude was thinking about the most important person in the world to her – Maude Delmont.

Based on the schemes that she was involved in (like the blackmail threats to Earl Lynn's father) and the ones that she was rumored to be associated with, it's clear that Maude is one of the most disreputable people in this story. Even the prosecution team thought so, which is why they never took a chance and let her testify, even though she was the only complaining witness to Roscoe's alleged crimes. I think it's very likely that the only reason she was in San Francisco that weekend is because she'd come with Al Semnacher to generate some "proof" of his infidelity and speed up his divorce.

But then when Virginia was injured and began suffering from terrible pain after spending time alone in a hotel room with a major celebrity, she came up with a new scheme. Maude spent nearly every minute of what remained of Virginia's life at her bedside, refusing to leave her "dear friend" (the one she'd known for all of three days) to suffer alone. In this way, Maude controlled the narrative. Whatever story Maude told was the "true story" and there was no one to contradict her. I'm convinced that she planned to use anything she gathered from her time with Virginia as blackmail material to get Roscoe to pay her. Even if the famous actor hadn't raped Virginia, it looked like he had, and she figured he'd do anything to keep the story from coming to light.

But then Virginia died.

This turn of events didn't stop Maude's scheme, but it did force her to alter it. She went to the police and spilled her version of events. As the only witness, she still controlled the narrative, and she could tell the police as much or as little as she liked. I believe that she tried to blackmail Roscoe, offering to tailor her story to whatever Roscoe wanted it to be. But Roscoe, knowing that he'd done nothing wrong, turned her down, naively believing he wouldn't be blamed for Virginia's death.

But by then, the damage was done. Maude painted Roscoe as the villain while still being such a liability to the police and the prosecution that she couldn't be a witness at trial. They undoubtedly didn't trust her or her story, but things had gone so far that pausing or stopping the prosecution would have destroyed the public's trust in the system since the newspapers had been screaming about Roscoe's guilt since the day Virginia died.

MAUDE MAY HAVE BEEN PARTIALLY RESPONSIBILITY FOR THE destruction of Roscoe Arbuckle's life and career, but it was Roscoe – and his bad decisions – who did the most damage.

We can debate the idea that most of what Roscoe did while at the hotel was one bad decision after another, but that's going too far for our purposes here, although there were some bad decisions made in hindsight – skipping the parade and screening and going out of town, throwing the party, buying illegal booze, following Virginia into the other room, and so on. But, in his defense, none of these were things that he wouldn't have done without the very unhappy ending to the weekend, so I doubt he considered any of that to be a mistake.

Roscoe's first damaging mistake came after he learned of Virginia's death. With the police and the press asking questions, he feared that telling the truth would be a bad idea. Would anyone believe his interaction with Virginia was consensual? What would his fans think of him if they found out he was engaging in boozy foreplay with a young woman in a hotel room? He must have wondered how she was injured and why she blacked out. He assumed it was from the liquor, which was the logical conclusion. But maybe there was some other explanation. What was it?

He didn't know – so he lied

At first, he said he'd never been alone with her. Later, when it fit the testimony of the state's witnesses, his story became more details – some truth, some fiction – to make himself look better. The first lie was a bad decision, and he compounded the mess by lying some more.

The thing is, though, he should have just told the truth in the first place. There was nothing about what I think occurred that would fit the definition of involuntary manslaughter – homicide committed without malice but in the perpetration of an unlawful act. That was the charge filed against Roscoe when the murder charge didn't stand. The unlawful act the state claimed occurred was a sexual assault that was only halted by Virginia's injury and her loss of consciousness. I don't believe it was an assault, but even if it had been, the state produced no evidence – not the bruises, the handprints, or ruptured bladder – that connected Roscoe to such an assault. Other witness accounts of what Virginia allegedly said, such as "He hurt me," didn't prove the interaction wasn't consensual.

But in addition to the bad decisions he made, Roscoe was not entirely blameless. He was guilty of perjury for some of the concocted details he added to his story, and some could say he deserved to be condemned for breaking Prohibition laws to throw a liquor-fueled pajama party with showgirls, and depending on what happened with the ice, he's not exactly innocent there either.

Bad decisions.

In any case, based on what the prosecution knew and what it didn't know, Roscoe Arbuckle should never have been tried for manslaughter, and he certainly never should have been branded a killer and a rapist. He should never have been portrayed as a monster by the press and blacklisted by the movie industry.

THERE WERE TWO PEOPLE IN ROOM 1219 THAT DAY AND neither of them knew that one of them had suffered a fatal injury until after she was dead.

We will never know for certain what happened behind the locked door to that room on Labor Day afternoon, other than the fact that one person endured an injury that led to death four days later and eventually led to the ruin of her reputation – a final indignity that she didn't deserve.

The other person suffered from her death, too. He wasn't injured and he didn't die because of what happened in room 1219 that day – but I do think it killed him, nevertheless.

Roscoe Arbuckle died a little bit that day and while he didn't know his life was over yet, there's no question that nothing was ever the same for him again.

AFTERWORD
THE SPIRITS OF THE PAST

LOCATED NEXT DOOR TO PARAMOUNT STUDIOS IN LOS ANGELES is a quiet, peaceful burial ground, shaded by trees, and sprawling over acre after acre of rolling grounds. It was founded in 1899 as Hollywood Memorial Park by two local real estate men, I.N. Van Nuys and Colonel Isaac Lankershim.

Thanks to its location, it became the more desirable place to be buried by the most famous personalities in Hollywood history, including Douglas Fairbanks, Rudolph Valentino, Peter Lorre, Tyrone Power, Clifton Webb, Mel Blanc, William Desmond Taylor, Marion Davies, Cecil B. DeMille, John Huston, Fay Wray, Don Adams, Darren McGavin, Mama Cass Elliot (who did not die choking on a ham sandwich), Jayne Mansfield, Chris Cornell, David Lynch, and many others.

By the last years of the twentieth century, the cemetery had fallen into a state of disrepair and was on the verge of being closed, thanks to the mishandling of funds by eccentric owner, Jules Roth.

Roth, a convicted felon who had served five years in San Quentin for grand theft and securities fraud, purchased the cemetery in the late 1930s and, over the years, pocketed millions of dollars of the burial ground's revenues. During his ownership, Roth sold off more than third of the original 100 acres and he purchased a yacht to be used for "burials at sea," although it was used for lavish parties instead.

Over time, Roth's workforce dwindled, and the grounds became overgrown and unkempt. The cemetery became a haven for the unhoused and crime became commonplace. Roth soon began making more money from re-opening graves than opening new ones as families began moving their loved ones to better locations. State officials finally began asking questions in the 1980s and the property

Hollywood Memorial Park, which is known as Hollywood Forever Cemetery today. It's the top place to go if you're looking for the graves of celebrities and movie stars

was seized in 1995. Roth was under investigation by the state's attorney when he died in 1998.

The cemetery was scheduled for closure when Tyler Cassity, from a family in the cemetery business in St. Louis, purchased Hollywood Memorial Park at auction. He spent more than $7 million renovating the property, changed the name to Hollywood Forever Cemetery, and updated the services offered to include live internet broadcasts of funeral services for family members who could not be present and computer kiosks around the property that contain biographies of those interred on the grounds.

Today, it is *the* place to go to find celebrity graves, and the cemetery even offers events, concerts, and movie screenings.

It is in Hollywood Forever Cemetery where the body of Virigina Rappe was laid to rest in 1921. Her grave is located near a lagoon. Henry Lehrman, who paid for Virginia's burial and plot, is buried next to her. But it's not Lehrman's ghost that has allegedly been encountered at this spot.

Virgina Rappe lost not only her life over the course of the Labor Day Weekend of 1921, but she lost a promising career, and her reputation was destroyed. Most likely, she had no idea that Maude

Delmont had concocted such a lurid story about the weekend. Virginia was in too much pain from the infection caused by her ruptured bladder and was rarely consciousness over the next four days. She was unable to defend herself from the newspaper stories and scandalous rumors and she died with a half-finished life.

When we consider her troubled life and the tragic way that it ended, it's not surprising to hear reports that her spirit is still lingering behind. Over the years, visitors to Hollywood Forever Cemetery have claimed to hear a woman weeping near Virginia's simple grave. No living woman is ever found to be nearby.

Still others have claimed to see a woman walking along the edge of the nearby lagoon. She's described as pretty, with dark hair, wearing a stylish but old-fashioned white dress – and she's always crying. She never acknowledges those who have seen her and the few that have spoken to her say she ignores them – and then vanishes without explanation.

Even those who know nothing of Virginia's history – or even who is buried nearby – have identified her from photographs, saying with certainty that she is the woman they saw in the white dress.

If this really is the spirit of Virginia Rappe, though, this is not the only place where she still walks.

THERE ARE ALSO REPORTS OF A GHOST IN ROOM 1219 AT THE Westin St. Francis Hotel in San Francisco. Guests who have stayed in the room where the party took place over Labor Day weekend 1921 often say they are awakened by the sound of old music playing and laughter, as well as a woman crying and moaning in pain.

Room 1219 at the Westin St. Francis in San Francisco today

There are also reports of a pretty girl with dark hair who has been spotted looking out the window of the room during the early morning hours. When anyone speaks to her – or tries to approach her – she disappears.

This spirit – like the one seen in Hollywood Forever Cemetery – is believed to be Virginia, still attached to this world, and still grieving for a life that cut short far too soon.

BUT VIRGINIA'S SPIRIT IS NOT THE ONLY PRESENCE THAT LINGERS from this tragic story.

In the wake of his ruined career, Roscoe Arbuckle worked on the stage and in vaudeville. He tried repeatedly to return to making movies but was forced to work behind the scenes, writing and directing under a pseudonym. He was overjoyed when he was finally given a contract to star in some comedy shorts, believing that his chance to return to Hollywood was on the verge of finally happening.

But he didn't live long enough to see that comeback happen. He died from a heart attack on June 29, 1933.

Even in death, it's been said, Roscoe has not found peace. He is still slandered today as the rapist who killed Virginia Rappe, even though the story wasn't true. It didn't matter, though. The Arbuckle case managed to change the image of Hollywood from one that was linked to dreams – to an image that was forever tarnished by scandal.

Perhaps this is the reason that Fatty's ghost haunted the old Vitaphone studio building in Brooklyn for many years.

In 1916, Vitagraph occupied two acres of land in Brooklyn and became famous for some of its early comedy shorts, producing a number of stars, including Norma Talmadge, Anita Stewart, Clara Kimball Young, and, of course, Mabel Normand. There were more than 100 shareholders in the company but unfortunately, the partners lacked the foresight to link their studio to a movie theater chain, which by the late 1910s was needed to survive. By the early 1920s, Vitagraph was unable to find screens to show its films and so in 1925, the studio was sold to Warner Brothers, which had been founded only two years earlier.

By that time, most of the movie industry had moved to Los Angeles but Warner kept the Brooklyn studio and used it to produce short films, which is what brought Roscoe there in the early 1930s.

In 1952, when television was in its infancy, NBC bought the studio and thanks to

The Vitaphone Studio building in Brooklyn

additions that were made at the time, it was the largest television studio on the East Coast through the 1950s and 1960s. A soap opera called *Underworld* was filmed there, along with the Perry Como and Sammy Davis shows and the historic production of *Peter Pan* with Mary Martin. Other productions included *Hall of Fame* dramas and special films for Judy Garland, Laurence Olivier, and Frank Sinatra.

It was at this time when rumors of Roscoe's ghost began making the rounds. Many claimed to encounter him as simply a "sad presence," attached to the place where he almost made it back to doing what he truly loved. Others claimed to see Roscoe himself, catching a glimpse of him backstage, in dimly lit hallways, and standing back out of the way, watching the filming that was taking place on the stages and sets.

But the spirit of Roscoe Arbuckle likely vanished with building itself.

In the 1960s, the remaining film productions were moved to Los Angeles, and the studio went dark. *Only Another World, As the World Turns,* and a few small productions kept the studio alive.

In the late 1960s, the original Vitagraph Studio building, where Roscoe worked, was sold to the Shulamith School for Girls, ending its connection to show business – and Fatty Arbuckle.

The later buildings that had been added to the studios by NBC still exist today and are used for production work but the oldest building on the lot was demolished in 2015.

Today, only the old smokestack remains, on which black brick letters "Vitagraph" are still clearly visible. Since the ghost of Roscoe Arbuckle hasn't been reported since the 1960s, that chimney is the only surviving reminder of the storied past of this corner of Brooklyn.

BIBLIOGRAPHY

Adams, Charles F. - *Murder by the bay: Historical Homicide in and About the City of San Francisco*, Sanger, CA, Word Dancer, 2005

Allen, Frederick Lewis - *Only Yesterday: An Informal History of the 1920s*, New York, NY, Harper & Row, 1931

Anger, Kenneth - *Hollywood Babylon*, San Francisco, CA, Straight Arrow Books, 1975

Atlas Obscura

Basinger, Jeanine - *Silent Stars*, Middletown, CT, 1999

Bessie, Michael Simon - *Jazz Journalism: The Story of the Tabloid Newspapers*, New York, NY, Dutton, 1938

Black, Gregory D. - *Hollywood Censored*, New York, NY, Cambridge University Press, 1996

Blesh, Rudi - *Keaton*, New York, BY, McMillan, 1966

Blum, Daniel - *A Pictorial History of the Silent Screen*, New York, NY, Grosset & Dunlap, 1953

Brownlow, Kevin - *The Parade's Gone By...*, Berkeley, Ca, University of California Press, 1968

Butler, Ivan - *Silent Magic*, New York, NY, Ungar, 1987

Card, James - *Seductive Cinema: The Art of Silent Film*, New York, NY, Alfred A. Knopf, 1994

Chaplin, Charlie - *My Autobiography*, New York, NY Simon & Schuster, 1964

Charyn, Jerome – *Movieland: Hollywood and the Great American Dream Culture*, New York, NY, New York University Press, 1989

Crafton, Donald – *The Talkies, American Cinema's Transition to Sound 1926-1931*, Berkeley, CA, University of California Press, 1999

Doggett, Danielle – *Cut: Hollywood Murders, Accidents and Other Tragedies*, New York, NY, Global Book Publishing, 2005

Drew, William M. – *"The Prehistory of Hollywood" Early Hollywood Films and Movie Stars*, 2009

Edmonds, Andy – *Frame Up! The Untold Story of Roscoe "Fatty" Arbuckle*, New York, NY, William Morrow and Co., 1991

Everson, William K. – *American Silent Film*, New York, NY, Oxford University Press, 1978

Eyman, Scott – *The Speed of Sound: Hollywood and the Talkie Revolution 1926-1930*, Baltimore, MD, Johns Hopkins University Press, 1999

Fine, Gerald – *Fatty*, self-published, 1971

Ghareeb, Gordon and Martin Cox – *Hollywood to Honolulu: The Story of the Los Angeles Steamship Company*, Palo Alton, CA, Glencannon, 2009

Goodman, Ezra – *The Fifty-Year Decline and Fall of Hollywood*, Mew York, NY, McFadden, 1961

Grazia, Edward de and Roger K. Newman – *Banned Films: Movies, Censors and the First Amendment*, New York, NY, R.R. Bowker, 1982

Guild, Leo – *The Fatty Arbuckle Case*, New York, NY, Paperback Library 1962

Hallet, Hilary A. – *Inventing the It Girl*, New York, NY, Liverwright Publishing, 2022

Hays, Will H. – *The Memoirs of Will H. Hays*, Garden City, NY, Doubleday, 1955

Hays, Will, Jr. – *Come Home With Me Now: The Untold Story of Movie Czar Will Hays by His Son*, Indianapolis, IN, Guild Press of Indiana, 1993

Jacobson, Laurie – *Dishing Hollywood*, Nashville, TN, Cumberland House, 2003

----------------------- - *Hollywood Heartbreak*, New York, NY, Simon & Schuster, 1984

Jacobson, Laurie and Mark Wanamaker – *Hollywood Haunted*, Santa Monica, Angel City Press, 1994

Keaton, Buster with Charles Samuels – *My Wonderful World of Slapstick*, Garden City, NT, 1960

Keaton, Eleanor and Jeffrey Vance – *Buster Keaton Remembered*, New York, Harry N. Abrams, 2001

Lahue, Kalton C. and Terry Brewer – *Kops and Custards: The Legend of Keystone Films*, Norman, OK, University of Oklahoma Press, 1968

Jemper, Tom – *Hidden Talent: The Emergence of Hollywood Agents*, Berkeley, CA, University of California Press, 2010

Kerr, Walter – *The Silent Clowns*, New York, NY, Alfred A. Knopf, 1975

Kirkpatrick, Sidney – *A Cast of Killers*, New York, NY, E.P. Dutton, 1986

Kobal, John – *Hollywood: The Years of Innocence*, New York, NY, Abbeville, 1985

Kobel, Peter – *Silent Movies: The Birth of Film and the Triumph of Movie Culture*, New York, NY, Little, Brown & Co. 2007

Koszarski, Richard – *An Evening's Entertainment: The Age of the Silent Feature Picture 1915-1928*, Berkely, CA, University of California Press, 1990

Krist, Gary – *The Mirage Factory*, New York, NY, Crown, 2018

Loos, Anita – *Kiss Hollywood Goodbye*, New York, NY, Viking, 1974

Louvish, Simon – *Keystone: The Life and Clowns of Mack Sennett*, New York, By, Faber & Faber, 2003

Macnabb, Matt – *Hollywood's Dark History*, Philadelphia, PA, Pen and Sword History, 2019

Mann, William J. – *Tinseltown*, New York, NY, Harper Collins, 2014

Meade, Marion – *Buster Keaton: Cut to the Chase*, New York, Ny, Harper Collins, 1995

Merritt, Greg – *Room 1219*, Chicago, IL, Chicago Review Press, 2013

Oderman, Stuart – *Roscoe "Fatty" Arbuckle: A Biography of the Silent Film Comedian 1887-1933*, Jefferson, NC, McFarland, 1994

Okrent, Daniel -- *Last Call: The Rise and Fall of Prohibition*, New York, NY, Scribner, 2011

Robinson, David – *From Peep Show to Palace: The Birth of the American Film*, New York, NY, Columbia University Press, 1996

Rogers St. John, Adela – *Love, Laughter and Tears: My Hollywood Story*, Garden City, NY, Doubleday, 1978

Schickel, Richard – *D.W. Griffith: An American Life*, New York, Simon & Schuster, 1984

Scott, Henry E. – *Shocking True Story: The Rose and Fall of Confidential, "America's Most Scandalous Magazine,"* New York, NY, Pantheon, 2010

Sennett, Mack with Cameron Shipp, *King of Comedy*, Garden City, NY, Doubleday, 1954

Slide, Anthony – *Inside the Hollywood Film Magazine*, Jackson, MS, University of Mississippi Press, 2010

Stenn, David – *Clara Bow: Runnin' Wild*, New York, NY, Cooper Square, 1988

Studlar, Gaylyn – *Precocious Charms*, Berkeley, CA, University of California Press, 2013

Taylor, Troy – *Bloody Hollywood*, Decatur, IL, Whitechapel Press, 2008

Vieira, Mark A. – *Forbidden Hollywood*, New York, NY, 2019

Wagner, Rob Leicester – *Red Ink, White Lies: The Rise and Fall of Los Angeles Newspapers*, Upland, CA, Dragonflyer Press, 2000

Wagner, Walter – *You Must Remember This*, New York, Putnam, 1975

Walker, Alexander – *The Shattered Silents: How the Talkies Came to Stay*, New York, NY, William Morrow, 1979

Weissman, Stephen – *Chaplin: A Life*, New York, NY, Arcade, 2008

Williams, Joe – *Hollywood Myths*, Minneapolis, MN, Voyageur Press, 2012

Yallop, David – *The Day the Laughter Stopped: The True Story of Fatty Arbuckle*, New York, NY, 1976

Young, Robert, Jr. – *Roscoe "Fatty" Arbuckle: A Bio-Bibliography*, Westport, CT, Greenwood, 1994

Zuda, Dave (Editor) – *Forty Quarts of Liquor*, Bamber Books, 2018

NEWSPAPERS AND PERIODICALS
Albuquerque Morning Journal (NM)
American Cinematographer
Atlanta Constitution
Bakersfield Californian (CA)
Baltimore American
Berkeley Daily Gazette (CA)
Bisbee Daily Review (AZ)
Boston Globe
Cedar Rapids Daily Republican (IA)
Chicago Herald & Examiner
Chicago Tribune
Cinema Journal
Cook County Journal (IL)
Decatur Daily Review (IL)
Denver Post
Deseret Evening News
Detroit Free Press
Dubuque Telegraph-Herald (IA)
Eau Claire Leader (WI)
Film Fun
Fort Wayne News (IN)
Helena Daily Independent (MT)
Joplin Globe (MO)
Liberty
Literary Digest
Los Angeles Examiner
Los Angeles Express
Los Angeles Herald
Los Angeles Times
Miami News
Milwaukee Journal
Motion Picture World

Movie Pictorial
Movie Weekly
Moving Picture World
New York American
New York Clipper
New York Dramatic Mirror
New York Herald
New York Morning Telegraph
New York Times
New York Tribune
Oakland Tribune
Ogden Standard-Examiner (UT)
Omaha Excelsior
Palm Beach Post (FL)
Philadelphia Evening Public Ledger
Photoplay
Pittsburgh Press
Providence News (RI)
Reno Evening Gazette (NV)
Sacramento Bee
Salt Lake Tribune
San Francisco Call and Post
San Francisco Chronicle
San Francisco Examiner
Screenland
Special Interest Auto, February 1990
Spokane Spokesman-Review (WA)
Syracuse Herald (NY)
Toledo Blade (OH)
Toledo News-Bee (OH)
True Detective Mysteries
Vanity Fair
Variety
Warsaw Daily Times (IN)
Washington Times

Minta Durfee Arbuckle Collection, Margaret Herrick Library, Academy of Motion Picture Arts and Sciences, Beverly Hills, CA

SPECIAL THANKS:

April Slaughter: Cover Design
Samantha Smith
Athena & the "Aunts" - Sue, Carmen & Rocky
Orrin and Rachel Taylor
Rene Kruse
Rachael Horath
Bethany Horath
Elyse and Thomas Reihner
John Winterbauer
Cody Beck
Trey Shrader
Tom and Michelle Bonadurer
Lydia Rhoades
Cheryl Stamp and Sheryel Williams-Staab
Joelle Leitschuh
Tina Rea
Scott and Hannah Robl
Victoria & Reese Welch
And the entire crew of American Hauntings

ABOUT THE AUTHOR

Troy Taylor is the author of books on ghosts, hauntings, true crime, the unexplained, and the supernatural in America. He is the founder of American Hauntings Ink, which offers books, ghost tours, events, and the Haunted America Conference, as well as the creator of the American Oddities Museum in Alton, Illinois. He was born and raised in the Midwest and divides his time between Alton, Illinois and wherever the wind decides to take him. See Troy's other titles at: www.americanhauntingsink.com

www.ingramcontent.com/pod-product-compliance
Lightning Source LLC
Chambersburg PA
CBHW062041080426
42734CB00012B/2525